ENGLISH
FOR EVERYONE
LIBRO DE EJERCICIOS
GRAMÁTICA INGLESA

Autor

Tom Booth ha sidodo durante 10 años profesor de inglés en Polonia
y en Rusia. Actualmente vive en Inglaterra, donde trabaja como
editor y autor de materiales para el aprendizaje de la lengua inglesa.
Ha colaborado en varios libros de la serie *English for Everyone*.

Consultor

Tim Bowen ha enseñado inglés y ha formado profesores en más de
30 países en todo el mundo. Es coautor de libros sobre la enseñanza de la
pronunciación y sobre la metodología de la enseñanza de idiomas, y
autor de numerosos libros para profesores de inglés. Actualmente se
dedica a la escritura de materiales, la edición y la traducción.
Es miembro del Chartered Institute of Linguists.

ENGLISH
FOR EVERYONE
LIBRO DE EJERCICIOS
GRAMÁTICA INGLESA

    reported speech

conditional   perfect

 phrasal verbs   Aa

    modal

Edición del proyecto Ben Ffrancon Davies
Edición de arte sénior Amy Child
Ilustración Square Egg
Diseño de la cubierta Surabhi Wadhwa-Gandhi
Edición de la cubierta Emma Dawson
Dirección de desarrollo de diseño de la cubierta Sophia MTT
Producción, preproducción Robert Dunn
Producción Jude Crozier
Corrección Steph Lewis
Edición ejecutiva Christine Stroyan
Edición ejecutiva de arte Anna Hall
Dirección editorial Andrew Macintyre
Dirección de arte Karen Self
Dirección general editorial Jonathan Metcalf

DK India
Edición de arte sénior Chhaya Sajwan
Edición sénior Arani Sinha
Asistencia a la edición de arte Sonali Mahthan, Vidushi Gupta
Edición Nandini Devdutt Tripathy
Asistencia editorial Udit Verma, Andrew Korah
Diseño de cubierta Priyanka Bansal
Coordinación editorial de cubiertas Priyanka Sharma
Edición ejecutiva de cubiertas Saloni Singh
Edición ejecutiva de arte sénior Arunesh Talapatra
Edición ejecutiva Soma B. Chowdhury
Dirección de preproducción Sunil Sharma
Diseño de maquetación sénior Tarun Sharma, Harish Aggarwal
Diseño de maquetación Manish Upreti

Servicios editoriales Tinta Simpàtica
Traducción Anna Nualart

Publicado originalmente en Gran Bretaña en 2019
por Dorling Kindersley Ltd, 80 Strand, Londres, WC2R 0RL
Parte de Penguin Random House

UN MUNDO DE IDEAS
www.dkespañol.com

Cómo utilizar este libro

Este libro de ejercicios acompaña a la *Gramática inglesa* de la serie *English for Everyone*. En cada una de sus unidades se ejercita lo aprendido en la unidad de la *Gramática inglesa* del mismo número.

UNIDAD DE LA GRAMÁTICA

UNIDAD DEL LIBRO DE EJERCICIOS

EJERCICIOS

Los ejercicios están cuidadosamente graduados para profundizar en los contenidos gramaticales expuestos en la correspondiente unidad de la *Gramática inglesa*, de manera que te permitan comprender y recordar lo que has aprendido.

Número de ejercicio
La numeración de los ejercicios facilita encontrar las respuestas rápidamente.

Instrucciones del ejercicio
Una breve explicación te indica lo que debes hacer.

Respuesta de ejemplo
La primera pregunta está resuelta. Así te será más fácil comprender el ejercicio.

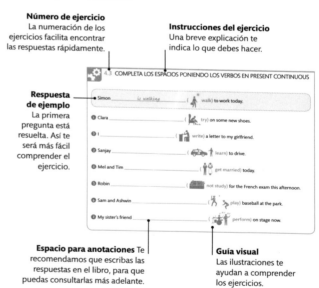

Espacio para anotaciones Te recomendamos que escribas las respuestas en el libro, para que puedas consultarlas más adelante.

Guía visual
Las ilustraciones te ayudan a comprender los ejercicios.

RESPUESTAS

En la sección de Respuestas al final del libro tienes las soluciones de todos los ejercicios. Compruébalas cuando hayas terminado una unidad o un ejercicio para verificar tu nivel de acierto.

Número de ejercicio Busca el número de ejercicio para comprobar tus respuestas.

Contenidos

01 El present simple — 8

02 El present simple negativo — 11

03 Preguntas en present simple — 14

04 El present continuous — 16

05 Present: repaso — 20

06 Imperativo — 24

07 El past simple — 26

08 El past simple negativo — 30

09 Preguntas en past simple — 32

10 El past continuous — 34

11 El present perfect simple — 36

12 El present perfect continuous — 40

13 El past perfect simple — 42

14 El past perfect continuous — 44

15 "Used to" y "would" — 46

16 Past: repaso — 48

17 El futuro con "going to" — 52

18 El futuro con "will" — 54

19 El presente para hablar del futuro — 56

20 El future continuous — 58

21 El future perfect — 60

22 El future in the past — 62

23 Future: repaso — 64

24 La voz pasiva — 68

25 La voz pasiva en pretérito — 71

26 La voz pasiva en futuro — 74

27 La voz pasiva en verbos modales — 76

28 Otras construcciones en pasiva — 78

29 Frases condicionales — 80

30 Otras frases condicionales — 86

31 Frases condicionales: repaso — 88

32 Posibilidades futuras — 90

33 Deseos y lamentaciones — 92

34 Hacer preguntas — 94

35 Expresiones interrogativas — 97

36 Preguntas abiertas — 100

37 Preguntas de objeto y de sujeto — 102

38 Preguntas indirectas — 104

39 Question tags — 106

40 Preguntas cortas — 108

41	Respuestas cortas	109
42	Preguntas: repaso	110
43	Reported speech	112
44	Tiempos en reported speech	114
45	Verbos de reported speech	117
46	Reported speech de frases negativas	118
47	Preguntas en reported speech	119
48	Reported speech: repaso	122
49	Tipos de verbos	124
50	Verbos de acción y de estado	126
51	Infinitivos y participios	128
52	Pautas verbales	130
53	Pautas verbales con objetos	133
54	Pautas verbales con preposiciones	135
55	Phrasal verbs	136
56	Verbos modales	140
57	Habilidades	142
58	Permiso, peticiones, ofrecimientos	144
59	Sugerencias y consejos	146
60	Obligaciones	148
61	Hacer deducciones	150
62	Posibilidad	152
63	Artículos	154
64	Artículos: repaso	158
65	"This / that / these / those"	160
66	"No / none"	162
67	"Each / every"	164
68	"Either / neither / both"	166
69	Sustantivos singulares y plurales	168
70	Sustantivos contables e incontables	170
71	Concordancia sujeto-verbo	172
72	Sustantivos abstractos y concretos	174
73	Sustantivos compuestos	176
74	Números	178
75	Cantidades	180
76	Cantidades aproximadas	184
77	Pronombres personales	186
78	Pronombres reflexivos	188
79	Pronombres indefinidos	192
80	Posesión	194
81	Cláusulas relativas definidas	198
82	Cláusulas relativas indefinidas	200

83	Otras estructuras de relativo	202
84	Expresiones interrogativas y "-ever"	204
85	"There"	206
86	"It" introductorio	209
87	Cambiar el énfasis	211
88	Inversión	213
89	Elipsis	215
90	Abreviar infinitivos	217
91	Sustitución	220
92	Adjetivos	222
93	Adjetivos graduables y no graduables	225
94	Adjetivos comparativos	228
95	Dos comparativos combinados	232
96	Comparaciones con "as... as"	234
97	Adjetivos superlativos	236
98	Adverbios de modo	240
99	Adverbios comparativos y superlativos	242
100	Adverbios de grado	244
101	Adverbios de tiempo	247
102	Adverbios de frecuencia	250
103	"So" y "such"	252

104	"Enough" y "too"	254
105	Preposiciones	256
106	Preposiciones de lugar	258
107	Preposiciones de tiempo	260
108	Otras preposiciones	263
109	Preposiciones dependientes	265
110	Conjunciones copulativas	268
111	Conjunciones subordinantes	270
112	Otros conectores	272
113	Conjunciones: repaso	274
114	Prefijos	276
115	Sufijos	278
116	Expresiones que se confunden	280
117	Ordenar y organizar	282
118	Corregir y cambiar de tema	284
119	Decisiones y matices	286
120	Mantener una conversación	288

| Respuestas | 290 |

01 El present simple

El present simple se utiliza para transmitir información simple, hablar de cosas que suceden de manera regular y describir cosas que son siempre ciertas.

1.1 COMPLETA LOS ESPACIOS PONIENDO LOS VERBOS EN PRESENT SIMPLE

Jessica _____walks_____ (walk) around the park every day at lunchtime.

1 Tony _____ (make) a huge breakfast for his family on Sundays.

2 I usually _____ (eat) my lunch at 1pm at an Italian restaurant.

3 Fiona _____ (meet) her friends at a café on Thursday evenings.

4 We sometimes _____ (play) tennis with our friends on Saturday mornings.

5 My cousin _____ (start) work at 6am every morning.

6 The shop assistant _____ (leave) work at 6pm in the evening.

7 You _____ (drink) a lot of coffee every morning.

8 Paolo usually _____ (read) a book in the evenings.

1.2 MARCA LAS FRASES QUE SEAN CORRECTAS

Steve usually finishes work at 5pm. ☑
Steve usually finishs work at 5pm. ☐

1 Greg workes in a factory. ☐
Greg works in a factory. ☐

2 My dad watches TV every evening. ☐
My dad watchs TV every evening. ☐

3 Michel plays the piano beautifully. ☐
Michel playes the piano beautifully. ☐

4 Jane brushs her hair in the morning. ☐
Jane brushes her hair in the morning. ☐

5 Selma gos shopping after work. ☐
Selma goes shopping after work. ☐

6 Imran washes his clothes on Sunday. ☐
Imran washs his clothes on Sunday. ☐

7 Mary teaches French at a college. ☐
Mary teachs French at a college. ☐

1.3 COMPLETA LOS ESPACIOS CON "AM", "IS" O "ARE"

> They ___are___ here for the party.

1. I _____ a doctor at the local hospital.
2. Vicky _____ my eldest child.
3. We _____ from a town in Scotland.
4. Both my parents _____ lawyers.
5. You _____ a very good friend.
6. I _____ an American.
7. That policeman _____ so tall.
8. She _____ twenty-three years old.
9. It _____ cold outside.
10. I _____ fifteen today.
11. Our cat _____ black and white.
12. We _____ very excited.
13. They _____ students from France.
14. Jim _____ an architect.
15. My sister-in-law _____ from Japan.
16. I _____ so hungry!
17. You _____ very lazy.
18. My children _____ so tired.
19. I _____ forty-three years old.
20. They _____ late for work.
21. Claudia and Paolo _____ Italian.
22. My grandfather _____ retired.
23. We _____ from Pakistan.
24. Paul _____ disappointed.

 1.4 COMPLETA LOS ESPACIOS CON "HAVE" O "HAS"

> He ___has___ a lot of homework to do.

1. Jack _____ a new car.
2. Jennifer _____ Abbie's bag.
3. We _____ a beautiful farm.
4. I _____ three sisters.
5. Bob _____ toothache.
6. My house _____ a large garage.
7. They _____ a new laptop.
8. We _____ so many books.
9. My dad _____ red hair.
10. You _____ an old phone.
11. My neighbors _____ a daughter.
12. Juan's house _____ three floors.
13. That bird _____ big eyes.
14. I _____ a new baby.
15. We both _____ headaches.
16. They _____ the same dress.
17. My grandparents _____ chickens.
18. You _____ a friendly cat.
19. My town _____ two museums.
20. Yuko _____ a painful back.
21. Our dogs _____ lots of toys.
22. We _____ an English class tonight.
23. Vineetha _____ a new haircut.
24. I _____ dinner at 6pm every day.

1.5 CONECTA CADA IMAGEN CON LA FRASE CORRECTA

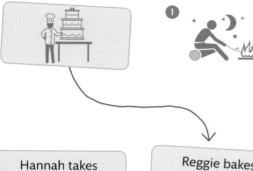

| Hannah takes beautiful photos of the places she visits. | Reggie bakes the most incredible cakes. | Emil leaves the office at 6pm each day. | Brad goes camping in the forest every summer. |

 1.6 COMPLETA LOS ESPACIOS CON LAS PALABRAS DEL RECUADRO

Katya _____*teaches*_____ young children how to read.

1. I _____ work at 9am during the week.

2. You _____ an engineer.

3. Maria _____ coffee with Jules in the morning.

4. They _____ to work by train.

5. My dad _____ 67 years old.

6. Robert _____ work at 7pm.

7. We _____ an English lesson later.

8. Paul often _____ a film in the evening.

9. Emma _____ to bed early on Sundays.

| watches | is | are | goes | have |
| go | start | has | finishes | ~~teaches~~ |

10

02 El present simple negativo

Para formar frases negativas utilizando "be" en present simple se añade "not" a continuación del verbo. Con otros verbos, se utiliza el verbo auxiliar "do not" o "does not".

2.1 ESCRIBE DE NUEVO LAS FRASES PONIENDO LAS PALABRAS EN EL ORDEN CORRECTO

French. | not | I | am

I am not French.

1 doctor. | is | She | a | not

2 are | New Zealand. | We | from | not

3 not | My | American. | is | dad

4 my | not | are | dogs. | They

5 are | You | Egyptian. | not

6 is | my | This | computer. | not

7 engineer. | an | am | I | not

2.2 COMPLETA LOS ESPACIOS CON "DO NOT" O "DOES NOT"

Michael ___*does not*___ have a dog.

1 You _____ work in the library.

2 He _____ eat meat.

3 Val _____ watch TV in the evening.

4 I _____ play football very often.

5 We _____ get up early on Saturdays.

6 My grandparents _____ have a car.

7 Nico _____ work in the factory.

8 She _____ go to work on Fridays.

9 I _____ go to restaurants very often.

10 You _____ have a cat.

11 They _____ work outside.

2.3 ESCRIBE DE NUEVO LAS FRASES EN FORMA NEGATIVA EMPLEANDO CONTRACCIONES

| She is happy with her meal. | *She's not happy with her meal.* | *She isn't happy with her meal.* |

1 He is a teacher.

2 Carla is very tall.

3 You are from Australia.

4 They are farmers.

5 We are happy.

6 You are lawyers.

7 She is a doctor.

8 It is very cold outside.

2.4 MARCA LAS FRASES QUE SEAN CORRECTAS

He does not likes baseball. ☐
He does not like baseball. ☑

1 I don't like Sam's cooking. ☐
I no like Sam's cooking. ☐

2 You doesn't look very happy. ☐
You don't look very happy. ☐

3 Antonio does not live in Madrid. ☐
Antonio do not lives in Madrid. ☐

4 Phil don't drive a car. ☐
Phil doesn't drive a car. ☐

5 I'm not a doctor. ☐
I amn't a doctor. ☐

6 Diana doesn't have a computer. ☐
Diana don't has a computer. ☐

7 I don't like cats. ☐
I like not cats. ☐

8 Paolo does not get up at 6am. ☐
Paolo do not get up at 6am. ☐

9 My dad don't feels well. ☐
My dad doesn't feel well. ☐

10 They isn't from China. ☐
They aren't from China. ☐

11 My friends don't like chess. ☐
My friends doesn't like chess. ☐

2.5 ESCRIBE DE NUEVO LAS FRASES EN FORMA NEGATIVA

> This book **is** very interesting.
> *This book isn't very interesting.*

1 Amy **works** as a receptionist in our office.

_____

2 I **like** going to the health center.

_____

3 Your company **is** very successful.

_____

4 You **play** the guitar very well.

_____

5 Jean **cooks** the dinner in the evening.

_____

6 This TV show **is** very interesting.

_____

7 Sonia and Rick **live** in Paris.

_____

8 My son **is** a firefighter.

_____

9 Our house **is** very big.

_____

10 Sandra **works** late on Fridays.

_____

11 My husband and I **relax** on weekends.

_____

12 Edith and Sam **like** dancing in their free time.

_____

Las preguntas en present simple con "be" se forman invirtiendo las posiciones del verbo y el sujeto. Con otros verbos, se añade el verbo auxiliar "do" o "does" antes del sujeto.

3.1 COMPLETA LOS ESPACIOS CON "AM", "IS" O "ARE"

___Are___ you a chef?

1. _____ you the new teacher?
2. _____ she your sister?
3. _____ we nearly home?
4. _____ I on the list?
5. _____ your dogs friendly?
6. Where _____ the front door?
7. _____ Carlo still a teacher?
8. _____ we late for the party?
9. Where _____ my shoes?
10. _____ that Shelly's new car?
11. Who _____ the manager here?
12. _____ I too late for the concert?
13. When _____ your birthday?
14. _____ he here for the presentation?
15. Where _____ the bathroom?
16. _____ I supposed to be at work?
17. Why _____ they angry?
18. _____ it time to eat yet?
19. _____ they coming to the seminar?

3.2 COMPLETA LOS ESPACIOS CON "DO" O "DOES"

___Does___ he work in a hotel?

1. _____ Laura have a brother?
2. _____ they know your address?
3. _____ Craig still live in Dublin?
4. Where _____ your mother work?
5. _____ they know your father?
6. _____ the restaurant serve fish?
7. _____ you still have my book?
8. _____ your house have a garage?
9. _____ we have enough time?
10. How _____ Ben travel to work?
11. _____ your parents have a car?
12. When _____ the lesson end?
13. _____ you work on Saturdays?
14. _____ she play any instruments?
15. What _____ you want for dinner?
16. _____ I need to wear a dress?
17. What _____ he want this time?
18. _____ they know what time it is?
19. Where _____ she buy her clothes?

3.3 MARCA LAS FRASES QUE SEAN CORRECTAS

Does she goes to your school? ☐
Does she go to your school? ☑

❶ Does Danielle plays baseball very often? ☐
Does Danielle play baseball very often? ☐

❷ Do you know how to play the electric guitar? ☐
Do know you how to play the electric guitar? ☐

❸ Does your daughter know how to drive a car? ☐
Do your daughter knows how to drives a car? ☐

❹ What time does you get up in the morning? ☐
What time do you get up in the morning? ☐

3.4 ESCRIBE DE NUEVO LAS FRASES EN FORMA DE PREGUNTA

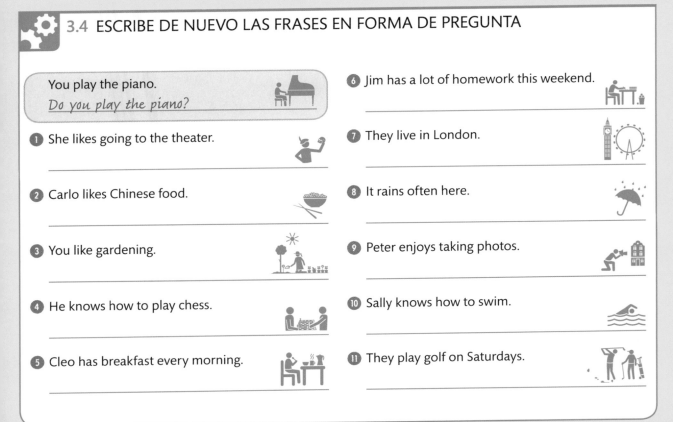

You play the piano.
Do you play the piano?

❶ She likes going to the theater.
_____

❷ Carlo likes Chinese food.
_____

❸ You like gardening.
_____

❹ He knows how to play chess.
_____

❺ Cleo has breakfast every morning.
_____

❻ Jim has a lot of homework this weekend.
_____

❼ They live in London.
_____

❽ It rains often here.
_____

❾ Peter enjoys taking photos.
_____

❿ Sally knows how to swim.
_____

⓫ They play golf on Saturdays.
_____

04 El present continuous

El present continuous se utiliza para hablar sobre
acciones continuadas que ocurren en este momento.
Se forma con "be" y un present participle.

4.1 CONECTA CADA IMAGEN CON LA FRASE CORRECTA

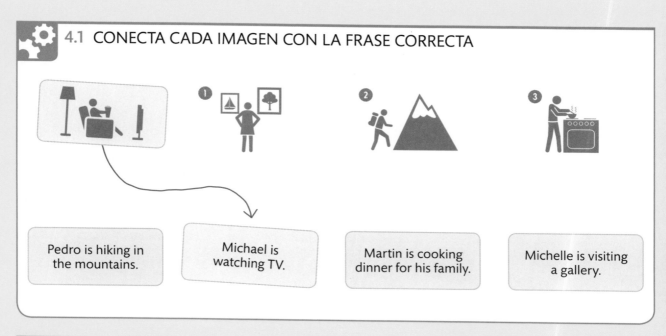

Pedro is hiking in
the mountains.

Michael is
watching TV.

Martin is cooking
dinner for his family.

Michelle is visiting
a gallery.

4.2 COMPLETA LOS ESPACIOS CON LAS PALABRAS DEL RECUADRO

The children _____ *are playing* _____ football.

① You _____ a beautiful red dress.

② Matilda _____ a travel book about Brazil.

③ My cat _____ the apple tree.

④ I _____ such an interesting book.

⑤ Hetty and Paula _____ some orange juice.

⑥ Phil _____ for his piano lesson.

am reading

~~are playing~~

is climbing

is practicing

is reading

are wearing

are drinking

4.3 COMPLETA LOS ESPACIOS PONIENDO LOS VERBOS EN PRESENT CONTINUOUS

Simon _____*is walking*_____ (walk) to work today.

1. Clara _____ (try) on some new shoes.

2. I _____ (write) a letter to my girlfriend.

3. Sanjay _____ (learn) to drive.

4. Mel and Tim _____ (get married) today.

5. Robin _____ (not study) for the French exam this afternoon.

6. Sam and Ashwin _____ (play) baseball at the park.

7. My sister's friend _____ (perform) on stage now.

4.4 MARCA LAS FRASES QUE SEAN CORRECTAS

Diane is buying a new house. ☑
Diane buys a new house. ☐

1. Sam and Pete not playing cards in the living room. ☐
   Sam and Pete aren't playing cards in the living room. ☐

2. The children eat pizza once a week. ☐
   The children are eating pizza once a week. ☐

3. Julian is wearing a suit for the meeting. ☐
   Julian is wears a suit for the meeting. ☐

4.5 CONECTA EL INICIO Y EL FINAL DE CADA FRASE

Is she coming — to the party tonight?

① Are they going — eating for dinner?

② What are we — snowing outside?

③ Is it — wearing such fancy clothes?

④ Why is Lisa — to the festival?

4.6 ESCRIBE DE NUEVO LAS FRASES PONIENDO LAS PALABRAS EN EL ORDEN CORRECTO

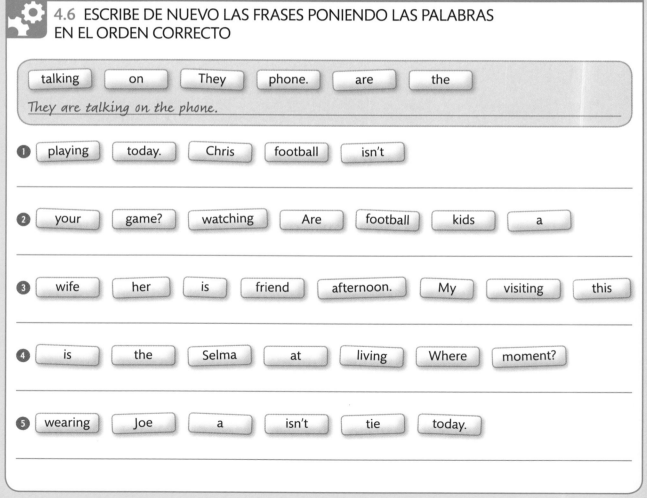

talking · on · They · phone. · are · the

They are talking on the phone.

① playing · today. · Chris · football · isn't

② your · game? · watching · Are · football · kids · a

③ wife · her · is · friend · afternoon. · My · visiting · this

④ is · the · Selma · at · living · Where · moment?

⑤ wearing · Joe · a · isn't · tie · today.

18

4.7 ESCRIBE DE NUEVO LAS FRASES COMO PREGUNTAS

> She is eating an apple.
> *Is she eating an apple?*

1 They are driving to the beach.
_____

2 You are going swimming.
_____

3 She is watching a movie.
_____

4 Nelson is going shopping.
_____

5 Ben is listening to classical music.
_____

6 Chrissie is climbing the tree.
_____

7 Sven and Olly are singing.
_____

8 You are drinking apple juice.
_____

9 They are playing tennis.
_____

10 My son is reading a book.
_____

11 Pavel is speaking Russian.
_____

12 You are wearing a dress.
_____

 ## 4.8 ESCRIBE DE NUEVO LAS FRASES EN FORMA NEGATIVA

> We are enjoying the show.
> *We are not enjoying the show.*

1 I am going to the zoo.
_____

2 The dog is chasing a cat.
_____

3 They are walking their dog.
_____

4 Angela is wearing a dress.
_____

5 We are playing chess.
_____

6 I am eating Chinese food.
_____

7 James is wearing your shirt.
_____

8 You are reading a book.
_____

9 She is cleaning her room.
_____

10 Ed and Gus are watching a movie.
_____

11 I am speaking French.
_____

12 It is raining outside.
_____

Present: repaso

El present simple y el present continuous se utilizan en diferentes situaciones. Las preguntas y las frases negativas se escriben de distintas maneras en cada caso.

5.1 MIRA LAS IMÁGENES Y COMPLETA LAS FRASES CON LAS EXPRESIONES DEL RECUADRO

Mike and Ellie ___*are painting*___ their house this afternoon.

❸ Is Dimitri still _____ the garage wall?

❶ Annabelle _____ caves in her free time.

❹ Brendan _____ watching comedies on TV in the evenings.

❷ João _____ dogs. He's really scared of them.

❺ Sid and Les _____ at the beauty salon.

| explores | ~~are painting~~ | work | doesn't like | loves | building |

5.2 TACHA LAS PALABRAS INCORRECTAS DE CADA FRASE

 Jim ~~tries~~ / is trying to build a chair.

① Kit goes / is going scuba diving with her friends on Fridays.

② Ben and Kelly dance / are dancing at the club tonight.

③ Sai puts / is putting the dishes in the dishwasher each evening.

④ Bruce waits / is waiting to go for a walk.

5.3 COMPLETA LOS ESPACIOS PONIENDO LOS VERBOS EN PRESENT SIMPLE O PRESENT CONTINUOUS

Alastair usually _____*plays*_____ (play) tennis, but this afternoon he ___*is playing*___ (play) badminton.

① Mary _____ (not send) letters often, but she _____ (write) one to her mother now.

② I _____ (work) from home today, but usually I _____ (work) in an office.

③ We usually _____ (go) to Spain on vacation, but this year we _____ (go) to Mexico.

④ Helen _____ (work) in an elementary school. She _____ (teach) math right now.

⑤ I _____ (not eat) meat very often, but tonight I _____ (have) a steak.

⑥ It _____ (not rain) often in California, but today it _____ (pour).

⑦ My cousin _____ (perform) on stage now. I _____ (love) her voice.

⑧ Rajiv _____ (wear) a T-shirt now, but he always _____ (wear) a shirt at work.

⑨ My dad _____ (sleep) now. He _____ (be) tired after the journey.

⑩ Juan normally_____ (start) work at 8am, but today he _____ (go) to the dentist.

⑪ Bob _____ (take) a taxi to work this morning, but he usually _____ (take) the bus.

5.4 CONECTA EL INICIO Y EL FINAL DE CADA FRASE

	Mario sometimes		living at the moment?
1	My brother doesn't		in the kitchen?
2	My mom usually bakes		plays tennis with his uncle.
3	Where is your sister		play golf with your colleagues?
4	Tom's new girlfriend		work on Friday afternoons.
5	What's dad cooking		a cake on the weekends.
6	How often do you		lives in a resort in Spain.

5.5 ESCRIBE DE NUEVO LAS FRASES PONIENDO LAS PALABRAS EN EL ORDEN CORRECTO

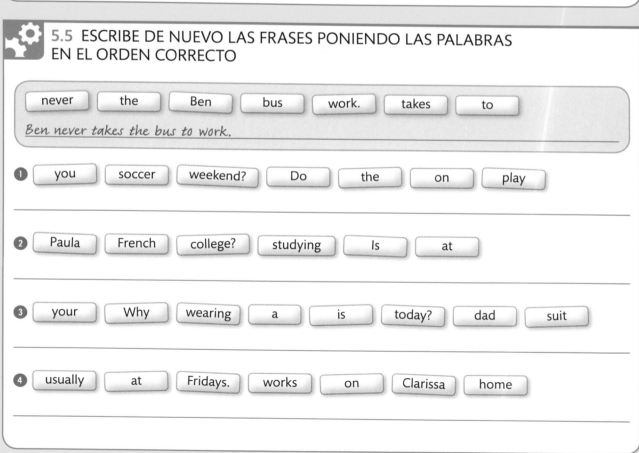

never · the · Ben · bus · work. · takes · to

Ben never takes the bus to work.

1. you · soccer · weekend? · Do · the · on · play

_____

2. Paula · French · college? · studying · Is · at

_____

3. your · Why · wearing · a · is · today? · dad · suit

_____

4. usually · at · Fridays. · works · on · Clarissa · home

_____

22

5.6 MARCA LAS FRASES QUE SEAN CORRECTAS

Do Christina still have a cat? ☐
Does Christina still have a cat? ☑

1 Lou wakes up at 7am each morning. ☐
Lou wake up at 7am each morning. ☐

2 Henry is performing at a country and western club tonight. ☐
Henry are performing at a country and western club tonight. ☐

3 Tanya doesn't feels well, so she's not coming to the party. ☐
Tanya doesn't feel well, so she's not coming to the party. ☐

5.7 ESCRIBE DE NUEVO LAS FRASES Y CORRIGE LOS ERRORES

Unfortunately, Mr. Clarke **doesn't understands** Russian.
Unfortunately, Mr. Clarke doesn't understand Russian.

1 Steve **read** in bed before he **go** to sleep.

_____

2 Lisa and Tim **goes** to the gym after work.

_____

3 My mom **plays** golf with her friend this afternoon.

_____

4 Vernon **don't like** snakes. He really **hate** them.

_____

5 We often **are going** to the café by the park.

_____

6 Craig **walking** in the mountains with Rob this week.

_____

06 Imperativo

El imperativo se utiliza para dar órdenes o hacer peticiones. También se usa para hacer una advertencia o indicarle una dirección a alguien.

 6.1 BUSCA IMPERATIVOS EN LA TABLA Y AÑÁDELOS A LA LISTA

```
G  G  N  I  D  R  A  W  B  Y  R  U  N
N  S  A  I  H  E  L  P  T  A  K  E  V
N  W  E  M  J  S  M  D  S  M  A  R  D
G  I  V  E  E  R  T  I  S  T  A  R  T
S  K  A  M  E  B  O  T  R  Q  I  N  G
W  R  I  T  E  Y  A  D  F  G  I  N  D
W  R  L  O  L  A  O  Z  B  E  G  I  N
P  W  O  R  K  N  V  O  N  S  E  N  D
T  C  D  H  T  N  D  E  G  J  A  Q  I
E  H  I  J  L  I  S  T  E  N  U  S  S
R  E  C  E  P  S  T  I  I  G  G  E  D
G  E  F  D  B  C  A  H  T  J  J  L  M
Q  K  P  P  Y  T  U  R  N  D  I  W  G
E  D  I  S  R  Y  A  D  F  A  E  N  T
M  Z  L  O  L  A  O  Z  I  O  R  I  Z
C  O  M  E  S  N  V  O  N  O  E  Y  D
T  C  D  H  T  N  D  E  G  J  A  G  I
E  H  I  J  A  R  E  A  D  E  O  S  S
R  E  C  E  A  E  E  I  S  N  G  K  O
B  S  M  I  L  E  H  E  I  D  J  L  M
```

IMPERATIVOS

write

1. _____
2. _____
3. _____
4. _____
5. _____
6. _____
7. _____
8. _____
9. _____
10. _____
11. _____
12. _____
13. _____
14. _____

6.2 CONECTA CADA IMAGEN CON LA FRASE CORRECTA

Don't sit there! It's Andrew's chair.

Pass me the stapler, please.

Let me help you with your bags, Vera.

Be careful on the wet floor!

Take the second road on the right.

6.3 CONECTA EL INICIO Y EL FINAL DE CADA FRASE

Give me a	the window.
① Turn right	the theater.
② Eat your	minute, please.
③ Give the cake	the grass.
④ Please close	road on the left.
⑤ Let's go to	at the crossroads.
⑥ Don't walk on	that vase!
⑦ Take the first	to Layla.
⑧ Don't touch	breakfast, Greg!

6.4 ESCRIBE DE NUEVO LAS FRASES PONIENDO LAS PALABRAS EN EL ORDEN CORRECTO

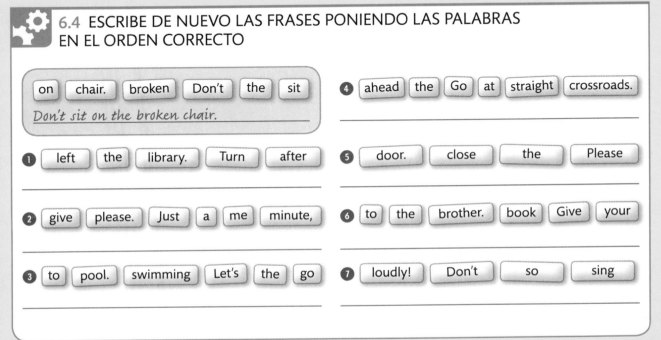

on | chair. | broken | Don't | the | sit

Don't sit on the broken chair.

① left | the | library. | Turn | after

② give | please. | Just | a | me | minute,

③ to | pool. | swimming | Let's | the | go

④ ahead | the | Go | at | straight | crossroads.

⑤ door. | close | the | Please

⑥ to | the | brother. | book | Give | your

⑦ loudly! | Don't | so | sing

25

07 El past simple

El past simple sirve para hablar de acciones terminadas
que pasaron en un momento definido del pasado.
Es el tiempo del pasado más habitual en inglés.

7.1 COMPLETA LOS ESPACIOS CON LOS VERBOS EN PAST SIMPLE DEL RECUADRO

After work, Phil _____*listened*_____ to music.

1 I _____ my bedroom this morning.

2 We _____ football in the afternoon.

3 After his dinner, Alex _____ a movie on TV.

4 My wife _____ her parents yesterday.

5 Lucia _____ with her friends at the party.

> played
> ~~listened~~   watched
> visited   danced
> cleaned

7.2 CONECTA EL INICIO Y EL FINAL DE CADA FRASE

After I finished work — I decided to go for a swim.

1 Terry usually takes the metro to work,   so I checked my email.

2 I arrived at work early   the old town and visited the museum.

3 In the morning we walked to   but yesterday he walked instead.

4 Angela cried when she   after she finished her dinner.

5 We usually go to France   then started reading his new book.

6 Jemma washed the dishes   heard the sad news.

7 Roger listened to some music   but last year we traveled around Russia.

7.3 ESCRIBE DE NUEVO LAS FRASES PONIENDO LAS PALABRAS EN EL ORDEN CORRECTO

| hurried | catch | The | last | to | the | children | bus. |

The children hurried to catch the last bus.

❶ | so | felt | to | she | Amy | doctor. | sick, | went | the |

_____

❷ | walk | I | but | to | usually | the | yesterday | I | café, | drove. |

_____

❸ | laughed | Martin's | she | joke. | Mia | heard | when |

_____

7.4 TACHA LA PALABRA INCORRECTA DE CADA FRASE

Jason ~~steped~~ / stepped off the bus and headed toward the café.

❶ Simone **tryed** / **tried** to open the door, but it was completely stuck.

❷ Elena **decideed** / **decided** to wear a nice dress to the dinner party that evening.

❸ Chan **washed** / **washd** the dishes after she and Dan had eaten.

❹ Stephan and Klara **hurried** / **hurryed** to catch the last train home.

❺ The waiter **dropped** / **droped** the dishes onto the floor.

❻ Megan **carryed** / **carried** the files into the office.

7.5 COMPLETA LOS ESPACIOS PONIENDO LOS VERBOS EN PAST SIMPLE

When I was a kid I _____ had _____ (have) two hamsters named Kim and Star.

1 Marilyn _____ (go) with Clive to the exhibition at the gallery.

2 I _____ (see) Phil and Dan at the party last night.

3 Sheila _____ (swim) across the lake to the island.

4 I _____ (drink) a large bottle of water after the race.

5 We _____ (drive) to a beautiful resort in the mountains.

6 Carol _____ (put) her cup down on the table.

7 Seb _____ (do) his homework on the bus to school.

8 Omar _____ (buy) a scarf for his wife at the market.

9 She _____ (draw) a beautiful picture of a cherry tree.

7.6 COMPLETA LOS ESPACIOS CON "WAS" O "WERE"

Irena and Jon _____ were _____ students together in Madrid.

1 You _____ at Paulina's party on Saturday.

2 Joanna _____ very tired after the flight to Australia.

3 My parents _____ delighted when I passed all my exams.

4 There _____ so many people waiting to buy a ticket.

5 I _____ upset when I lost my purse.

6 Liam _____ a pilot for more than 40 years.

7 There _____ a loud bang in the kitchen.

8 My cousins _____ famous dancers in the 1990s.

9 We _____ at the convention last year.

7.7 ESCRIBE DE NUEVO LAS FRASES UTILIZANDO EL PAST SIMPLE

> Sam **goes** running with friends in the local park.
> *Sam went running with friends in the local park.*

1 Robin **wants** to go skiing in the winter.

_____

2 Julie and Scott **drink** a lot of coffee at the café.

_____

3 Eli **goes** camping in the woods last summer.

_____

4 Jon **plays** rugby on Saturday afternoon.

_____

5 I **watch** TV dramas until late last night.

_____

6 We **go** to a jazz club to listen to live music.

_____

7 Sadiq's dog **barks** in the yard all evening.

_____

8 The pollution in my city **is** very bad.

_____

9 Angelo **eats** an apple for his lunch.

_____

10 Kyle **makes** his bed after getting up in the morning.

_____

11 Tina **plays** the piano with her little brother.

_____

08 El past simple negativo

El past simple negativo se utiliza para hablar de cosas que no ocurrieron en el pasado. Se construye siempre de la misma manera, salvo cuando el verbo principal es "be".

8.1 CONECTA EL INICIO Y EL FINAL DE CADA FRASE

I didn't walk to work today. → I took the train instead.

because she felt tired.

1 Emily didn't go to the party — Jenny didn't call him on his birthday.

2 The sports car cost a huge amount, — I took the train instead.

3 Ben was upset because — so we didn't buy it.

4 My uncle didn't enjoy the film — she didn't talk to anyone at the party.

5 The teacher shouted at me — because he hates science fiction.

6 Katie is very shy, so — because I didn't do my homework.

8.2 MARCA LAS FRASES QUE SEAN CORRECTAS

Joanne and Greg didn't knew which road to take to get to the restaurant. ☐
Joanne and Greg didn't know which road to take to get to the restaurant. ☑

1 Zehra didn't played football yesterday. She went fishing. ☐
Zehra didn't play football yesterday. She went fishing. ☐

2 Michael did not like the burger he ordered, so he sent it back. ☐
Michael not liked the burger he ordered, so he sent it back. ☐

3 I didn't went out last night; I stayed in and watched TV instead. ☐
I didn't go out last night; I stayed in and watched TV instead. ☐

8.3 TACHA LAS PALABRAS INCORRECTAS DE CADA FRASE

Lloyd **wasn't** / ~~weren't~~ happy with the new computer he'd just bought.

❶ There **wasn't** / **weren't** enough sandwiches for everyone.

❷ I **not did** / **did not finish** mowing the lawn because I was tired.

❸ The book **wasn't** / **weren't** interesting, so I watched TV instead.

❹ Joe **didn't make** / **didn't made** enough potatoes for everyone.

❺ The students **not understood** / **didn't understand** the teacher.

❻ There **wasn't** / **weren't** many people at the concert last night.

❼ It **wasn't** / **weren't** very warm outside, so we stayed at home.

❽ My brother **didn't enjoy** / **didn't enjoyed** the movie very much.

8.4 ESCRIBE CADA FRASE EN SU OTRA FORMA

Paula **was** on time for work today.	Paula **wasn't** on time for work today.
❶ We spoke to Ellen.	
❷	They **were not** happy.
❸ They **were** late.	
❹	I **didn't wait** for Carl.
❺ Lola **understood**.	
❻	Brendan **wasn't there**.
❼ They **paid** the bill.	
❽	Hugh **did not talk** to me.
❾ Claire **ate** the cake.	
❿	She **didn't go** swimming.

09 Preguntas en past simple

Para hacer preguntas en past simple se utiliza "did".
En el caso de "be", en cambio, se intercambian las
posiciones del sujeto y del verbo "was" o "were".

9.1 CONECTA CADA AFIRMACIÓN CON LA PREGUNTA QUE LE CORRESPONDE

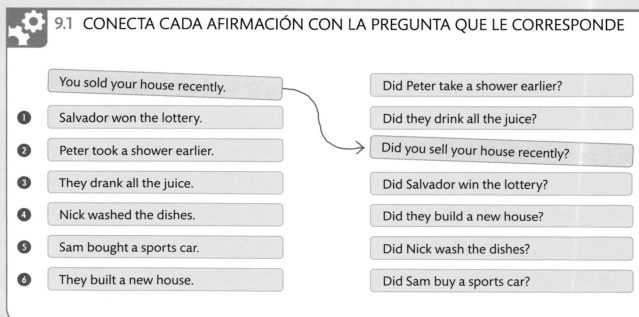

You sold your house recently.

1 Salvador won the lottery.

2 Peter took a shower earlier.

3 They drank all the juice.

4 Nick washed the dishes.

5 Sam bought a sports car.

6 They built a new house.

Did Peter take a shower earlier?

Did they drink all the juice?

Did you sell your house recently?

Did Salvador win the lottery?

Did they build a new house?

Did Nick wash the dishes?

Did Sam buy a sports car?

9.2 CONECTA CADA IMAGEN CON LA PREGUNTA CORRECTA

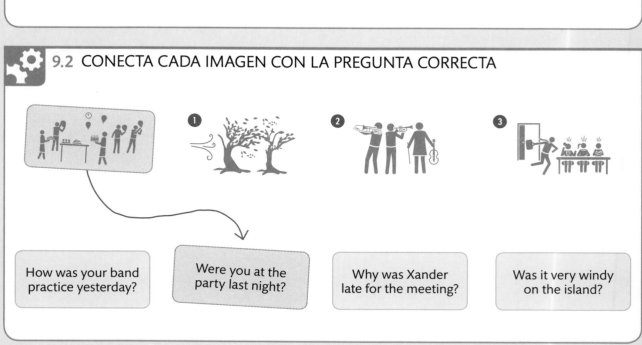

How was your band
practice yesterday?

Were you at the
party last night?

Why was Xander
late for the meeting?

Was it very windy
on the island?

9.3 ESCRIBE DE NUEVO LAS FRASES PONIENDO LAS PALABRAS EN EL ORDEN CORRECTO

| you | down? | Where | broke | when | were | car | your |

Where were you when your car broke down?

① | the | Did | for | take | walk? | you | dog | a |

_____

② | did | home | night? | you | last | How | get |

_____

③ | food | the | Greece? | was | in | like | What |

_____

9.4 ESCRIBE DE NUEVO LAS FRASES Y CORRIGE LOS ERRORES

Did Josie went to work today? She said she was feeling unwell last night.
Did Josie go to work today? She said she was feeling unwell last night.

① Why you were both so late for work this morning?

_____

② Were Katie pleased with the present you got her?

_____

③ Did you took any good photos while you were on vacation?

_____

④ What the weather was like while you were in Greece?

_____

⑤ Where you did buy that lovely suit, Vincent?

_____

10 El past continuous

El past continuous se utiliza en inglés para hablar de acciones que estaban en progreso en un momento determinado del pasado. Se forma con "was" o "were" y un present participle.

10.1 CONECTA CADA IMAGEN CON LA FRASE CORRECTA

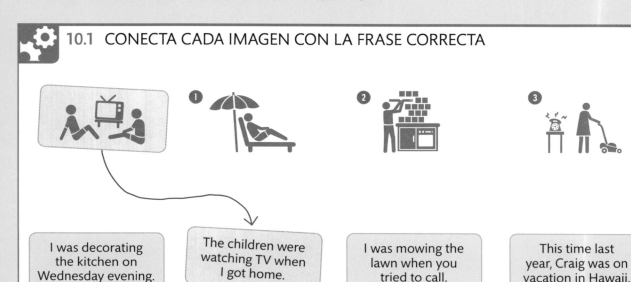

I was decorating the kitchen on Wednesday evening.

The children were watching TV when I got home.

I was mowing the lawn when you tried to call.

This time last year, Craig was on vacation in Hawaii.

10.2 TACHA LAS PALABRAS INCORRECTAS DE CADA FRASE

I was eating / ~~ate~~ my dinner when there ~~was being~~ / was a knock on the door.

1. We were sunbathing / sunbathed when it was beginning / began to rain.

2. When I was meeting / met Tracy yesterday, she was wearing / wore a lovely dress.

3. It was being / was a beautiful day and the birds were singing / sang in the trees.

4. I was hearing / heard a loud bang when I was watching / watched TV last night.

5. It was starting / started to rain while I was talking / talked on the telephone.

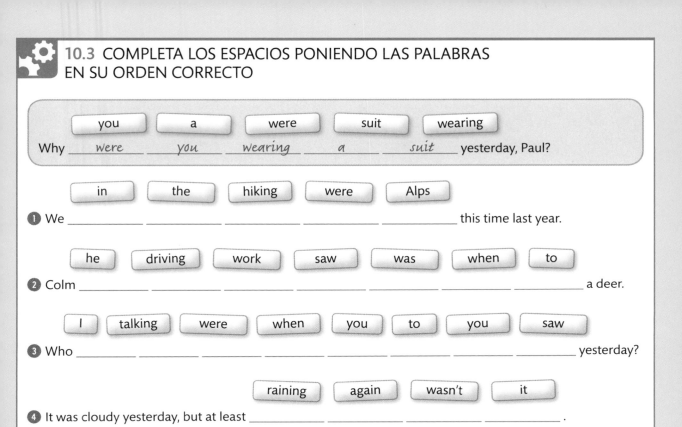

10.3 COMPLETA LOS ESPACIOS PONIENDO LAS PALABRAS EN SU ORDEN CORRECTO

you | a | were | suit | wearing

Why ___were___ ___you___ ___wearing___ ___a___ ___suit___ yesterday, Paul?

in | the | hiking | were | Alps

1 We _____ _____ _____ _____ _____ this time last year.

he | driving | work | saw | was | when | to

2 Colm _____ _____ _____ _____ _____ _____ _____ a deer.

I | talking | were | when | you | to | you | saw

3 Who _____ _____ _____ _____ _____ _____ _____ _____ yesterday?

raining | again | wasn't | it

4 It was cloudy yesterday, but at least _____ _____ _____ _____ .

10.4 COMPLETA LOS ESPACIOS PONIENDO LOS VERBOS EN LOS TIEMPOS CORRECTOS

We ___were walking___ (walk) in the forest when we ___saw___ (see) a bear.

1 Mia _____ (visit) Sydney while she _____ (travel) around Australia.

2 The children _____ (read) when I _____ (enter) the classroom.

3 Ravi _____ (see) an old castle when he _____ (walk) through the forest.

4 The sun _____ (shine) when we _____ (set off) on the journey home.

11 El present perfect simple

El present perfect simple se utiliza para hablar de acontecimientos del pasado reciente que tienen efecto aún en el momento actual. Se construye con "have" y un past participle.

11.1 COMPLETA LAS FRASES CON "HAS" O "HAVE"

Tess ____*has*____ visited France many times, but she ____*has*____ never been to Paris.

1. Daria _____ baked a delicious cake for everyone at the office.

2. My parents _____ decided to buy a little cottage in the country.

3. Ola _____ taken the day off and _____ gone to the new gallery in town.

4. We _____ decided when we're going to get married.

11.2 COMPLETA LOS ESPACIOS CON LAS PALABRAS DEL RECUADRO

Karen ____*has called*____ the police about her noisy neighbors.

1. Hank _____ the letter from his college yet.

2. My children _____ the car at last.

3. Kelly still _____ her bedroom. It's so messy!

4. Danny _____ the bedroom and the living room.

5. Jess _____ Peru and Ecuador so far this year.

hasn't cleaned

has painted   ~~has called~~

hasn't opened

has visited   have washed

11.3 COMPLETA LOS ESPACIOS PONIENDO LOS VERBOS EN PRESENT PERFECT SIMPLE

Michelle _____ *has bought* _____ (buy) a puppy for her daughter.

❶ Fran and Leo _____ (go) to the fair together.

❷ Angelo _____ (not cook) dinner for his family yet.

❸ Jenny _____ (clean) all the windows in her apartment.

❹ I _____ (not meet) Nick's new girlfriend yet.

❺ Morgan _____ (watch) this movie at least six times already.

❻ Mr. Fernandez and his son _____ (leave) the building.

11.4 BUSCA EN LA TABLA LOS PAST PARTICIPLES Y AÑÁDELOS A LA LISTA CORRESPONDIENTE

```
G G P I D R A O B W O T S
N S U N T I N H E L P E D
N D T M J S M D S M S R D
W A N T E D T I U T W U I
S M A Y E B O H R F U J G
E D I S R Y A S V U M N D
M Z L O W A L K E D R I Z
P A A E S N V O N S E N M
K A S K E D D E G J A G I
E H C E A R I D O N E S S
R E C M P S K I I N G E D
A N C G I V E N I J J E M
R E P E P S K D O S E N N
W A T C H E D H I J J L M
```

REGULAR

_____ *wanted* _____

❶ _____

❷ _____

❸ _____

❹ _____

IRREGULAR

_____ *given* _____

❺ _____

❻ _____

❼ _____

❽ _____

37

11.5 MARCA LAS FRASES QUE SEAN CORRECTAS

Did you always live in this apartment, Vicky? ☐
Have you always lived in this apartment, Vicky? ☑

1. I have studied French in college a long time ago. ☐
   I studied French in college a long time ago. ☐

2. I haven't lived in Venezuela since 2009. ☐
   I didn't live in Venezuela since 2009. ☐

3. Kevin has first visited Munich in 1997. ☐
   Kevin first visited Munich in 1997. ☐

4. Enzo finished the report on Friday. ☐
   Enzo has finished the report on Friday. ☐

5. Sebastian is working as a chef for 10 years. ☐
   Sebastian has worked as a chef for 10 years. ☐

11.6 ESCRIBE DE NUEVO LAS FRASES Y CORRIGE LOS ERRORES

Paula **hasn't did** her French homework yet.
Paula hasn't done her French homework yet.

1. Owen **has started** work here in 2017.

   _____

2. I **have spoke** to Tina about this twice today already.

   _____

3. How many countries **have you visit** so far?

   _____

4. Gloria **has never trying** windsurfing before.

   _____

5. Fabio **have lived** in England for more than 15 years.

   _____

11.7 SEÑALA LA MEJOR RESPUESTA A CADA PREGUNTA

Where is Janet today?

She's been to France, but she'll be back next week.

She's gone to France, but she'll be back next week. ✓

1 What's wrong, Frank?

I've just been to the dentist for a filling.

I've just gone to the dentist for a filling.

2 Where are Rob and Susan this afternoon?

They've been to the library.

They've gone to the library.

3 I saw Claire come in with lots of bags.

Yes, she's been shopping with her friends.

Yes, she's gone shopping with her friends.

4 You look hot, Paul.

Yes, I've just been for a run.

Yes, I've just gone for a run.

5 Hi, is Sammy there?

No, she's been for a walk with the dog.

No, she's gone for a walk with the dog.

11.8 SEÑALA LA MEJOR RESPUESTA A CADA PREGUNTA

Have you seen the new exhibition in the museum?

Yes, I saw it last weekend. ✓

Yes, I have seen it last weekend.

1 Have you visited the old temple here yet?

Of course, I've visited it many times.

Of course, I visited it many times.

2 Have you tried Greek food before?

Yes, I tried it when I went to Athens last year.

Yes, I've tried it when I've been to Athens last year.

3 Have you lived here long?

Yes, I've moved here in 1997.

Yes, I moved here in 1997.

4 Have you ever seen a play by William Shakespeare?

Yes, I saw *Macbeth* when I went to London.

Yes, I've seen *Macbeth* when I went to London.

5 Have you been snorkeling before?

Yes, I've tried it twice since I've been in Malaysia.

Yes, I tried it twice since I've been in Malaysia.

12 El present perfect continuous

El present perfect continuous se utiliza para hablar de una actividad en progreso del pasado que tiene aún efecto en el momento actual. Suele referirse al pasado reciente.

12.1 CONECTA EL INICIO Y EL FINAL DE CADA FRASE

David has been cleaning all day, so — the house is really neat!

1. Val has been learning to dance tango — address for a long time?
2. Jess has been running today — so I want to go on a diet.
3. Have you been living at this — and looks very tired.
4. I've been eating too much cake lately, — so I don't feel very fit.
5. I haven't been running for ages, — for more than six months.

12.2 ESCRIBE DE NUEVO LAS FRASES PONIENDO LAS PALABRAS EN EL ORDEN CORRECTO

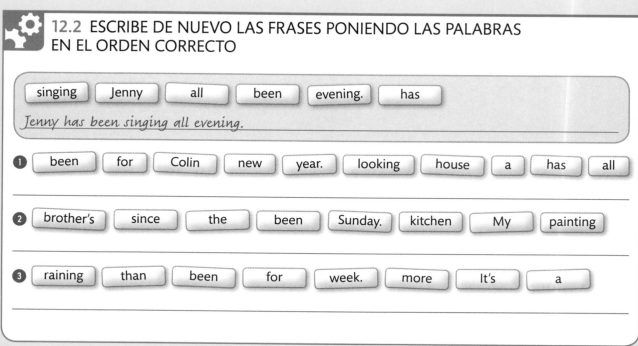

singing | Jenny | all | been | evening. | has

Jenny has been singing all evening.

1. been | for | Colin | new | year. | looking | house | a | has | all

2. brother's | since | the | been | Sunday. | kitchen | My | painting

3. raining | than | been | for | week. | more | It's | a

12.3 COMPLETA LOS ESPACIOS PONIENDO LOS VERBOS EN PRESENT PERFECT CONTINUOUS

I _____*have been driving*_____ (drive) for hours. I'm so tired!

1. I _____ (clean) the house because my parents are coming tomorrow.

2. You _____ (build) that wall all day. Are you nearly finished?

3. Joe _____ (fish) all afternoon, but he hasn't caught anything yet.

4. We _____ (not play) tennis together for very long.

5. How long _____ you _____ (train) for the marathon, Jon?

6. Josh _____ (paint) a lovely landscape this afternoon.

7. Matt and Heather _____ (study) for their exam all evening.

8. I _____ (not read) this book for very long.

9. Jane _____ (travel) all summer.

10. _____ Robin _____ (walk) all day? He looks exhausted.

11. I _____ (try) to cook a new recipe today.

12. Ed _____ (not feel) well, so I told him to go to the doctor.

13. My friend _____ (tour) Europe with his band.

14. My manager _____ (sleep) at his desk all afternoon.

13 El past perfect simple

En inglés, utilizamos el past perfect y el past simple
para hablar de dos o más hechos que ocurrieron
en diferentes momentos del pasado.

 13.1 COMPLETA LOS ESPACIOS CON LAS PALABRAS DEL RECUADRO

George was relieved because he _____*had found*_____ his passport.

1 The play _____ by the time we arrived at the theater.

2 Ben liked Sal, even though he _____ her only a few times.

3 I _____ Indian food before, so I didn't know what to expect.

4 Justin called his sister, but she _____ to bed.

5 Edith _____ her niece for years so was delighted when she visited.

6 Amber felt so happy that she _____ her exam.

7 My uncle was upset because I _____ him recently.

8 Christine worked late because she _____ her project yet.

9 There were a lot of delays because a bus _____ .

10 When we arrived at the station, we discovered the train _____ .

11 Amy couldn't take her flight because she _____ her passport.

12 My son looked bored because he _____ inside the house all day.

13 The house looked shabby because we _____ it in years.

14 Jane was excited about going to Rome. She _____ to Italy before.

hadn't eaten	had started	hadn't finished	had left
had been	hadn't seen	hadn't called	hadn't been	~~had found~~	had gone
had broken down	had passed	had met	had forgotten	hadn't painted

13.2 CONECTA CADA IMAGEN CON LA FRASE CORRECTA

I had just sat down with my drink when it started to rain.

1

Yasmin was exhausted because she had just run a marathon.

2

Janine felt really cold because she'd been outside too long.

3

Tony had called for a taxi an hour earlier, but it still hadn't arrived.

4

Pete had almost finished tiling the wall by the time I got home.

13.3 COMPLETA LOS ESPACIOS PONIENDO LOS VERBOS EN PAST SIMPLE O PAST PERFECT SIMPLE

I _____*tried*_____ (try) to buy some onions, but the store _____*had run out*_____ (run out).

1 Craig _____ (arrive) late to work because he _____ (miss) the train.

2 Marie _____ (not ride) a bike for years, so she _____ (find) it difficult.

3 Dana _____ (be) delighted that she _____ (pass) her driving test at last.

4 James _____ (prepare) breakfast when Caitlin _____ (get up).

5 She _____ (visit) San Francisco once before, when she _____ (be) seven.

6 I _____ (not meet) Karl before, but we _____ (have) lots in common.

7 We _____ (see) the play once before, but we _____ (enjoy) it anyway.

14 El past perfect continuous

Utilizamos el past perfect continuous con el past simple para hablar de una actividad que estaba en progreso antes de que ocurriera otra acción o acontecimiento.

14.1 MARCA LAS FRASES QUE SEAN CORRECTAS

When Fiona finally got home, she had been traveling for 12 hours. ☑
When Fiona finally got home, she has been traveling for 12 hours. ☐

1. Maya had been working here for five years when I started. ☐
   Maya was working here for five years when I had started. ☐

2. It had been raining for a week before the sun came out. ☐
   It rained for a week before the sun had been coming out. ☐

3. I got sunburned because I been lying in the sun all day. ☐
   I got sunburned because I'd been lying in the sun all day. ☐

4. We had been to see that movie everyone talked about at work. ☐
   We went to see that movie everyone had been talking about at work. ☐

5. Vlad had been studying English for a year when he moved to Toronto. ☐
   Vlad had studying English for a year when he had moved to Toronto. ☐

6. My computer hadn't been working properly for ages, so I bought a new one. ☐
   My computer didn't work properly for ages, so I had bought a new one. ☐

7. We only found the hotel after we been driven for more than an hour. ☐
   We only found the hotel after we'd been driving for more than an hour. ☐

8. I'd trained for years before I had been winning my first marathon. ☐
   I'd been training for years before I won my first marathon. ☐

9. Carol had been cooking all morning, so she was exhausted. ☐
   Carol had been cooked all morning, so she was exhausted. ☐

10. I went to the doctor because I hadn't been feeling well all week. ☐
    I went to the doctor because I didn't been feeling well all week. ☐

14.2 CONECTA EL INICIO Y EL FINAL DE CADA FRASE

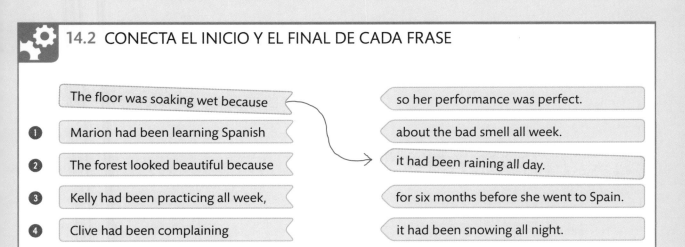

The floor was soaking wet because → it had been raining all day.

1. Marion had been learning Spanish

2. The forest looked beautiful because

3. Kelly had been practicing all week,

4. Clive had been complaining

so her performance was perfect.

about the bad smell all week.

it had been raining all day.

for six months before she went to Spain.

it had been snowing all night.

14.3 COMPLETA LOS ESPACIOS PONIENDO LOS VERBOS EN PAST SIMPLE O PAST PERFECT CONTINUOUS

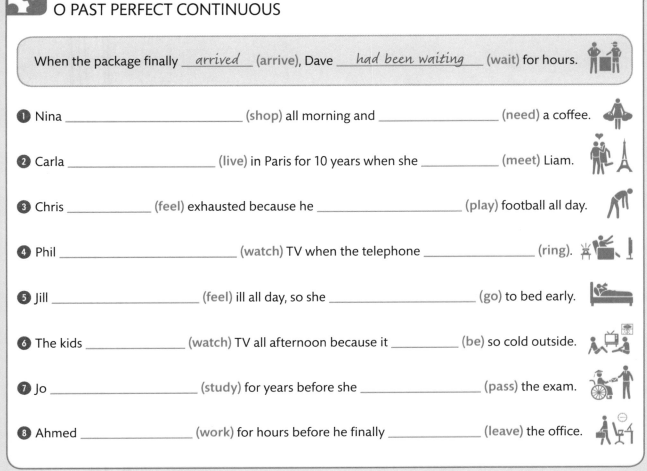

When the package finally __arrived__ (arrive), Dave __had been waiting__ (wait) for hours.

1. Nina _____ (shop) all morning and _____ (need) a coffee.

2. Carla _____ (live) in Paris for 10 years when she _____ (meet) Liam.

3. Chris _____ (feel) exhausted because he _____ (play) football all day.

4. Phil _____ (watch) TV when the telephone _____ (ring).

5. Jill _____ (feel) ill all day, so she _____ (go) to bed early.

6. The kids _____ (watch) TV all afternoon because it _____ (be) so cold outside.

7. Jo _____ (study) for years before she _____ (pass) the exam.

8. Ahmed _____ (work) for hours before he finally _____ (leave) the office.

45

15 "Used to" y "would"

Solemos utilizar "used to" o "would" para hablar de hábitos o estados del pasado. En inglés se utilizan a menudo estas formas para contraponer pasado y presente.

 15.1 MIRA LAS IMÁGENES Y COMPLETA LAS FRASES CON LAS EXPRESIONES DEL RECUADRO

Ricardo _____*used to play*_____ the piano, but now he prefers the violin.

❸ There _____ any factories here. There were beautiful woods.

❶ I _____ in London, but I moved to Paris 10 years ago.

❹ When I worked, I _____ at 5am. Now I relax in the morning.

❷ When I was a teenager, I _____ fishing on Saturdays. Now I prefer photography.

❺ Did you _____ a bike when you were a child?

---

would get up   used to live   use to ride

~~used to play~~   didn't use to be   would go

46

15.2 MARCA LAS FRASES QUE SEAN CORRECTAS

Harry would be an engineer before he became a teacher. ☐
Harry used to be an engineer before he became a teacher. ☑

1. Dana was playing soccer with her friends when she was a child. ☐
Dana used to play soccer with her friends when she was a child. ☐

2. Chris didn't use to have such long hair. ☐
Chris didn't used to have such long hair. ☐

3. I would visit Prague three times when I was a child. ☐
I visited Prague three times when I was a child. ☐

4. Maria used to believe in ghosts when she was little. ☐
Maria use to believe in ghosts when she was little. ☐

5. I used to know Andre well when I was a student. ☐
I would know Andre well when I was a student. ☐

15.3 ESCRIBE DE NUEVO LAS FRASES Y CORRIGE LOS ERRORES

Jenny didn't **used to** like ice cream, but now she loves it.
Jenny didn't use to like ice cream, but now she loves it.

1. I would **tried** to save money when I was at college.
_____

2. My brother **used** read comics when he was a kid.
_____

3. Did **use you** play computer games when you were young?
_____

4. I **didn't used** to read novels, but I really enjoy them now.
_____

16 Past: repaso

Hay ocho maneras distintas de hablar del pasado en inglés.
Las diferencias entre el past simple y el present perfect simple
son especialmente importantes.

16.1 TACHA LAS PALABRAS INCORRECTAS DE CADA FRASE

 Tom went to the doctor last week because he ~~has been feeling~~ / had been feeling unwell.

1 When I saw Sam earlier this morning, he was mopping / has mopped the floor.

2 Ron and Tim are working / have worked at the salon for more than 10 years.

3 Danny wasn't understanding / didn't understand what the man was saying.

4 When I was a kid, I used to be / would be scared of spiders.

5 I love travel, but I haven't been / did not go to New York before.

6 I discovered the loggers were cutting / had cut down almost all the trees.

7 Pavel went outside and had built / built a snowman in the park.

8 We were delayed, and the concert had started / started by the time we arrived.

9 Ash had been studying / was studying Spanish for years before he moved to Madrid.

10 We have been hiking / hiked all morning. Let's have a break, shall we?

11 It was a beautiful day, and the sun had shone / was shining through the window.

16.2 CONECTA EL INICIO Y EL FINAL DE CADA FRASE

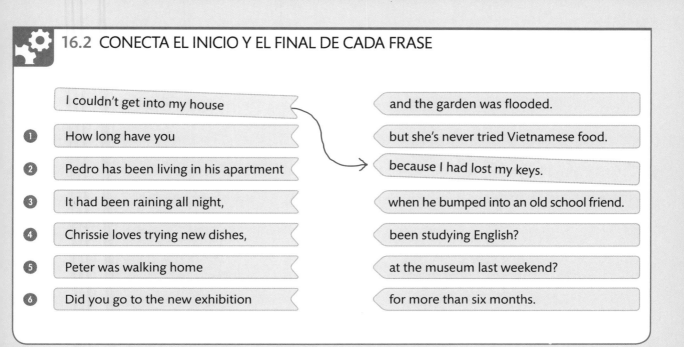

I couldn't get into my house — because I had lost my keys.

1. How long have you — been studying English?

2. Pedro has been living in his apartment — for more than six months.

3. It had been raining all night, — and the garden was flooded.

4. Chrissie loves trying new dishes, — but she's never tried Vietnamese food.

5. Peter was walking home — when he bumped into an old school friend.

6. Did you go to the new exhibition — at the museum last weekend?

16.3 ESCRIBE DE NUEVO LAS FRASES PONIENDO LAS PALABRAS EN EL ORDEN CORRECTO

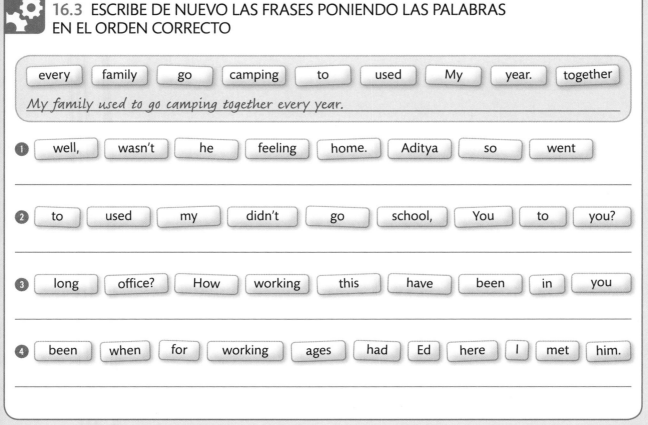

every | family | go | camping | to | used | My | year. | together

My family used to go camping together every year.

1. well, | wasn't | he | feeling | home. | Aditya | so | went

_____

2. to | used | my | didn't | go | school, | You | to | you?

_____

3. long | office? | How | working | this | have | been | in | you

_____

4. been | when | for | working | ages | had | Ed | here | I | met | him.

_____

49

When Harriet _____got_____ (get) to the station, the train had already left.

1 When I arrived at the venue, I realized I _____ (not bring) the tickets.

2 By the time we arrived at the theater, the play _____ (begin).

3 I _____ (not see) that movie yet. Jon told me it's great.

4 Sophie _____ (cook) all morning. She's exhausted.

5 Harry looked great. He _____ (wear) his new suit.

6 Natalia _____ (sunbathe) when she noticed a monkey in a tree.

7 I _____ (not go) to the party on Friday. I was at a concert.

8 Len _____ (decorate). He has paint on his clothes.

9 Jamie _____ (practice) for months before yesterday's show.

10 I _____ (call) my dad this morning to wish him a happy birthday.

11 Bill _____ (take) a bath when he heard a knock at the door.

 16.5 CONECTA CADA IMAGEN CON LA FRASE CORRECTA

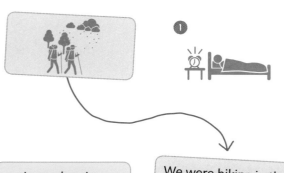

I was sleeping soundly when my alarm clock rang.

We were hiking in the countryside when it started to rain.

I've been dreaming of going abroad all year.

After we'd eaten, Marco helped me clear the table.

16.6 ESCRIBE DE NUEVO LAS FRASES Y CORRIGE LOS ERRORES

Where **did** you **went** on vacation last year?
Where did you go on vacation last year?

1 It **has been** my gran's birthday yesterday.

_____

2 I **use to** like mathematics, but now I prefer chemistry.

_____

3 When I walked into the room, Juan **talked** on the phone.

_____

4 We were sailing to Crete when I **was seeing** a dolphin.

_____

5 You look hot, Karen. **Have** you **be running**?

_____

6 When Dan **has finished** the cleaning, he went to the park.

_____

7 We **have been** lost for three weeks before the helicopter spotted us.

_____

8 **Are** you **lived** in this house for a long time?

_____

9 I **have cycled** all the way to London yesterday.

_____

10 We **walked** through the woods when we saw a bear.

_____

11 When Ben was a child, he **was wanting** to be an astronaut.

_____

12 **Were** you **enjoying** your vacation last week?

_____

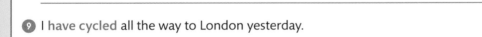

17 El futuro con "going to"

Las formas del futuro se construyen en inglés con la ayuda de verbos auxiliares. Una de las construcciones más comunes es "going to" más la forma base del verbo principal.

17.1 INDICA SI LAS FRASES SON PLANES FUTUROS O PREDICCIONES

I'm going to go see a play this weekend.
Plan futuro ☑
Predicción ☐

① Kirsty's going to fail her exams again.
Plan futuro ☐
Predicción ☐

② I'm not going to eat any more cake today.
Plan futuro ☐
Predicción ☐

③ That child's going to fall off the wall.
Plan futuro ☐
Predicción ☐

④ I'm going to cook a pizza for dinner tonight.
Plan futuro ☐
Predicción ☐

⑤ We're going to get married in April.
Plan futuro ☐
Predicción ☐

⑥ Marlon is going to win the race tonight.
Plan futuro ☐
Predicción ☐

⑦ Martin's going to travel around Morocco this summer.
Plan futuro ☐
Predicción ☐

17.2 CONECTA CADA IMAGEN CON LA FRASE CORRECTA

Ben's brought his guitar. I think he's going to sing.

The forecast says it's going to rain tomorrow.

I think Angela is going to fall off the ladder!

Ted told me he's going to travel around Egypt next year.

Cal has the ball. Is he going to score?

Look at those clouds. I think it's going to rain.

Oh dear! The waiter's going to drop all the plates.

Sam's writing on the wall. His dad's going to be furious.

17.3 ESCRIBE DE NUEVO LAS FRASES EN FORMA DE PREGUNTAS

Emma is going to start her own business.
Is Emma going to start her own business?

1 Gerald is going to win the race.
_____

2 Aziz is going to sail to Ireland.
_____

3 Fiona is going to teach us about statistics.
_____

4 We're going to run out of milk soon.
_____

17.4 COMPLETA LOS ESPACIOS PONIENDO LOS VERBOS EN FUTURO CON "GOING TO"

We _____*are going to buy*_____ (buy) a new television.

1 My son _____ (cook) for us tonight.

2 _____ Jess _____ (study) French at college?

3 Katie _____ (not teach) us next year.

4 It looks like it _____ (rain) again.

5 _____ they _____ (sing) another song for us?

6 I _____ (sell) my bike. I never use it.

7 Emily _____ (fix) the shower for us.

8 Pete _____ (play) rugby with us today.

9 Dad _____ (get) perfume for Mom's birthday again.

18 El futuro con "will"

"Will" se utiliza en algunos tiempos del futuro en inglés.
Se puede utilizar de varias formas, todas ellas diferentes
al futuro con "going to".

18.1 COMPLETA LOS ESPACIOS PONIENDO LOS VERBOS EN FUTURO CON "WILL"

Alice _____will pass_____ (pass) her exams this summer.

1 Ronaldo _____ (not go) to bed before midnight.

2 The kids _____ (have) a great time in Florida next summer.

3 You _____ (love) the new coat I just bought for the winter.

4 Mia _____ (not eat) anything with meat in it.

5 My car broke down, so I _____ (take) the train to work today.

6 Eric _____ (want) to eat steak and fries for his dinner.

7 Noah _____ (win) the 400m race at the track competition.

8 My children _____ (not like) that flavor of ice cream.

9 Charlotte _____ (marry) her boyfriend this year.

10 I _____ (stay) at home and watch TV tonight.

11 Arnie _____ (go) swimming with Bob and Sue.

18.2 INDICA SI LAS FRASES SON PREDICCIONES, OFERTAS, PROMESAS O DECISIONES

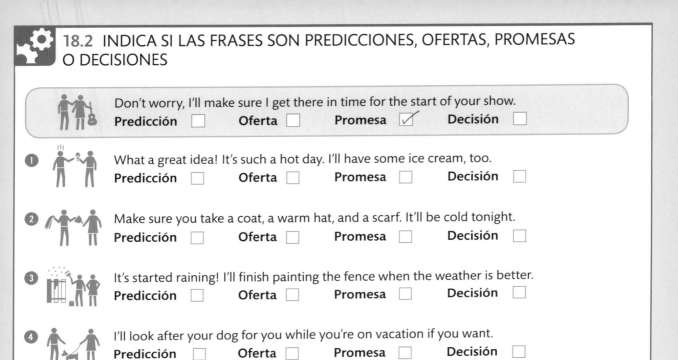

Don't worry, I'll make sure I get there in time for the start of your show.
Predicción ☐   **Oferta** ☐   **Promesa** ☑   **Decisión** ☐

① What a great idea! It's such a hot day. I'll have some ice cream, too.
Predicción ☐   **Oferta** ☐   **Promesa** ☐   **Decisión** ☐

② Make sure you take a coat, a warm hat, and a scarf. It'll be cold tonight.
Predicción ☐   **Oferta** ☐   **Promesa** ☐   **Decisión** ☐

③ It's started raining! I'll finish painting the fence when the weather is better.
Predicción ☐   **Oferta** ☐   **Promesa** ☐   **Decisión** ☐

④ I'll look after your dog for you while you're on vacation if you want.
Predicción ☐   **Oferta** ☐   **Promesa** ☐   **Decisión** ☐

18.3 ESCRIBE DE NUEVO LAS FRASES PONIENDO LAS PALABRAS EN EL ORDEN CORRECTO

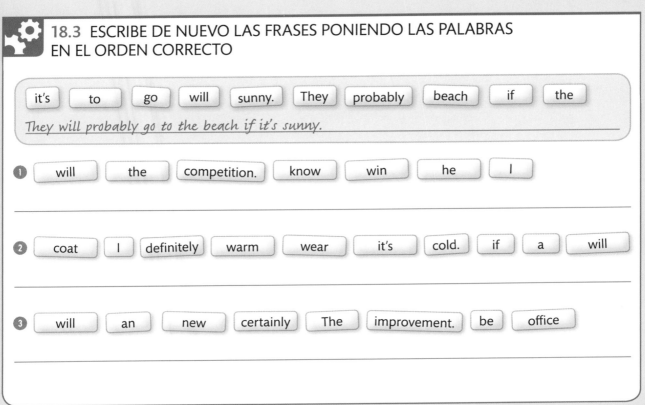

| it's | to | go | will | sunny. | They | probably | beach | if | the |

They will probably go to the beach if it's sunny.

① | will | the | competition. | know | win | he | I |

_____

② | coat | I | definitely | warm | wear | it's | cold. | if | a | will |

_____

③ | will | an | new | certainly | The | improvement. | be | office |

_____

55

19 El presente para hablar del futuro

El present simple y el present continuous pueden emplearse
para hablar de acontecimientos previstos para el futuro.
Suelen utilizarse con alguna expresión temporal.

19.1 INDICA SI LAS FRASES SE REFIEREN AL PRESENTE O AL FUTURO

The next train to Liverpool departs in three hours.
Presente ☐   **Futuro** ☑

① Kevin lives in a large house in Dublin.
Presente ☐   **Futuro** ☐

② The store closes early tomorrow because it's Sunday.
Presente ☐   **Futuro** ☐

③ Megan's traveling around India with her brother Joseph.
Presente ☐   **Futuro** ☐

④ We have two cats and a dog.
Presente ☐   **Futuro** ☐

⑤ The next flight to Zurich leaves at 9pm tonight.
Presente ☐   **Futuro** ☐

⑥ Chiara is playing tennis with her boyfriend tomorrow afternoon.
Presente ☐   **Futuro** ☐

⑦ Vihaan likes watching action movies.
Presente ☐   **Futuro** ☐

⑧ I can't come to dinner with you on Friday because I'm seeing Nina.
Presente ☐   **Futuro** ☐

⑨ We have a rehearsal after work for the concert on Wednesday.
Presente ☐   **Futuro** ☐

⑩ Janet is dancing with one of her friends.
Presente ☐   **Futuro** ☐

19.2 TACHA LAS PALABRAS INCORRECTAS DE CADA FRASE

 Bharti ~~sees~~ / is seeing a play tomorrow evening.

1 The exam **is** / is being next week. I'm nervous!

2 The bus to London usually **departs** / is departing at 5pm.

3 Phil takes / **is taking** his children to the library tomorrow.

4 Lech won't be at work tomorrow. He travels / **is traveling** to Berlin.

5 I can't come to the meeting tomorrow; I **have** / am having a doctor's appointment.

6 Mel and Phil get / **are getting** married this weekend.

19.3 ESCRIBE DE NUEVO LAS FRASES Y CORRIGE LOS ERRORES

Polly **is having** an exam next week.
Polly has an exam next week.

1 We **go** to a party later if you want to join us.

_____

2 The train from Glasgow **arrive** at 10:15pm.

_____

3 I **go** fishing with my father this afternoon.

_____

4 Terry **works** all next weekend to earn a bit of extra money.

_____

57

20 El future continuous

El future continuous se puede formar utilizando "will" o "going to". Describe un acontecimiento o situación que estará en progreso en algún momento en el futuro.

20.1 CONECTA EL INICIO Y EL FINAL DE CADA FRASE

I'd love to go to the theater tomorrow, → but I'm going to be doing my homework.

① Will you be coming into college later? — driving past the library anyway.

② In the year 3000, I think — people will be living on the moon.

③ I can give you a lift. I'll be — I'll be living in a nice house in the country.

④ Will we be having a meeting — he'll be working as a translator in a few years.

⑤ I'm sure people won't be driving — I need some help with my project.

⑥ Mia is going to be bringing her — about the new company logo?

⑦ I'm working as a waiter now, but I hope — new boyfriend to the party tonight.

⑧ Will you be playing soccer — as an actor in a few years' time.

⑨ Enzo's studying French. He hopes — with us this weekend?

⑩ I can post your letter. I'll be going — today. She looked terrible yesterday.

⑪ In 10 years' time, I hope — Thursday to see her mother.

⑫ Tomorrow evening, Femi's band — I'll be running my own restaurant in 10 years.

⑬ I guess Liz won't be coming to work — flying cars in 20 years' time.

⑭ Marco hopes that he'll be working — to the post office this afternoon anyway.

⑮ Sophie will be traveling to Paris next — are going to be performing at Funky Joe's.

20.2 INDICA SI LAS FRASES SON PREGUNTAS NEUTRAS O PETICIONES

Will you be walking past a post office
on your way home?
Pregunta neutra ☑   **Petición** ☐

❸ Will you be taking the train to
Colin's wedding?
Pregunta neutra ☐   **Petición** ☐

❶ Will you go to the supermarket
later, please?
Pregunta neutra ☐   **Petición** ☐

❹ Will we be having a meeting about
the new company logo?
Pregunta neutra ☐   **Petición** ☐

❷ Will you be going to Anastasia's
party later?
Pregunta neutra ☐   **Petición** ☐

❺ Will you help me with my
project, please?
Pregunta neutra ☐   **Petición** ☐

20.3 ESCRIBE DE NUEVO LAS FRASES Y CORRIGE LOS ERRORES

Everyone is going to be watch the World Cup.
Everyone is going to be watching the World Cup.

❶ I'll be live in a mansion by the time I'm 40.

_____

❷ Marie is going to talking about the sales figures.

_____

❸ We'll all relaxing on the beach next week!

_____

❹ Cas will probably earning lots of money before too long.

_____

❺ Is Martin going to be play any of his new songs?

_____

❻ I think humans be exploring other planets by 2050.

_____

21 El future perfect

El future perfect se utiliza para hablar sobre un acontecimiento que se solapará con otro en el futuro, o que terminará antes que aquel. Puede utilizarse en las formas simple o continuous.

⚙ 21.1 COMPLETA LOS ESPACIOS PONIENDO LOS VERBOS EN FUTURE PERFECT O FUTURE PERFECT CONTINUOUS

> By this time next week, I _____ *will have been traveling* _____ (travel) for a month.

1. Amelia _____ (move) to Cairo by the end of September.

2. By the end of the year, we _____ (live) here for 25 years.

3. _____ Pedro _____ (finish) the painting by the time we return?

4. The paint _____ (dry) by tomorrow morning.

5. By four o'clock, we _____ (wait) here for two hours.

6. I'm sure he _____ (win) more than 10 medals by the end of the year.

7. I think by the end of the year Rio _____ (ask) Yukio to marry him.

8. By the time she's 22, Suzy _____ (finish) college.

9. We _____ (complete) the project by the end of May.

10. Sam _____ (graduate) by this time next year.

11. _____ you _____ (finish) the assignment by early October?

12. How many countries _____ (visit) by the time you're 40?

13. By the time I'm 25, I _____ (study) for six years.

14. They _____ (leave) the country by the time you get here.

15. Dan _____ (retire) by the time he's 60.

16. By this time next week, we _____ (be) married for a year!

17. Sam _____ (cook) all day by the time the dinner's ready.

18. By the end of tonight, I _____ (write) this essay.

21.2 CONECTA CADA IMAGEN CON LA FRASE CORRECTA

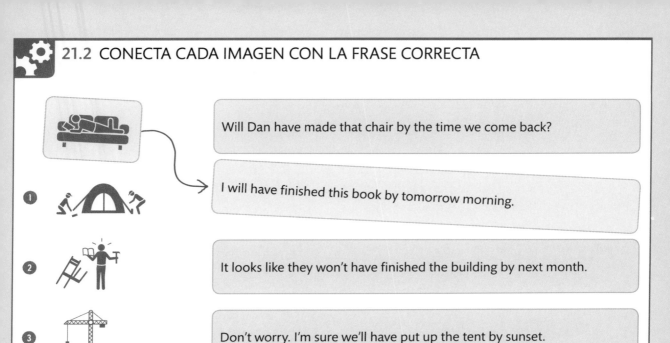

Will Dan have made that chair by the time we come back?

I will have finished this book by tomorrow morning.

It looks like they won't have finished the building by next month.

Don't worry. I'm sure we'll have put up the tent by sunset.

21.3 COMPLETA LOS ESPACIOS CON LAS PALABRAS DEL RECUADRO

I _____ *will have cleaned* _____ the whole house by the time the guests arrive.

❶ Anika _____ for 10 years by the end of the year.

❷ I'm afraid I _____ the kitchen by the time you return.

❸ By December, I _____ the piano for six months.

❹ The guests _____ all the food by the time Tom arrives.

❺ Leroy _____ 18 by the end of next month.

❻ In a year's time, Katie _____ in Rome for 20 years.

will have been acting	will have turned	will have been learning	will have eaten
~~will have cleaned~~	will have been living	won't have painted	

22 El future in the past

Determinadas construcciones pueden utilizarse en inglés para expresar pensamientos sobre el futuro que alguien tuvo en el pasado.

22.1 CONECTA LAS FRASES CON SUS EQUIVALENTES QUE EMPLEAN EL FUTURE IN THE PAST

We think we will have enough money to go on vacation this year.	I thought Hugo would have been promoted by the end of the year.
1 I think Hugo will have been promoted by the end of the year.	We thought we would have enough money to go on vacation this year.
2 Pari is going to buy a kitten for her daughter.	I thought Sam would pass the final English exam.
3 Do you think you'll still be working here in 2021?	Pari was going to buy a kitten for her daughter.
4 I think Sam will pass the final English exam.	I knew Michelle would become a successful singer one day.
5 Penny is going to clean her house if she has time.	Did you think you'd still be working here in 2021?
6 I know Michelle will become a successful singer one day.	Beccy wasn't going to do the English course, was she?
7 Beccy isn't going to do the English course, is she?	Penny was going to clean her house if she had time.

I'm going to become a doctor if I get the grades.
I was going to become a doctor if I got the grades.

① Christopher **thinks he'll go** traveling when he **finishes** college.
_____

② Farouk **is going to start** cycling to work in the new year.
_____

③ I am going to **cook** dinner when I **get** home from work.
_____

④ Pablo **has** the ball. I **think he's going to** score.
_____

⑤ I'm sure Danny **will finish** the wall soon.
_____

⑥ I **think** Ania **will win** the athletics competition.
_____

⑦ My sister **is going** to get a cat when she **moves** house.
_____

⑧ The radio **says it's going to snow** tonight.
_____

⑨ Craig **thinks he'll visit** Japan in the summer.
_____

⑩ We're **going to see** a new band playing at Club 9000.
_____

⑪ I'm sure **he's going to talk** about the company's problems.
_____

⑫ Kelly **is sure she is going to see** some dolphins on vacation.
_____

63

23 Future: repaso

El inglés utiliza diversas construcciones para hablar sobre el futuro. La mayoría se construyen con el verbo auxiliar "will" o con una forma de "be" con "going to".

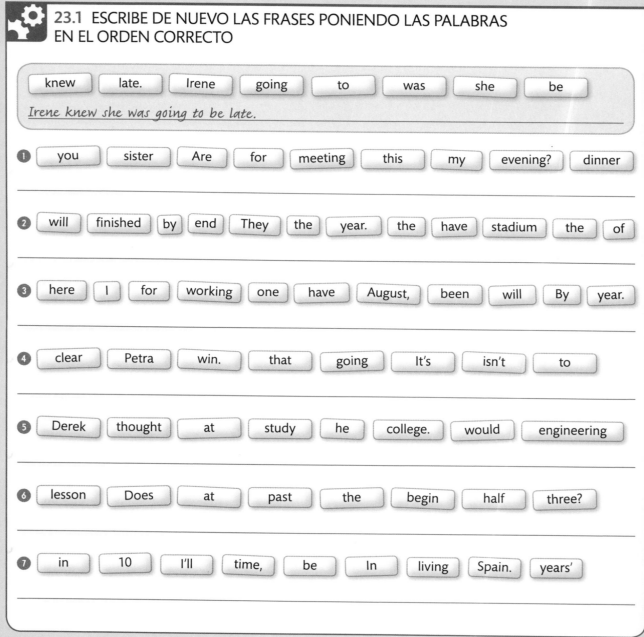

23.1 ESCRIBE DE NUEVO LAS FRASES PONIENDO LAS PALABRAS EN EL ORDEN CORRECTO

| knew | late. | Irene | going | to | was | she | be |

Irene knew she was going to be late.

1 | you | sister | Are | for | meeting | this | my | evening? | dinner |

_____

2 | will | finished | by | end | They | the | year. | the | have | stadium | the | of |

_____

3 | here | I | for | working | one | have | August, | been | will | By | year. |

_____

4 | clear | Petra | win. | that | going | It's | isn't | to |

_____

5 | Derek | thought | at | study | he | college. | would | engineering |

_____

6 | lesson | Does | at | past | the | begin | half | three? |

_____

7 | in | 10 | I'll | time, | be | In | living | Spain. | years' |

_____

23.2 CONECTA EL INICIO Y EL FINAL DE CADA FRASE

The next train to Pasadena	but I made it to work just on time.
① I thought I was going to be late	volcanoes will be very interesting.
② Tomorrow's lecture about	leaves the station at 4pm.
③ Tim thought the meeting	I will have finished in 10 minutes.
④ Sorry, I'm busy at the moment, but	would have started by now.

23.3 TACHA LAS PALABRAS INCORRECTAS DE CADA FRASE

  Oh no! He is going to / ~~will~~ drop those glasses!

① Sue tells me she is going to / will start learning Spanish next year.

② You look tired. I'm going to / I'll get you some coffee.

③ Look at those clouds. It's going to / It will rain soon.

④ I'm going to / I'll help you with those bags, Edith.

⑤ Look! He is going to / will ask his girlfriend to marry him.

⑥ I am going to / will see a play at the theater. I've already got the tickets.

⑦ In the future I think people are going to / will travel to other planets.

⑧ I'm going to / I'll have the chocolate cake on the right, please.

23.4 CONECTA CADA IMAGEN CON LA FRASE CORRECTA

I hope Silvia's going to sing all her hits tonight.

I'm going to be working all weekend.

The forecast said it was going to rain later.

If you're not careful, you'll smash a window.

23.5 ESCRIBE DE NUEVO LAS FRASES Y CORRIGE LOS ERRORES

They thought **they will finish** the housework by 6pm.
They thought they would finish the housework by 6pm.

1 Our company **not going to make** a profit this year.

_____

2 I don't think my son **will to be** an artist when he grows up.

_____

3 I can't meet you tommorow. **I'll play** tennis with Antoine.

_____

4 **We going to be miss** the beginning of the play. Let's hurry!

_____

5 Sal **will have be working** at the diner for 10 years in August.

_____

6 **I was going eat** another piece of cake, but I remembered I was on a diet.

_____

In November, I will have finished my degree. ☑
In November, I will have been finishing my degree. ☐

1 My son thinks we will be driving flying cars in the future. ☐
My son thinks we will have driven flying cars in the future. ☐

2 Seb won't have finished the decorating by the time you get back. ☐
Seb won't finish the decorating by the time you get back. ☐

3 Look! That child will fall off that wall. ☐
Look! That child's going to fall off that wall. ☐

4 It's Angie's party tonight. I'll to bring some snacks and cakes. ☐
It's Angie's party tonight. I'll bring some snacks and cakes. ☐

5 The train had broken down, so I knew I am going to be late. ☐
The train had broken down, so I knew I was going to be late. ☐

6 I'm going to buy that house I saw a couple of times last week. ☐
I will buy that house I saw a couple of times last week. ☐

7 Suki joins us for dinner at the Hotel Bristol. ☐
Suki is joining us for dinner at the Hotel Bristol. ☐

8 When I turn 40, I will be living in Lisbon for 20 years. ☐
When I turn 40, I will have been living in Lisbon for 20 years. ☐

9 I travel to Paris by train this afternoon. ☐
I am traveling to Paris by train this afternoon. ☐

10 I know! I'll buy my grandmother a new scarf. ☐
I know! I'm going to buy my grandmother a new scarf. ☐

11 John knew there were going be bad delays on the trains. ☐
John knew there were going to be bad delays on the trains. ☐

12 Do you think you'll have finished the essay by the time I arrive? ☐
Do you think you'll being finished the essay by the time I arrive? ☐

13 This time next year, I hope I'll have been studying medicine at college. ☐
This time next year, I hope I'll be studying medicine at college. ☐

24 La voz pasiva

En la mayoría de las frases, el sujeto lleva a cabo la acción y el objeto la recibe, o recibe el resultado de la misma. En las frases en pasiva, esto se invierte y es el sujeto el que recibe la acción.

 24.1 MIRA LAS IMÁGENES Y COMPLETA LAS FRASES CON LAS EXPRESIONES DEL RECUADRO

The course _____*is taught*_____ online.

3 The Eiffel Tower _____ by millions of tourists each year.

1 The alarm _____ once a month at my workplace.

4 Lunch _____ in the college cafeteria.

2 The sculpture _____ in the main hall.

5 The band _____ to perform its greatest hits.

---

is expected   is visited   is tested

~~is taught~~   is displayed   is eaten

68

24.2 CONECTA LAS FRASES EN VOZ ACTIVA CON SUS EQUIVALENTES EN VOZ PASIVA

A plumber is fixing the leak in my roof.

This program is used by many students.

① Many students use this program.

The leak in my roof is being fixed.

② A famous designer is making her new dress.

The train is usually driven by Martin.

③ Someone cleans our apartment every Thursday.

Her new dress is being made by a famous designer.

④ Martin usually drives the train.

Our apartment is cleaned every Thursday.

24.3 CONECTA CADA IMAGEN CON LA FRASE CORRECTA

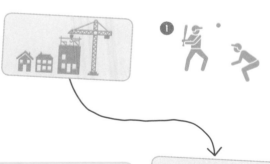 ① ② ③

The play is being performed on stage later tonight.

A new apartment buiding is being built near my house.

Solar panels are being used by an increasing number of people.

The game is usually played in Central Park each September.

24.4 COMPLETA LOS ESPACIOS PONIENDO LOS VERBOS EN PRESENT SIMPLE O EN PRESENT CONTINUOUS PASSIVE

The newspaper _____*is delivered*_____ (deliver) every morning at 7am.

1 English _____ (not understand) by many people here.

2 A new shopping mall _____ (build) near the park.

3 Some shows _____ (watch) by millions of people each day.

4 The food _____ (prepare) at home today.

5 The castle _____ (surround) by dense forests.

6 Our products _____ usually _____ (dispatch) within two days.

7 Latin _____ (not study) by many young people.

8 Guests _____ always _____ (provide) with a complimentary lunch.

9 My computer _____ (repair) at the moment.

10 Kelvin _____ (teach) how to juggle today.

11 The children _____ always _____ (supervise) by two adults.

12 A lot of old factories _____ (knock down).

13 The crime _____ (investigate) by the police.

14 Students _____ (expect) to be punctual at all times.

15 I'm staying with Claire while my house _____ (decorate).

16 The play _____ (perform) in French tonight.

17 That course _____ usually _____ (teach) by Eduardo.

18 All our plastic and glass _____ (recycle) by the council.

19 Ron _____ (investigate) for fraud.

20 My hair _____ (cut) by a stylist from Ecuador.

21 The car _____ (wash) right now.

22 Karim's performance _____ (record) tonight.

25 La voz pasiva en pretérito

En inglés se utiliza la voz pasiva en pretérito para poner énfasis en el efecto de una acción que tuvo lugar en el pasado y no en la causa de dicha acción.

25.1 CONECTA CADA IMAGEN CON LA FRASE CORRECTA

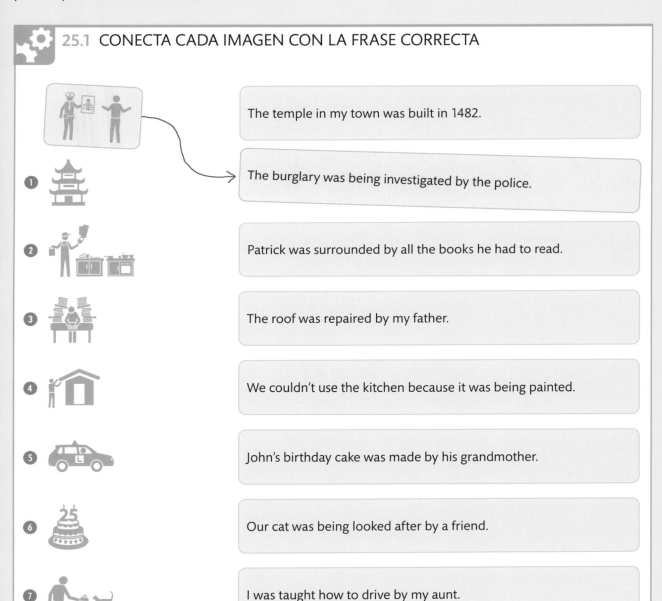

The temple in my town was built in 1482.

The burglary was being investigated by the police.

Patrick was surrounded by all the books he had to read.

The roof was repaired by my father.

We couldn't use the kitchen because it was being painted.

John's birthday cake was made by his grandmother.

Our cat was being looked after by a friend.

I was taught how to drive by my aunt.

25.2 CONECTA EL INICIO Y EL FINAL DE CADA FRASE

The lecture had been canceled

because she hadn't been invited to the party.

1 When we got home,

so I didn't have a present for him.

2 Karen was so upset

because the professor was sick.

3 I hadn't been told it was Rajiv's birthday,

we discovered the house had been broken into.

4 Many houses have been damaged

about tomorrow's meeting?

5 Have all the staff been informed

It's been in the auto repair shop for ages!

6 Has your car been fixed yet?

by the recent hurricane.

25.3 COMPLETA LOS ESPACIOS CON LAS PALABRAS DEL RECUADRO

The puppies _____ *have been given* _____ to families with big yards.

1 The play _____ by the smoke alarm. We had to evacuate the theater.

2 Dan's room was filthy. It _____ in weeks.

3 That old factory near my house _____.

4 All of the plants on the balcony _____.

5 The mail _____ yet. I'm still waiting.

6 Most of the forest _____ last year.

7 The spy _____ by two men in hats.

8 Malcolm _____. He was so lazy!

has been demolished   was being followed   hadn't been cleaned   hasn't been delivered

have been watered   have been given   was cut down   has been fired   was interrupted

72

The chefs were cooking lots of food for the party.
Lots of food was being cooked for the party.

1 People ate all of the cake that Jemima had made.

2 The thieves stole all the money from the bank's safe.

3 Someone injured my brother in a car accident yesterday.

4 People have booked all the tables in the restaurant.

5 They were building lots of tower blocks in the suburbs.

6 Nobody had explored that part of the country before.

7 They were so happy that someone had found their cat.

8 They didn't inform me that the office was closed on Friday.

9 We have sold all the tickets for tonight's movie.

10 People have never climbed that mountain before.

11 The earthquake has destroyed a lot of buildings.

12 It's cold. Someone has left the window open.

26 La voz pasiva en futuro

En inglés se utiliza la voz pasiva en futuro para poner
énfasis en el efecto de una acción que ocurrirá en el
futuro y no en la causa de tal acción.

26.1 COMPLETA LOS ESPACIOS PONIENDO LOS VERBOS EN FUTURE SIMPLE PASSIVE

The letter _____ will be sent _____ (send) to you this afternoon.

1. The new stadium _____ (open) by the president.

2. All the food _____ (cook) by our new chef, Luigi.

3. Our house _____ (not finish) by the end of the year.

4. The prisoner _____ (release) after 30 years.

5. _____ the show _____ (present) by a new DJ?

6. My latest novel _____ (publish) in January.

7. The water _____ (turn off) on Thursday morning.

8. The lecture _____ (give) by Professor O'Brien.

9. Dinner _____ (serve) in the dining room between 7 and 9pm.

10. All the laundry _____ (do) by the time you get back.

11. _____ the students _____ (give) a test at the end of the course?

26.2 CONECTA CADA IMAGEN CON LA FRASE CORRECTA

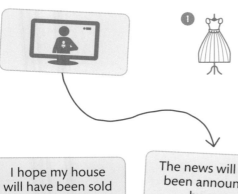 **1** **2** **3**

| I hope my house will have been sold by next month. | The news will have been announced by now. | I'm sure we'll have been visited by aliens by 2100. | Will the dress have been altered before the wedding day? |

26.3 COMPLETA LOS ESPACIOS PONIENDO LOS VERBOS EN FUTURE PERFECT PASSIVE

By tomorrow evening, everyone _____ *will have been notified* _____ (notify) of the changes.

1 By 2030, intelligent robots _____ (develop).

2 I'm sure our car _____ (repair) by the beginning of next week.

3 The computer _____ (replace) before you start work.

4 I think Jane _____ (fire) by this time next year.

5 By 2050, many more galaxies _____ (discover).

6 Do you think the criminals _____ (catch) by then?

7 All our staff _____ (train) by the end of the week.

8 _____ the project _____ (complete) by the time we return?

9 All the issues _____ (resolve) before we release the product.

10 I hope the kitchen _____ (paint) by the time we move in.

11 Our new bed _____ (deliver) by the end of the month.

12 The decision _____ (make) by Friday evening.

La voz pasiva en verbos modales

Los verbos modales pueden utilizarse en inglés en voz
pasiva. Como ocurre con otras construcciones pasivas,
el énfasis pasa al objeto que recibe la acción.

27.1 ESCRIBE DE NUEVO LAS FRASES PONIENDO LAS PALABRAS EN EL ORDEN CORRECTO

| box | kept | should | place. | a | This | in | be | safe |

This box should be kept in a safe place.

1 | turned | off | should | All | before | the | leaving | computers | office. | be |

_____

2 | at | must | Protective | all | worn | glasses | be | times. |

_____

3 | have | exam. | about | been | We | the | told | should |

_____

4 | meeting | until | be | week? | the | postponed | in | Can | later | the |

_____

5 | tourists | should | a | guidebook. | All | given | the | be |

_____

6 | have | You | running | could | across | been | that | street! | killed |

_____

7 | car | been | weeks | have | Our | repaired | should | ago. |

_____

27.2 MARCA LAS FRASES QUE SEAN CORRECTAS

They should have been told that the class was canceled. ☑
They should have told that the class was canceled. ☐

① All the floors must have be mopped at the end of the day. ☐
All the floors must be mopped at the end of the day. ☐

② That ugly building should have been demolish years ago. ☐
That ugly building should have been demolished years ago. ☐

③ The mountain can be climbed with the help of ropes. ☐
The mountain can been climbed with the help of ropes. ☐

④ Our forests must be protected from destruction. ☐
Our forests must be protect from destruction. ☐

⑤ You wouldn't have been stung if you'd remained calm. ☐
You wouldn't been stung if you'd remained calm. ☐

27.3 CONECTA EL INICIO Y EL FINAL DE CADA FRASE

Marco's computer broke, but   one of my teeth must be removed.

① Bicycles should only be ridden   a tiger has escaped from the zoo.

② The dentist told me that   it might have been repaired by now.

③ Clara should have been given   for one minute on each side.

④ Everyone should be warned that   if you are wearing a helmet.

⑤ The dish could have been improved   more time to finish her assignment.

⑥ The steak should be fried   if the car hadn't been going so fast.

⑦ The accident might have been avoided   if we'd used better ingredients.

28 Otras construcciones en pasiva

Muchos modismos del inglés utilizan formas pasivas.
Algunos de ellos utilizan las normas estándares de la
voz pasiva, mientras que otros son un poco distintos.

28.1 CONECTA CADA IMAGEN CON LA FRASE CORRECTA

That old house across the road is said to be haunted.

1 There is said to be a problem with crime in the local area.

2 The mountain is known to be dangerous to climb.

3 It has been revealed that the company is losing a lot of money.

4 It has been reported that many houses have been destroyed.

5 There are said to be many beautiful temples in Japan.

6 The movie star is rumored to be in a relationship with her co-star.

7 The new gallery is reported to contain a lot of modern art.

28.2 COMPLETA LOS ESPACIOS CON LAS PALABRAS DEL RECUADRO

It's freezing! I hope that the heating will _____ *get fixed* _____ soon.

1 I'm hoping that I will _____ to senior manager soon.

2 My colleague often _____ for the quality of her work.

3 The bedroom's _____ next week.

4 My aunt's car _____ from the parking lot at work.

5 Samantha _____ by a dog in the local park.

gets criticized	got stolen	got bitten
getting redecorated	~~get fixed~~	get promoted

28.3 ESCRIBE DE NUEVO LAS FRASES Y CORRIGE LOS ERRORES

My new dress **got deliver** yesterday. It's beautiful!
My new dress got delivered yesterday. It's beautiful! _____

1 This store **is know** to sell high-quality shoes.

_____

2 It **been reported** that Ella is going to start performing again.

_____

3 The grass **get cut** once a month by our gardener.

_____

4 It **is rumor** that we are going to have an exam today.

_____

5 All the dishes **got wash** by Danny.

_____

29 Frases condicionales

Las frases condicionales se utilizan para describir resultados reales o hipotéticos de situaciones reales o hipotéticas. Pueden utilizar muchas formas verbales distintas.

29.1 CONECTA CADA IMAGEN CON LA FRASE CORRECTA

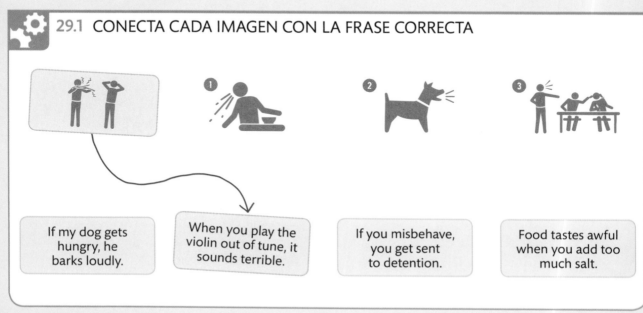

If my dog gets hungry, he barks loudly.

When you play the violin out of tune, it sounds terrible.

If you misbehave, you get sent to detention.

Food tastes awful when you add too much salt.

29.2 CONECTA EL INICIO Y EL FINAL DE CADA FRASE

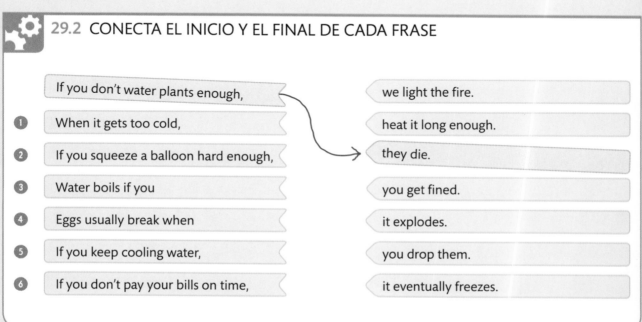

If you don't water plants enough,

1 When it gets too cold,

2 If you squeeze a balloon hard enough,

3 Water boils if you

4 Eggs usually break when

5 If you keep cooling water,

6 If you don't pay your bills on time,

we light the fire.

heat it long enough.

they die.

you get fined.

it explodes.

you drop them.

it eventually freezes.

29.3 COMPLETA LOS ESPACIOS CON LAS PALABRAS DEL RECUADRO

If it starts to rain, _____ *put on* _____ your coat.

1. If the phone rings, please _____ it.

2. _____ if you have any problems at all.

3. _____ it if you don't like it.

4. When you buy something expensive, always _____ the receipt.

5. If it's sunny tomorrow, _____ to use sunscreen.

Let me know
make sure
answer ~~put on~~
Don't eat   keep

 29.4 TACHA LAS PALABRAS INCORRECTAS DE CADA FRASE

If they don't hurry up, they will / ~~won't~~ miss their flight.

1. If it stops / will stop raining, I'll finish painting the fence.

2. If Janine works very hard, she passes / will pass her exams.

3. If I don't get / won't get the job, I'll be very upset.

4. Sally loses / will lose her job if she keeps missing deadlines.

5. If it doesn't rain tomorrow, we have / will have a picnic.

6. If I get / don't get a raise, I'll definitely go on an expensive vacation.

7. Sarah will go fishing on Saturday if she has / doesn't have time.

8. If we take this path, we get / will get there more quickly.

29.5 MARCA LAS FRASES QUE SEAN CORRECTAS

If I owned a television, I will watch the football game. ☐
If I owned a television, I would watch the football game. ☑

❶ Phil would buy a new television if he had more money. ☐
Phil would buy a new television if he would have more money. ☐

❷ If I didn't have a headache, I'd definitely come to the party. ☐
If I wouldn't have a headache, I'd definitely come to the party. ☐

❸ I'd visit you more often if I'd had more time. ☐
I'd visit you more often if I had more time. ☐

❹ If I was young again, I will go traveling around the world. ☐
If I was young again, I would go traveling around the world. ☐

29.6 ESCRIBE DE NUEVO LAS FRASES PONIENDO LAS PALABRAS EN EL ORDEN CORRECTO

| they | money, | buy | more | bigger | a | house. | If | would | had | they |

If they had more money, they would buy a bigger house.

❶ | a | lottery. | buy | if | would | he | Tony | villa | won | the |

_____

❷ | we | money, | If | more | own | we | would | had | start | business. | our |

_____

❸ | sure | would | if | I'm | you | David | him. | you | help | asked |

_____

❹ | went | If | she'd | Ania | go | traveling, | Vietnam. | to |

_____

29.7 COMPLETA LOS ESPACIOS PONIENDO LOS VERBOS EN THIRD CONDITIONAL

If Carlos _had studied_ (study) harder, he _would have passed_ (pass) his exams.

1. If Fleur _____ (go) to bed earlier, she _____ (not feel) tired all day.

2. Simon _____ (go) to jail if the police _____ (catch) him.

3. If Marco _____ (know) there was a test, he _____ (study) for it.

4. I _____ (bring) an umbrella if I _____ (know) it was going to rain.

5. If Chris _____ (not score), we _____ (not win) the championship.

6. If I _____ (know) you were coming, I _____ (clean) the apartment.

7. I _____ (buy) you a present if I _____ (know) it was your birthday.

8. Dom _____ (not be) alone on his birthday if he _____ (invite) his friends.

9. If I _____ (not sleep) through my alarm, I _____ (not arrive) late for work.

10. Abbie _____ (study) art if she _____ (go) to college.

11. If we _____ (arrive) early, we _____ (not miss) the train.

12. Libby _____ (win) the race if she _____ (be) faster than George.

13. We _____ (not go) camping if _____ (know) it was going to be so hot.

14. If Lou _____ (not work) so hard, the project _____ (not be) such a success.

83

29.8 CONECTA EL INICIO Y EL FINAL DE CADA FRASE

If she hadn't forgotten her phone,

if she'd remembered her key this morning.

1 If I hadn't brought the umbrella

he'd be going to a good college now.

2 If Ed had scored higher on his tests,

she would be able to call someone for help.

3 I'd be at work now

if he hadn't stolen the painting from the gallery.

4 Chloe wouldn't be sitting outside now

if I hadn't missed the 7am train.

5 Gordon wouldn't be in prison

I'd be very wet now.

29.9 COMPLETA LOS ESPACIOS CON LAS PALABRAS DEL RECUADRO

If I had done this work earlier, I _____ *could be relaxing* _____ this evening.

1 Jemma _____ so tired now if she'd gone to bed earlier.

2 If they _____ the decorating, we wouldn't be sleeping in a camper.

3 If Emma _____ to our advice, she would be more successful now.

4 I wouldn't be such a good athlete if I _____ so hard.

5 If Len had fixed my car, I _____ to work today.

6 Tim _____ it here if he had decided to join us.

7 Karen wouldn't have to stand if she _____ a seat.

8 If I hadn't lost my job, I _____ with my sister.

9 If you _____ practicing, I'm sure you'd be a famous singer today.

had reserved	wouldn't be	had listened	wouldn't be walking	had kept
wouldn't be living	~~could be relaxing~~	would love	had finished	hadn't trained

84

If Fiona won more races, she will enjoy running more.
If Fiona won more races, she would enjoy running more.

❶ If I have to make a choice, I would say I prefer dogs.

_____

❷ I would graduated by now if I'd continued with my studies.

_____

❸ If you won't hurry up, you're going to be late for school.

_____

❹ You would have had a great time at the party if you will come.

_____

❺ We'd be on vacation now if we haven't missed the flight.

_____

❻ When water will get hot enough, it boils.

_____

❼ I go to the doctor if my leg still hurts tomorrow.

_____

❽ The soup tastes better if I had added more salt.

_____

❾ I always drink plenty of water if I got too hot.

_____

❿ It would have be a perfect party if the dog hadn't eaten the cake.

_____

⓫ I repair the roof this afternoon if the weather's good.

_____

⓬ I will be very scared if I ever saw a UFO.

_____

30 Otras frases condicionales

El inglés permite algunas variaciones en la estructura de las frases condicionales. Dichas variaciones dan más información sobre el contexto del condicional.

 30.1 MIRA LAS IMÁGENES Y COMPLETA LAS FRASES CON LAS EXPRESIONES DEL RECUADRO

If you entered the competition, you _____*could win*_____ some money!

3 We _____ camping if I take a few days off work.

1 You _____ an ice cream if you're really good.

4 If she had practiced more, Helena _____ a great singer.

2 If you'd asked her to marry you, she _____ yes.

5 If I have some free time later, I _____ some gardening.

could have been	might have said	can have
could go	~~could win~~	might do

86

30.2 CONECTA EL INICIO Y EL FINAL DE CADA FRASE

Your infection will get worse	unless we start paying her more.
1 Unless you get up now,	the neighbors will complain.
2 She'll leave the firm	unless you go to the doctor today.
3 Unless you turn the music down,	you're going to be late.
4 You'll get sunburned	you're not going to graduate on time.
5 Unless you start working harder,	unless you wear sun protection.
6 Angelica will get annoyed	we'll reach the summit before noon.
7 Unless there's bad weather,	unless you reply to her email.

 30.3 ESCRIBE DE NUEVO LAS FRASES EN THIRD CONDITIONAL EMPLEANDO LA INVERSIÓN FORMAL

If Simon had ordered his sofa sooner, it would be here by now.
Had Simon ordered his sofa sooner, it would be here by now.

1 If business had been better, the company wouldn't have gone bankrupt.

2 If Pamela had been richer, she would have bought a larger house.

3 If you had studied harder, the exam wouldn't have been so difficult.

4 If Paul had attended the meeting, he would have known about the new project.

5 If the weather had been better, their trip would have been more enjoyable.

31 Frases condicionales: repaso

Hay cuatro tipos de frases condicionales. El zero conditional
se refiere a situaciones reales, pero los first, second y third
conditionals se refieren a situaciones hipotéticas.

31.1 INDICA SI LAS FRASES EMPLEAN EL ZERO, EL FIRST, EL SECOND O EL THIRD CONDITIONAL

If she had more money, she would buy a new phone.

Zero ☐   **First** ☐   **Second** ☑   **Third** ☐

❶ If I didn't feel so tired, I would go to Jake's party.

Zero ☐   **First** ☐   **Second** ☐   **Third** ☐

❷ If you eat another cupcake, you will feel ill.

Zero ☐   **First** ☐   **Second** ☐   **Third** ☐

❸ Plants die if you don't give them water.

Zero ☐   **First** ☐   **Second** ☐   **Third** ☐

❹ If Juan had studied harder, he could have been a doctor.

Zero ☐   **First** ☐   **Second** ☐   **Third** ☐

❺ If the weather is nice tomorrow, we will go to the beach.

Zero ☐   **First** ☐   **Second** ☐   **Third** ☐

❻ We will miss the train if you don't hurry up.

Zero ☐   **First** ☐   **Second** ☐   **Third** ☐

❼ If you mix red and yellow, you get orange.

Zero ☐   **First** ☐   **Second** ☐   **Third** ☐

❽ I'd study mathematics at college if I were you.

Zero ☐   **First** ☐   **Second** ☐   **Third** ☐

❾ I would have returned this suit if I hadn't lost the receipt.

Zero ☐   **First** ☐   **Second** ☐   **Third** ☐

❿ If I had a lot of money, I'd buy a sports car.

Zero ☐   **First** ☐   **Second** ☐   **Third** ☐

31.2 ESCRIBE DE NUEVO LAS FRASES Y AÑADE COMAS DONDE SEA NECESARIO

> If David finishes his homework he can play with his toys.
> *If David finishes his homework, he can play with his toys.*

1 If I had more money I'd go on vacation to Rome.

_____

2 We would have packed warmer clothes if we'd known it was so cold here.

_____

3 They could play baseball if it stopped raining.

_____

4 If you keep practicing you will win the championship.

_____

 31.3 MARCA LAS FRASES QUE SEAN CORRECTAS

> If you will win the race, you'll get a medal. ☐
> If you win the race, you'll get a medal. ☑

1 I would have passed the test if I'd studied. ☐
I would passed the test if I'd studied. ☐

2 If Mia had more time, she'd start a hobby. ☐
If Mia has more time, she'd start a hobby. ☐

3 If it's sunny tomorrow, I go swimming. ☐
If it's sunny tomorrow, I'll go swimming. ☐

4 If you heat ice, it turns into water. ☐
If you will heat ice, it turns into water. ☐

5 I'd have caught the bus if I hadn't overslept. ☐
I'd have catch the bus if I hadn't overslept. ☐

6 If my team won't win, I'll be disappointed. ☐
If my team doesn't win, I'll be disappointed. ☐

7 If Mel won the lottery, she'd buy a villa. ☐
If Mel won the lottery, she'll buy a villa. ☐

8 If I had seen Rob, I would said hello. ☐
If I had seen Rob, I would have said hello. ☐

9 If I'm late again, my boss is so angry. ☐
If I'm late again, my boss will be so angry. ☐

10 If she had asked me, I would have helped her. ☐
If she asked me, I would have helped her. ☐

11 If you go to bed earlier, you'd feel less tired. ☐
If you went to bed earlier, you'd feel less tired. ☐

32 Posibilidades futuras

Hay muchas maneras de hablar de situaciones imaginarias
futuras. Pueden utilizarse diversas estructuras para indicar
si una situación es probable o improbable.

32.1 INDICA SI LO QUE DICEN LAS FRASES ES PROBABLE, IMPROBABLE O NO HA SUCEDIDO

Suppose the factory closed down. Where would we work instead?
Probable ☐   **Improbable** ☑   **No ha sucedido** ☐

① What if we miss the train? We won't get to the wedding on time.
Probable ☐   **Improbable** ☐   **No ha sucedido** ☐

② Suppose I hadn't met Ella. Who would I be with now?
Probable ☐   **Improbable** ☐   **No ha sucedido** ☐

③ What if I hadn't moved to New York? Would I still be living in Chicago?
Probable ☐   **Improbable** ☐   **No ha sucedido** ☐

④ What if you won the election? How would you feel?
Probable ☐   **Improbable** ☐   **No ha sucedido** ☐

⑤ Suppose I'd practiced every day for the recital. Would I have sounded better?
Probable ☐   **Improbable** ☐   **No ha sucedido** ☐

⑥ What if I took piano classes? Do you think I'm too old to start?
Probable ☐   **Improbable** ☐   **No ha sucedido** ☐

⑦ Suppose you saw a tiger. What would you do?
Probable ☐   **Improbable** ☐   **No ha sucedido** ☐

⑧ What if someone doesn't eat meat? We'd better make something vegetarian too.
Probable ☐   **Improbable** ☐   **No ha sucedido** ☐

⑨ Let's take some waterproof jackets in case it rains at the festival.
Probable ☐   **Improbable** ☐   **No ha sucedido** ☐

⑩ What if I got a new job? I'd like to work for a museum.
Probable ☐   **Improbable** ☐   **No ha sucedido** ☐

32.2 CONECTA LAS PARTES DE UNA MISMA FRASE

Make sure you lock the doors

Where do you think you'd work?

1. What if Vicky became a famous actress?

We may not be able to find the path.

2. Suppose you lost your job at the café.

in case someone tries to break in.

3. Suppose we get lost in the forest.

She really enjoys drama, after all.

4. Let's prepare some more food

What if the audience don't like me?

5. Take some water with you

in case more people arrive.

6. I'm nervous about going on stage tonight.

in case you get hot while you're jogging.

32.3 MARCA LAS FRASES QUE SEAN CORRECTAS

What if we runned out of money? We won't be able to get home! ☐
What if we run out of money? We won't be able to get home! ☑

1. Check the gallery's website in case it will be closed on Mondays. ☐
Check the gallery's website in case it is closed on Mondays. ☐

2. Suppose the factory would close. What would the town do? ☐
Suppose the factory closed. What would the town do? ☐

3. What if we come across a bear? There are lots of them in the mountains. ☐
What if we will come across a bear? There are lots of them in the mountains. ☐

4. Your interview's tomorrow. Set an alarm in case you don't wake up on time. ☐
Your interview's tomorrow. Set an alarm in case you didn't wake up on time. ☐

5. What if we would win the lottery? What would we do with the money? ☐
What if we won the lottery? What would we do with the money? ☐

6. Take a good book in case you got bored waiting. ☐
Take a good book in case you get bored waiting. ☐

33 Deseos y lamentaciones

En inglés se utiliza el verbo "wish" para hablar sobre lamentaciones presentes y pasadas. El tiempo del verbo que acompaña a "wish" afecta al significado de la frase.

33.1 CONECTA CADA IMAGEN CON LA FRASE CORRECTA

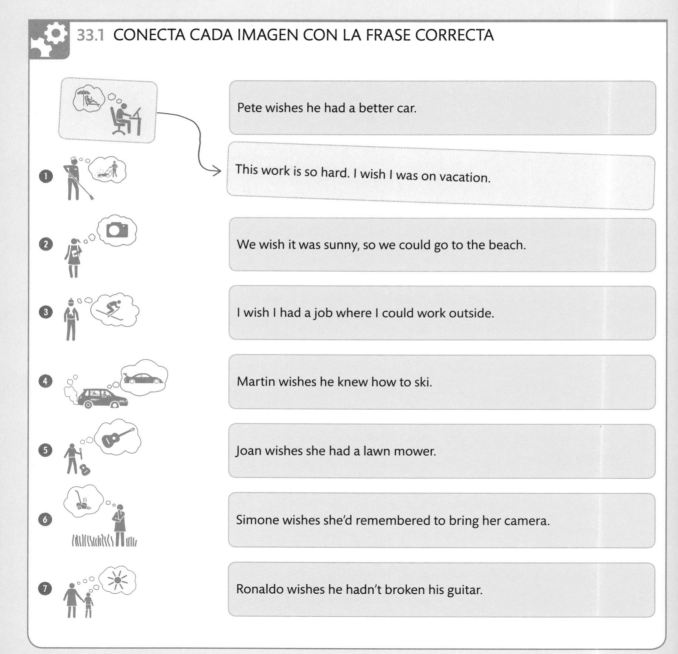

Pete wishes he had a better car.

This work is so hard. I wish I was on vacation.

We wish it was sunny, so we could go to the beach.

I wish I had a job where I could work outside.

Martin wishes he knew how to ski.

Joan wishes she had a lawn mower.

Simone wishes she'd remembered to bring her camera.

Ronaldo wishes he hadn't broken his guitar.

33.2 INDICA SI LO QUE DICEN LAS FRASES AÚN PODRÍA SUCEDER O YA NO PODRÍA SUCEDER

Brian wishes his sister would call him more often.
Aún podría suceder ☑ **Ya no podría suceder** ☐

1 Kasia wishes she had studied harder at school.
Aún podría suceder ☐ **Ya no podría suceder** ☐

2 Carmen wishes she hadn't eaten so much at dinner.
Aún podría suceder ☐ **Ya no podría suceder** ☐

3 Bob wishes he lived in a bigger house.
Aún podría suceder ☐ **Ya no podría suceder** ☐

4 If only you had told me it was your birthday.
Aún podría suceder ☐ **Ya no podría suceder** ☐

5 I wish you wouldn't interrupt me all the time.
Aún podría suceder ☐ **Ya no podría suceder** ☐

33.3 ESCRIBE DE NUEVO LAS FRASES Y CORRIGE LOS ERRORES

Public transportation here is terrible. If only I know how to drive.
Public transportation here is terrible. If only I knew how to drive.

1 I wish I don't work so late all the time. I'm so tired in the evenings.

_____

2 We're lost! We should planned our route a little better.

_____

3 Ed, I wish that you stop singing out of tune all the time.

_____

4 If only I can cook! Everything I make is a disaster.

_____

34 Hacer preguntas

Si una afirmación utiliza "be" o un verbo auxiliar, se construye su forma interrogativa invirtiendo verbo y sujeto. Cualquier otra pregunta se construye añadiendo "do" o "does".

34.1 CONECTA LAS FRASES CON LAS PREGUNTAS CORRECTAS

She is a police officer. → Is she a police officer?

Is there a good restaurant on Park Street?

1 The children are waiting.

2 There is a good restaurant on Park Street.

Can Fu speak fluent French?

3 Fu can speak fluent French.

Are the children waiting?

4 Jean is going to win the game.

Should Peter tell Amy about the party?

5 Peter should tell Amy about the party.

Has Kelly bought a gift for her dad?

6 Kelly has bought a gift for her dad.

Is Jean going to win the game?

34.2 CONECTA LAS FRASES CON LAS PREGUNTAS CORRECTAS

He goes swimming on Mondays. → Does he go swimming on Mondays?

Does Wayne want to come to the zoo with us?

1 Anthony started his new job at the bank.

2 Wayne wants to come to the zoo with us.

Did Anthony start his new job at the bank?

3 Harleen worked for us a few years ago.

Do Lara and Michael go to the same school?

4 Henry likes classical music.

Do they own the bookstore by the park?

5 Lara and Michael go to the same school.

Did Harleen work for us a few years ago?

6 They own the bookstore by the park.

Does Henry like classical music?

34.3 MARCA LAS FRASES QUE SEAN CORRECTAS

Do they goes to the cinema often? ☐
Do they go to the cinema often? ☑

1. Does Tina still work at the boutique? ☐
   Does Tina still works at the boutique? ☐

2. Does you prefer cats or dogs? ☐
   Do you prefer cats or dogs? ☐

3. Did the children enjoyed the fair? ☐
   Did the children enjoy the fair? ☐

4. Did you manage to move that box? ☐
   Did manage you to move that box? ☐

5. Does Selma go jogging often? ☐
   Do Selma goes jogging often? ☐

6. Did you helped clean up after the party? ☐
   Did you help clean up after the party? ☐

7. Do you often go abroad on vacation? ☐
   Do go you often abroad on vacation? ☐

8. Doesn't Clara has two large dogs? ☐
   Doesn't Clara have two large dogs? ☐

9. Have you ever read *Little Women*? ☐
   Have read you ever *Little Women*? ☐

10. Don't you like fast food, Phillippe? ☐
    Don't you liking fast food, Phillippe? ☐

11. Have you ever have a driving lesson? ☐
    Have you ever had a driving lesson? ☐

12. Did you enjoyed the art exhibition? ☐
    Did you enjoy the art exhibition? ☐

13. Did you remember to feed the dog? ☐
    Did you remembered to feed the dog? ☐

 ## 34.4 TACHA LA PALABRA INCORRECTA DE CADA FRASE

~~Has~~/ Have you set a date for your wedding yet?

1. Do / Does Dora work in a bank?

2. Is / Are your colleagues coming to the party?

3. Do / Does we start work at 10am on Fridays?

4. Do / Does Marlon really live in a mansion?

5. Did Bill work / worked for the government?

6. Was / Were there many animals in the forest?

7. Do / Does Marcel come from Argentina?

8. Did you went / go to the theater last night?

9. Has / Have you seen Anika's new car?

10. Is / Are Tom going to finish the report today?

11. Did Bruce live / lived in Glasgow?

12. Was / Were John at the airport to meet you?

13. Do / Does you take a shower in the evening?

14. Is / Are there any juice left?

15. Has / Have we got enough time left?

16. Is / Are your brother coming later?

17. Do / Does Claire and Sam have any children?

18. Do / Does Tim play soccer on the weekend?

19. Is / Are those your tools on the table?

20. Did Elsa have / had a boyfriend named Gus?

21. Do / Does Ash still work at the café?

22. Is / Are your daughter still in college?

23. Has / Have Sheila seen your new house yet?

34.5 ESCRIBE DE NUEVO LAS FRASES Y CORRIGE LOS ERRORES

someone? | call | we | Should
Should we call someone?

❸ you | the | party | Are | later? | coming | to
_____

❶ finished | painting | Has | she | yet? | the
_____

❹ teacher? | Is | Jackie | still | a
_____

❷ India? | you | Have | to | been
_____

❺ remember | door? | Did | the | you | lock | to
_____

34.6 ESCRIBE DE NUEVO LAS FRASES EN FORMA INTERROGATIVA

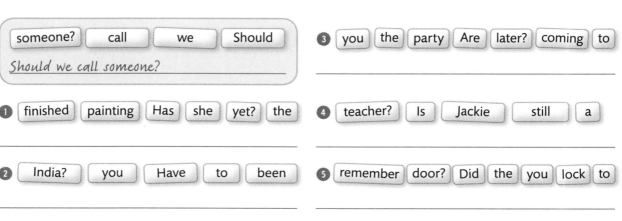

He was snowboarding in Canada last week.
Was he snowboarding in Canada last week?

❶ Ed has lived in New York for more than 10 years.
_____

❷ Katia and Pavel are getting married in June.
_____

❸ Claudia took a flight to Rio de Janeiro.
_____

❹ Mia goes swimming every evening after work.
_____

❺ You remembered to buy some water.
_____

❻ Ron and Lily are playing tennis this afternoon.
_____

35 Expresiones interrogativas

Las preguntas abiertas son preguntas que no se responden con un simple "sí" o "no". En inglés, se construyen con la ayuda de las expresiones interrogativas.

35.1 TACHA LAS PALABRAS INCORRECTAS DE CADA FRASE

Where / ~~Who~~ has your dog gone?

1. What / Where did you buy at the market?
2. Why / Who is Lena laughing so much?
3. Where / Which of these bags is yours?
4. Why / How does your dad feel today?
5. Whose / Who is going to teach the course?
6. Whose / Where car is parked outside?
7. How / What quickly can you finish it?
8. When / Where does your cousin live?
9. When / What does the hardware store close?
10. Whose / What diary is on the desk?
11. How / When did you last see Maria?
12. What / How many times has he been to Kenya?
13. Why / How did she quit the course?
14. Where / What is the entrance?
15. When / Who did you invite to the party?
16. How / What long does it take to get there?
17. Which / Who car should I buy?
18. Whose / Where did I put my glasses?

35.2 PON LAS PALABRAS EN SU ORDEN CORRECTO

you · How · are · today?

How are you today?

1. the · is · classroom? · Where

_____

2. this? · Whose · is · phone

_____

3. do · you · Why · that? · did

_____

4. long · wait? · did · How · you

_____

5. earlier? · did · meet · Who · you

_____

6. house · Which · yours? · is

_____

7. movie · the · When · start? · does

_____

35.3 CONECTA CADA IMAGEN CON LA FRASE CORRECTA

| How does the soup taste, Gustav? | Which of these dresses should I buy? | Which way do you think we should go? | When did you start playing the guitar, Tom? |

 35.4 MARCA LAS FRASES QUE SEAN CORRECTAS

What is bigger, the moon or the sun? ☐
Which is bigger, the moon or the sun? ☑

❶ What is the date today? ☐
Which is the date today? ☐

❷ What's the name of your business? ☐
Which is the name of your business? ☐

❸ What train are you taking, the 1pm or the 3pm? ☐
Which train are you taking, the 1pm or the 3pm? ☐

❹ What do you prefer, skiing or snowboarding? ☐
Which do you prefer, skiing or snowboarding? ☐

❺ What time are they arriving? ☐
Which time are they arriving? ☐

❻ If you had to choose between dogs and cats, what would you choose? ☐
If you had to choose between dogs and cats, which would you choose? ☐

35.5 INDICA LA PREGUNTA QUE SE AJUSTA MÁS A CADA CONVERSACIÓN

☑ When do you go cycling?

☐ How often do you go cycling?

I go on Saturdays.

❸
☐ When is the movie being released?

☐ How often is the movie being released?

It's coming out next month.

❶
☐ When do you read?

☐ How often do you read?

I read every day.

❹
☐ When do you perform in public?

☐ How often do you perform in public?

Only around once a month.

❷
☐ When can we have our meeting?

☐ How often can we have our meeting?

Tomorrow afternoon would be good.

❺
☐ When do you finish work?

☐ How often do you finish work?

I finish at 5:30pm most days.

 ## 35.6 CONECTA EL INICIO Y EL FINAL DE CADA PREGUNTA

Who is the new manager → in your department?

❶ How many people work → to build the new airport?

❷ Where are they going → of the Italian restaurant downtown?

❸ Whose coat has been left → the concert start?

❹ Which way is it → on the back of that chair?

❺ What time does → to Glasgow leave?

❻ When does the train → to the bus station?

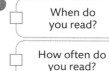
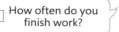
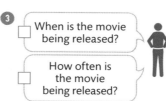

36 Preguntas abiertas

Las preguntas abiertas no pueden responderse con "sí" o "no".
Se construyen de diferente manera en función de cuál sea el
verbo principal de la pregunta.

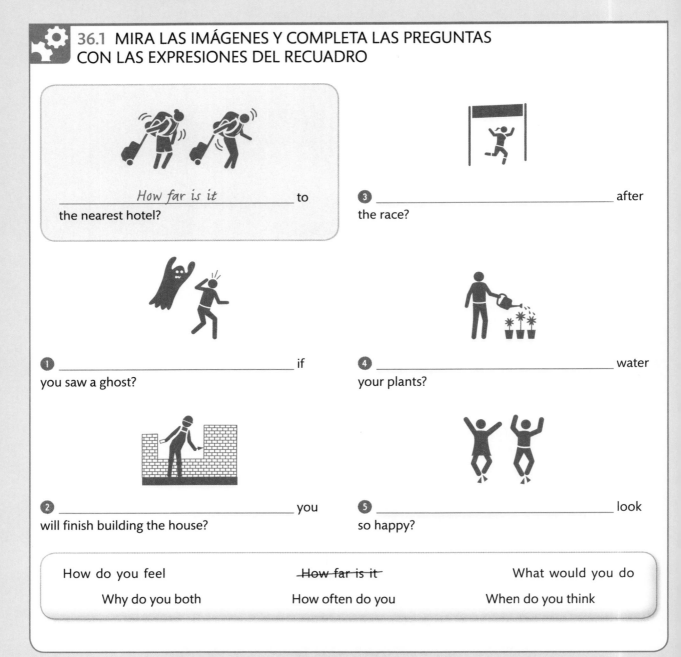

36.1 MIRA LAS IMÁGENES Y COMPLETA LAS PREGUNTAS CON LAS EXPRESIONES DEL RECUADRO

_____How far is it_____ to
the nearest hotel?

3 _____ after
the race?

1 _____ if
you saw a ghost?

4 _____ water
your plants?

2 _____ you
will finish building the house?

5 _____ look
so happy?

| How do you feel | How far is it | What would you do |
| Why do you both | How often do you | When do you think |

36.2 MARCA LAS PREGUNTAS QUE SEAN CORRECTAS

> Who should I talk to about this? ✓
> Who I should talk to about this? ☐

1. What time does the train leave? ☐
   What time the train does it leave? ☐

2. What your name is? ☐
   What is your name? ☐

3. How the movie was? ☐
   How was the movie? ☐

4. When did you get this dog? ☐
   When you did get this dog? ☐

5. Why you did phone me earlier? ☐
   Why did you phone me earlier? ☐

6. Who can speak English here? ☐
   Who speak can English here? ☐

7. Who should I call to complain? ☐
   Who I should call to complain? ☐

8. When you start work? ☐
   When do you start work? ☐

9. What is this button for? ☐
   What this button is for? ☐

10. Which dress you prefer? ☐
    Which dress do you prefer? ☐

11. Why aren't you at work today? ☐
    Why you aren't at work today? ☐

12. What do you eat for breakfast? ☐
    What you eat for breakfast? ☐

13. Where do David live? ☐
    Where does David live? ☐

 ## 36.3 REESCRIBE LAS PREGUNTAS Y CORRIGE LOS ERRORES

> When she does finishes work?
> *When does she finish work?*

1. What she is going to sing for us next?
   _____

2. Where you bought that lovely dress?
   _____

3. What did happened to your leg, Paul?
   _____

4. Who's bicycle is that in the yard?
   _____

5. Why you have to watch so much TV?
   _____

6. How feel you about losing your job?
   _____

7. Where you do cycle to on Sundays?
   _____

8. How many times you visited New York?
   _____

9. Why you so angry, Anthony?
   _____

10. How old the twins are today?
    _____

11. What time you do eat your lunch?
    _____

12. When you last went camping, Sam?
    _____

37 Preguntas de objeto y de sujeto

Hay dos clases de preguntas: las preguntas de objeto y las preguntas de sujeto. Cada una se construye de manera diferente y se utiliza para preguntar sobre cosas distintas.

37.1 CONECTA LAS PREGUNTAS CON LAS RESPUESTAS CORRECTAS

Who taught you how to drive? → My dad taught me how to drive.

An artist from Australia painted it.

1 Who did you go to the party with?

2 Who painted that amazing picture?

I went with an old friend from school.

3 Who gave you that lovely necklace?

We saw a play by William Shakespeare.

4 What did you see at the theater?

Angelica. She has so much experience.

5 What are you going to have for dinner?

It was a present from my boyfriend.

6 Who are you going to offer the job to?

There was a terrible storm last week.

7 What caused all that damage to your house?

I'm going to have fish and chips.

37.2 MARCA LA OPCIÓN CORRECTA PARA CADA PREGUNTA

What did she have for dinner?
Pregunta de sujeto ☐
Pregunta de objeto ☑

1 Who was performing last night?
Pregunta de sujeto ☐
Pregunta de objeto ☐

2 Who teaches you English?
Pregunta de sujeto ☐
Pregunta de objeto ☐

3 Who did you borrow the money from?
Pregunta de sujeto ☐
Pregunta de objeto ☐

4 What just made that awful noise outside?
Pregunta de sujeto ☐
Pregunta de objeto ☐

5 Who paid for all these drinks?
Pregunta de sujeto ☐
Pregunta de objeto ☐

6 What are you doing tomorrow?
Pregunta de sujeto ☐
Pregunta de objeto ☐

7 Who did the police arrest?
Pregunta de sujeto ☐
Pregunta de objeto ☐

37.3 TACHA LAS PALABRAS INCORRECTAS DE CADA FRASE

> Who came / ~~did come~~ into the office today?

1 Who **played** / did play golf with you yesterday?

2 What saw you / **did you see** at the movies last night?

3 Who **married** / did marry Sonia at the end of the movie?

4 What caught you / **did you catch** while fishing yesterday?

37.4 ESCRIBE DE NUEVO LAS FRASES Y CORRIGE LOS ERRORES

> What watched you on TV last night?
> *What did you watch on TV last night?*

1 Who I saw you playing golf with on Sunday?

_____

2 Who did stole the money from the bank?

_____

3 Who did leave this terrible mess?

_____

4 What you are going to wear to the wedding?

_____

5 Who in that huge castle lives?

_____

6 What you did give the cat to eat?

_____

7 Who the race won this afternoon?

_____

38 Preguntas indirectas

Las preguntas indirectas son más educadas que las preguntas directas. Son muy habituales en el inglés hablado formal, en especial cuando se pide información.

38.1 COMPLETA LOS ESPACIOS PONIENDO LAS PALABRAS EN SU ORDEN CORRECTO

is　library　where　the

Could you tell me __where__ __the__ __library__ __is__ ?

the　begins　what　time　lesson

1 Do you know _____ _____ _____ _____ _____ ?

bus　where　is　the　station

2 Do you know _____ _____ _____ _____ _____ ?

get　to　how　gallery　to　the　national

3 Could you tell me _____ _____ _____ _____ _____ _____ _____ ?

costs　ticket　a　Oslo　to　much　how

4 Do you know _____ _____ _____ _____ _____ _____ _____ ?

still　if　served　breakfast　being　is

5 Could you tell me _____ _____ _____ _____ _____ _____ ?

is　why　so　expensive　this

6 Could you tell me _____ _____ _____ _____ _____ ?

train　Swansea　goes　to　the　whether

7 Do you know _____ _____ _____ _____ _____ _____ ?

38.2 MARCA LAS FRASES QUE SEAN CORRECTAS

Do you know when does the supermarket open? ☐
Do you know when the supermarket opens? ☑

❶ Could you tell me where Lizzy lives? ☐
Could you tell me where does Lizzy live? ☐

❷ Do you know why is the school closed? ☐
Do you know why the school is closed? ☐

❸ Do you know has the course begun yet? ☐
Do you know if the course has begun yet? ☐

❹ Could you tell me why you did that? ☐
Could you tell me why did you do that? ☐

38.3 ESCRIBE DE NUEVO LAS FRASES Y CORRIGE LOS ERRORES

Do you know why are you in trouble?
Do you know why you are in trouble?

❶ Do you know has Emma brushed the yard?
_____

❷ Could you tell me whose is that old car?
_____

❸ Do you know will the car be ready by 5pm?
_____

❹ Could you tell me where is the station?
_____

❺ Do you know when will you finish the report?
_____

39 Question tags

En el inglés hablado es frecuente añadir pequeñas preguntas al final de las frases. Son las llamadas question tags, y normalmente se utilizan para invitar al interlocutor a manifestar su acuerdo.

39.1 CONECTA EL INICIO DE LAS FRASES CON LAS QUESTION TAGS CORRECTAS

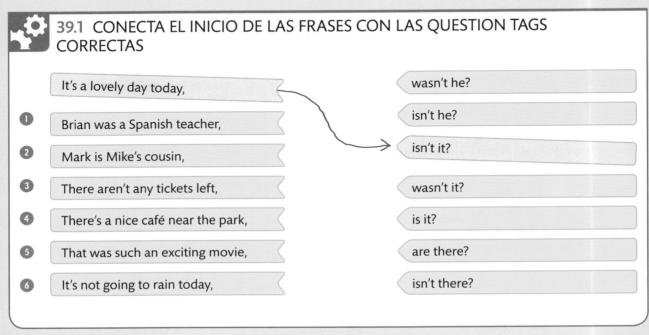

It's a lovely day today,

① Brian was a Spanish teacher,

② Mark is Mike's cousin,

③ There aren't any tickets left,

④ There's a nice café near the park,

⑤ That was such an exciting movie,

⑥ It's not going to rain today,

wasn't he?

isn't he?

isn't it?

wasn't it?

is it?

are there?

isn't there?

39.2 COMPLETA LOS ESPACIOS CON LAS QUESTION TAGS DEL RECUADRO

I could become a lawyer, ___*couldn't I?*___

① Your grandmother likes tea, _____

② Gerald has finished the gardening, _____

③ Luca didn't pass the English exam, _____

④ Carla worked in a bakery, _____

⑤ We should buy a new fridge, _____

⑥ You haven't seen my glasses, _____

⑦ Mike can swim, _____

couldn't I?	shouldn't we?		have you?	can't he?
didn't she?	did he?	hasn't he?		doesn't she?

The photocopier shouldn't do that, _____ *should it* _____ ?

1. The hat on the left is gorgeous, _____ ?

2. That ride was really scary, _____ ?

3. You're Daniel's cousin, _____ ?

4. I think our team's going to win, _____ ?

5. We aren't going to catch our plane, _____ ?

6. You've read that book before, _____ ?

7. The guests don't look very happy, _____ ?

8. Bill plays the guitar really well, _____ ?

9. Chloe will do the shopping for you, _____ ?

10. I should have brought an umbrella, _____ ?

11. Martin doesn't like cooking much, _____ ?

12. Paul looks absolutely exhausted, _____ ?

13. We've been waiting here for 30 minutes, _____ ?

14. You're not listening to anything I say, _____ ?

40 Preguntas cortas

Las preguntas cortas son una manera de mostrar interés durante una conversación. Se utilizan para mantener activa la conversación más que para pedir más información.

40.1 MARCA LA MEJOR RESPUESTA A CADA AFIRMACIÓN

I study every evening after work.
Are you? ☐
Do you? ☑

① The chef cooks the most amazing dishes.
Does he? ☐
Doesn't he? ☐

② I just saw a mouse under the bed!
Saw you? ☐
Did you? ☐

③ My company isn't doing very well.
Isn't it? ☐
Doesn't it? ☐

④ We've just come back from New York.
Have you? ☐
Are you? ☐

⑤ Martha saw a cat in the garden earlier.
Did she see? ☐
Did she? ☐

⑥ Ola is teaching us math next year.
Does she? ☐
Is she? ☐

⑦ Andrew still hasn't found his dog.
Hasn't he? ☐
Has he? ☐

⑧ It was raining all the time we were in Paris.
Was it? ☐
Did it? ☐

⑨ Liam's going rock climbing on the weekend.
Goes he? ☐
Is he? ☐

41 Respuestas cortas

Cuando respondemos a preguntas cerradas en inglés, se suele
prescindir de algunas palabras para hacer más corta la respuesta.
Estas respuestas cortas se utilizan a menudo en el inglés hablado.

41.1 MARCA LA MEJOR RESPUESTA A CADA AFIRMACIÓN

Do you like being a chef?

Yes, I am. ☐

Yes, I do. ☑

① Is there a library in your town?

Yes, it is. ☐

Yes, there is. ☐

② Do you know where the tickets are?

No, I don't. ☐

No, they don't. ☐

③ Will you visit the castle while you're there?

No, we don't. ☐

No, we won't. ☐

④ Do you own this amazing house?

Yes, I own. ☐

Yes, I do. ☐

⑤ Are you going on vacation?

Yes, we do. ☐

Yes, we are. ☐

⑥ Were there many people at the meeting?

Yes, there were. ☐

Yes, there did. ☐

⑦ Can Jamie play badminton?

Yes, he can. ☐

Yes, he plays. ☐

⑧ Have you got a large black cat?

No, I haven't. ☐

No, I haven't got. ☐

⑨ Would you like an ice cream?

No, I wouldn't. ☐

No, I don't. ☐

109

42 Preguntas: repaso

En inglés pueden hacerse preguntas de diversas maneras, según
sea el verbo principal. Las preguntas abiertas y cerradas se hacen
de manera distinta, y se pronuncian con distinta entonación.

42.1 ESCRIBE DE NUEVO LAS FRASES EN FORMA DE PREGUNTA

Helen went to Sydney last year.
Did Helen go to Sydney last year?

❶ Joe's playing tennis on Thursday.

❷ They've knocked down the apartment block.

❸ Jean-Paul is learning to cook.

❹ Rob is going to win the race.

❺ Chrissy does exercises each morning.

❻ They will play all their greatest hits.

❼ Claire and Ben got married last week.

❽ Aziz works late every evening.

❾ Jessica took the dog for a walk.

42.2 ESCRIBE LAS PREGUNTAS DEL RECUADRO EN LA LISTA CORRECTA

PREGUNTAS DE SUJETO

Who wrote this book?

PREGUNTAS DE OBJETO

Who did you invite?   Who do you live with?   What does John do for work?

What happened next?   What did you buy?

~~Who wrote this book?~~   Who called earlier?   Who drove you to work?

42.3 INDICA SI LAS PREGUNTAS SON ABIERTAS O CERRADAS

Where did you put my phone charger?
Pregunta abierta ☑   **Pregunta cerrada** ☐

1 What are you going to buy at the supermarket?
Pregunta abierta ☐   **Pregunta cerrada** ☐

2 Would you like to go see a jazz concert with me tonight?
Pregunta abierta ☐   **Pregunta cerrada** ☐

3 Have you already finished your final assignment?
Pregunta abierta ☐   **Pregunta cerrada** ☐

4 Why did you decide to study environmental science at college?
Pregunta abierta ☐   **Pregunta cerrada** ☐

5 Did your brother really make that delicious dinner we just ate?
Pregunta abierta ☐   **Pregunta cerrada** ☐

6 Shall we go ice skating again tonight? I enjoyed it last time.
Pregunta abierta ☐   **Pregunta cerrada** ☐

43 Reported speech

Las palabras que pronuncia una persona se llaman direct speech.
El reported speech se utiliza a menudo para describir lo que alguien
dijo en un momento anterior.

43.1 CONECTA LAS FRASES EN DIRECT SPEECH CON LAS CORRESPONDIENTES EN REPORTED SPEECH

You look very happy today!	→	He told me I looked very happy today.

She said her husband was from Alabama.

1 I want to come to the park with you.

He told me I looked very happy today.

2 My husband is from Alabama.

She told me that she was a lawyer.

3 It is extremely hot in Adelaide.

Our boss told us we had to work harder.

4 I'm a lawyer.

Emilia said she wanted to come to the park with us.

5 I want to quit school.

They told me they owned a villa in Spain.

6 You have to work harder.

He said it was extremely hot in Adelaide.

7 We own a villa in Spain.

My son said he wanted to quit school.

43.2 MARCA LAS FRASES QUE SEAN CORRECTAS

They said that there was a big carnival today. ☑
They said me that there was a big carnival today. ☐

❶ She told me she was a Canadian citizen. ☐
She said me she was a Canadian citizen. ☐

❷ Rob said me he had won a huge amount of money. ☐
Rob said he had won a huge amount of money. ☐

❸ Ella said that Phil's 18th birthday party was great fun. ☐
Ella told that Phil's 18th birthday party was great fun. ☐

❹ Ted told me he went backpacking around Europe last year. ☐
Ted told he went backpacking around Europe last year. ☐

43.3 ESCRIBE DE NUEVO LAS FRASES EN REPORTED SPEECH, PONIENDO LOS VERBOS EN PAST SIMPLE

I want to buy a new basketball.
He _____*told*_____ (tell) me that he _____*wanted*_____ (want) to buy a new basketball.

❶ I travel around the world a lot for work.

She _____ (say) that she _____ (travel) around the world a lot for work.

❷ My new boyfriend is from Ethiopia.

She _____ (tell) me that her new boyfriend _____ (be) from Ethiopia.

❸ I live in Milan with my family.

Silvio _____ (tell) Maria that he _____ (live) in Milan with his family.

❹ I feel sick, so I'm going home.

Mike _____ (say) that he _____ (feel) sick, so he went home.

❺ My brother works in a travel agency.

She _____ (tell) me that her brother _____ (work) in a travel agency.

En reported speech, el verbo que se cita suele "retroceder"
un tiempo verbal. Las referencias de tiempo y lugar y los
pronombres cambian también a veces.

44.1 MARCA LA FRASE EN REPORTED SPEECH EQUIVALENTE A CADA FRASE EN DIRECT SPEECH

It is raining very heavily.
Shaun said it rained very heavily. ☐
Shaun said it was raining very heavily. ☑

1 I'll give you a call later tonight.
Jan said she would give me a call later that evening. ☐
Jan said she gave me a call later that evening. ☐

2 I'm seeing my grandma later today.
Benedict said he saw his grandma later that day. ☐
Benedict said he was seeing his grandma later that day. ☐

3 I arrived at the hotel hours ago.
George told me he'd arrived at the hotel hours earlier. ☐
George told me he would arrive at the hotel hours later. ☐

4 We're going to the movies to see the new thriller.
Matt and Mabel said they had gone to the movies to see a thriller. ☐
Matt and Mabel said they were going to the movies to see a thriller. ☐

5 I can't afford to come on vacation with you this summer.
Danny said he didn't afford to come on vacation with us this summer. ☐
Danny said he couldn't afford to come on vacation with us this summer. ☐

6 Your new dress looks great.
Gemma told me that my new dress looks great. ☐
Gemma told me that my new dress had looked great. ☐

7 I'll give the camera back to you tomorrow.
Katie said she had given the camera back to me the next day. ☐
Katie said she'd give the camera back to me the next day. ☐

44.2 CONECTA CADA IMAGEN CON LA FRASE CORRECTA

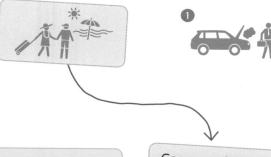 

Malcolm told Mel that he works in a salon.

George and Tamsin told me they go on vacation a lot.

Archie told me that his car had broken down.

Betty said she'd seen a wolf in the woods last year.

44.3 ESCRIBE DE NUEVO LAS FRASES Y CORRIGE LOS ERRORES

Christopher told me that he **will** call me yesterday.
Christopher told me that he would call me yesterday.

1 Cath told me she **has** posted the letter a few days ago.

2 The weather forecast said it **is** going to be sunny yesterday.

3 Angela told me she **was** already mowed the lawn.

4 Miles told us that the company **is** losing money before it went bankrupt.

5 In February, Lisa told me that she **has** had a great idea for a vacation.

6 Emil said he **will** visit me in Japan that summer.

44.4 CONECTA LAS FRASES EN DIRECT SPEECH CON LAS CORRESPONDIENTES EN REPORTED SPEECH

An engineer will come to your house tomorrow.

The shop assistant told me they didn't have a shirt in my size.

They told me an engineer would come to my house the following day.

1 We're going to the zoo on Thursday.

The manager said the hotel was fully booked in July.

2 We don't have a shirt in your size, sorry.

Harry told me they were going to the zoo on Thursday.

3 I don't want to go to the party tonight.

Michelle said she didn't want to go to the party last night.

4 I'm afraid the hotel's fully booked in July.

Billy's mom said he would pass all his exams.

5 I worked on a farm when I was a student.

She said that she lives in a house near the bus station.

6 Billy will pass all his exams this summer.

Jenny told me that she'd worked on a farm when she was a student.

7 I'm writing a novel set in Ancient Rome.

Carlo said he was going to buy a new car that afternoon.

8 I live in a house near the bus station.

Robert told me he was writing a novel set in Ancient Rome.

9 I'm going to buy a new car this afternoon.

45 Verbos de reported speech

En reported speech, "said" puede reemplazarse por una gran cantidad de verbos que ofrecen más información sobre cómo se expresó alguien.

45.1 COMPLETA LOS ESPACIOS PONIENDO LAS PALABRAS EN SU ORDEN CORRECTO

| she | that | admitted |

Katrina _admitted_ _that_ _she_ didn't understand the question.

| me | buy | to | reminded |

1 Don _____ _____ _____ _____ some milk on the way home.

| study | me | encouraged | to |

2 My parents _____ _____ _____ _____ medicine in college.

| be | explained | would | that | she |

3 Tina's sister _____ _____ _____ _____ _____ late to the recital.

45.2 CONECTA CADA IMAGEN CON LA FRASE CORRECTA

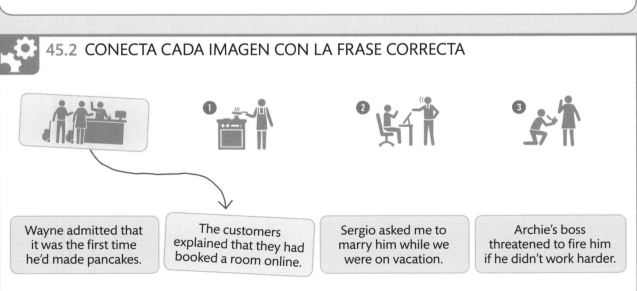

Wayne admitted that it was the first time he'd made pancakes.

The customers explained that they had booked a room online.

Sergio asked me to marry him while we were on vacation.

Archie's boss threatened to fire him if he didn't work harder.

46 Reported speech de frases negativas

Las frases negativas en reported speech se forman igual que las negativas en direct speech. Se utiliza "not" con el auxiliar, o con el verbo principal cuando no hay auxiliar.

46.1 CONECTA EL INICIO Y EL FINAL DE CADA FRASE

The weather report advised people	not to draw on the walls.
① Pedro explained that he	not to forget my passport.
② Paul's mom told him	not to travel during the storm.
③ Monika reminded me	didn't work on Fridays.
④ I said that I didn't want	come because I was feeling ill.
⑤ I told my brother I couldn't	to drive to the restaurant.

46.2 MARCA LAS FRASES QUE SEAN CORRECTAS

My husband reminded me to don't be late for dinner. ☐
My husband reminded me not to be late for dinner. ☑

① My colleague mentioned that the printer wasn't working. ☐
My colleague mentioned that the printer not working. ☐

② Mark explained me that he didn't like dogs. ☐
Mark explained that he didn't like dogs. ☐

③ Myra phoned to say that she not to come to the meeting. ☐
Myra phoned to say that she wasn't coming to the meeting. ☐

④ Jon tried to persuade me not to eat any more cake. ☐
Jon tried to persuade me not eating any more cake. ☐

118

47 Preguntas en reported speech

El reported speech se utiliza a veces para citar lo que alguien preguntó. Las preguntas en direct y en reported speech ordenan las palabras de maneras diferentes.

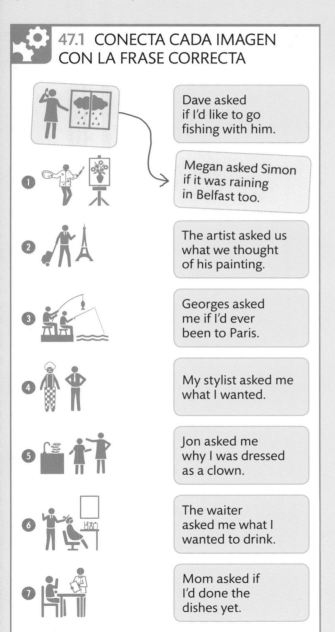

47.1 CONECTA CADA IMAGEN CON LA FRASE CORRECTA

Dave asked if I'd like to go fishing with him.

Megan asked Simon if it was raining in Belfast too.

The artist asked us what we thought of his painting.

Georges asked me if I'd ever been to Paris.

My stylist asked me what I wanted.

Jon asked me why I was dressed as a clown.

The waiter asked me what I wanted to drink.

Mom asked if I'd done the dishes yet.

47.2 ESCRIBE DE NUEVO LAS FRASES Y CORRIGE LOS ERRORES

Rick asked me where I do work.
Rick asked me where I work.

1. He asked me where do you live.
_____

2. Sue asked me what did I think.
_____

3. Amy asked us should she bring something.
_____

4. Paul asked why did I leave.
_____

5. They asked me where had I been.
_____

6. The girl asked me where is the station.
_____

7. She asked where was the exit.
_____

8. Mia asked me do I own a car.
_____

9. They asked me who is he.
_____

47.3 COMPLETA LOS ESPACIOS PONIENDO LAS PALABRAS EN SU ORDEN CORRECTO

| me | what | asked |

The officer _asked_ _me_ _what_ my name was.

| to | coming | were | if | you | the |

1 Peter asked _____ _____ _____ _____ _____ _____ performance later.

| to | I'd | if | decided | me | asked |

2 My teacher _____ _____ _____ _____ _____ _____ study math in college.

| I | to | me | go | where | wanted |

3 Lou asked _____ _____ _____ _____ _____ _____ on Saturday.

| if | order | we | wanted | to | asked |

4 The waiter _____ _____ _____ _____ _____ _____ more drinks.

| time | me | we | usually | what | have |

5 Susan asked _____ _____ _____ _____ _____ _____ our lunch break.

| wanted | go | if | to | I | the | to |

6 She asked me _____ _____ _____ _____ _____ _____ movies with her.

| kids | wanted | her | they | if | mint | or |

7 Claire asked _____ _____ _____ _____ _____ _____ strawberry ice cream.

| we | lived | how | had | in | long |

8 Fran asked _____ _____ _____ _____ _____ _____ San Francisco.

| help | could | him | I | house | whether | move |

9 Pete asked _____ _____ _____ _____ _____ _____ this weekend.

47.4 ESCRIBE DE NUEVO LAS FRASES EMPLEANDO REPORTED SPEECH, CON LOS VERBOS EN LOS TIEMPOS CORRECTOS

> Are you studying physics or chemistry here?
> He asked me whether I _____*was studying*_____ (study) physics or chemistry there.

❶ Can I borrow your T-shirt?

Paul asked if he _____ (can) borrow my T-shirt.

❷ Is it raining where you are?

Danny wanted to know if it _____ (rain) here.

❸ Is Tim coming to the lecture later today?

Hiroshi asked whether you _____ (come) to the lecture later today.

❹ Will you post this letter for me?

Shona asked me if I _____ (post) this letter for her.

❺ How long have you been knitting for, Grandma?

My granddaughter asked me how long I _____ (knit) for.

❻ Where is Silvio living at the moment?

Antonia asked me where you _____ (live) at the moment.

❼ Who is the singer in this band?

Greg asked me who the singer _____ (be) in the band we saw last night.

❽ Do you know when you are going to finish the block?

I asked the architect if he knew when they _____ (finish) the block.

❾ Who won the marathon today?

Ella asked me who _____ (win) the marathon yesterday.

❿ Do you believe in ghosts, Mom?

My children asked me today if I _____ (believe) in ghosts.

⓫ Who directed the new comedy?

Patsy wanted to know who _____ (direct) the new comedy.

48 Reported speech: repaso

Al hacer el reported speech a partir del direct speech, ciertas palabras cambian de orden para mantener el significado de la frase. Otras palabras, en cambio, quedan igual.

48.1 CONECTA LAS FRASES EN DIRECT SPEECH CON LAS CORRESPONDIENTES EN REPORTED SPEECH

I am moving house next week. → Sanjay told me that he was moving house the following week.

Les told me Christine had paid for lunch the week before.

1 I really miss my friends and family.

2 Christine paid for lunch last week.

Jiya once told me she'd be a famous singer by 2015.

3 I really don't want to work this Saturday.

Steph told me that she really missed her friends and family.

4 My daughter dreams of becoming an actor.

Angela tells me she's never been to the Tower of London.

5 I'll be a famous singer by 2015.

Rohan tells me he really doesn't want to work this Saturday.

6 We're going to the theater tomorrow.

Mia told Dan that her daughter dreamed of becoming an actor.

7 I've never been to the Tower of London.

Lou told me they were going to the theater the following day.

48.2 MARCA LAS FRASES QUE SEAN CORRECTAS

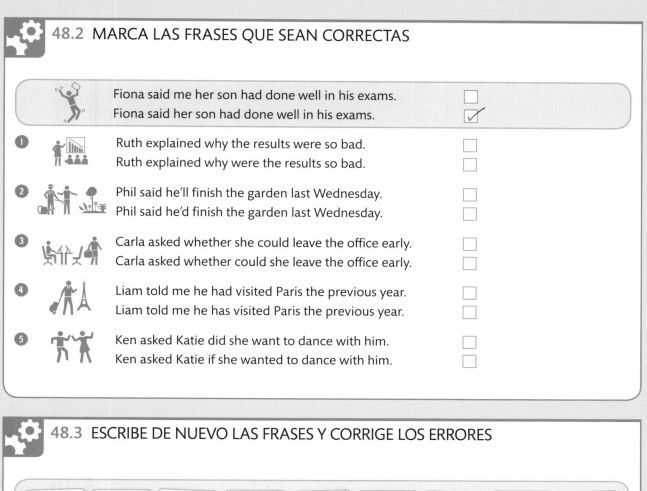

Fiona said me her son had done well in his exams. ☐
Fiona said her son had done well in his exams. ☑

1. Ruth explained why the results were so bad. ☐
   Ruth explained why were the results so bad. ☐

2. Phil said he'll finish the garden last Wednesday. ☐
   Phil said he'd finish the garden last Wednesday. ☐

3. Carla asked whether she could leave the office early. ☐
   Carla asked whether could she leave the office early. ☐

4. Liam told me he had visited Paris the previous year. ☐
   Liam told me he has visited Paris the previous year. ☐

5. Ken asked Katie did she want to dance with him. ☐
   Ken asked Katie if she wanted to dance with him. ☐

48.3 ESCRIBE DE NUEVO LAS FRASES Y CORRIGE LOS ERRORES

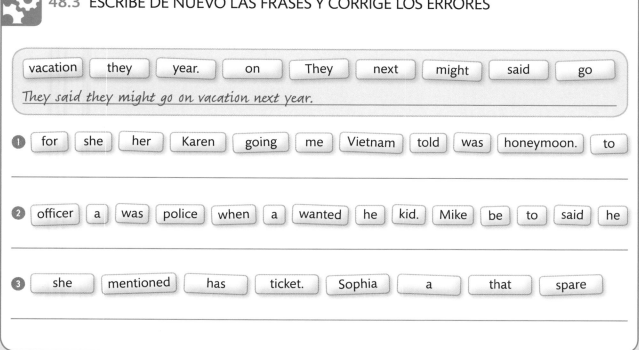

vacation · they · year. · on · They · next · might · said · go

They said they might go on vacation next year.

1. for · she · her · Karen · going · me · Vietnam · told · was · honeymoon. · to

2. officer · a · was · police · when · a · wanted · he · kid. · Mike · be · to · said · he

3. she · mentioned · has · ticket. · Sophia · a · that · spare

123

49 Tipos de verbos

Distinguimos entre verbos principales y verbos auxiliares. Los verbos principales describen acciones, sucesos o estados, mientras que los verbos auxiliares modifican el significado de los principales.

49.1 INDICA SI EL VERBO ES PRINCIPAL O AUXILIAR

Unfortunately, nobody told Harry that the meeting time **had** changed.
Principal ☐ **Auxiliar** ☑

1. Jen **called** a taxi to take her home from the supermarket.
Principal ☐ **Auxiliar** ☐

2. Sally **had** been studying for her exams all day.
Principal ☐ **Auxiliar** ☐

3. **Would** you like me to help you with your bag?
Principal ☐ **Auxiliar** ☐

4. You **should** always do warm-up exercises before running.
Principal ☐ **Auxiliar** ☐

5. I like to **listen** to the radio early in the morning.
Principal ☐ **Auxiliar** ☐

6. Julio **plays** baseball with his friends after school.
Principal ☐ **Auxiliar** ☐

7. They **had** just sold the last tickets for the show.
Principal ☐ **Auxiliar** ☐

8. Mia **gave** her sister her birthday present.
Principal ☐ **Auxiliar** ☐

9. Ella and Paul **are** buying an apartment together.
Principal ☐ **Auxiliar** ☐

10. Ed **works** as a scientist at the university.
Principal ☐ **Auxiliar** ☐

49.2 COMPLETA LOS ESPACIOS CON LOS VERBOS DEL RECUADRO

My friends _____ *are* _____ very funny, you'd like them!

1 You _____ call your grandma. It's her birthday.

2 The students _____ all handed in their papers.

3 Sandra _____ coming to the party tonight.

4 My son _____ already swim when he was three.

5 I _____ already left by the time Jim arrived.

6 I _____ like her boyfriend. He was rude.

7 You _____ speak so loudly in the library.

| have |
| didn't |
| had |
| isn't |
| mustn't |
| ~~are~~ |
| should |
| could |

49.3 BUSCA EN LA TABLA OTROS SEIS VERBOS Y PONLOS EN LA CATEGORÍA CORRECTA

```
G P N I D R A O B W T N S
C A R R I V E G T A S N V
N D E M J S R D S N M R D
R I N T H R O W U T I U I
S W G T X B A A R D L J G
D G I V E Y D D F A E N X
M Z L O U A O L I O R I Z
P A Q E S N V A N S E S D
T C D H T N D U G J A G I
B R I N G R I G I E O S S
R E Q E P S K H C O M E H
A E C D E F X F I J J L M
```

TRANSITIVOS

_____ *give* _____

1 _____

2 _____

3 _____

INTRANSITIVOS

_____ *laugh* _____

4 _____

5 _____

6 _____

125

50 Verbos de acción y de estado

Los verbos que describen acciones o acontecimientos se conocen como verbos de "acción" o "dinámicos", mientras que aquellos que describen estados se denominan verbos de "estado" o "estativos".

50.1 INDICA SI LOS VERBOS SON DE ACCIÓN O DE ESTADO

One day, I want to be famous.
Acción ☐
Estado ☑

① We play soccer after school.
Acción ☐
Estado ☐

② I like your new blouse, Katie.
Acción ☐
Estado ☐

③ Liam goes home at 4:30pm.
Acción ☐
Estado ☐

④ Fay cooks wonderful meals.
Acción ☐
Estado ☐

⑤ This cheese tastes a bit strange.
Acción ☐
Estado ☐

⑥ Chiara wants to study art history.
Acción ☐
Estado ☐

⑦ Rob takes the bus to work.
Acción ☐
Estado ☐

50.2 ESCRIBE DE NUEVO LAS FRASES Y CORRIGE LOS ERRORES

I'm having a cold at the moment.
I have a cold at the moment.

① We are knowing Jenny very well.
_____

② This soup is tasting awful.
_____

③ Chris is wanting an ice cream.
_____

④ Our vacation was costing a lot of money.
_____

⑤ Craig is understanding Spanish.
_____

⑥ I was recognizing that man.
_____

⑦ My son is hating vegetables.
_____

⑧ Dom's pie was smelling great.
_____

⑨ Your book is sounding interesting.
_____

50.3 ESCRIBE LOS VERBOS DEL RECUADRO EN EL GRUPO CORRECTO

VERBOS DE ACCIÓN	VERBOS DE ESTADO
try	

drive   be   contain   hear   own

~~try~~   kick   know   eat   read

50.4 TACHA LAS PALABRAS INCORRECTAS DE CADA FRASE

 Chrissy doesn't want / ~~isn't wanting~~ to go to work today.

① Fatima writes / is writing a book about her childhood.

② It rains / is raining outside. Let's watch something on TV.

③ Marco plays / is playing guitar on stage now.

④ Rosita has / is having two sisters, who live in the United States.

⑤ Claude hates / is hating all salad and vegetables.

⑥ I read / am reading a travel guide to Los Angeles.

51 Infinitivos y participios

Los infinitivos y los participios son formas verbales que raramente se usan solas, pero que son importantes para crear otras formas o construcciones.

 51.1 ESCRIBE LOS VERBOS EN SUS OTRAS FORMAS

FORMA BASE	PRESENT PARTICIPLE	PAST PARTICIPLE
walk	*walking*	*walked*
❶	planning	
❷ play		
❸	doing	
❹	liking	
❺		found
❻		written
❼ finish		
❽		bought
❾ read		
❿		told
⓫		hoped
⓬ swim		
⓭		gone
⓮	crying	
⓯	beginning	
⓰		said
⓱	loving	

51.2 COMPLETA LOS ESPACIOS CON LOS PARTICIPIOS DEL RECUADRO

> I have been ___*waiting*___ for a train for ages.

1 Carla has _____ all of her assignments.

2 Marsha's _____ a surprise party for Ed.

3 Marion is _____ to get married this fall.

4 We hadn't _____ to stay in, but it started raining.

5 We want _____ to the art exhibition tomorrow.

to go	planned
going	finished
~~waiting~~	planning

51.3 ESCRIBE DE NUEVO LAS FRASES Y CORRIGE LOS ERRORES

> I need help **chooseing** my college major. I can't decide!
> *I need help choosing my college major. I can't decide!*

1 **Writting** new vocabulary in a notebook helps me remember it.

_____

2 Tim's English teacher asked if he'd **donne** his homework.

_____

3 My husband keeps **forgeting** his keys. It's so frustrating.

_____

4 My children don't **want go** to school this morning.

_____

5 I go **swiming** most weekends with my friends.

_____

6 Everyone had **sang** Happy Birthday by the time I arrived.

_____

52 Pautas verbales

Algunos verbos solo pueden ir con un gerundio o un infinitivo. Otros pueden ir con ambas formas. Estos verbos suelen describir deseos, planes, o sentimientos.

 52.1 MIRA LAS IMÁGENES Y COMPLETA LAS FRASES CON LAS EXPRESIONES DEL RECUADRO

Penelope ___*offered*___ to help her friend move house.

❸ We _____ to meet for a drink after work.

❶ I finally _____ to buy a house after saving for years.

❹ My brother _____ buying a sports car when he turned 40.

❷ Alberto has _____ painting the landscape.

❺ I really _____ meeting your friends at the party.

| arranged | managed | considered | enjoyed | offered | finished |

130

52.2 ESCRIBE DE NUEVO LAS FRASES PONIENDO LAS PALABRAS EN EL ORDEN CORRECTO

| don't | too | running; | tiring! | I | like | it's |

I don't like running; it's too tiring!

1 | start | Spanish. | decided | dad | studying | My | to | has |

_____

2 | colleague | help | the | My | finish | to | report. | me | offered |

_____

3 | really | weekend. | on | enjoy | I | running | the |

_____

52.3 TACHA LAS PALABRAS INCORRECTAS DE CADA FRASE

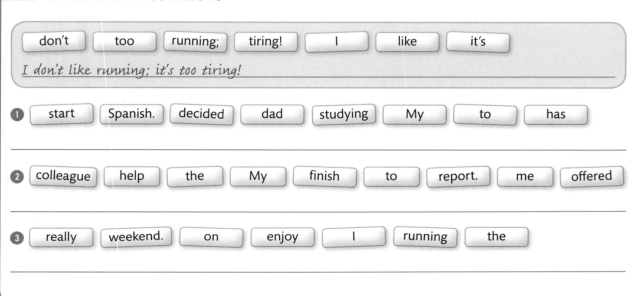

Brian was considering ~~to buy~~ / buying a new surfboard.

1 Carlo enjoys going / to go to the theater every Friday.

2 Rob and Phil intend buying / to buy a house this year.

3 Ellie is planning visiting / to visit Sydney while she's in Australia.

4 I don't feel like playing / to play football this evening.

5 Margo refused eating / to eat the ice cream Jed offered her.

6 My boss agreed letting / to let me go home early from work.

We regret to inform you that you have not got the job.

I was driving home when I decided to stop for a cup of coffee.

We have to tell you that you have not got the job, and we are sorry.

1 I regret telling Jon about my new job. He's told everyone.

2 On the way back home, I stopped to have a cup of coffee.

I will remember to pick Angela up later from the airport.

3 I won't forget to pick Angela up from the airport.

I wish I hadn't told Jon about my job.

4 Do you remember meeting Paul at the conference last year?

The professor thanked the organizers and then talked about the experiment.

5 I stopped drinking coffee ages ago. I only drink tea now.

You were supposed to meet Paul. Did you remember to do that?

6 After thanking the organizers, the professor went on to talk about the experiment.

I used to drink coffee, but I decided to stop a long time ago.

7 Did you remember to meet Paul at the conference?

The professor was talking about the experiment and continued to do so.

8 I'll never forget seeing Angela at the airport for the first time.

Do you remember the time you first met Paul at the conference?

9 The professor went on talking about the experiment for hours.

I'll always remember when I saw Angela for the first time.

53 Pautas verbales con objetos

Algunos verbos, los llamados transitivos, llevan un objeto. Cuando estos verbos van seguidos de un infinitivo o un gerundio, el objeto debe ir entre el verbo y el infinitivo o gerundio.

53.1 MARCA LAS FRASES QUE SEAN CORRECTAS

My teacher expects me to do a lot of homework. ☑
My teacher expects me doing a lot of homework. ☐

1. Alfred spends a lot of time playing golf after work. ☐
   Alfred spends a lot of time to play golf after work. ☐

2. Janice watched the kids to play in the park. ☐
   Janice watched the kids playing in the park. ☐

3. Marco tried sold his old car to me. ☐
   Marco tried to sell his old car to me. ☐

4. My boss wants me working more quickly. ☐
   My boss wants me to work more quickly. ☐

5. Helena heard people talking in the room next door. ☐
   Helena heard people to talk in the room next door. ☐

6. My aunt borrowed a lot of money to my dad. ☐
   My aunt borrowed a lot of money from my dad. ☐

7. My mom wants me clean my room immediately. ☐
   My mom wants me to clean my room immediately. ☐

8. Hanif asked me to help him use the new software. ☐
   Hanif asked me helping him use the new software. ☐

9. Yuri bought an ice cream for his girlfriend. ☐
   Yuri bought an ice cream to his girlfriend. ☐

10. Tom reminded Peter buying some tickets for the concert. ☐
    Tom reminded Peter to buy some tickets for the concert. ☐

53.2 ESCRIBE DE NUEVO LAS FRASES PONIENDO LAS PALABRAS EN EL ORDEN CORRECTO

| Caroline | son | advice. | her | gave | some |

Caroline gave her son some advice.

1 | keep | parents | room | to | clean. | my | My | expect | me |

_____

2 | Gus's | finish | him | boss | early | allows | Fridays. | on | to |

_____

3 | on | the | children | Danny | lawn. | watched | playing | the |

_____

4 | to | my | Don | reminded | grandmother. | me | phone |

_____

5 | told | walk | The | to | principal | more | slowly. | us |

_____

6 | an | becoming | I | Katie | day. | imagine | actor | can | one |

_____

7 | on | summer | Ravi | beach. | spent | lying | the | his |

_____

8 | friendly. | to | dog | Eleanor | more | wants | be | her |

_____

9 | from | milk | to | Mona | me | the | buy | store. | some | asked |

_____

54 Pautas verbales con preposiciones

Algunas pautas verbales incluyen preposiciones. Estas no pueden ir seguidas por infinitivos, por lo que dichas pautas utilizan únicamente gerundios.

 54.1 COMPLETA LOS ESPACIOS CON LAS PREPOSICIONES DEL RECUADRO

Stop worrying _____ *about* _____ what might happen tomorrow!

1. Emma is talking _____ quitting her job.

2. Ania finally admitted _____ stealing the jewelry.

3. My dad tried to prevent me _____ studying art in college.

4. Our company believes _____ doing the best possible job.

5. Frank apologized _____ forgetting my birthday.

6. I want to ask my tutor _____ doing the exam again.

7. We congratulated Sandra _____ winning the competition.

8. Paul objected _____ Danny eating a burger in the office.

9. We decided _____ buying a house in the country.

10. We're all looking forward _____ visiting you soon.

11. I need to concentrate _____ passing all my exams this spring.

12. Peter is worrying _____ his interview tomorrow.

13. The council banned people _____ taking dogs onto the beach.

14. Chloe accused me _____ stealing her idea for the presentation.

15. Leo's parents tried to stop him _____ marrying the girl he loved.

about	from	to	about	to	in	about	on
of	~~about~~	on	against	from	to	for	from

135

55 Phrasal verbs

Algunos verbos se componen de dos o más palabras, que juntas tienen un significado distinto que el de esas palabras por separado. Son los llamados phrasal verbs.

55.1 CONECTA CADA IMAGEN CON LA FRASE CORRECTA

Tony works out at the local gym each evening.

I love chilling out by watching a funny movie and eating popcorn.

I've heard from Bill. He's got some shocking news.

It's taken me a long time to get over this cold.

My mother takes care of my sons on Fridays.

I meet up with my friends most weekends.

We checked into the hotel and went to our room.

I get along very well with my brother.

55.2 MARCA LAS FRASES QUE SEAN CORRECTAS

> I've dress upped for the party. ☐
> I've dressed up for the party. ☑

1. Jen and Hugo eat out very often. ☐
   Jen and Hugo eat very often out. ☐

2. You should try it on before buying it. ☐
   You should try on it before buying it. ☐

3. The music was loud so I turned it down. ☐
   The music was loud so I turned down it. ☐

4. I've always looked up to my brother. ☐
   I've always up to my brother looked. ☐

5. We've run out milk of. ☐
   We've run out of milk. ☐

6. We checked into the hotel at noon. ☐
   We checked the hotel into at noon. ☐

7. Rob meets up with Nina on Fridays. ☐
   Rob meet ups with Nina on Fridays. ☐

8. Does Pete always shows up on time? ☐
   Does Pete always show up on time? ☐

9. I was annoyed because he woke up me. ☐
   I was annoyed because he woke me up. ☐

10. I'm staying in to watch the game tonight. ☐
    I'm in staying to watch the game tonight. ☐

11. Sharon hand inned her essay early. ☐
    Sharon handed in her essay early. ☐

12. The caterpillar turned into a butterfly. ☐
    The caterpillar turned a butterfly into. ☐

13. It's heavy. Please help me pick it up. ☐
    It's heavy. Please help me pick up it. ☐

55.3 ESCRIBE DE NUEVO LAS FRASES Y CORRIGE LOS ERRORES

> If you drop litter, pick up it.
> *If you drop litter, pick it up.*

1. Ramon is getting the flu over.
   _____

2. It was lovely from you to hear.
   _____

3. She told the children to down sit.
   _____

4. Here's your coat. Put on it please.
   _____

5. We need to check the hotel into.
   _____

6. I spotted a coin and picked up it.
   _____

7. Riku up gets at 9:30am on Saturdays.
   _____

8. The baby's crying. You woke up him.
   _____

9. I love cooking so I don't out eat often.
   _____

10. The café has out run of coffee.
    _____

11. Femi up grew in New York.
    _____

12. The airplane take offs in one hour.
    _____

55.4 ESCRIBE DE NUEVO LAS FRASES PONIENDO LAS PALABRAS EN EL ORDEN CORRECTO

forward | I'm | seeing | tomorrow. | you | looking | to

I'm looking forward to seeing you tomorrow.

1 most | work | I | gym | in | evenings. | the | out

_____

2 up | Camila | to | teacher. | really | her | looks | English

_____

3 after | father. | Rachel | her | takes

_____

4 to | It's | so | up | hard | Libby. | keep | with

_____

5 more. | some | We | I | ran | of | out | so | made | food

_____

6 were | I | when | on | didn't | with | get | we | brother | young. | my

_____

7 got | trip | We | to | from | Wales | our | Thursday. | on | back

_____

8 I | up | the | get | later | usually | on | weekend.

_____

9 down. | car | My | breaking | is | dad's | always

_____

55.5 ESCRIBE LOS PHRASAL VERBS DEL RECUADRO EN EL GRUPO CORRECTO

SEPARABLES	INSEPARABLES
_____	*do without*
_____	_____
_____	_____
_____	_____

get through   turn on   fill up   come across   go over   ~~do without~~   throw away   wake up

55.6 COMPLETA LOS ESPACIOS CON LAS PALABRAS DEL RECUADRO

Our business is not doing well, so we have had to make a lot of _____ *cutbacks* _____ .

1 A break on the coast sounds like the ideal _____ .

2 There has been another _____ of the disease in the city.

3 The café was a _____! We paid $20 for a bowl of soup.

4 After the _____, the sun came out again.

5 It's important to make a _____ of any work you do.

6 There have been so many _____ from the course this year.

7 All the students were given a _____ with important information.

8 Following her _____ with Charlie, Ola was very unhappy.

9 We haven't had _____ like this for years. There's snow and ice everywhere.

downpour   snowfall   getaway   break-up   rip-off

handout   ~~cutbacks~~   dropouts   outbreak   backup

139

56 Verbos modales

Los verbos modales son muy frecuentes en inglés. Se utilizan para hablar de muchas cosas, principalmente de posibilidades, obligaciones y deducciones.

56.1 ESCRIBE DE NUEVO LAS FRASES PONIENDO LAS PALABRAS EN EL ORDEN CORRECTO

you | me | Could | where | is? | library | tell | the

Could you tell me where the library is?

① learn | computer. | You | a | should | to | how | use

_____

② cake? | Could | piece | have | another | I | of

_____

③ run | corridor. | the | You | not | in | must

_____

④ languages | My | fluently. | sister | four | can | speak

_____

⑤ I | Can | with | give | you | shopping? | a | hand | your

_____

⑥ moment? | your | lend | Could | pen | you | me | a | for

_____

⑦ be | from | That | must | letter | college. | Ken's

_____

56.2 CONECTA CADA IMAGEN CON LA FRASE CORRECTA

  ① ② ③

| Can I get you a drink? | Maybe I should call my mother. | Can I help you with your bag? | You mustn't be late for work again. |

 56.3 ESCRIBE DE NUEVO LAS FRASES COMO PREGUNTAS

Simon can speak Irish fluently.
Can Simon speak Irish fluently?

① I can help you clean up.

_____

② Phil should study math in college.

_____

③ Graham can play the violin.

_____

④ Peter has to go to the meeting.

_____

⑤ She can have another chocolate.

_____

⑥ Angela could drive us to the party.

_____

 56.4 ESCRIBE DE NUEVO LAS FRASES EN FORMA NEGATIVA

Students must bring a calculator.
Students must not bring a calculator.

① Leroy can repair your oven.

_____

② My grandma could speak Welsh.

_____

③ You should eat more red meat.

_____

④ Louisa can swim well.

_____

⑤ Students have to wear uniforms.

_____

⑥ You can have another piece of cake.

_____

141

57 Habilidades

"Can" es un verbo modal que describe lo que alguien es capaz de hacer. Se utiliza de distintas maneras para describir habilidades del presente y del pasado.

57.1 CONECTA CADA IMAGEN CON LA FRASE CORRECTA

Emma can make beautiful dresses.

Tina can dance really well.

Chris can repair your car.

Jamie can't lift that box. I'll help him.

I can't solve this. It's too difficult.

Rita can cook the most amazing dishes.

Chloe can speak three languages.

I can't climb that mountain.

57.2 ESCRIBE DE NUEVO LAS FRASES EN EL ORDEN CORRECTO

box. | can't | I | that | reach

I can't reach that box.

1. the | Jonathan | can | guitar. | play

2. can't | We | door. | open | the

3. well. | really | can | Amy | sing

4. Lizzie | car. | cannot | a | drive

5. can | trees. | Femi | climb

6. languages. | can | five | speak | Marion

7. that | piano. | Derek | can't | move

57.3 CONECTA EL INICIO Y EL FINAL DE CADA FRASE

I couldn't buy a new laptop		make wonderful cakes.
1 My grandmother could		You need a new one.
2 I couldn't fix your phone.		because they were too expensive.
3 When I was a child,		because I felt ill.
4 Martha could play the piano		I could run much faster.
5 I couldn't come to the party		Jen could already speak six languages.
6 When she was six,		when she was four years old.

57.4 CONECTA LAS FRASES EN PRESENTE CON LAS FRASES EN FUTURO QUE CORRESPONDAN

I can play most of this piece now.		I'll be able to speak it fluently by the summer.
1 I can already speak some Spanish.		I'll be able to play the whole thing by next week.
2 I can't find my passport.		In the future, we'll be able to travel to other planets.
3 We can already travel to the moon.		I'm hoping I will be able to fix it soon.
4 I still haven't been able to repair your old clock.		I won't be able to take my flight without it.

58 Permiso, peticiones, ofrecimientos

"Can", "could" y "may" se utilizan para pedir permiso para hacer
algo o bien para pedirle a alguien que haga algo por nosotros.
Pueden utilizarse también para ofrecernos a ayudar a alguien.

58.1 INDICA SI LAS FRASES SON FORMALES O INFORMALES

Could you be quiet, please?
Formal ☑
Informal ☐

❶ Could you tell me where the bank is, please?
Formal ☐
Informal ☐

❷ Can I play outside now?
Formal ☐
Informal ☐

❸ May I introduce my sister, Kay?
Formal ☐
Informal ☐

❹ Can I have some more cake?
Formal ☐
Informal ☐

❺ Could you turn down the radio, please?
Formal ☐
Informal ☐

❻ May I go home earlier today?
Formal ☐
Informal ☐

❼ Can I sit here?
Formal ☐
Informal ☐

58.2 INDICA SI LAS FRASES SON PETICIONES U OFRECIMIENTOS

Can I help you at all?
Petición ☐
Ofrecimiento ☑

❶ May I make a reservation for 8pm?
Petición ☐
Ofrecimiento ☐

❷ Can I offer you something to eat?
Petición ☐
Ofrecimiento ☐

❸ Can you lend me 10 dollars?
Petición ☐
Ofrecimiento ☐

❹ Can I get you something to drink?
Petición ☐
Ofrecimiento ☐

❺ Can you help me with this report?
Petición ☐
Ofrecimiento ☐

❻ May I leave the table, please?
Petición ☐
Ofrecimiento ☐

❼ Shall I take your coat for you?
Petición ☐
Ofrecimiento ☐

58.3 CONECTA CADA IMAGEN CON LA FRASE CORRECTA

May I take your order?

Shall I open the door for you?

Shall I carry it for you?

Can I take your coat?

58.4 ESCRIBE DE NUEVO LAS FRASES Y CORRIGE LOS ERRORES

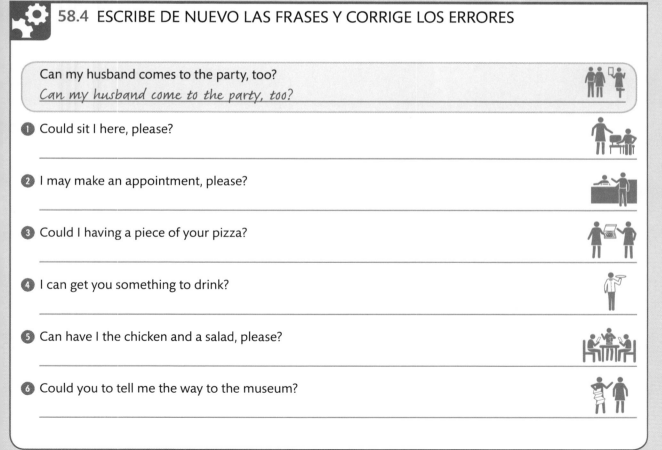

Can my husband comes to the party, too?
Can my husband come to the party, too?

1 Could sit I here, please?

2 I may make an appointment, please?

3 Could I having a piece of your pizza?

4 I can get you something to drink?

5 Can have I the chicken and a salad, please?

6 Could you to tell me the way to the museum?

59 Sugerencias y consejos

El verbo modal "could" se puede utilizar para hacer sugerencias. "Could" no es tan fuerte como "should", y se percibe como un consejo más amable.

59.1 CONECTA CADA SITUACIÓN CON EL CONSEJO CORRECTO

It looks like it's very cold outside. → You should wear a coat and some gloves.

You should take it out for a walk.

1 My dog keeps barking. It's so irritating.

2 It's really hot and sunny outside.

You should try talking to a native speaker.

3 I want to learn how to speak good English.

You should put on some sunscreen.

4 My son doesn't have many friends.

She should try to relax before bed.

5 My wife can't sleep at night.

He should join a club or take up a hobby.

6 I don't know what to buy my girlfriend.

You should go home and get some sleep.

7 My cousin wants to lose some weight.

You could make a little card for her as a gift.

8 I'm not feeling well at all.

You should try to save money regularly.

9 I can't afford to go on vacation this summer.

He should eat less cake and exercise more.

59.2 ESCRIBE DE NUEVO LOS CONSEJOS EMPLEANDO "HAD BETTER" O "HAD BETTER NOT"

> You ought to leave now, or you'll miss the bus.
> *You had better leave now, or you'll miss the bus.*

① It's going to rain. You should take an umbrella.

_____

② The train's been canceled. We ought to take a taxi.

_____

③ It's icy outside. You shouldn't drive tonight.

_____

④ I'm late for the meeting. I should call my boss.

_____

 59.3 MARCA EL MEJOR CONSEJO PARA CADA SITUACIÓN

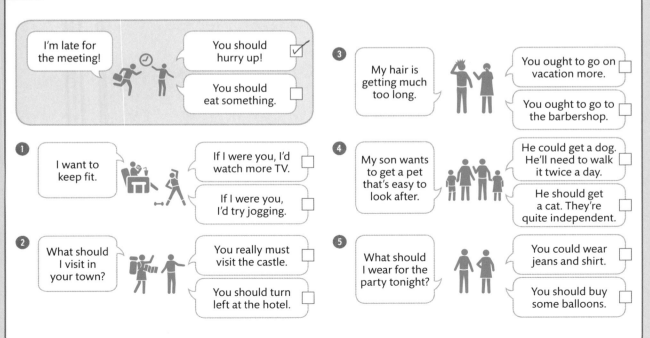

147

60 Obligaciones

En inglés, "have to" o "must" se utilizan para hablar de obligaciones o cosas que son necesarias. También suelen utilizarse para dar instrucciones importantes.

60.1 CONECTA CADA SITUACIÓN CON LA OBLIGACIÓN CORRECTA

My eyesight is absolutely terrible.

You have to go. It's about the new IT system.

① There's a meeting in 10 minutes, but I'm too busy.

You really must go to the optician.

② I've just remembered it's my grandmother's birthday today.

Yes. All our workers must wear a helmet at all times.

③ I've got too much homework to do.

The council must do something to stop people from littering.

④ I'm feeling much better now. The pain has gone.

You must call her right away!

⑤ There's so much litter in town.

He had to go home because his daughter's unwell.

⑥ Why are you driving so slowly here?

You won't have to do any when the summer break comes!

⑦ I forgot to bring my helmet. Does it matter?

You must not lift anything heavy for two weeks.

⑧ Why isn't Juan at the meeting today?

In that case, you don't have to take your medication any longer.

⑨ I hurt my back while I was moving house.

I have to keep to the speed limit.

60.2 COMPLETA LAS FRASES CON "MUST NOT" O "DON'T HAVE TO"

You ___*don't have to*___ come swimming, but you are invited.

1. I _____ wear a suit for work, but I wear one anyway.

2. I'm staying in bed because I _____ go to work today.

3. You _____ stay in the sun too long. You'll get burned.

4. You _____ touch that pan. It's hot.

5. You _____ be great at tennis to enjoy it.

6. I have a secret, but you _____ tell anyone else.

 60.3 ESCRIBE DE NUEVO LAS FRASES EN FUTURO

Students must use a laptop.
Students will have to use a laptop.

1. Everyone must leave before 5pm.
_____

2. You must inform your manager.
_____

3. Brenda has to go home early today.
_____

4. She must pay for the damage.
_____

 60.4 ESCRIBE DE NUEVO LAS FRASES EN PASADO

Joe must come in early.
Joe had to come in early.

1. The managers must apologize.
_____

2. Greg must eat all the broccoli.
_____

3. Joe has to work very hard today.
_____

4. I must rest all this week.
_____

61 Hacer deducciones

Los verbos modales también pueden utilizarse para hablar de cuán probable o improbable es algo. Pueden utilizarse para estimar y hacer deducciones sobre lo que ha ocurrido o está ocurriendo.

61.1 CONECTA CADA IMAGEN CON LA FRASE CORRECTA

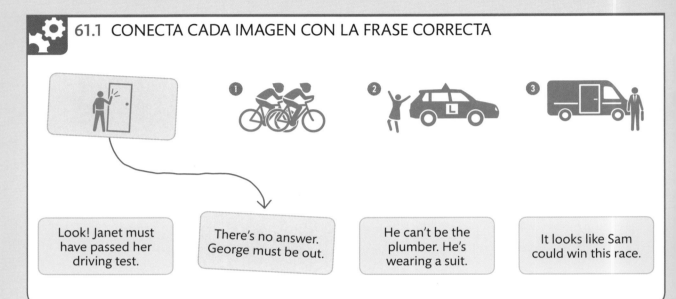

Look! Janet must have passed her driving test.

There's no answer. George must be out.

He can't be the plumber. He's wearing a suit.

It looks like Sam could win this race.

61.2 TACHA LAS PALABRAS INCORRECTAS DE CADA FRASE

Dan has been off work for days. He **must** / ~~cannot~~ be sick.

1 Alina drank all the water. She **must** / **can** have been really thirsty.

2 I can't read this. I **could not** / **might** need new glasses.

3 Ben **can't** / **might** have stolen the vase. He was with me last night.

4 The journey home takes ages. The children **must** / **can** be so bored.

5 I can't find my wallet. I **must** / **can't** have dropped it somewhere.

61.3 COMPLETA LOS ESPACIOS PONIENDO LAS PALABRAS EN SU ORDEN CORRECTO

> [broken] [have] [must]
>
> It's freezing in this house! The heating __must__ __have__ __broken__ .

[on] [have] [it] [might] [left]

❶ I can't find my purse. I _____ _____ _____ _____ _____ the bus.

[a] [have] [I] [might]

❷ I keep sneezing. I think _____ _____ _____ _____ cold.

[failed] [have] [her] [must]

❸ Veronika is crying. She _____ _____ _____ _____ test.

[bear] [be] [could] [a]

❹ What's that animal with brown fur? It _____ _____ _____ _____ .

61.4 CONECTA LAS FRASES QUE SE CORRESPONDAN

I haven't heard from Kate today.	That must be so interesting.
❶ Jon works for the local zoo.	It must have cost a lot of money.
❷ What was that noise?	She might have lost her phone.
❸ Ivana's driving a brand-new sports car.	You can't have followed the recipe properly.
❹ Mabel's team lost the match.	There might be a burglar downstairs.
❺ The cake I made tastes horrible.	She can't be feeling very happy.

62 Posibilidad

Los verbos modales pueden utilizarse para hablar sobre posibilidad, o para expresar incertidumbre. "Might" es el verbo modal más común para ello.

62.1 MIRA LAS IMÁGENES Y COMPLETA LAS FRASES CON LAS EXPRESIONES DEL RECUADRO

The weather forecast said it ___*might rain*___ on Saturday.

4 I can't find my keys. I _____ them at work.

1 It looks like my team _____ tonight's game!

5 If you don't hurry, you _____ the deadline!

2 I _____ some driving lessons if I can afford them.

6 I think we _____ lost. We'd better ask someone.

3 I think the train _____ canceled.

7 I _____ the building by the end of the year.

might take	might not finish	might win	might have left
might be	~~might rain~~	might have been	might miss

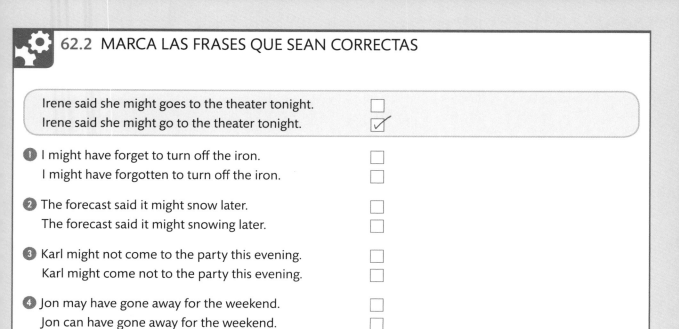

62.2 MARCA LAS FRASES QUE SEAN CORRECTAS

Irene said she might goes to the theater tonight. ☐
Irene said she might go to the theater tonight. ☑

1. I might have forget to turn off the iron. ☐
   I might have forgotten to turn off the iron. ☐

2. The forecast said it might snow later. ☐
   The forecast said it might snowing later. ☐

3. Karl might not come to the party this evening. ☐
   Karl might come not to the party this evening. ☐

4. Jon may have gone away for the weekend. ☐
   Jon can have gone away for the weekend. ☐

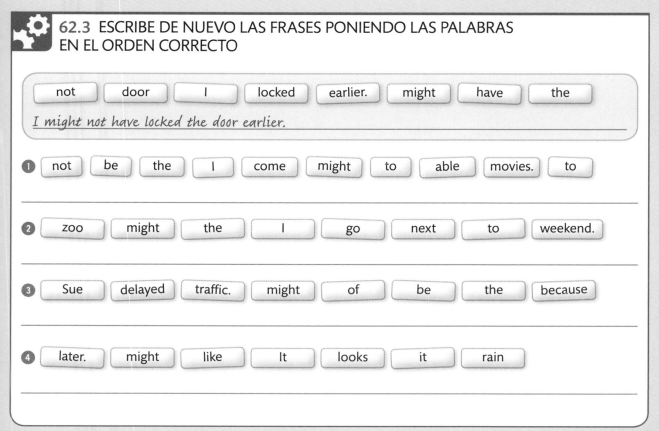

62.3 ESCRIBE DE NUEVO LAS FRASES PONIENDO LAS PALABRAS EN EL ORDEN CORRECTO

| not | door | I | locked | earlier. | might | have | the |

I might not have locked the door earlier.

1. | not | be | the | I | come | might | to | able | movies. | to |

2. | zoo | might | the | I | go | next | to | weekend. |

3. | Sue | delayed | traffic. | might | of | be | the | because |

4. | later. | might | like | It | looks | it | rain |

63 Artículos

Los artículos son palabras cortas que van antes de los sustantivos e indican si estos se refieren a objetos genéricos o específicos. Hay normas que marcan qué artículo debe usarse, o si debe evitarse.

 63.1 TACHA LAS PALABRAS INCORRECTAS DE CADA FRASE

> There is a / ~~an~~ / ~~the~~ black cat in the garden. I wonder whose it is.

1. Russia is a / an / the huge country. It took me seven days to cross it by train.

2. While hiking in Scotland, I spotted a / an / the eagle soaring above us.

3. Bill took me on a / an / the date to a / an / the most expensive bar in town.

4. Where can you get a / an / the good cup of coffee in a / an / the evening?

5. A / An / The food in Italy was absolutely delicious.

6. When I was a / an / the child, I wanted to be a / an / the actor.

7. A / An / The first train to Madrid leaves at 4:30 from platform 4.

8. It's going to rain this evening. Don't forget to take a / an / the umbrella.

9. Do you live in a / an / the house or a / an / the apartment?

10. I saw a / an / the wolf and a / an / the bear in Canada. A / An / The bear was catching fish.

11. Neil Armstrong was a / an / the first man to set foot on a / an / the moon.

12. Last week, I went to see a / an / the show with my cousin.

13. My brother used to be a / an / the chef. He's a / an / the optician now.

14. While I was in Rome, I visited a / an / the Colosseum.

15. A / An / The cakes in that bakery are a / an / the best in town.

16. I had a / an / the cup of coffee and a / an / the croissant. A / An / The coffee was cold, though.

17. Is there a / an / the good hotel where I can stay in your town?

18. A / An / The book that I just finished was really interesting.

63.2 REESCRIBE LAS FRASES EMPLEANDO PLURALES

> There is a book on the table.
> *There are some books on the table.*

1 There's a mug in the dishwasher.

_____

2 I have a pencil here.

_____

3 There's a sandwich for you.

_____

4 Mary has a beautiful dress.

_____

5 Hassan caught a big fish.

_____

6 There's a café in town.

_____

7 There is a watch on the counter.

_____

8 Marco climbed a high mountain.

_____

9 There's a bag in the kitchen.

_____

10 There's a person running outside.

_____

11 There is a big hotel by the shore.

_____

12 Ola sang a beautiful song

_____

63.3 REESCRIBE LAS FRASES CORRIGIENDO LOS ERRORES

> I don't have some pets.
> *I don't have any pets.*

1 Clara works in a office.

_____

2 Do you have some brothers or sisters?

_____

3 There are any banks on my street.

_____

4 There aren't some cookies in the cupboard.

_____

5 Is there the hospital near here?

_____

6 We visited a interesting exhibition today.

_____

7 Are there some good restaurants nearby?

_____

8 London is the very big city.

_____

9 Is there any swimming pool in your town?

_____

10 There aren't some students in the classroom.

_____

11 There are any nice cafés near my house.

_____

12 I tasted a best pasta while I was on vacation.

_____

63.4 CONECTA EL INICIO Y EL FINAL DE CADA FRASE

The Eiffel Tower is one of

1. The president is visiting the
2. The rich always complain
3. The buildings in the
4. The coffee served in this café
5. I had a great trip, but
6. The press were waiting

north of the country next week.

capital are really beautiful.

the most famous buildings in France.

that they don't earn enough.

outside the star's apartment.

is the best in town.

the weather was disappointing.

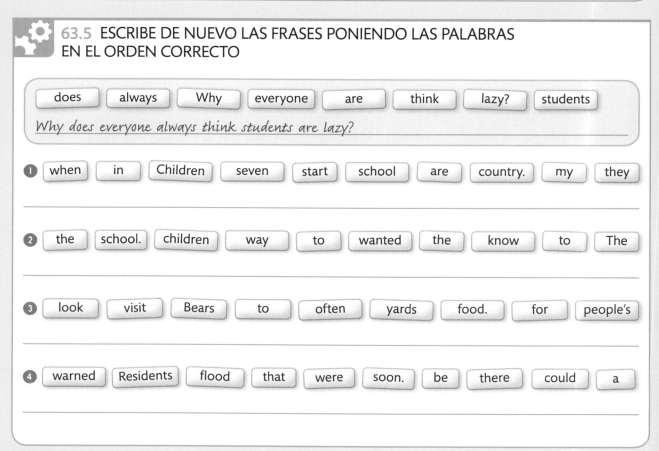

63.5 ESCRIBE DE NUEVO LAS FRASES PONIENDO LAS PALABRAS EN EL ORDEN CORRECTO

| does | always | Why | everyone | are | think | lazy? | students |

Why does everyone always think students are lazy?

1. | when | in | Children | seven | start | school | are | country. | my | they |

2. | the | school. | children | way | to | wanted | the | know | to | The |

3. | look | visit | Bears | to | often | yards | food. | for | people's |

4. | warned | Residents | flood | that | were | soon. | be | there | could | a |

63.6 MARCA LAS FRASES QUE SEAN CORRECTAS

Did you see letter that arrived for you this morning? ☐
Did you see the letter that arrived for you this morning? ☑

1 My sister-in-law is doctor at local hospital. ☐
My sister-in-law is a doctor at the local hospital. ☐

2 Perfume you bought for your wife is in my bag. ☐
The perfume you bought for your wife is in my bag. ☐

3 Try not to get water all over the bathroom floor. ☐
Try not to get the water all over a bathroom floor. ☐

4 I'm going to climb the highest mountain in my country. ☐
I'm going to climb a highest mountain in my country. ☐

5 You really should go to the bed. You're exhausted. ☐
You really should go to bed. You're exhausted. ☐

6 The food was excellent during our trip to Morocco. ☐
Food was excellent during our trip to the Morocco. ☐

7 Phone has been ringing all the morning. ☐
The phone has been ringing all morning. ☐

8 Is there the museum I can visit in your town? ☐
Is there a museum I can visit in your town? ☐

9 I rode an elephant when I visited India last year. ☐
I rode the elephant when I visited India last year. ☐

10 You might see lions while you're on safari. ☐
You might see the lions while you're on safari. ☐

11 Christopher has hot dog for the lunch every day. ☐
Christopher has a hot dog for lunch every day. ☐

12 I ride my bike to the office each morning. ☐
I ride my bike to office each morning. ☐

13 Only rich people can afford to go to that restaurant. ☐
Only the rich people can afford to go to that restaurant. ☐

64 Artículos: repaso

Los artículos definido e indefinido se utilizan en distintas situaciones, lo que depende de si se usan con un sustantivo singular, plural o incontable.

 64.1 TACHA LAS PALABRAS INCORRECTAS DE CADA FRASE

I'm sorry, but we don't have a reservation for a / ~~the~~ Peter Radley. Did you book the right dates?

1 It's so warm outside. I'm going to invite some / the friends over for a barbecue.

2 The / A new secretary seems good but doesn't have much experience.

3 I read some / the really good books during my last vacation.

4 What happened in a / the kitchen? It's such a mess.

5 A / The shirt Liam bought for a / the party cost more than $80.

6 My cousin has a / the really friendly dog.

7 While walking in the park, I spotted a / the rare bird.

8 I have a / the lot of friends who still live with their parents.

9 Paula has left a / some money on a / the kitchen table for you.

10 I think Brazil would be a / the fascinating country to visit.

11 I've just baked the / some cupcakes. Would you like to try one?

12 The / Some cake you made for the fair was absolutely delicious.

13 My family's big. I have three brothers and a / the sister.

14 A / The blue whale is a / the biggest animal that has ever existed.

15 I asked an / the waiter for a / the large cup of coffee.

16 A / The saxophone is a / the difficult instrument to play.

17 India is a / the country I'd most like to visit.

18 We saw a / the bear on our trip through a / the mountains.

64.2 COMPLETA LOS ESPACIOS CON LOS ARTÍCULOS CORRECTOS
Y DEJA UN BLANCO PARA EL ZERO ARTICLE

I'm lost! I was supposed to get the bus to _____*the*_____ Taj Mahal.

1 I don't go to _____ work on Fridays. I look after my daughter.

2 My son rides _____ bike to _____ school each day.

3 In my country, _____ people usually retire when they're about 60.

4 Colm works as _____ scientist at a large research center.

5 You should make sure you get plenty of _____ sleep before _____ exam tomorrow.

6 Irma buys her paint from the store by _____ café.

7 Bill got married to _____ woman he met at work.

8 _____ band I went to see last night was awful.

9 I'm still in touch with _____ friends I made while on _____ vacation.

10 My aunt thought she saw _____ wolf in the woods today.

11 _____ shoes I bought yesterday are far too big.

12 My mom says that _____ cats are much cleaner than _____ dogs.

13 While I was traveling in Australia, I saw _____ kangaroo.

14 _____ president gave _____ long speech at the conference.

65 "This / that / these / those"

"This", "that", "these" y "those" pueden utilizarse como determinantes para especificar de qué se habla en concreto. También pueden utilizarse como pronombres para sustituir a un sustantivo en una frase.

 65.1 TACHA LA PALABRA INCORRECTA DE CADA FRASE

I really like ~~that~~ / those shoes.

① **This / These** is my new boyfriend, Dan.

② **That / Those** book is so interesting.

③ **That / Those** was such a tasty pizza!

④ I'd like **that / those** grapes, please.

⑤ Do you like **this / these** shirt?

⑥ I want to see **that / those** movie tonight.

⑦ **This / These** are your glasses right here.

⑧ Where did you buy **that / those** jeans?

⑨ Is **this / these** my cup of coffee?

⑩ **That / Those** shoes look great on you!

⑪ **This / These** is the perfect car for a family.

⑫ Is **that / those** your new motorcycle, Andy?

⑬ Who made **this / these** cakes?

⑭ **This / These** are my parents, Anna and Charles.

⑮ **This / These** wardrobe's so heavy!

 65.2 CONECTA CADA IMAGEN CON LA FRASE CORRECTA

That is my new house. It's just by the ocean.

That is a very nice painting. It looks great!

That was an amazing goal. You should have seen it!

This is your desk and computer.

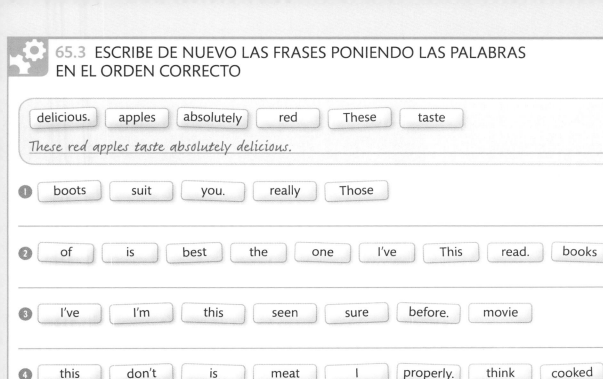

65.3 ESCRIBE DE NUEVO LAS FRASES PONIENDO LAS PALABRAS EN EL ORDEN CORRECTO

| delicious. | apples | absolutely | red | These | taste |

These red apples taste absolutely delicious.

① | boots | suit | you. | really | Those |

② | of | is | best | the | one | I've | This | read. | books |

③ | I've | I'm | this | seen | sure | before. | movie |

④ | this | don't | is | meat | I | properly. | think | cooked |

65.4 CONECTA EL INICIO Y EL FINAL DE CADA FRASE

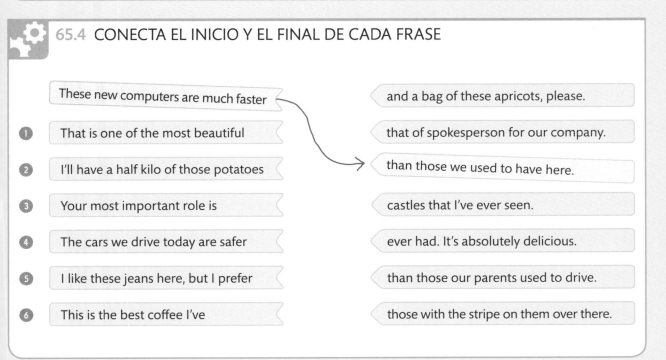

These new computers are much faster — and a bag of these apricots, please.

① That is one of the most beautiful — that of spokesperson for our company.

② I'll have a half kilo of those potatoes → than those we used to have here.

③ Your most important role is — castles that I've ever seen.

④ The cars we drive today are safer — ever had. It's absolutely delicious.

⑤ I like these jeans here, but I prefer — than those our parents used to drive.

⑥ This is the best coffee I've — those with the stripe on them over there.

161

66 "No / none"

"No" y "none" indican la ausencia o la falta de algo.
"No" se utiliza siempre con un sustantivo, mientras
que "none" sustituye a un sustantivo en una frase.

66.1 CONECTA CADA IMAGEN CON LA FRASE CORRECTA

I've missed the train again. I'm having no luck this week!

❶  I'm sorry! I was going to make you a cup of coffee, but there's no milk left!

❷ 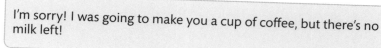 We wanted a room with a view, but the receptionist said that there were none available.

❸  I wanted to order apple pie, but there was none left.

❹ We had no time to make lunch, so we went out for burgers instead.

❺ None of my friends believed I saw a ghost.

❻ None of the clothes I tried on suited me.

❼ I couldn't call you because there was no reception where I was.

66.2 ESCRIBE LAS FRASES EN SU OTRA FORMA

I don't have any time for this.	I have no time for this.
①	There are no free seats.
② I don't have any money left.	
③	There were no more tickets.
④	Kinga has no friends at work.
⑤ It doesn't take any time to get there.	
⑥ There wasn't any doubt that he did it.	

66.3 TACHA LAS PALABRAS INCORRECTAS DE CADA FRASE

I wanted some orange juice, but there was no / none in the fridge.

① No / None vegetarian food had been ordered for the convention.

② There are no / any places left on the English course.

③ No / None of the staff wanted to work on Saturdays.

④ Amelia wanted to buy salad, but there wasn't any / none in the store.

⑤ There was no / none time to think about the exam questions.

⑥ I called five hotels, but no / none had a free room for tonight.

⑦ There wasn't no / any milk left, so I went to the shops.

⑧ I had no / none energy left after work, so I watched some TV.

⑨ No / None of my friends wanted to see a movie with me.

⑩ There weren't no / any seats free on the train home.

⑪ I wanted to try one of Sarah's cakes, but there were no / none left.

⑫ No / None dentists were available to see me, so I went home.

67 "Each / every"

"Each" y "every" son palabras que van delante de sustantivos singulares para referirse a todos los miembros de un grupo de personas.

67.1 ESCRIBE DE NUEVO LAS FRASES PONIENDO LAS PALABRAS EN EL ORDEN CORRECTO

| in | pyramids | I | Egypt. | time | every | I | the | visit | am |

I visit the pyramids every time I am in Egypt.

① | and | wife | the | David | Poconos | his | every | visit | March. |

_____

② | the | go | Indian | every | I | Monday. | in | to | restaurant | town |

_____

③ | us | a | of | was | sandwich | given | Each | and | a | drink. |

_____

④ | Luis | buys | Every | a | coffee | morning, | before | work. |

_____

⑤ | for | type | shampoo | works | This | of | every | hair. |

_____

⑥ | member | the | was | Each | team | given | of | a | prize. |

_____

⑦ | gave | of | Maddy | dollars. | each | thousand | a | her | children |

_____

164

67.2 CONECTA CADA IMAGEN CON LA FRASE CORRECTA

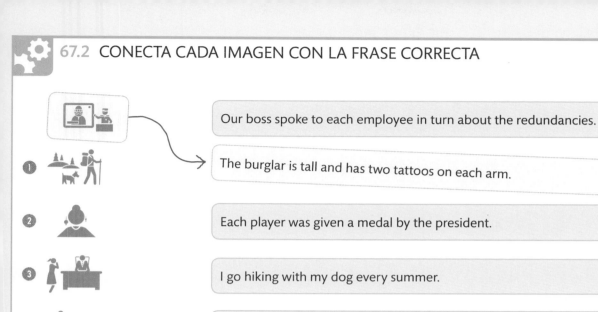

Our boss spoke to each employee in turn about the redundancies.

The burglar is tall and has two tattoos on each arm.

Each player was given a medal by the president.

I go hiking with my dog every summer.

Mona has a different type of earring in each ear.

67.3 CONECTA EL INICIO Y EL FINAL DE CADA FRASE

The concert was incredible,

1 Our manager has spoken to

2 We gave every child at the party

3 My sister loves jewelry and

4 Every Thursday, I play golf

5 Oscar makes sure he does

6 The bakery near my house sells

7 Each city we visited in Spain

8 Every time I hear that song, I

9 I love that author. I've read

a present and some cake.

with one of my work colleagues.

and each singer was extremely talented.

each employee about the factory closing.

every kind of bread you can think of.

had incredibly beautiful architecture.

wears a bracelet on each wrist.

every one of her books.

some exercise every morning.

remember the first time I heard it.

68 "Either / neither / both"

"Either", "neither" y "both" se utilizan en situaciones en las que se describen dos opciones. Indican que una, ambas o ninguna de las opciones son posibles.

68.1 TACHA LAS PALABRAS INCORRECTAS DE CADA FRASE

 I couldn't decide which suit I preferred, so I bought ~~either~~ / both of them.

① Neither / Either Dan nor Belinda could remember the way to the theater.

② Both / Either of my brothers go hiking in the hills on the weekend.

③ Either / Neither of us could resist another piece of cake.

④ Janet could afford to buy neither / either the skirt or the dress.

⑤ I invited both / either Sheila and Bill to my apartment in Paris.

⑥ Either / Both Steve and Louis work really hard in their English class.

⑦ Let's eat out neither / either on Wednesday or Thursday.

⑧ Either / Neither of the managers were at the meeting, unfortunately.

⑨ I had to take either / both the cat and the dog to the veterinarian.

⑩ Ramon can play either / both the electric and acoustic guitar.

⑪ Chetana didn't really like either / neither of the paintings on sale.

68.2 CONECTA EL INICIO Y EL FINAL DE CADA FRASE

Everything looks delicious. I'm going → to have either the steak or the fish.

to the party last night.

1 Neither Gabriela nor Carlos came

the cheesecake appealed to my aunt.

2 My niece wants to be either an

3 Lisa wants both a puppy

still live with our parents.

4 Neither the apple pie nor

actress or an accountant.

5 I want to see either an action film

works properly in my new house.

6 Both my brother and sister

and a laptop for her birthday.

7 Neither the electricity nor the water

or a comedy tonight.

68.3 TACHA LA PALABRA INCORRECTA DE CADA FRASE

Neither the soup nor the other appetizers ~~is~~ / are ready yet.

1 Either my cousin or my parents is / are going to pick you up from the airport.

2 Neither Paula's car nor her bike is / are working properly.

3 I hope either the steak or the fish is / are on the menu today.

4 Both the food and the drink was / were really overpriced.

5 Neither my brother nor my sister is / are coming tomorrow.

6 Either a cat or a dog makes / make a great pet for a family.

7 Neither of us wants / want to go to the conference.

8 I don't really like either of the dress / dresses she bought.

9 Neither the boss nor the workers was / were pleased about the deal.

10 We're thinking about adopting both of the puppy / puppies we saw.

69 Sustantivos singulares y plurales

Los sustantivos en inglés no tienen género. Cambian de forma en función de si son singulares, indicando que hay uno, o plurales, indicando que hay más de uno.

69.1 MARCA EL SUSTANTIVO DE CADA FRASE

It's a lovely day today, so let's go out.
lovely ☐ **day** ☑ **so** ☐

❶ Jim has just bought a second-hand car.
bought ☐ **second-hand** ☐ **car** ☐

❷ That castle looks like it's really old.
castle ☐ **like** ☐ **really** ☐

❸ Andrea asked me if I wanted to play chess.
asked ☐ **wanted** ☐ **chess** ☐

❹ I've just had the strangest thought.
just ☐ **strangest** ☐ **thought** ☐

❺ We walked past an incredible waterfall earlier.
walked ☐ **past** ☐ **waterfall** ☐

69.2 BUSCA OTROS SEIS SUSTANTIVOS EN LA TABLA Y ESCRÍBELOS EN EL GRUPO CORRECTO

H	O	P	E	D	R	A	O	B	W	O	N	S
N	S	C	I	S	S	O	R	S	Q	E	N	V
N	E	F	M	C	T	U	N	R	Y	O	R	F
R	P	N	T	E	R	T	I	Y	T	C	U	L
J	T	A	O	E	O	R	A	N	G	E	N	O
U	E	W	W	R	Y	A	D	F	A	E	S	W
P	M	L	N	L	A	O	G	E	O	R	G	E
I	B	V	E	S	T	M	Q	E	R	I	A	R
T	E	D	H	T	N	D	E	G	J	A	K	I
E	R	I	J	F	R	A	N	C	E	O	E	S
R	E	C	E	P	Y	F	O	I	F	G	Y	D

NOMBRES COMUNES

town

❶ _____

❷ _____

❸ _____

NOMBRES PROPIOS

France

❹ _____

❺ _____

❻ _____

168

69.3 TACHA LOS SUSTANTIVOS INCORRECTOS DE CADA FRASE

This is an excellent book / ~~books~~ / ~~bookes~~.

 ❶ When I finished my dinner, I washed all the dish / dishes / dishs.

 ❷ I bought my new watch / watchs / watche in Switzerland.

 ❸ A lot of persons / peoples / people were waiting on the platform.

 ❹ We need to protect endangered species / specieses / speciess.

69.4 ESCRIBE LAS FRASES EN SU OTRA FORMA

The **child likes** ice cream.	*The children like ice cream.*
❶ _____	Tim asked to borrow the **dictionaries**.
❷ The **train** always **leaves** on time.	_____
❸ The **woman was** talking about the past.	_____
❹ _____	The mayor visited the **factories** in our city.
❺ _____	I think there **are some mice** in the kitchen.
❻ That **story was** wonderful.	_____
❼ _____	The **sheep were** standing in the road.
❽ The **box is** full. We need to buy more.	_____
❾ _____	Carla rested her **feet** on a cushion.
❿ _____	Ellie asked the **men** for directions.
⓫ Maria put her **baby** into the **cot**.	_____

169

70 Sustantivos contables e incontables

En inglés, los sustantivos pueden ser contables o incontables.
Los sustantivos contables pueden contarse de manera individual.
Los objetos que no se cuentan son incontables.

70.1 ESCRIBE LOS SUSTANTIVOS DEL RECUADRO EN EL GRUPO CORRECTO

CONTABLES	INCONTABLES
question	

money   city   apple   ~~question~~   knowledge   sugar

70.2 CONECTA CADA IMAGEN CON LA FRASE CORRECTA

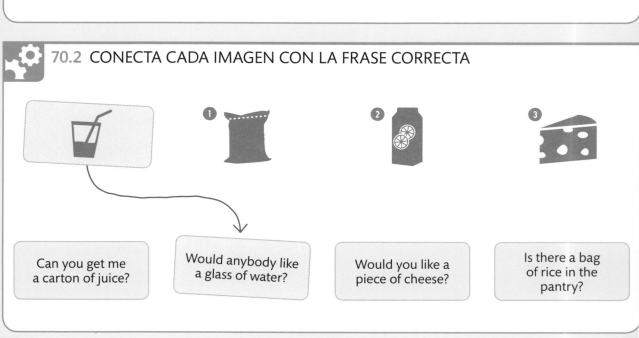

Can you get me a carton of juice?

Would anybody like a glass of water?

Would you like a piece of cheese?

Is there a bag of rice in the pantry?

70.3 ESCRIBE LAS FRASES EN SU OTRA FORMA

I **have some** paper here.	*I don't have any paper here.*
1	There **isn't any** milk in the fridge.
2 I **bought some** eggs at the store.	
3 We **saw some** bears in the mountains.	
4	There **isn't any** juice left.
5	I **didn't get any** gifts for my birthday.
6 I **have some** fruit in my bag.	
7	We **don't have any** important information.
8 There's **some** rice in the cupboard.	
9	I **don't have any** money saved for the vacation.

70.4 MARCA LAS FRASES QUE SEAN CORRECTAS

How many bread do you need? ☐
How much bread do you need? ☑

1 How much meat is there? ☐
How many meat is there? ☐

2 How many cups of tea are there? ☐
How much cups of tea are there? ☐

3 How many coffee have you made? ☐
How much coffee have you made? ☐

4 How much bars of chocolate do we have? ☐
How many bars of chocolate do we have? ☐

5 How many jars of jam are there? ☐
How much jars of jam are there? ☐

6 How many juice will we need? ☐
How much juice will we need? ☐

7 How much milk is there? ☐
How many milk is there? ☐

8 How many bowls of cereal are there? ☐
How much bowls of cereal are there? ☐

9 How much bananas do you have? ☐
How many bananas do you have? ☐

10 How much bags of flour did you buy? ☐
How many bags of flour did you buy? ☐

11 How many cartons of milk are there? ☐
How much cartons of milk are there? ☐

71 Concordancia sujeto-verbo

En inglés sujeto y verbo deben concordar en número. Ciertos sujetos, de todas maneras, pueden actuar como sustantivos singulares o plurales en función del contexto.

 71.1 OBSERVA LAS IMÁGENES Y COMPLETA LAS FRASES CON LAS EXPRESIONES DEL RECUADRO

Physics _is an extremely interesting_ subject in my opinion.

❸ The United States _____ of more than 300 million people.

❶ Athletics _____, such as running and the high jump.

❹ Measles _____ that usually affects children rather than adults.

❷ I think the news _____, but my parents always watch it.

❺ *The Adventures of Sherlock Holmes* _____ _____. I read it every summer.

is an illness	consists of a number of sports	is my favorite book
~~is an extremely interesting~~	is really boring	has a population

71.2 ESCRIBE DE NUEVO LAS FRASES Y CORRIGE LOS ERRORES

Darts are a very popular game in some countries.
Darts is a very popular game in some countries.

1 The Netherlands are one of the world's biggest exporters of fresh flowers.

_____

2 Gymnastics weren't my first choice of sport.

_____

3 *The Three Musketeers* have remained a popular novel since its publication in 1844.

_____

4 Mathematics were my favorite subject when I was at school.

_____

71.3 ESCRIBE DE NUEVO LAS FRASES PONIENDO LAS PALABRAS EN EL ORDEN CORRECTO

| is | in | The | this | band | summer. | Rome | performing |

The band is performing in Rome this summer.

1 | gets | each | Christmas. | My | together | family | usually |

_____

2 | hired | The | of | company | managers. | couple | have | new | a |

_____

3 | refusing | details. | any | The | reveal | is | to | government |

_____

4 | are | work. | staff | after | going | meal | All | out | the | a | for |

_____

72 Sustantivos abstractos y concretos

La mayoría de los sustantivos abstractos son incontables. Algunos,
de ellos, sin embargo, pueden ser tanto contables como incontables,
y ambas formas suelen significar cosas ligeramente distintas.

72.1 CONECTA EL INICIO Y EL FINAL DE CADA FRASE

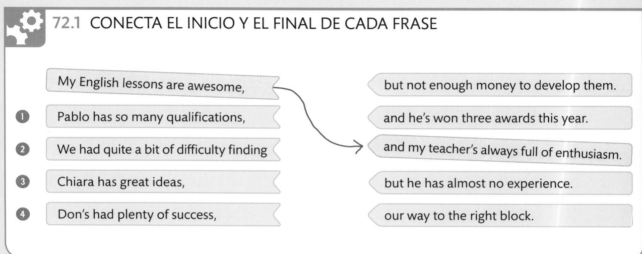

My English lessons are awesome,

1 Pablo has so many qualifications,

2 We had quite a bit of difficulty finding

3 Chiara has great ideas,

4 Don's had plenty of success,

but not enough money to develop them.

and he's won three awards this year.

and my teacher's always full of enthusiasm.

but he has almost no experience.

our way to the right block.

72.2 BUSCA OTROS SEIS SUSTANTIVOS EN LA TABLA Y ESCRÍBELOS EN EL GRUPO CORRECTO

G	G	N	I	D	A	R	B	Y	W	O	Q	H
N	S	E	F	L	O	V	E	T	Q	E	N	A
N	D	E	V	J	S	M	L	S	M	A	R	P
R	I	N	T	E	R	T	I	U	T	C	L	P
S	B	T	A	O	K	R	E	D	N	A	J	I
E	D	I	S	R	Y	E	F	F	T	R	N	N
M	Z	L	O	L	A	E	Z	I	O	H	I	E
P	E	N	C	I	L	V	O	N	S	E	N	S
T	I	M	E	T	N	D	X	G	J	A	G	S
E	H	I	O	A	Y	T	A	B	L	E	H	G

SUSTANTIVOS CONCRETOS

pencil

1 _____

2 _____

3 _____

SUSTANTIVOS ABSTRACTOS

happiness

4 _____

5 _____

6 _____

72.3 TACHA LAS PALABRAS INCORRECTAS DE CADA FRASE

> This office is much too small! There isn't enough room / ~~rooms~~ for everyone.

 ❶ I met people from many different cultures / culture at college.

 ❷ After a lot of thoughts / thought, I've decided to quit my job.

 ❸ Being able to play an instrument is a great skill / skills to have.

 ❹ I've visited the museum a few times / time this year.

 ❺ Don't give up hopes / hope! Your team might win.

 ❻ I have a terrible memory / memories for people's names.

 ❼ It takes a lot of times / time to learn a foreign language.

 ❽ Venice is famous for its culture / cultures and history.

 ❾ Trisha loves to share her memory / memories of the past.

 ❿ There's a lot of space / spaces in my new apartment.

 ⓫ My uncle is always driving everywhere at high speeds / speed.

 ⓬ I made some lasting friendships / friendship while traveling.

 ⓭ There isn't enough times / time to finish the project.

73 Sustantivos compuestos

Los sustantivos compuestos son dos o más sustantivos que actúan como uno solo. El primero (o los primeros si son más de dos) modifica el siguiente, de manera parecida a un adjetivo.

My mother-in-law had her birthday party in the town hall.

1

Two thieves had just carried out a bank robbery, but a policeman caught them before they could make their getaway.

2

I went to pick up my theater tickets from the ticket office.

3

During the heat wave, we kept the air-conditioning switched on all day.

4

Marc looked at the night sky as he relaxed on his camping trip.

5

Alberto stood at the front door, with his suitcase, waiting for the taxi.

6

As Ellie felt the first raindrops fall, she regretted not bringing a raincoat.

7

Sally had a terrible headache, so she asked her boyfriend to get her some painkillers.

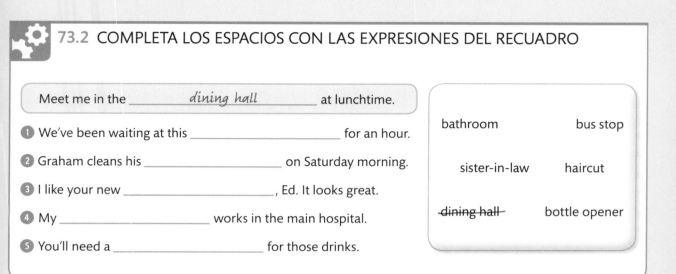

73.2 COMPLETA LOS ESPACIOS CON LAS EXPRESIONES DEL RECUADRO

Meet me in the _____ *dining hall* _____ at lunchtime.

1 We've been waiting at this _____ for an hour.

2 Graham cleans his _____ on Saturday morning.

3 I like your new _____, Ed. It looks great.

4 My _____ works in the main hospital.

5 You'll need a _____ for those drinks.

bathroom   bus stop

sister-in-law   haircut

~~dining hall~~   bottle opener

73.3 ESCRIBE DE NUEVO LAS FRASES PONIENDO LAS PALABRAS EN EL ORDEN CORRECTO

| this | enjoy | year? | Did | the | summer | you | party |

Did you enjoy the summer party this year?

1 | the | bookstore. | investigating | The | break-in | at | police | the | are |

_____

2 | The | floor. | kitchen | teapot | the | onto | fell |

_____

3 | drugstore. | the | bought | I | at | some | toothpaste |

_____

4 | had | cereal. | sunrise | got | and | I | up | a | bowl | breakfast | at | of |

_____

5 | his | birthday | for | Darren | a | bought | card | son. |

_____

74 Números

Los números cardinales se utilizan para contar y para decir qué cantidad hay de algo. Los números ordinales indican la posición de algo en una lista ordenada.

74.1 INDICA SI LOS NÚMEROS SON CARDINALES U ORDINALES

sixth
Cardinal ☐
Ordinal ☑

4 three thousand
Cardinal ☐
Ordinal ☐

1 seventy-two
Cardinal ☐
Ordinal ☐

5 thirty-fourth
Cardinal ☐
Ordinal ☐

2 ninety-second
Cardinal ☐
Ordinal ☐

6 one-hundredth
Cardinal ☐
Ordinal ☐

3 one hundred and five
Cardinal ☐
Ordinal ☐

7 fourteen
Cardinal ☐
Ordinal ☐

74.2 ESCRIBE CADA NÚMERO EN SU OTRA FORMA

207	Two hundred and seven
1 9,000	
2 _____	eight hundred and forty-eight
3 _____	four hundred and seventeen
4 6,500	
5 958	
6 _____	ninety-seven
7 3,590	
8 359	

74.3 CONECTA LAS CIFRAS CON EL TEXTO CORRECTO

4,096,733 **1** 6,840,250 **2** 14,220,902 **3** 90,310,000

fourteen million, two hundred and twenty thousand, nine hundred and two

four million, ninety-six thousand, seven hundred and thirty-three

ninety million, three hundred and ten thousand

six million, eight hundred and forty thousand, two hundred and fifty

82%	→	two-thirds

❶ 12.5 — eighty-two percent

❷ 27.5% — six and three-quarters

❸ ²⁄₃ — two fifths

❹ 32% — twelve point five

❺ 6¾ — six point three four

❻ 14.95 — twenty-seven point five percent

❼ 19% — eight and a third

❽ ²⁄₅ — thirty-two percent

❾ 6.34 — fourteen point nine five

❿ 8⅓ — eight and a half

⓫ 79.4% — nineteen percent

⓬ 8½ — seventy-nine point four percent

75 Cantidades

En inglés hay varias maneras de expresar cantidades generales
o concretas, decir si las cantidades son adecuadas y comparar
cantidades distintas.

 75.1 COMPLETA LOS ESPACIOS CON LAS EXPRESIONES DEL RECUADRO

___A few people___ in my office work from home on Fridays.

① _____ also have a part-time job.

② Only _____ came to my barbecue on Saturday.

③ There are _____ performing tonight.

④ I sent _____ while I was traveling.

⑤ There is _____ in the fridge if you want some.

> some good bands
>
> Lots of students   lots of juice
>
> ~~A few people~~   a few postcards
>
> a few of my friends

 75.2 TACHA LAS PALABRAS INCORRECTAS DE CADA FRASE

This essay is due tomorrow; I don't have enough / ~~too many~~ time!

① There isn't / aren't enough sugar to make a birthday cake.

② The burger costs six euros? I'm afraid that's enough / too much.

③ Do we have enough / too much money to buy a car?

④ There are too much / too many people on the bus this morning.

⑤ There isn't enough / is too much chicken to make dinner for everyone.

⑥ I bought too much / enough fruit. Please take some!

⑦ Is / Are there enough orange juice in the fridge for breakfast?

⑧ There are only two seats left. There are not enough / too many of us here.

I'm going traveling for a year because there are ~~few~~ / a few countries I'd like to visit.

 1 A lot of / A lot people visit the mountains on the weekend.

 2 I'm not rich, but I try to donate little / a little money to charity every month.

 3 Sadly, there are few / a few Sumatran tigers left in the world today.

 4 I met quite a few / quite a bit of new clients at the conference.

 5 I have little / a little patience for people who are always late. I'm always on time!

 6 There's quite a bit of / quite a few snow. Let's build a snowman!

 7 Lots / Lots of people came to Craig's 40th birthday party.

 8 Do you need some help with that report? I have little / a little time I can spare.

 9 Be careful! That vase is worth quite a bit of / quite a few of money.

 10 There are few / a few paintings in the museum I haven't seen. Can we stay a bit longer?

 11 There are very few / a few people I would lend money to, but my brother is one of them.

 12 I don't have lots of friends, but I've got few / a few who I'm really close to.

75.4 COMPLETA LOS ESPACIOS CON "FEWER" O "LESS"

There are much _____*fewer*_____ entries for the competition than there were last year.

1 I spent _____ time on this essay than I did last time.

2 The lecture was almost empty. There were _____ than 10 students there.

3 I'm earning _____ money with my new job, but the conditions are better.

4 _____ people eat meat today in comparison with a decade ago.

5 The train leaves in _____ than half an hour. We should hurry!

6 There was much _____ traffic than usual on the way to work.

7 There are _____ than 5,000 black rhinos left in the wild.

8 _____ young people are studying languages than in the past.

9 It's _____ than 10 minutes' walk to the historic part of the city.

75.5 MARCA LAS FRASES QUE SEAN CORRECTAS

The brighter the moon is, the fewer stars you can see at night. ☑
The brighter the moon is, the fewer stars than you can see at night. ☐

1 We didn't go shopping because we had enough money. ☐
We didn't go shopping because we didn't have enough money. ☐

2 The weather was awful, but at least I made few friends there. ☐
The weather was awful, but at least I made a few friends there. ☐

3 There is much less traffic in the city than 15 years ago. ☐
There is much fewer traffic in the city than 15 years ago. ☐

4 A male African elephant can weigh more then seven tons. ☐
A male African elephant can weigh more than seven tons. ☐

5 I received lot of presents for my 30th birthday. ☐
I received a lot of presents for my 30th birthday. ☐

75.6 ESCRIBE DE NUEVO LAS FRASES Y CORRIGE LOS ERRORES

> You should have **lots of career opportunity** once you graduate.
> _You should have lots of career opportunities once you graduate._

1 Marco was making **far too many noise**, so Ellie went out to the café.

___

2 I'm afraid it's bad news. Our company is making **fewer money than** it did last year.

___

3 Unfortunately, **very a little** can be done about the bad weather.

___

4 Do we have **pasta enough** to make lunch for all the family?

___

5 We have **lots things** to pack. Do you think there's room in the box?

___

6 **A few people** come to the restaurant on a Monday evening. It's almost empty.

___

7 There are **quite a bit of sandwiches** left. Help yourself to one!

___

8 There were a **lots of people** waiting on the platform for the train.

___

9 There were **a quite few clothes** I liked, but I didn't buy any.

___

10 **Less than 10 people** work for our company. It's very cozy here.

___

11 The safari park costs **fewer than** $5 to visit. It's a real bargain.

___

12 We have **quite a few time** before we need to leave.

___

76 Cantidades aproximadas

Cuando se dispone de cifras concretas, puede ser útil darlas.
Pero si no conocemos las cifras exactas o queremos evitar
repeticiones podemos necesitar términos más generales.

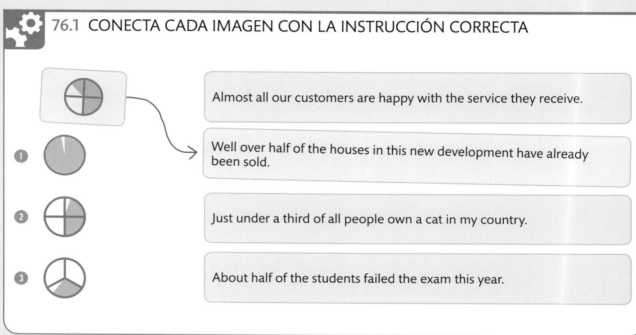

76.1 CONECTA CADA IMAGEN CON LA INSTRUCCIÓN CORRECTA

Almost all our customers are happy with the service they receive.

Well over half of the houses in this new development have already been sold.

Just under a third of all people own a cat in my country.

About half of the students failed the exam this year.

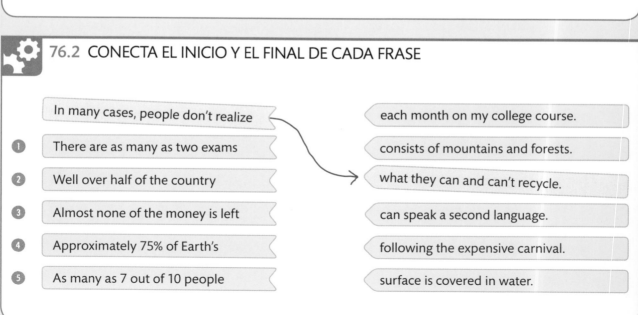

76.2 CONECTA EL INICIO Y EL FINAL DE CADA FRASE

In many cases, people don't realize

1 There are as many as two exams

2 Well over half of the country

3 Almost none of the money is left

4 Approximately 75% of Earth's

5 As many as 7 out of 10 people

each month on my college course.

consists of mountains and forests.

what they can and can't recycle.

can speak a second language.

following the expensive carnival.

surface is covered in water.

76.3 ESCRIBE DE NUEVO LAS FRASES Y CORRIGE LOS ERRORES

will · as · 1,000 · There · as · be · there. · many · people

There will be as many as 1,000 people there.

1. little · be · could · as · as · months. · You · fluent · two · in · in · English

_____

2. quickly · poisoning. · In · from · cases, · most · recover · food · people

_____

3. almost · eaten · cakes. · The · the · children · have · all

_____

4. students · exam. · About · final · half · failed · the · the

_____

5. ten · As · applications · in · few · one · are · as · successful.

_____

6. three-quarters · use · over · of · Well · media. · students · social

_____

7. cases, · of · to · a · go · minority · In · prison. · people

_____

8. in · are · my · as · public · There · as · many · 25 · city. · parks

_____

9. the · away · is · My · from · house · a · just · station. · under · mile

_____

77 Pronombres personales

Los pronombres personales se utilizan para sustituir sustantivos en una frase. Pueden referirse a personas o cosas y presentan distintas formas según sean un sujeto o un objeto.

77.1 ESCRIBE LOS PRONOMBRES EN SU OTRA FORMA

SUJETO	OBJETO
I	me
① we	_____
② _____	you
③ he	_____
④ _____	her
⑤ it	_____
⑥ _____	them

77.2 MARCA LAS FRASES QUE SEAN CORRECTAS

Sonja and me are going shopping. ☐
Sonja and I are going shopping. ☑

① Kelly's so angry with he. ☐
Kelly's so angry with him. ☐

② Paula asked me to marry her. ☐
Paula asked I to marry her. ☐

③ Do you know what happened to them? ☐
Do you know what happened to they? ☐

④ Mike gave she the money. ☐
Mike gave her the money. ☐

77.3 CONECTA CADA IMAGEN CON LA FRASE CORRECTA

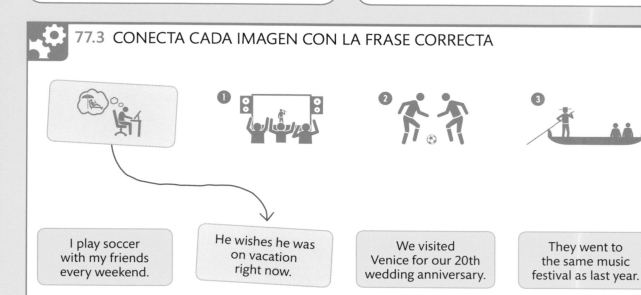

I play soccer with my friends every weekend.

He wishes he was on vacation right now.

We visited Venice for our 20th wedding anniversary.

They went to the same music festival as last year.

77.4 CONECTA LAS FRASES QUE SE CORRESPONDAN

Rachel invited Paige and Scott to the heavy metal concert.

She saw him working in a shop in Edinburgh.

She invited them to the heavy metal concert.

1 Jenny saw Andrew working in a shop in Edinburgh.

2 Michael gave Peter and me a ride to the movie theater.

He offered her a flower.

3 Robert offered Angela a flower.

He gave us a ride to the movie theater.

77.5 ESCRIBE DE NUEVO LAS FRASES SUSTITUYENDO LAS PALABRAS DESTACADAS POR LOS PRONOMBRES CORRECTOS

Darren gave Kate a necklace for her birthday, and Kate absolutely loved the necklace.
Darren gave Kate a necklace for her birthday, and she absolutely loved it.

1 Jane cooked a new dish, but the dish tasted awful. Jane was so disappointed.
_____

2 Tom asked Roger to water the plants. Roger watered the plants and went home.
_____

3 The commuters waited for the train. The commuters were angry because the train was delayed.
_____

4 Mike told his parents he wanted to study drama. His parents thought that drama was a great choice.
_____

5 Shona bought a coffee for Brian. Brian thanked Shona for buying the coffee.
_____

78 Pronombres reflexivos

Los pronombres reflexivos indican que el sujeto de un verbo es también su objeto. En otras ocasiones pueden utilizarse para dar énfasis.

78.1 ESCRIBE LOS PRONOMBRES EN SU OTRA FORMA

OBJETO	REFLEXIVO
me	*myself*
➊ you (singular)	
➋ you (plural)	
➌	himself
➍	herself
➎ it	
➏ us	
➐	themselves

78.2 COMPLETA LOS ESPACIOS CON LOS PRONOMBRES DEL RECUADRO

She introduced _____ *herself* _____ to her new boss.

➊ I asked _____ if I should leave my job.

➋ You should pride _____ on your work, Phil.

➌ Did Daniel injure _____ when he fell off the wall?

➍ Ed and Flora are teaching _____ to cook.

➎ Sarah is preparing _____ for the interview.

➏ Did you and Claire enjoy _____ at the party?

> herself   himself
> yourself
> themselves
> ~~herself~~   myself
> yourselves

78.3 TACHA LAS PALABRAS INCORRECTAS DE CADA FRASE

I really need to pass this test, but I can't concentrate / ~~concentrate myself~~!

1. Tim shaves / shaves himself when he gets up in the morning.

2. Angela cut / cut herself while she was chopping the onions.

3. The door opened / opened itself, and my uncle walked into the room.

4. Chan hurt / hurt himself when he slipped on the ice.

5. Janet feels / feels herself better after her illness.

78.4 MARCA LAS FRASES QUE SEAN CORRECTAS

We were told to take care of us while climbing the dangerous mountain. ☐
We were told to take care of ourselves while climbing the dangerous mountain. ☑

1. I baked the cake myself. I hope you like it. ☐
   I myself baked the cake. I hope you like it. ☐

2. Most stores close at 5pm in my town. ☐
   Most stores close themselves at 5pm in my town. ☐

3. Did the children behave himself during the class? ☐
   Did the children behave themselves during the class? ☐

4. Annie asked Peter and myself to move the boxes. ☐
   Annie asked Peter and me to move the boxes. ☐

5. The child sat by himself reading a book. ☐
   The child sat with himself reading a book. ☐

6. How was the party? Did you enjoy? ☐
   How was the party? Did you enjoy yourselves? ☐

7. We were talking to each other when the phone rang. ☐
   We were talking to ourselves when the phone rang. ☐

78.5 ESCRIBE DE NUEVO LAS FRASES PONIENDO LAS PALABRAS EN EL ORDEN CORRECTO

| president | at | will | event. | The | be | the | herself |

The president herself will be at the event.

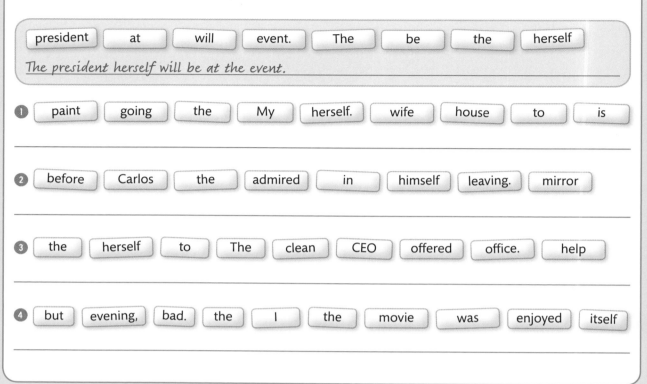

1. | paint | going | the | My | herself. | wife | house | to | is |

_____

2. | before | Carlos | the | admired | in | himself | leaving. | mirror |

_____

3. | the | herself | to | The | clean | CEO | offered | office. | help |

_____

4. | but | evening, | bad. | the | I | the | movie | was | enjoyed | itself |

_____

78.6 CONECTA EL INICIO Y EL FINAL DE CADA FRASE

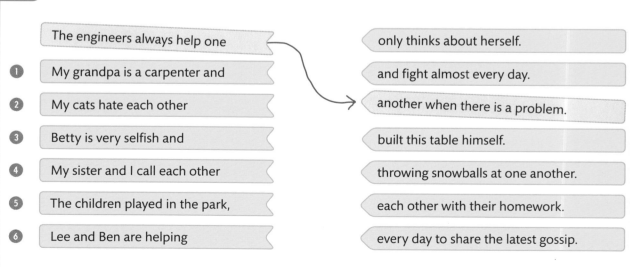

The engineers always help one		only thinks about herself.
1. My grandpa is a carpenter and		and fight almost every day.
2. My cats hate each other		another when there is a problem.
3. Betty is very selfish and		built this table himself.
4. My sister and I call each other		throwing snowballs at one another.
5. The children played in the park,		each other with their homework.
6. Lee and Ben are helping		every day to share the latest gossip.

78.7 COMPLETA LOS ESPACIOS CON PRONOMBRES REFLEXIVOS, O DEJA ESPACIOS EN BLANCO SI NO SON NECESARIOS

Jennifer told _____*herself*_____ that she would start eating more healthy food.

1. Sharon is teaching _____ how to knit.

2. It's hard to tear _____ away from a really good book.

3. Martin shaves _____ each morning when he gets up.

4. I made some tea while the cake baked _____ in the oven.

5. We found _____ in a strange part of town. We were lost.

6. My grandparents have convinced _____ to go swimming each day.

7. How was the fair? Did the children enjoy _____ there?

8. The truck started to reverse _____, so we moved out of the way.

9. I'm familiarizing _____ with the new software.

10. Jim and Ula are decorating their new house _____. It's so much cheaper.

11. My arm really hurts _____. I hope I haven't broken it.

12. Our café prides _____ on its excellent service.

13. I find it so hard to concentrate _____ with all that noise.

14. It looks like the weather is improving _____. Let's go out.

191

79 Pronombres indefinidos

Los pronombres indefinidos, como "anyone", "someone" y "everyone", se utilizan para referirse a una persona u objeto, o un grupo de personas u objetos, sin explicar de quiénes o de qué se trata.

79.1 CONECTA CADA PREGUNTA CON LA RESPUESTA CORRECTA

Does anybody here speak Greek?	What would you prefer? Tea or coffee?
① Could I have something to drink?	No, nobody here speaks that language.
② Where's everyone gone?	It was nothing. Probably just the cat playing.
③ Is there anything wrong, Edward?	Yes, it's half past five.
④ Did you hear something downstairs?	There's a meeting in room 10.
⑤ Does anyone know what time it is?	I'm not feeling very well at all.
⑥ Can someone help me open this jar?	No one's heard of him, sorry.
⑦ Does anyone know Bill Jones here?	Of course. Pass it here.

79.2 CONECTA CADA IMAGEN CON LA FRASE CORRECTA

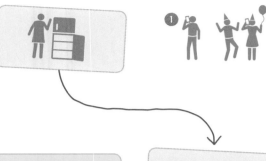 

Did you buy anything when you were at the grocer's?	There's nothing here to eat!	I was exhausted after checking everything.	Everyone's asking why you're not at the party!

79.3 ESCRIBE DE NUEVO LAS FRASES Y CORRIGE LOS ERRORES

> Michael was bored because he didn't know nobody at the party.
> _Michael was bored because he didn't know anybody at the party._

1 I'm sorry. I know absolutely anything about electronics.

_____

2 Libby doesn't want something to eat at the moment.

_____

3 I don't get on with my brother. We have something in common.

_____

4 I didn't buy nothing while I was at the store.

_____

5 There's anything to do here. I'm bored!

_____

6 I think I just heard nothing downstairs.

_____

80 Posesión

Los determinantes posesivos, los pronombres posesivos,
el apóstrofo con "s" y los verbos "have" y "have got" se
utilizan en inglés para expresar posesión.

 80.1 ESCRIBE CADA PALABRA EN SUS OTRAS FORMAS

PRONOMBRE DE SUJETO	DETERMINANTE POSESIVO	PRONOMBRE POSESIVO
I	my	mine
❶	your	
❷ he		
❸		hers
❹	its	
❺ we		
❻		theirs

 80.2 CONECTA CADA IMAGEN CON LA FRASE CORRECTA

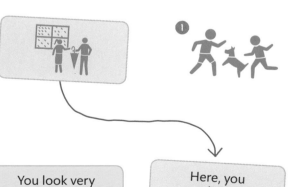

You look very
excited with your
new present.

Here, you
can borrow
my umbrella.

There's Silvia taking
her dogs for a walk.

I saw the
children playing
with their dog.

80.3 ESCRIBE DE NUEVO LAS FRASES PONIENDO LAS PALABRAS EN EL ORDEN CORRECTO

this | Is | phone? | your

Is this your phone?

1. their | Where | house? | is

_____

2. yours. | is | This | desk

_____

3. my | that | there? | charger | Is

_____

4. aren't | These | theirs. | books

_____

5. coat. | her | That | is

_____

6. Are | glasses? | these | his

_____

7. these | mine? | of | Which | cups | is

_____

80.4 TACHA LAS PALABRAS INCORRECTAS DE CADA FRASE

This is my / ~~mine~~ jacket, so this one must be ~~your~~ / yours.

1. Their / Theirs IT system is modern, but our / ours needs replacing soon.

2. These earrings are my / mine, but that bracelet is her / hers.

3. My / Mine bag is the yellow one. Which one is your / yours?

4. The large boxes are their / theirs, but these small ones are our / ours.

5. Her / hers parents live in the countryside, while my / mine live in the city.

6. If this is your / yours, then I don't know which laptop is my / mine.

7. Stacey put her / hers lunch in the fridge. Are these sandwiches your / yours?

8. Katia parked her / hers car by the park. Where did your parents park their / theirs?

9. We drive our / ours cars on the right, whereas they drive their / theirs on the left.

10. Your / Yours father drives a sports car, but my / mine rides a bike.

The cat of Laura
Laura's cat

1 The uncle of Mary and Don

_____

2 The son of Ben

_____

3 The grades of the students

_____

4 The cat of Sam and Ayshah

_____

5 The house of Debbie

_____

6 The dog of my parents

_____

7 The car of Marco and Kate

_____

8 The house of my grandparents

_____

9 The grandchild of Elsa

_____

10 The parrot of Beth

_____

11 The choice of the people

_____

Look at the dog! It's chasing its tail. ☑
Look at the dog! Its chasing it's tail. ☐

1 The women's clothes are downstairs. ☐
The womens' clothes are downstairs. ☐

2 Pick the babie's toys up, please. ☐
Pick the babies' toys up, please. ☐

3 Your car's new, while my is old. ☐
Your car's new, while mine is old. ☐

4 That book is yours, and this one is mine! ☐
That book is your, and this one is my! ☐

5 Toms' computer is slow. ☐
Tom's computer is slow. ☐

6 Hurry up! Its time you left for work. ☐
Hurry up! It's time you left for work. ☐

7 My town is bigger than yours. ☐
My town is bigger than your. ☐

8 The childrens' food is here. ☐
The children's food is here. ☐

9 That bag over there is your. ☐
That bag over there is yours. ☐

10 These are the ladie's coats. ☐
These are the ladies' coats. ☐

11 My parent's house is small. ☐
My parents' house is small. ☐

12 The mens' changing room is there. ☐
The men's changing room is there. ☐

13 The dog can't find it's home. ☐
The dog can't find its home. ☐

80.7 CONECTA EL INICIO Y EL FINAL DE CADA FRASE

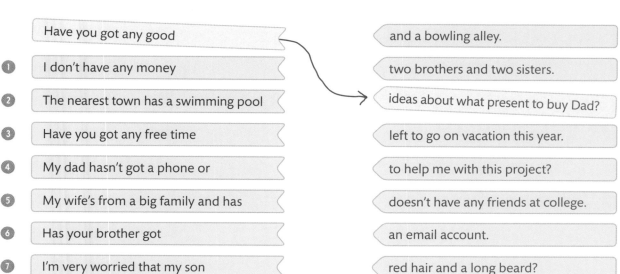

Have you got any good — ideas about what present to buy Dad?

1. I don't have any money — left to go on vacation this year.
2. The nearest town has a swimming pool — and a bowling alley.
3. Have you got any free time — to help me with this project?
4. My dad hasn't got a phone or — an email account.
5. My wife's from a big family and has — two brothers and two sisters.
6. Has your brother got — red hair and a long beard?
7. I'm very worried that my son — doesn't have any friends at college.

80.8 INDICA LA MEJOR RESPUESTA PARA CADA PREGUNTA

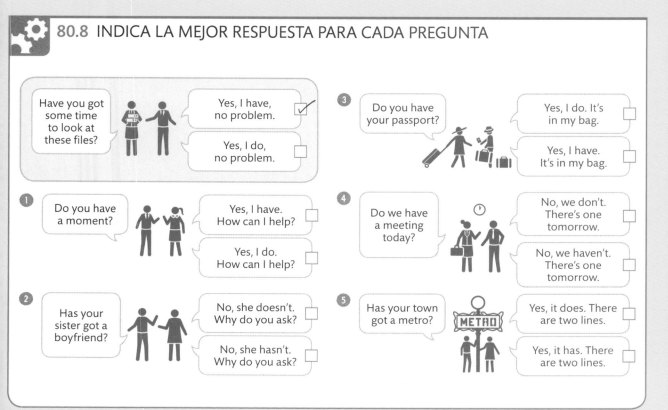

Have you got some time to look at these files?
- Yes, I have, no problem. ✓
- Yes, I do, no problem.

1. Do you have a moment?
- Yes, I have. How can I help?
- Yes, I do. How can I help?

2. Has your sister got a boyfriend?
- No, she doesn't. Why do you ask?
- No, she hasn't. Why do you ask?

3. Do you have your passport?
- Yes, I do. It's in my bag.
- Yes, I have. It's in my bag.

4. Do we have a meeting today?
- No, we don't. There's one tomorrow.
- No, we haven't. There's one tomorrow.

5. Has your town got a metro?
- Yes, it does. There are two lines.
- Yes, it has. There are two lines.

81 Cláusulas relativas definidas

Una cláusula relativa es una parte de la frase que proporciona más información sobre el sujeto. Una cláusula relativa definida identifica el sujeto del que hablamos.

81.1 ESCRIBE DE NUEVO LAS FRASES PONIENDO LAS PALABRAS EN EL ORDEN CORRECTO

| the | English. | assistant | could | We | speak | hired | who |

We hired the assistant who could speak English.

1. | who | a | I | man | sailed | met | around | world. | has | the |

2. | exciting. | you | The | really | book | was | that | me | lent |

3. | that | delicious. | ordered | The | Misha | looks | dessert |

4. | knows | some | she | invited | college. | people | who | Laura | from |

5. | visit | to | was | The | hoping | palace | was | that | closed. | I |

6. | Sanjay | sea. | house | close | that | is | a | moving | the | to | to | is |

7. | performed | stage. | on | I | band | loved | the | which |

I wish my neighbors had a dog that didn't bark so much. ☑

I wish my neighbors had a dog who didn't bark so much. ☐

1. My son has a camera which takes wonderful photos. ☐

   My son has a camera which it takes wonderful photos. ☐

2. The milk what you bought yesterday has turned sour. ☐

   The milk that you bought yesterday has turned sour. ☐

3. The woman who was just speaking to you is incredibly rich. ☐

   The woman was just speaking to you is incredibly rich. ☐

4. Where did you get the hat you're wearing? ☐

   Where did you get the hat who you're wearing? ☐

My sister is starting a fashion business — that helps people find clothes that suit them.

which produces kitchen equipment.

1. Ben works for a company

who dreams of becoming an astronaut.

2. Do you like the shirt

3. Fatima showed me the dog

which we're planning to buy.

4. Betty is playing a woman

that I bought at the market today?

5. This is the villa

who lives over the road.

6. There are only two stores

that she wants to adopt.

7. My dad studied with the woman

that she could lend me?

8. Does Mira have an umbrella

that sell that particular part.

82 Cláusulas relativas indefinidas

Igual que las cláusulas relativas definidas, las cláusulas relativas indefinidas dan información adicional sobre algo. De todas maneras, se limitan a añadir detalles y no cambian el significado de la frase.

82.1 CONECTA CADA IMAGEN CON LA FRASE CORRECTA

The Statue of Liberty, which is on a small island, is popular with tourists.

Someone crashed into my brand new car, which I only bought last week.

Sam has a lovely dog, which he takes for a walk each morning.

Den has a new sports car, which he spent all his savings on.

82.2 TACHA LAS PALABRAS INCORRECTAS DE CADA FRASE

The lecture, which / ~~who~~ had been scheduled for 3pm, was canceled at the last minute.

1. My new sweater, who / which is made of wool, cost $40.

2. I teach many international students, many of that / whom are Indian.

3. David's cat, who / which is usually very calm, just scratched me!

4. My wife, who / that is an optician, enjoys her job very much.

5. He has two daughters, both of who / whom are lawyers.

82.3 ESCRIBE DE NUEVO LAS FRASES Y AÑADE COMAS SI ES NECESARIO

> My rabbit which I haven't seen for days is still missing.
> *My rabbit, which I haven't seen for days, is still missing.*

1 I've recently bought a house which I'm now decorating.

_____

2 My nephew who is only seven years old is learning to play the violin.

_____

3 The singer thanked her fans many of whom were at the event.

_____

4 My car which I only bought last week has already broken down.

_____

5 Jill who has worked here for 15 years is extremely reliable.

_____

82.4 INDICA SI LAS CLÁUSULAS RELATIVAS SON DEFINIDAS O INDEFINIDAS

> The Algarve, which is in Portugal, has some amazing beaches.
> **Definida** ☐ **Indefinida** ☑

1 I'm working with someone who is always late for work.
Definida ☐ **Indefinida** ☐

2 The fans, many of whom had traveled far, were delighted.
Definida ☐ **Indefinida** ☐

3 I own so many books, most of which I've never read.
Definida ☐ **Indefinida** ☐

4 Sula's wearing the necklace that you bought her.
Definida ☐ **Indefinida** ☐

83 Otras estructuras de relativo

Las expresiones relativas introducen cláusulas que describen un nombre en la parte principal de la frase. Se utilizan distintas expresiones relativas para referirse a distintos tipos de nombres.

83.1 TACHA LA PALABRA INCORRECTA DE CADA FRASE

This building is ~~whereby~~ / where the local council used to meet before they moved offices.

1. I'll never forget that afternoon when / which Paula told me she wanted to move to another country.

2. Jane, who / whose sister you work with, is giving the speech this afternoon.

3. A long break and some sunshine is exactly which / what Kelly needs right now.

4. Toni's café, where / that you worked as a student, has closed down.

5. I'm interviewing a woman whose / that brother used to work here.

6. I'm looking forward to a time which / when we don't have to work so late.

7. That sofa is just which / what we need for the living room.

8. The companies have an agreement whereby / which they share customer data.

83.2 COMPLETA LOS ESPACIOS CON LOS RELATIVOS DEL RECUADRO

Sam is a new author ____whose____ first book has just become a bestseller.

1. I thought it was Monday _____ Manuela was supposed to come.

2. I have no idea _____ he's bought me for my birthday.

3. We visited the part of India _____ my parents grew up.

4. Liam, _____ report you've just read, is an excellent lawyer.

5. Stratford-upon-Avon, _____ Shakespeare was born, is lovely.

whose	where
~~whose~~	when
where	what

202

83.3 MARCA LAS FRASES QUE SEAN CORRECTAS

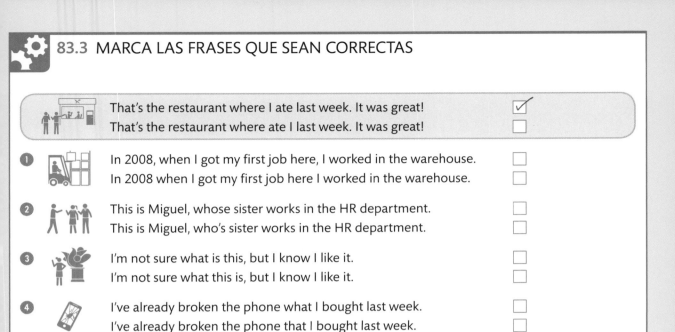

That's the restaurant where I ate last week. It was great! ✓
That's the restaurant where ate I last week. It was great! ☐

1 In 2008, when I got my first job here, I worked in the warehouse. ☐
In 2008 when I got my first job here I worked in the warehouse. ☐

2 This is Miguel, whose sister works in the HR department. ☐
This is Miguel, who's sister works in the HR department. ☐

3 I'm not sure what is this, but I know I like it. ☐
I'm not sure what this is, but I know I like it. ☐

4 I've already broken the phone what I bought last week. ☐
I've already broken the phone that I bought last week. ☐

83.4 ESCRIBE DE NUEVO LAS FRASES PONIENDO LAS PALABRAS EN EL ORDEN CORRECTO

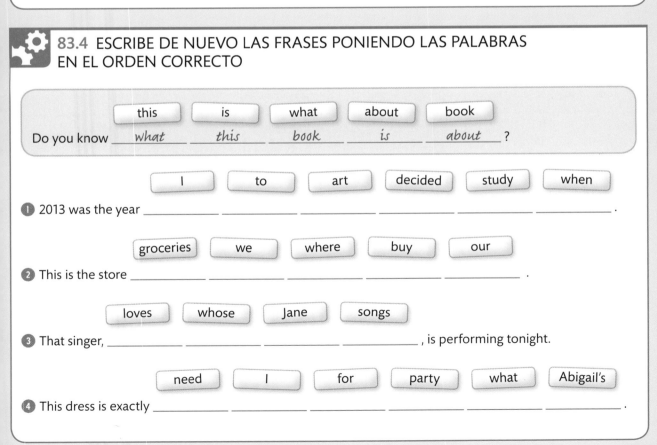

| this | is | what | about | book |

Do you know __what__ __this__ __book__ __is__ __about__ ?

| I | to | art | decided | study | when |

1 2013 was the year _____ _____ _____ _____ _____ _____ .

| groceries | we | where | buy | our |

2 This is the store _____ _____ _____ _____ _____ .

| loves | whose | Jane | songs |

3 That singer, _____ _____ _____ _____ , is performing tonight.

| need | I | for | party | what | Abigail's |

4 This dress is exactly _____ _____ _____ _____ _____ _____ .

84 Expresiones interrogativas y "-ever"

Al añadir "-ever" a las expresiones interrogativas se modifica su significado.
Estas expresiones pueden ser adverbios o determinantes en sus propias
cláusulas, o bien pueden conectar dos cláusulas.

84.1 CONECTA EL INICIO Y EL FINAL DE CADA FRASE

My son always sends me a postcard — from wherever he is in the world.

whichever decision I make.

1. I want to finish this puzzle,

for John's birthday dinner tonight.

2. Catrina said she'd support me,

3. You can wear whatever you like

however long it takes.

4. Tony tries to visit his parents

has left a terrible mess.

5. Whoever was in the kitchen last

whenever he gets the chance.

84.2 TACHA LA PALABRA INCORRECTA DE CADA FRASE

Let's grab a coffee together ~~wherever~~ / whenever you're in London next.

1. However / Whatever did Jon do to make you so angry with him?

2. We're going to be late, whenever / whichever route we take.

3. Elsie told me that she'd be there to help whenever / however I needed her.

4. The engagement's not a secret. You can tell whoever / whichever you want.

5. However / Whoever won first prize must be a really good artist.

6. Whenever / Whatever I hear that music, I always think of Paris.

7. My new kitten follows me whichever / wherever I go in the house.

84.3 OBSERVA LAS IMÁGENES Y COMPLETA LAS FRASES CON LAS PALABRAS DEL RECUADRO

We think you'll be very happy with your new car, _____*whichever*_____ one you choose.

❶ I'm going to study drama, _____ my parents say.

❷ John's in front of the TV _____ I go to see him.

❸ _____ Andy's gone, he's forgotten his wallet.

❹ _____ painted this clearly has a vivid imagination.

❺ I do some gardening _____ I have a spare moment.

❻ _____ student answers this question will win a prize.

❼ I'm going to finish writing this novel, _____ long it takes!

❽ _____ it is John's cooked, it tastes absolutely terrible.

❾ _____ much Anthony earns, he always wants more.

whenever	whatever	wherever	whoever	whatever
however	~~whichever~~	however	whichever	whenever

85 "There"

"There" puede utilizarse con una forma de "be" para hablar de la existencia o la presencia de una persona o cosa. Las frases con "there" pueden utilizarse en distintos tiempos verbales.

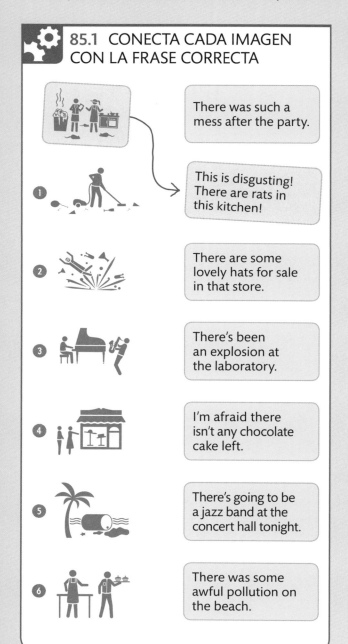

85.1 CONECTA CADA IMAGEN CON LA FRASE CORRECTA

There was such a mess after the party.

This is disgusting! There are rats in this kitchen!

There are some lovely hats for sale in that store.

There's been an explosion at the laboratory.

I'm afraid there isn't any chocolate cake left.

There's going to be a jazz band at the concert hall tonight.

There was some awful pollution on the beach.

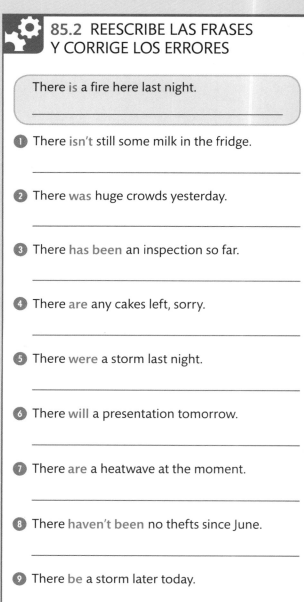

85.2 REESCRIBE LAS FRASES Y CORRIGE LOS ERRORES

There **is** a fire here last night.
_____

1 There **isn't** still some milk in the fridge.
_____

2 There **was** huge crowds yesterday.
_____

3 There **has been** an inspection so far.
_____

4 There **are** any cakes left, sorry.
_____

5 There **were** a storm last night.
_____

6 There **will** a presentation tomorrow.
_____

7 There **are** a heatwave at the moment.
_____

8 There **haven't been** no thefts since June.
_____

9 There **be** a storm later today.
_____

85.3 CONECTA EL INICIO Y EL FINAL DE CADA FRASE

There are going to be lots of people — about the poor service at the restaurant.

1 There have been a lot of complaints — to celebrate our silver wedding anniversary.

2 There will be a meeting to — at the teachers' convention next week.

3 There's going to be a party — seats for all the people here.

4 There weren't many — discuss the forthcoming redundancies.

5 There are not enough — cars in my village when I was a child.

85.4 TACHA LAS PALABRAS INCORRECTAS DE CADA FRASE

Please pay your bill on time. There is / ~~are~~ a penalty for late payments.

1 There are / were a lot of visitors at yesterday's exhibition.

2 There isn't / aren't any tickets for the show this evening.

3 There is / are a lot of sugar in the recipe for Cathy's cake.

4 Is / Was there a party to celebrate Olive's 90th birthday tomorrow?

5 There is / are going to be a soccer match this afternoon.

6 Was / Were there enough room for all the guests?

7 Do you know if there is / are another train tonight?

8 There has been / have been some terrible weather recently.

9 There wasn't / weren't many students at the lecture.

10 Bill's so busy at work. There is / was a deadline soon.

11 There is / are water all over the floor. What happened?

12 I'm sure there isn't / won't be another unexpected election this year.

| there | at | Will | any | entertainment | party? | the | be |

Will there be any entertainment at the party?

1 | in | fridge. | food | the | plenty | of | There's |

___

2 | a | is | the | street. | in | large | There | dog |

___

3 | there | in | town? | good | Are | cafés | any | your |

___

4 | and | vegetables. | selling | a | lot | are | of | people | fruit | There |

___

5 | bus | won't | another | be | today. | There |

___

6 | there | rice | left? | any | you | if | is | Do | know |

___

7 | waiting | people | There | are | of | outside. | lots |

___

8 | be | course? | the | an | Will | of | end | there | the | exam | at |

___

9 | there | a | afternoon? | to | Is | meeting | be | going | this |

___

86 "It" introductorio

"It" se utiliza a menudo cuando una frase no tiene un sujeto claro, y se lo conoce a veces como un sujeto vacío.

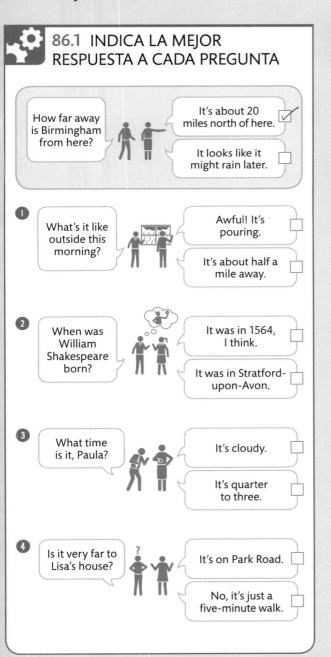

86.1 INDICA LA MEJOR RESPUESTA A CADA PREGUNTA

How far away is Birmingham from here?

It's about 20 miles north of here. ✓

It looks like it might rain later. ☐

1. What's it like outside this morning?

Awful! It's pouring. ☐

It's about half a mile away. ☐

2. When was William Shakespeare born?

It was in 1564, I think. ☐

It was in Stratford-upon-Avon. ☐

3. What time is it, Paula?

It's cloudy. ☐

It's quarter to three. ☐

4. Is it very far to Lisa's house?

It's on Park Road. ☐

No, it's just a five-minute walk. ☐

86.2 INDICA A QUÉ HACE REFERENCIA "IT" EN CADA FRASE

I've got so much to do, and it's ten past three already!

Hora ✓
Distancia ☐
Día / Fecha / Mes / Año ☐
Climatología ☐

1. It's about 20 miles to the guest house.

Hora ☐
Distancia ☐
Día / Fecha / Mes / Año ☐
Climatología ☐

2. It's Monday today, isn't it?

Hora ☐
Distancia ☐
Día / Fecha / Mes / Año ☐
Climatología ☐

3. It can get really cold in Siberia.

Hora ☐
Distancia ☐
Día / Fecha / Mes / Año ☐
Climatología ☐

4. It's half past seven.

Hora ☐
Distancia ☐
Día / Fecha / Mes / Año ☐
Climatología ☐

86.3 CONECTA EL INICIO Y EL FINAL DE CADA FRASE

It's easy to forget how difficult — it can be to learn a new language.

1. It is essential that all candidates — arrive 15 minutes before the interview.

2. It's often said that — absence makes the heart grow fonder.

3. If you don't start working harder, — it's unlikely you'll pass the exam.

4. It was so nice to meet — you and your husband at the party.

5. It is difficult for foreigners to — pronounce some words in my language.

6. It is dangerous to drive — too fast on the highway.

7. It would be great if — we could meet for coffee next weekend.

8. It's been impossible for me — to find a free moment to call you.

9. It's such a shame that it — rained every day on our vacation.

10. It was a surprise to discover — that we share the same birthday.

11. It is wonderful to lie in a field — and look up at the stars.

12. It's been 40 minutes. It looks — like the bus isn't coming.

86.4 COMPLETA LOS ESPACIOS CON "THAT" O "TO"

It is unlikely _____*that*_____ the house is going to be finished on time.

1. It is true _____ being a doctor involves a lot of hard work.

2. It is important _____ lock all the doors when you go out.

3. It is useful _____ write down important information in a notebook.

4. It is possible _____ Andre forgot that the party is tonight.

87 Cambiar el énfasis

Para poner el énfasis en una determinada palabra o expresión,
podemos utilizar una cláusula con "it" o una cláusula con "what",
o podemos mover un sustantivo al inicio de la frase.

87.1 CONECTA EL INICIO Y EL FINAL DE CADA FRASE

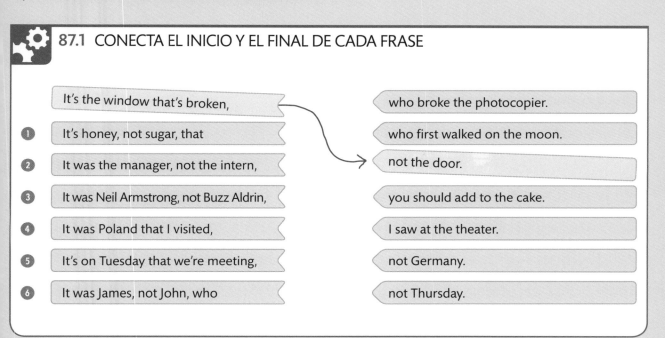

It's the window that's broken,	who broke the photocopier.
❶ It's honey, not sugar, that	who first walked on the moon.
❷ It was the manager, not the intern,	not the door.
❸ It was Neil Armstrong, not Buzz Aldrin,	you should add to the cake.
❹ It was Poland that I visited,	I saw at the theater.
❺ It's on Tuesday that we're meeting,	not Germany.
❻ It was James, not John, who	not Thursday.

87.2 CONECTA CADA IMAGEN CON LA FRASE CORRECTA

What I really hate is people singing out of tune.

What my children enjoy more than anything is playing outside.

What I enjoyed most were the fascinating ruins.

What Karen needs is to get more sleep.

87.3 COMPLETA LOS ESPACIOS CON LAS PALABRAS DEL RECUADRO

___The day___ we agreed on for our meeting was Monday, not Tuesday.

The day

The reason

The person

The country

The one thing

The subject

1 _____ I admire most in the world is my grandfather.

2 _____ I'll never forget is when I won the national prize.

3 _____ they gave for firing me was ridiculous.

4 _____ I loved visiting most was Montenegro.

5 _____ I enjoyed most at school was history.

87.4 ESCRIBE DE NUEVO LAS FRASES PONIENDO LAS PALABRAS EN EL ORDEN CORRECTO

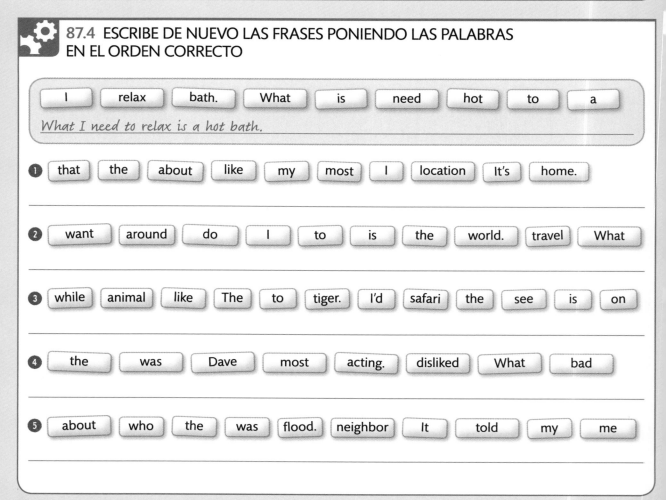

| I | relax | bath. | What | is | need | hot | to | a |

What I need to relax is a hot bath.

1 that | the | about | like | my | most | I | location | It's | home.

_____

2 want | around | do | I | to | is | the | world. | travel | What

_____

3 while | animal | like | The | to | tiger. | I'd | safari | the | see | is | on

_____

4 the | was | Dave | most | acting. | disliked | What | bad

_____

5 about | who | the | was | flood. | neighbor | It | told | my | me

_____

88 Inversión

Invertir el orden normal de las palabras sirve para cambiar el énfasis o para generar expectativas. Es frecuente tras algunos tipos de locuciones adverbiales.

88.1 CONECTA LAS FRASES QUE SE CORRESPONDAN

Robert is an excellent writer, and he's also a very confident public speaker.

Only after my departure did I realize that I had forgotten to say goodbye.

Not only is Robert an excellent writer, but he is also a very confident public speaker.

1 It had just stopped raining, and the children ran out to play.

2 I only realized after my departure that I had forgotten to say goodbye.

Never before have we achieved such amazing results.

3 I had just arrived at the airport when I decided I wasn't going to leave the country.

Hardly had it stopped raining when the children ran out to play.

4 We have never achieved such amazing results before.

Rarely have I had such a positive response to a proposal.

5 We did not suspect that the boy would one day become president.

No sooner had I arrived at the airport than I decided I wasn't going to leave the country.

6 I have rarely had such a positive response to a proposal.

Only when I opened the letter did I realize that I was going to college.

7 I only realized that I was going to college when I opened the letter.

Little did we know that the boy would one day become president.

88.2 COMPLETA LOS ESPACIOS PONIENDO LAS PALABRAS EN SU ORDEN CORRECTO

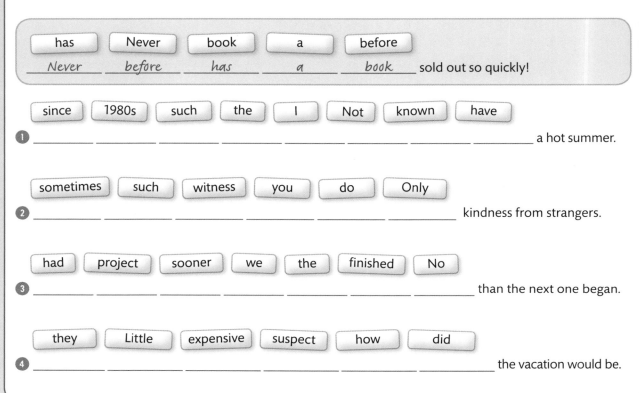

| has | Never | book | a | before |

Never _before_ _has_ _a_ _book_ sold out so quickly!

| since | 1980s | such | the | I | Not | known | have |

❶ _____ _____ _____ _____ _____ _____ _____ _____ a hot summer.

| sometimes | such | witness | you | do | Only |

❷ _____ _____ _____ _____ _____ _____ kindness from strangers.

| had | project | sooner | we | the | finished | No |

❸ _____ _____ _____ _____ _____ _____ _____ than the next one began.

| they | Little | expensive | suspect | how | did |

❹ _____ _____ _____ _____ _____ _____ the vacation would be.

88.3 MARCA LA MEJOR RESPUESTA PARA CADA AFIRMACIÓN

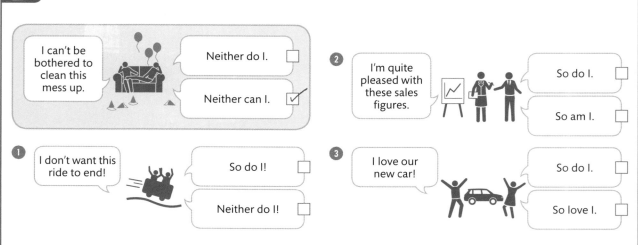

I can't be bothered to clean this mess up.
- Neither do I. ☐
- Neither can I. ✓

❶ I don't want this ride to end!
- So do I! ☐
- Neither do I! ☐

❷ I'm quite pleased with these sales figures.
- So do I. ☐
- So am I. ☐

❸ I love our new car!
- So do I. ☐
- So love I. ☐

89 Elipsis

Podemos prescindir de algunas palabras en una frase para
evitar la repetición, o cuando no son necesarias para que
se entienda el significado. Es lo que se conoce como elipsis.

89.1 CONECTA EL INICIO Y EL FINAL DE CADA FRASE

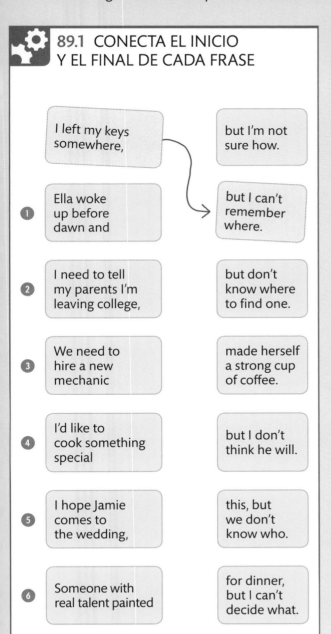

I left my keys somewhere, → but I can't remember where.

but I'm not sure how.

1. Ella woke up before dawn and

but I can't remember where.

2. I need to tell my parents I'm leaving college,

but don't know where to find one.

3. We need to hire a new mechanic

made herself a strong cup of coffee.

4. I'd like to cook something special

but I don't think he will.

5. I hope Jamie comes to the wedding,

this, but we don't know who.

6. Someone with real talent painted

for dinner, but I can't decide what.

89.2 INDICA LA MEJOR RESPUESTA PARA CADA PREGUNTA

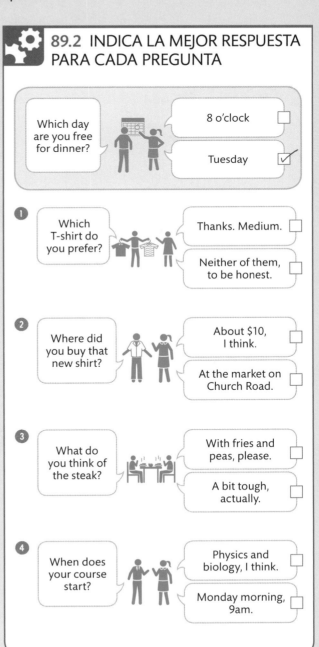

Which day are you free for dinner?

8 o'clock ☐

Tuesday ☑

1. Which T-shirt do you prefer?

Thanks. Medium. ☐

Neither of them, to be honest. ☐

2. Where did you buy that new shirt?

About $10, I think. ☐

At the market on Church Road. ☐

3. What do you think of the steak?

With fries and peas, please. ☐

A bit tough, actually. ☐

4. When does your course start?

Physics and biology, I think. ☐

Monday morning, 9am. ☐

89.3 ESCRIBE LAS FRASES DE NUEVO ELIMINANDO LAS PALABRAS INNECESARIAS

> I'm nervous about the exam in case I haven't studied enough for the exam.
> *I'm nervous about the exam in case I haven't studied enough.*

1 I asked Charlie to stop playing soccer, but he didn't stop playing.

_____

2 I'm trying to make an omelet, but I don't know how you make one.

_____

3 I want to move to a new area, but I don't know where to move.

_____

4 I really enjoy skiing, but my brother doesn't enjoy it.

_____

5 Someone's left a present, but I'm not sure who left it for me.

_____

6 I want to buy one of these laptops, but I'm not sure which one I should buy.

_____

7 Catalina said she'd come to the party, but I don't think she will come.

_____

8 There is a museum somewhere, but I'm not sure where the museum is.

_____

9 I tried to lift the box, but I wasn't strong enough to lift it.

_____

10 My wife can swim really well, but I can't swim.

_____

11 I want to study something at college, but I'm not sure what I want to study.

_____

12 Anne and Si passed the exam, but Matt didn't pass it.

_____

216

90 Abreviar infinitivos

Las frases que incluyen infinitivos a veces pueden
reducirse o abreviarse para evitar la repetición.
Esto hace que el idioma suene más natural.

90.1 CONECTA CADA IMAGEN CON LA FRASE CORRECTA

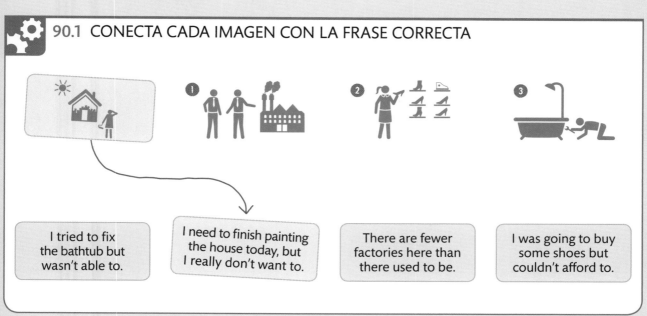

I tried to fix
the bathtub but
wasn't able to.

I need to finish painting
the house today, but
I really don't want to.

There are fewer
factories here than
there used to be.

I was going to buy
some shoes but
couldn't afford to.

90.2 CONECTA EL INICIO Y EL FINAL DE CADA FRASE

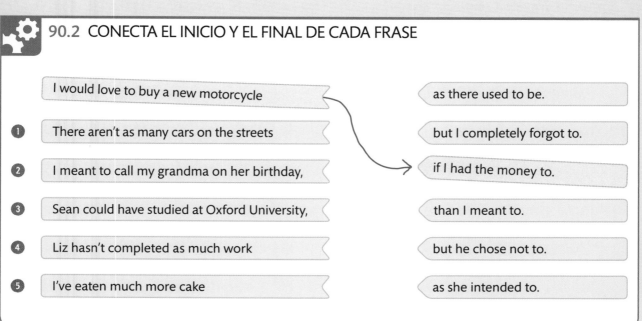

I would love to buy a new motorcycle — as there used to be.

① There aren't as many cars on the streets — but I completely forgot to.

② I meant to call my grandma on her birthday, → if I had the money to.

③ Sean could have studied at Oxford University, — than I meant to.

④ Liz hasn't completed as much work — but he chose not to.

⑤ I've eaten much more cake — as she intended to.

90.3 INDICA LA MEJOR RESPUESTA PARA CADA AFIRMACIÓN

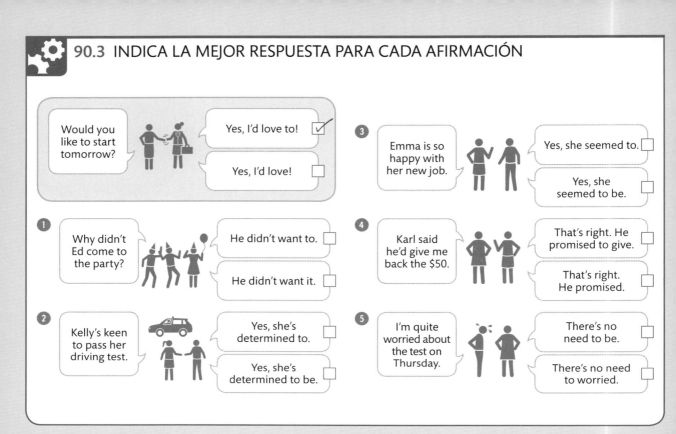

Would you like to start tomorrow?

Yes, I'd love to! ✓

Yes, I'd love! ☐

1 Why didn't Ed come to the party?

He didn't want to. ☐

He didn't want it. ☐

2 Kelly's keen to pass her driving test.

Yes, she's determined to. ☐

Yes, she's determined to be. ☐

3 Emma is so happy with her new job.

Yes, she seemed to. ☐

Yes, she seemed to be. ☐

4 Karl said he'd give me back the $50.

That's right. He promised to give. ☐

That's right. He promised. ☐

5 I'm quite worried about the test on Thursday.

There's no need to be. ☐

There's no need to worried. ☐

90.4 ESCRIBE DE NUEVO LAS FRASES PONIENDO LAS PALABRAS EN EL ORDEN CORRECTO

| to | I | plants, | meant | forgot. | but | I | the | water |

I meant to water the plants, but I forgot.

1 software · than · needs · is · This · it · complicated · more · be. · to

_____

2 party · though · come · didn't · even · the · promised. · she · Mia · to

_____

3 the · to · try · I'd · but · don't · love · I · hang · gliding, · have · courage.

_____

90.5 MARCA LAS FRASES QUE SEAN CORRECTAS

> There are fewer tigers in the wild these days than there used to. ☐
> There are fewer tigers in the wild these days than there used to be. ☑

❶ Maurice wasn't at the convention, even though he had hoped to be. ☐
  Maurice wasn't at the convention, even though he had hoped to. ☐

❷ I was thinking of studying French at college but decided to not. ☐
  I was thinking of studying French at college but decided not to. ☐

❸ Shelly isn't at school today, but she ought to. ☐
  Shelly isn't at school today, but she ought to be. ☐

❹ I wasn't able to go on the trip, but I did want to. ☐
  I wasn't able to go on the trip, but I did want be. ☐

❺ The dish isn't vegetarian, even though it's supposed to. ☐
  The dish isn't vegetarian, even though it's supposed to be. ☐

90.6 TACHA LAS PALABRAS INNECESARIAS

> There's no need to come with us if you don't want to ~~come with us.~~

❶ Lisa invited me to visit Spain, and I told her I'd love to visit her country.

❷ We asked Mario to play golf with us, but he didn't want to play with us.

❸ I wanted to see you this summer, but I won't be able to visit you.

❹ We can alter the dress for you. Would you like us to do that?

❺ I've never seen the Great Wall of China, but I'd love the chance to see it.

❻ Gerard doesn't have a motorcycle now, but he used to have one.

❼ Mary was going to buy a dog, but she decided not to buy one.

❽ I dream of buying that apartment, but I can't afford to buy it.

91 Sustitución

Además de con la elipsis (prescindir de palabras), la repetición puede evitarse reemplazando algunas expresiones con otras más cortas. Esto se denomina sustitución.

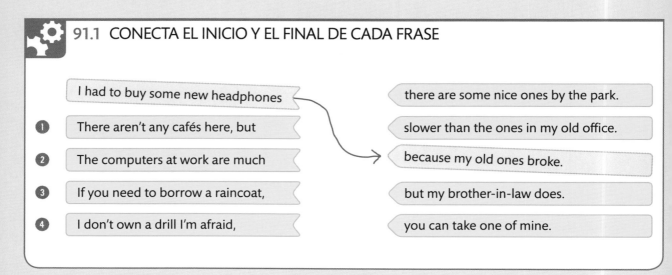

91.1 CONECTA EL INICIO Y EL FINAL DE CADA FRASE

I had to buy some new headphones — because my old ones broke.

1. There aren't any cafés here, but — there are some nice ones by the park.

2. The computers at work are much — slower than the ones in my old office.

3. If you need to borrow a raincoat, — you can take one of mine.

4. I don't own a drill I'm afraid, — but my brother-in-law does.

91.2 COMPLETA LOS ESPACIOS CON LAS EXPRESIONES DEL RECUADRO

I thought we'd run out of flour, but I _____*found some*_____ in the cupboard.

1. Cathy refuses to get a phone, though her husband _____ .

2. I really don't like this sofa, but I _____ over there.

3. There isn't any juice left, but I think _____ in the fridge.

4. I love your boots. I saw _____ in the boutique by the park.

5. I liked the look of the cakes in the bakery, so I _____ .

has got one	some similar ones		there's some
	like the red one	~~found some~~	bought some

We don't like fishing, but our dad does.

1 I really liked that house, but my husband didn't.

2 My car is ruined. I need to buy a new one.

3 I really like cooking, and so does my husband.

4 If that dress is too expensive, we have cheaper ones, too.

5 We'd like a dessert. Could you recommend one?

6 That looks delicious. Can I try some?

7 Zhao liked the artwork, but I didn't.

8 I own few books myself, but there are lots at the library.

Do you think the president will be there?

I hope so! ✓

I hope!

1 Do I need to dress smartly in the office?

We'd prefer if you so.

We'd prefer it if you did.

2 Do you have this T-shirt in medium?

I don't think so, sorry.

I don't think it, sorry.

3 Do you know the way to Angelo's bakery?

I'm afraid I don't.

I'm afraid so.

4 The forecast said it will get better later.

I hope that yes.

I hope so.

5 Did you manage to finish the final report?

I'm afraid not.

I'm afraid no.

6 Did you remember to clean your bedroom?

I did so this morning.

I did it this morning.

92 Adjetivos

Los adjetivos son palabras que describen sustantivos.
En inglés suelen preceder al sustantivo al que describen.
Existen varias categorías de adjetivos.

92.1 COMPLETA LOS ESPACIOS CON LAS EXPRESIONES DEL RECUADRO

They're building a _____*huge luxury*_____ apartment complex there.

1. My boyfriend gave me a _____ necklace for my birthday.

2. My grandma's knitting me a _____ sweater.

3. We went to see the _____ ruins while in Mexico.

4. We adopted a _____ kitten from the shelter.

- ~~huge luxury~~
- dark-green woolen
- beautiful gold
- cute friendly
- ancient Aztec

92.2 ANOTA LOS ADJETIVOS DEL RECUADRO EN EL GRUPO AL QUE CORRESPONDAN

TAMAÑO
little
_____
_____

FORMA
_____
_____
_____

EDAD
_____
_____
_____

COLOR
_____
_____
_____

NACIONALIDAD
_____
_____
_____

MATERIAL
_____
_____
_____

china tiny Argentinian diamond-shaped ~~little~~ round Vietnamese young pink

light-blue red French ancient massive cotton steel old square

92.3 BUSCA EN LA TABLA OTROS SEIS ADJETIVOS Y ANÓTALOS EN EL APARTADO CORRESPONDIENTE

```
A W F U L R A O B W O N S
N S H I L I N G O O D N V
N D E B E A U T I F U L D
R I N T P R T I U T C U I
A W O Q D U R H H L I J G
E O I S T Y A D F A E N D
M N L O Y A O Z I O R H Z
P D V E C L E V E R E N D
T E F R I E N D L Y A G I
E R I D D E L I C I O U S
R F C E P S R T I E G E D
B U B U T E R R I B L E M
B L T N T Q H W E D L N D
```

OPINIÓN GENERAL

awful

1. _____
2. _____
3. _____

OPINIÓN ESPECÍFICA

clever

4. _____
5. _____
6. _____

92.4 CONECTA CADA IMAGEN CON LA FRASE CORRECTA

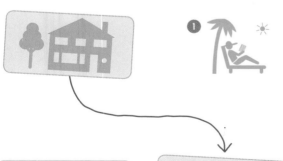

1   **2** **3**

I read this exciting new French novel while on vacation.

Mark's just bought this lovely large detached house.

Ebru made this lovely white silk dress.

That small old brown dog belongs to Harry.

92.5 COMPLETA LOS ESPACIOS PONIENDO LOS ADJETIVOS EN SU ORDEN CORRECTO

| antique | small | vase |

Liam bought a _small_ _antique_ _vase_ at the market.

| Indian | rug | beautiful | old |

1 Claude has a _____ _____ _____ _____ in his living room.

| American | big | red |

2 Nigel's bought himself a _____ _____ _____ sports car.

| wooden | small | black |

3 Catalina keeps her jewelry in a _____ _____ _____ box.

| tall | charming | young |

4 My granddaughter is engaged to a _____ _____ _____ man.

92.6 TACHA EL ADJETIVO INCORRECTO DE CADA FRASE

Sanjay's brother is completely ~~terrifying~~ / terrified of snakes.

1 Everyone found the presentation extremely boring / bored.

2 The instructions are so confusing / confused. I don't know what to do.

3 Selma and Paul are interesting / interested in wildlife.

4 We were all amazing / amazed when Sharon won the race.

93 Adjetivos graduables y no graduables

Los adjetivos graduables pueden hacerse más suaves o más intensos con el uso de un adverbio, mientras que los adjetivos no graduables describen cualidades absolutas que en general no admiten gradación.

93.1 CONECTA CADA IMAGEN CON LA FRASE CORRECTA

Ola is a very talented cook.

Turn the TV down! It's really loud!

They were ecstatic when they won the tournament.

It was boiling hot outside.

Marty was really hungry and ordered two hamburgers.

My new shoes are not very comfortable at all.

Our plumber is not particularly reliable.

93.2 INDICA SI LOS ADJETIVOS SON EXTREMOS, ABSOLUTOS O CLASIFICADORES

My grandmother is Scottish.
- Extremo ☐
- Absoluto ☐
- Clasificador ☑

❶ I really enjoyed Jessica's presentation; it was superb.
- Extremo ☐
- Absoluto ☐
- Clasificador ☐

❷ My wedding day was completely perfect.
- Extremo ☐
- Absoluto ☐
- Clasificador ☐

❸ My company now has a monthly meeting about taxes.
- Extremo ☐
- Absoluto ☐
- Clasificador ☐

❹ Pete's ideas for the business are always terrible.
- Extremo ☐
- Absoluto ☐
- Clasificador ☐

93.3 BUSCA EN LA TABLA OTROS SEIS ADJETIVOS Y ANÓTALOS
EN EL GRUPO AL QUE CORRESPONDAN

```
I N T E R E S T I N G N S
N S L G A N S G T L E Q V
N D E M J S E D S A A M D
R I N T B R W I L R R R E
X K H W D D A A H G I D G
E I N T E L L I G E N T D
C U U L L A E Z E O R I Z
O A V E S S Q U A R E N D
L C D A W E S O M E A G I
D H I J A R P E R F E C T
R E C E P S K I E N G E D
A W O O D E N H I J J L M
```

GRADUABLES

> *interesting*

1 _____

2 _____

3 _____

NO GRADUABLES

> *awesome*

4 _____

5 _____

6 _____

 93.4 CONECTA EL INICIO Y EL FINAL DE CADA FRASE

The movie was pretty → bad. It rained every day.

1 The weather was extremely — were not very tasty.

2 The cookies that Ellie made → good. I'd watch it again.

3 I found the exam almost — unique. There are no others like it.

4 Our business is reasonably — impossible to finish in time.

5 This antique vase is quite — terrified when he saw the bear.

6 Martin was absolutely — successful, but it could do better.

226

93.5 ESCRIBE DE NUEVO LAS FRASES PONIENDO LAS PALABRAS EN EL ORDEN CORRECTO

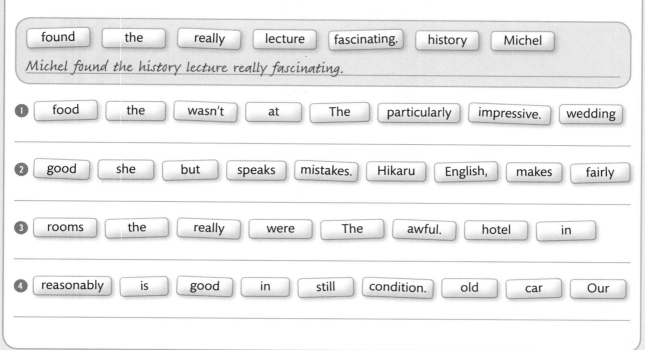

found | the | really | lecture | fascinating. | history | Michel

Michel found the history lecture really fascinating.

1. food | the | wasn't | at | The | particularly | impressive. | wedding

_____

2. good | she | but | speaks | mistakes. | Hikaru | English, | makes | fairly

_____

3. rooms | the | really | were | The | awful. | hotel | in

_____

4. reasonably | is | good | in | still | condition. | old | car | Our

_____

93.6 COMPLETA LOS ESPACIOS CON LOS ADJETIVOS DEL RECUADRO

Sonia keeps her jewelry in a _____*wooden*_____ box in her bedroom.

1. I can't criticize his cakes. They're absolutely _____ .

2. The clothes here are of good quality and _____ priced.

3. The concert was absolutely _____ . She simply can't sing!

4. There's a wonderful _____ castle in my town.

5. The software is _____ easy to use and won't cause too many problems.

6. It's _____ outside! Make sure you wear a hat.

reasonably | awful | perfect | ~~wooden~~ | freezing | medieval | fairly

94 Adjetivos comparativos

Los adjetivos comparativos se utilizan para comparar dos cosas. Pueden formarse añadiendo el sufijo "-er" o bien anteponiendo "more" o "less" al adjetivo.

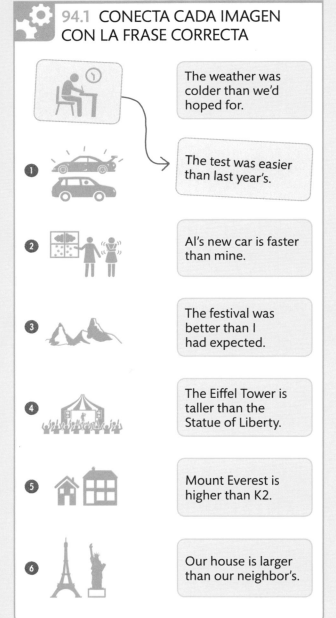

94.1 CONECTA CADA IMAGEN CON LA FRASE CORRECTA

The weather was colder than we'd hoped for.

❶

The test was easier than last year's.

❷

Al's new car is faster than mine.

❸

The festival was better than I had expected.

❹

The Eiffel Tower is taller than the Statue of Liberty.

❺

Mount Everest is higher than K2.

❻

Our house is larger than our neighbor's.

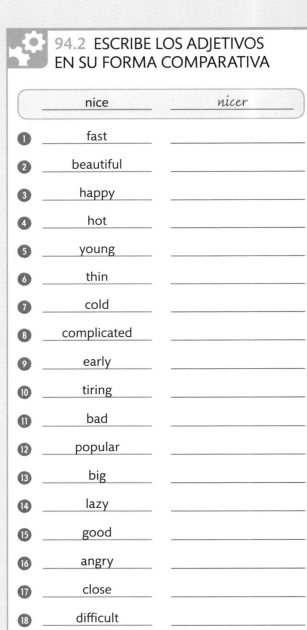

94.2 ESCRIBE LOS ADJETIVOS EN SU FORMA COMPARATIVA

	nice	nicer
❶	fast	
❷	beautiful	
❸	happy	
❹	hot	
❺	young	
❻	thin	
❼	cold	
❽	complicated	
❾	early	
❿	tiring	
⓫	bad	
⓬	popular	
⓭	big	
⓮	lazy	
⓯	good	
⓰	angry	
⓱	close	
⓲	difficult	

94.3 CONECTA EL INICIO Y EL FINAL DE CADA FRASE

The castle is far older	extravagant than I'd expected.
1 Danny's dog is much	older than her husband.
2 The wedding was more	than the cathedral.
3 Karen is only slightly	larger than mine.
4 Going to work by bike is	common than they were 10 years ago.
5 Electric cars are much more	less stressful than taking a train.
6 I'm less sporty than my	sensible than she used to be.
7 My daughter is much more	elder brother. I prefer reading to football.

94.4 ESCRIBE DE NUEVO LAS FRASES PONIENDO LOS COMPARATIVOS EN SU OTRA FORMA

Our new teacher is much friendlier than the last.
Our new teacher is much more friendly than the last.

1 The countryside is far quieter than the city.

_____

2 The Caspian Sea is shallower than the Black Sea.

_____

3 The new software we have to use couldn't be simpler.

_____

4 The road was narrower than I thought, and I scratched the car.

_____

5 Jane is really mad with you. I've never seen anyone angrier.

_____

Jay got up earlyer today because of the test. ☐
Jay got up earlier today because of the test. ✓

❶ Lisbon is much more farther away from here than Seville. ☐
Lisbon is much farther away from here than Seville. ☐

❷ The Sahara Desert is hotter than the Atacama. ☐
The Sahara Desert is hoter than the Atacama. ☐

❸ I feel happier since I moved to Barcelona. ☐
I feel happyer since I moved to Barcelona. ☐

❹ The weather in California is much better than in Montana. ☐
The weather in California is more better than in Montana. ☐

❺ A cheetah is more faster than a lion. ☐
A cheetah is faster than a lion. ☐

❻ Tom is only slightly more tall than his brother, Joe. ☐
Tom is only slightly taller than his brother, Joe. ☐

❼ These jeans are much tighter than my old ones. ☐
These jeans are much more tighter than my old ones. ☐

❽ The old buildings in my town are beautifuller than the modern ones. ☐
The old buildings in my town are more beautiful than the modern ones. ☐

❾ My new apartment is slightly smaller than my old one. ☐
My new apartment is slightly smaller then my old one. ☐

❿ My city has a worse transportation system than yours. ☐
My city has a worst transportation system than yours. ☐

⓫ The staff in this hotel are much more friendly than in the other one. ☐
The staff in this hotel are much more friendlier than in the other one. ☐

⓬ This book is much interestinger than the last one I read. ☐
This book is much more interesting than the last one I read. ☐

94.6 OBSERVA LAS IMÁGENES Y COMPLETA LAS FRASES CON LAS EXPRESIONES DEL RECUADRO

It's ___*much cheaper*___ to make your own curtains.

4 A salad is _____ than a hamburger.

1 The castle is _____ than the skyscrapers.

5 My colleagues are _____ than me.

2 She was _____ than me in the race.

6 A cruise liner is _____ than a sail boat.

3 The weather was _____ than was forecast.

7 I go to bed _____ on Sunday evenings.

a lot bigger	much more experienced	much better	just a bit quicker
slightly earlier	~~much cheaper~~	quite a bit older	a lot healthier

95 Dos comparativos combinados

En una misma frase pueden combinarse dos comparativos para referirse al efecto de una acción. También se utilizan para indicar que algo está cambiando.

 95.1 CONECTA EL INICIO Y EL FINAL DE CADA FRASE

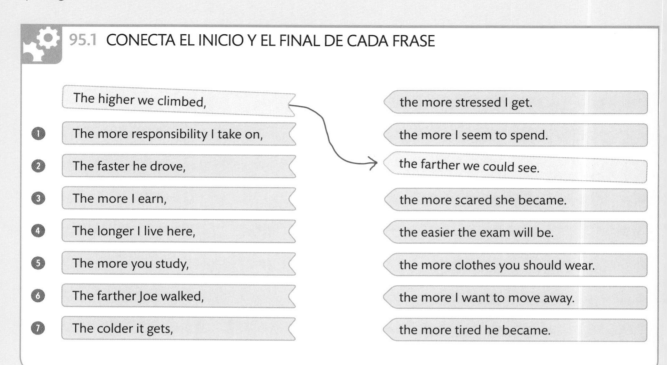

The higher we climbed, — the farther we could see.

1. The more responsibility I take on, — the more stressed I get.

2. The faster he drove, — the more I seem to spend.

3. The more I earn, — the more scared she became.

4. The longer I live here, — the easier the exam will be.

5. The more you study, — the more clothes you should wear.

6. The farther Joe walked, — the more I want to move away.

7. The colder it gets, — the more tired he became.

95.2 COMPLETA LOS ESPACIOS CON LOS COMPARATIVOS DEL RECUADRO

This book gets _more and more interesting_ with every page.

1. The _____, the more there will be to eat.

2. Ola's getting _____ at the guitar.

3. It's getting _____. Don't forget your scarf!

4. The faster you work, the _____ the project.

5. My nephew gets _____ every time I see him.

---

earlier you'll finish

more and more skilled

~~more and more interesting~~

colder and colder

taller and taller

bigger the cake

95.3 TACHA LAS PALABRAS INCORRECTAS DE CADA FRASE

 The hotter ~~the curry is~~, the better ~~it tastes~~.

1 The more people come to the party, the merrier it will be.

2 The sooner you finish this, the better it will be for all of us.

3 The stronger the coffee is, the better it tastes.

4 The more glamorous the dress you wear, the better you will look.

 95.4 ESCRIBE DE NUEVO LAS FRASES PONIENDO LAS PALABRAS EN EL ORDEN CORRECTO

| weather's | The | hotter | getting | and | hotter | day. | each |

The weather's getting hotter and hotter each day.

1 | is | and | Everyone | more | concerned | more | climate | about | change. | getting |

_____

2 | Philip's | keep | taller | growing | and | taller. | sunflowers |

_____

3 | gets | The | exam | harder | harder | and | year. | each |

_____

4 | Robots | becoming | are | and | more | more | sophisticated. |

_____

96 Comparaciones con "as... as"

Las comparaciones que utilizan construcciones con "as... as" sirven para indicar grados de similitud o diferencia. Pueden modificarse con adverbios para hacerlas más o menos intensas.

96.1 CONECTA CADA IMAGEN CON LA FRASE CORRECTA

I'm sure your pasta will be as tasty as usual.

The other dress isn't as pretty as this one.

This hat is twice as expensive as the other one.

I hope the new chef is as talented as Jean-Louis.

Dogs are not so easy to look after as cats.

I hope the movie is as good as the book.

The results are not as good as we had hoped.

96.2 MARCA LAS FRASES QUE SEAN CORRECTAS

Om can't run as fast so Ravi. ☐
Om can't run as fast as Ravi. ☑

1. I'm not as confident as I was before. ☐
   I'm not as confident I was before. ☐

2. The food wasn't half as good as we'd hoped. ☐
   The food wasn't as half good as we'd hoped. ☐

3. Rome isn't nowhere near as big as Paris. ☐
   Rome is nowhere near as big as Paris. ☐

4. He told us to finish as quickly as possible. ☐
   He told us to finish so quickly as possible. ☐

5. It's not quite as cold as last winter. ☐
   It's quite not as cold as last winter. ☐

6. Ula doesn't call as much so she used to. ☐
   Ula doesn't call as much as she used to. ☐

7. The journey took twice as long as usual. ☐
   The journey took as twice as long as usual. ☐

8. Ben was as quiet as a mouse. ☐
   Ben was so quiet as a mouse. ☐

9. Ed is as almost old as my aunt. ☐
   Ed is almost as old as my aunt. ☐

10. It cost just as much as it did last time. ☐
    It cost just as much it did last time. ☐

96.3 TACHA LAS PALABRAS INCORRECTAS DE CADA FRASE

 This dress is almost / ~~quite~~ as nice as the skirt.

① The exam was just so / as hard as I had expected.

② The skyscrapers here are nowhere near as big as / like in Shanghai.

③ This restaurant is twice / twice as expensive as the others.

④  The café is almost as / as almost big as the church.

⑤ The house is quite not / not quite as easy to find as we thought.

⑥ The singer was nowhere near / close as good as I hoped.

⑦ The play lasted twice so / as long as I expected.

⑧ It's nearly not / not nearly as cold as we'd imagined.

⑨ The supermarket was not almost / quite as busy as I feared.

⑩ The dress is twice as / twice so big as I thought it would be.

⑪ The other buildings are nowhere near so / as tall as the clock tower.

⑫ The company results were not quite so / like good as last year's.

⑬ The new store will be as popular as / like the others.

⑭ This was nearly not / not nearly as easy to make as I expected.

97 Adjetivos superlativos

Los adjetivos superlativos, como "the biggest" o "the smallest", se utilizan para hablar de los extremos. Los adjetivos largos añaden "most" y "least" para indicar un extremo.

97.1 CONECTA CADA IMAGEN CON LA FRASE CORRECTA

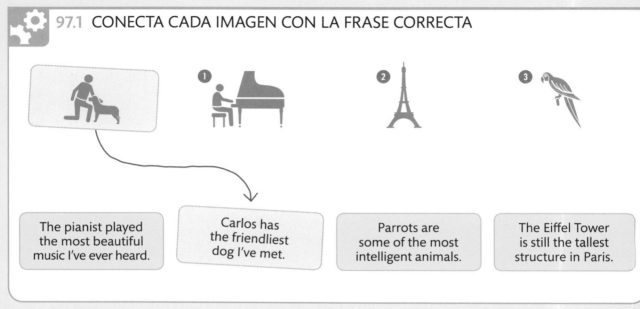

The pianist played the most beautiful music I've ever heard.

Carlos has the friendliest dog I've met.

Parrots are some of the most intelligent animals.

The Eiffel Tower is still the tallest structure in Paris.

97.2 CONECTA EL INICIO Y EL FINAL DE CADA FRASE

My uncle is the most

① Pablo has the strangest

② Glasgow is the biggest

③ Ania has the curliest hair

④ China has the largest

⑤ Our soccer team was the least

population in the world.

in my family.

intelligent person I know.

successful in the league.

city in Scotland.

taste in music in our class.

97.3 ESCRIBE LA FORMA SUPERLATIVA DE CADA ADJETIVO

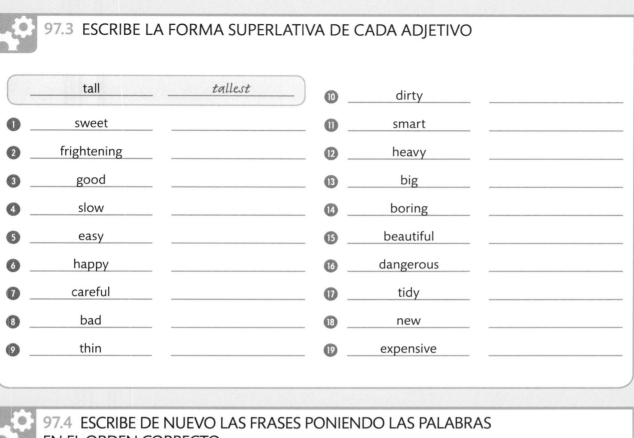

tall	tallest		
❶ sweet		⑩ dirty	
❷ frightening		⑪ smart	
❸ good		⑫ heavy	
❹ slow		⑬ big	
❺ easy		⑭ boring	
❻ happy		⑮ beautiful	
❼ careful		⑯ dangerous	
❽ bad		⑰ tidy	
❾ thin		⑱ new	
		⑲ expensive	

97.4 ESCRIBE DE NUEVO LAS FRASES PONIENDO LAS PALABRAS EN EL ORDEN CORRECTO

is   met.   person   ever   the   bravest   I've   Shelley

Shelley is the bravest person I've ever met.

❶ expensive   café   one   places   to   the   of   is   eat.   That   most

_____

❷ was   because   the   most   attractive.   vase   bought   We   this   it

_____

❸ the   things   My   sweetest   grandma   about   always   says   me.

_____

97.5 COMPLETA LOS ESPACIOS PONIENDO LOS ADJETIVOS EN SU FORMA SUPERLATIVA

That was _____ *the most difficult* _____ (difficult) test I've ever done!

1 The Mississippi is _____ (long) river in the United States.

2 The sailfish is _____ (fast) fish in the ocean.

3 Death Valley is _____ (hot) place on earth.

4 Bungee jumping is _____ (exciting) thing I've ever done.

5 Mont Blanc is _____ (high) mountain in France.

6 My sister is _____ (creative) person I know.

7 I felt like _____ (lucky) person alive when I won the lottery.

8 Some of _____ (old) paintings can be found in local caves.

97.6 TACHA LAS PALABRAS INCORRECTAS DE CADA FRASE

We bought ~~a cheapest~~ / the cheapest computer in the store.

1 This is the worst / baddest coffee I've ever drunk.

2 Daniel is the most fastest / fastest boy in my class.

3 I think this has been the hotest / hottest day of the year so far.

4 This feels like the slowest / most slow train I've ever been on.

5 Ashalata is the friendliest / friendlyest manager at work.

6 This is the less / least expensive car we have on sale at the moment.

7 That's the most exciting / excitingest news I've heard today.

8 Mr. Clarke is the most strictest / strictest teacher in school.

9 Michael lives the farest / farthest away from our office.

10 That was one of the saddest / sadest movies I've ever seen.

97.7 ESCRIBE DE NUEVO LAS FRASES Y CORRIGE LOS ERRORES

> Miguel is **easy the best** artist in my city.
> *Miguel is easily the best artist in my city.*

1 Elvira was the **most fast** cyclist in the race.

_____

2 I chose **least expensive** drink on the menu.

_____

3 This is **of far the tastiest** hamburger I've ever eaten.

_____

4 The Burj Khalifa is one of **the most tallest** buildings in the world.

_____

5 It's **worst** summer I've ever known.

_____

6 This is **the most best book** I've read for ages.

_____

7 Paul **is the happyest** person I know.

_____

8 Anna is **most worried** of us all about tomorrow's inspection.

_____

9 London is **the bigest** city in England.

_____

10 Don is **easiest the tallest** person in our class.

_____

11 Feng is **one the most talented** musicians I know.

_____

12 Claire's is **far the cheapest** salon in town.

_____

98 Adverbios de modo

Palabras como "quietly" y "loudly" son adverbios. Describen verbos, adjetivos, expresiones y otros adverbios y les añaden información.

98.1 COMPLETA LOS ESPACIOS CON LOS ADVERBIOS DEL RECUADRO

Paul has arrived _____*safely*_____ .

1 Tim _____ helped Jo with her bags.

2 The kids played _____ with the dog.

3 This bus is moving so _____!

4 Charles _____ ate all the chocolate.

5 It started to rain _____ .

6 Carla shouted _____ at her computer.

7 Ed's mom thinks he drives too _____ .

8 My doctor told me to eat _____ .

9 Kim waited _____ for her results.

~~safely~~	nervously	happily
healthily	slowly	heavily
greedily	kindly	angrily	quickly

98.2 ESCRIBE LOS ADJETIVOS COMO ADVERBIOS

powerful	*powerfully*
1 noisy	
2 reluctant	
3 good	
4 shy	
5 happy	
6 long	
7 calm	
8 straight	
9 easy	
10 hard	
11 soft	
12 dangerous	
13 repeated	
14 clumsy	
15 late	
16 bad	
17 fast	
18 stylish	

98.3 CONECTA EL INICIO Y EL FINAL DE CADA FRASE

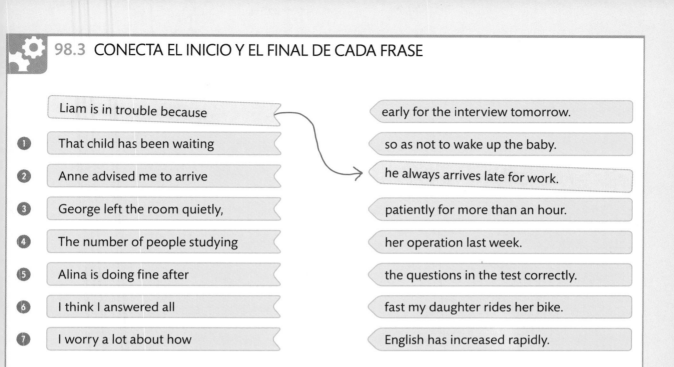

Liam is in trouble because — he always arrives late for work.

1. That child has been waiting — patiently for more than an hour.
2. Anne advised me to arrive — early for the interview tomorrow.
3. George left the room quietly, — so as not to wake up the baby.
4. The number of people studying — English has increased rapidly.
5. Alina is doing fine after — her operation last week.
6. I think I answered all — the questions in the test correctly.
7. I worry a lot about how — fast my daughter rides her bike.

98.4 COMPLETA LOS ESPACIOS ESCRIBIENDO LOS ADJETIVOS ENTRE PARÉNTESIS COMO ADVERBIOS

Miguel strolled ___*slowly*___ (slow) through the forest.

1. Ella _____ (gentle) stroked her new kitten.

2. Marvin played the piano _____ (beautiful) last night.

3. Louis has worked _____ (hard) to improve his English.

4. An eagle flew _____ (high) above the ruined castle.

5. My stapler has _____ (mysterious) disappeared.

6. Kathy sang very _____ (good) at the performance.

7. Tim shouted _____ (angry) at the TV when his team lost.

8. Sangita wasn't _____ (bad) injured in the accident.

9. I went _____ (straight) to my boss's office to talk to her.

10. Claudio passed the final test _____ (easy).

99 Adverbios comparativos y superlativos

Los adverbios tienen formas comparativas para comparar o mostrar diferencias. Tienen también forma superlativa para hablar sobre los extremos.

99.1 CONECTA EL INICIO Y EL FINAL DE CADA FRASE

I think the red silk shirt —————→ suits you the best.

when it started to snow.

1. Ola played the most beautifully — since you got the promotion.

2. Carlo speaks English more — of all the musicians.

3. You've been working harder — fluently than he does German.

4. Ahmed drove more carefully

99.2 ESCRIBE LOS ADVERBIOS EN SUS FORMAS COMPARATIVA Y SUPERLATIVA

ADVERBIO	COMPARATIVO	SUPERLATIVO
badly	worse	worst
1. early		
2. fast		
3. regularly		
4. hard		
5. well		
6. stylishly		

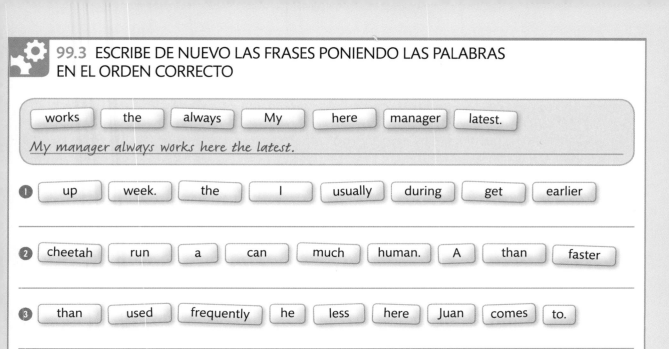

99.3 ESCRIBE DE NUEVO LAS FRASES PONIENDO LAS PALABRAS EN EL ORDEN CORRECTO

| works | the | always | My | here | manager | latest. |

My manager always works here the latest.

❶ | up | week. | the | I | usually | during | get | earlier |

_____

❷ | cheetah | run | a | can | much | human. | A | than | faster |

_____

❸ | than | used | frequently | he | less | here | Juan | comes | to. |

_____

99.4 COMPLETA LOS ESPACIOS CON LAS EXPRESIONES DEL RECUADRO

Could you explain a bit _____*more clearly*_____ how to do it?

❶ I should have looked _____ at my contract.

❷ My employees _____ when they're tired.

❸ Who _____ in the test, you or your sister?

❹ Joan gets up _____ in our family.

❺ My teacher said I should _____ in class.

❻ Lena has to _____ to get to our office.

❼ Our cat can _____ than our dog.

| work less efficiently | try harder | jump much higher | travel the farthest |
| more closely | ~~more clearly~~ | performed better | the earliest |

100 Adverbios de grado

Los adverbios de grado pueden ir antes de los adjetivos y los verbos para aumentar o disminuir la intensidad de su significado original. Algunos adverbios solo pueden acompañar a ciertos adjetivos.

100.1 CONECTA CADA IMAGEN CON LA FRASE CORRECTA

The two vases were only slightly different to each other.

My grandmother's house is extremely small.

Juan's cake was very popular. Everyone wanted more.

I don't think it's a particularly difficult mountain to climb.

Eric thought the test was fairly straightforward.

The house at the end of the road looks really unusual.

Phil's feeling remarkably fit despite how ill he was.

100.2 ESCRIBE LOS ADVERBIOS DEL RECUADRO EN LOS GRUPOS A LOS QUE CORRESPONDAN

MÁS FUERTE	MÁS DÉBIL
remarkably	

extremely   fairly   ~~remarkably~~   slightly

very   not particularly   barely   really

100.3 ESCRIBE LOS ADVERBIOS DEL RECUADRO EN LOS GRUPOS A LOS QUE CORRESPONDAN

GRADUANTES	NO GRADUANTES
slightly	

not particularly   totally   ~~slightly~~   fairly

utterly   completely   very   absolutely

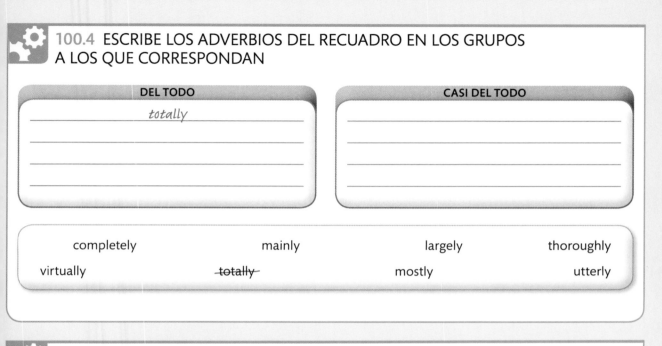

100.4 ESCRIBE LOS ADVERBIOS DEL RECUADRO EN LOS GRUPOS A LOS QUE CORRESPONDAN

DEL TODO

totally

CASI DEL TODO

completely   mainly   largely   thoroughly

virtually   ~~totally~~   mostly   utterly

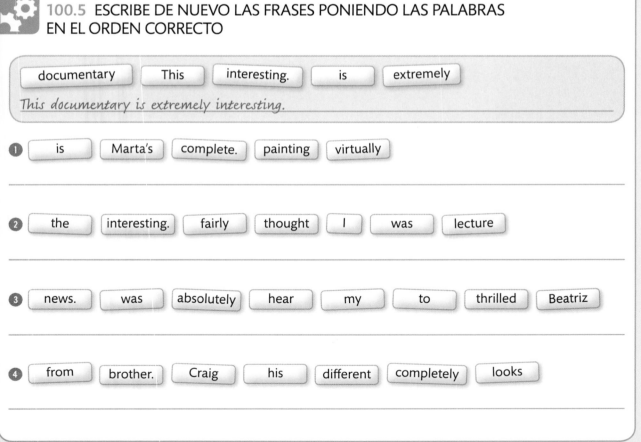

100.5 ESCRIBE DE NUEVO LAS FRASES PONIENDO LAS PALABRAS EN EL ORDEN CORRECTO

| documentary | This | interesting. | is | extremely |

This documentary is extremely interesting.

1. | is | Marta's | complete. | painting | virtually |

_____

2. | the | interesting. | fairly | thought | I | was | lecture |

_____

3. | news. | was | absolutely | hear | my | to | thrilled | Beatriz |

_____

4. | from | brother. | Craig | his | different | completely | looks |

_____

100.6 MARCA LAS FRASES QUE SEAN CORRECTAS

> The rides at the fair were totally awesome. ☑
> The rides at the fair were entirely awesome. ☐

❶ Unfortunately, the hotel we stayed in was utterly awful. ☐
Unfortunately, the hotel we stayed in was remarkably awful. ☐

❷ We found the music festival very brilliant this year. ☐
We found the music festival completely brilliant this year. ☐

❸ The students' handwriting was barely legible. ☐
The students' handwriting was nearly legible. ☐

❹ The food in the canteen is absolutely good. ☐
The food in the canteen is remarkably good. ☐

❺ It was nearly impossible, but we reached the summit in the end. ☐
It was slightly impossible, but we reached the summit in the end. ☐

100.7 CONECTA EL INICIO Y EL FINAL DE CADA FRASE

Saori's style of singing — wear jeans to work on Fridays.

❶ The play had almost started — useless without its charger.

❷ It's perfectly acceptable to → is really quite unique.

❸ This old phone is absolutely — by the time we found the theater.

❹ We were completely exhausted — writing his PhD thesis.

❺ Jon is extremely talented — when we reached the summit.

❻ Timothy has essentially finished — and should study art at college.

101 Adverbios de tiempo

Los adverbios de tiempo se utilizan para dar información más precisa sobre cuándo ha ocurrido algo exactamente. También pueden referirse a un acontecimiento o una acción en progreso.

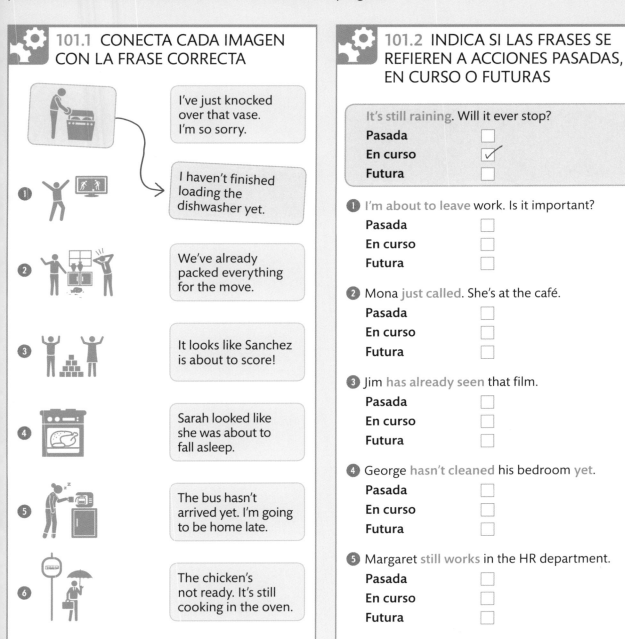

101.1 CONECTA CADA IMAGEN CON LA FRASE CORRECTA

I've just knocked over that vase. I'm so sorry.

I haven't finished loading the dishwasher yet.

We've already packed everything for the move.

It looks like Sanchez is about to score!

Sarah looked like she was about to fall asleep.

The bus hasn't arrived yet. I'm going to be home late.

The chicken's not ready. It's still cooking in the oven.

101.2 INDICA SI LAS FRASES SE REFIEREN A ACCIONES PASADAS, EN CURSO O FUTURAS

It's still raining. Will it ever stop?
Pasada ☐
En curso ☑
Futura ☐

❶ **I'm about to leave** work. Is it important?
Pasada ☐
En curso ☐
Futura ☐

❷ Mona **just called.** She's at the café.
Pasada ☐
En curso ☐
Futura ☐

❸ Jim **has already seen** that film.
Pasada ☐
En curso ☐
Futura ☐

❹ George **hasn't cleaned** his bedroom **yet.**
Pasada ☐
En curso ☐
Futura ☐

❺ Margaret **still works** in the HR department.
Pasada ☐
En curso ☐
Futura ☐

101.3 TACHA LAS PALABRAS INCORRECTAS DE CADA FRASE

 Has Daniel finished painting the bedroom yet / ~~just~~?

 1 I have yet / just received a letter from an old friend.

 2 Mizuho has already / just been to Paris three times before.

 3 Have you been introduced to Tonia's parents yet / just?

 4 The judges are about to / just reveal the winner of the competition.

 5 I've yet / just finished my final exam. It's such a relief.

 6 I haven't finished the book you lent me already / yet.

 7 Maria has yet / just told me she is quitting her job.

 8 The concert had already / just begun by the time we arrived.

 9 Lisa has yet / just returned from her trip around South America.

 10 I was about to / just leave, when I remembered the oven was still on.

 11 The new block on Park Street isn't finished just / yet.

 12 Hurry up, everyone! The train is just / about to leave.

 13 I've already / yet told Anna that the meeting has started.

101.4 CONECTA EL INICIO Y EL FINAL DE CADA FRASE

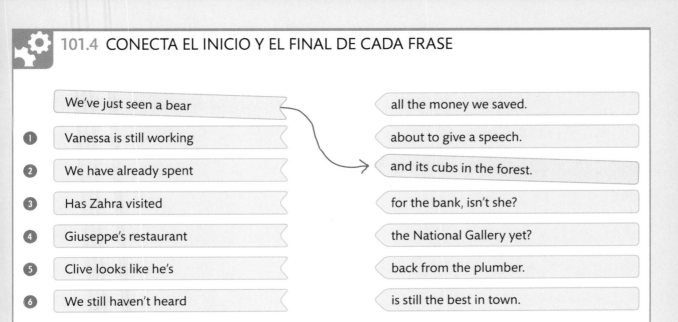

We've just seen a bear → and its cubs in the forest.

1. Vanessa is still working — for the bank, isn't she?
2. We have already spent — all the money we saved.
3. Has Zahra visited — the National Gallery yet?
4. Giuseppe's restaurant — is still the best in town.
5. Clive looks like he's — about to give a speech.
6. We still haven't heard — back from the plumber.

101.5 MARCA LAS FRASES QUE SEAN CORRECTAS

It looks like the band is about to go on stage. ☑
It looks like the band is about go on stage. ☐

1. Mesut still hasn't given back the $30 I lent him. ☐
   Mesut hasn't still given back the $30 I lent him. ☐

2. Leroy is still the best player on the team. ☐
   Leroy is yet the best player on the team. ☐

3. Has Timo still shown you around the new office? ☐
   Has Timo shown you around the new office yet? ☐

4. The guests have already eaten all of the birthday cake. ☐
   The guests have eaten already all of the birthday cake. ☐

5. I just have seen your brother walking out of the police station. ☐
   I've just seen your brother walking out of the police station. ☐

6. Jess is yet living in Aberdeen, isn't she? ☐
   Jess is still living in Aberdeen, isn't she? ☐

102 Adverbios de frecuencia

Los adverbios de frecuencia indican cuán a menudo se hace algo, desde algo que se hace muy frecuentemente ("always") hasta algo que no se hace nunca ("never").

 102.1 TACHA LAS PALABRAS INCORRECTAS DE CADA FRASE

Lou has to work late about once a month. = Lou ~~often~~ / occasionally works late.

① Ola goes to the gym six days a week. = Ola goes to the gym very often / sometimes.

② It rains in the desert once or twice a year. = It hardly ever / regularly rains in the desert.

③ I visit my gran on Tuesday and Thursday. = I regularly / always visit my gran.

④ Most Saturdays I go shopping with friends. = I always / usually go shopping on Saturday.

⑤ She goes running about three times a week. = She occasionally / frequently goes running.

⑥ We spend all our vacations in France. = We always / sometimes go to France on vacation.

102.2 ESCRIBE LOS ADVERBIOS DEL RECUADRO EN EL GRUPO AL QUE CORRESPONDAN

SIEMPRE O CASI SIEMPRE	A VECES	CASI NUNCA O NUNCA
always		

regularly   very often   almost never   ~~always~~   usually   occasionally

never   hardly ever   rarely   sometimes   nearly always

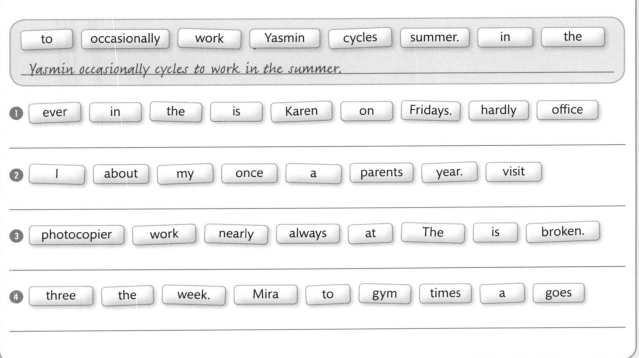

102.3 ESCRIBE DE NUEVO LAS FRASES PONIENDO LAS PALABRAS EN EL ORDEN CORRECTO

| to | occasionally | work | Yasmin | cycles | summer. | in | the |

Yasmin occasionally cycles to work in the summer.

1. | ever | in | the | is | Karen | on | Fridays. | hardly | office |

2. | I | about | my | once | a | parents | year. | visit |

3. | photocopier | work | nearly | always | at | The | is | broken. |

4. | three | the | week. | Mira | to | gym | times | a | goes |

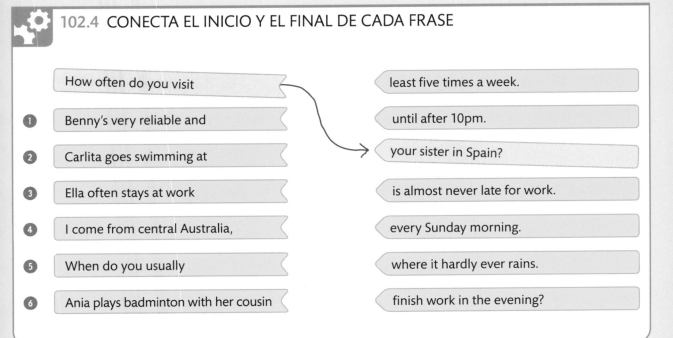

102.4 CONECTA EL INICIO Y EL FINAL DE CADA FRASE

How often do you visit ——————————→ your sister in Spain?

least five times a week.

1. Benny's very reliable and

until after 10pm.

2. Carlita goes swimming at

3. Ella often stays at work

is almost never late for work.

4. I come from central Australia,

every Sunday morning.

5. When do you usually

where it hardly ever rains.

6. Ania plays badminton with her cousin

finish work in the evening?

251

103 "So" y "such"

"So" y "such" son adverbios que pueden utilizarse con ciertas palabras para añadir énfasis. Tienen un significado similar, pero utilizan estructuras diferentes.

103.1 CONECTA EL INICIO Y EL FINAL DE CADA FRASE

Your apartment is so much → more spacious than mine.

1. It was so windy — that we couldn't fly a kite.

2. Your children are so — much better behaved than mine.

3. The bride wore such — all decided to go swimming.

4. It was so hot that we — beautifully decorated cake before.

5. I've never seen such a — a stylish dress for the wedding.

103.2 MARCA LAS FRASES QUE SEAN CORRECTAS

The photocopier's making such an awful noise. ✓
The photocopier's making a so awful noise. ☐

1. The cake that Carlos made for the party was such tasty. ☐
The cake that Carlos made for the party was so tasty. ☐

2. Your exam results are so better this year. ☐
Your exam results are so much better this year. ☐

3. This store sells such lovely clothes. ☐
This store sells such a lovely clothes. ☐

4. Your brother owns such a beautiful villa. ☐
Your brother owns a so beautiful villa. ☐

103.3 TACHA LAS PALABRAS INCORRECTAS DE CADA FRASE

> The children behaved ~~such~~ / so / ~~so much~~ badly that we sent them to bed.

1. Colm's job looks such / so / so much interesting, but it's very badly paid.

2. My new phone's such / so / so much better than my old one.

3. Everyone had such / so / so much a great time at the school reunion.

4. Hank is such / so / so much generous. He gave me a watch for my birthday.

5. The new intern works such / so / so much harder than the old one.

6. It was such / so / so much a shock when our boss said he was leaving.

7. Lorna's such / so / so much a talented musician.

8. The weather was such / so / so much bad that we decided to cancel the barbecue.

103.4 ESCRIBE DE NUEVO LAS FRASES Y CORRIGE LOS ERRORES

> This book is so better than the author's last one.
> *This book is so much better than the author's last one.*

1. My little sister is a so good dancer. She should take classes.

2. The match was such a disappointing. No one scored.

3. The weather is so warmer in Florida. You should move here.

4. Kirsty's such a funny. She always makes me laugh.

5. Sandra is so much a good cook. Everything she makes is delicious.

253

104 "Enough" y "too"

"Enough" se utiliza cuando se tiene el grado o la cantidad correctos de algo. "Too" se utiliza cuando hay más de lo necesario o de lo que se quiere.

104.1 CONECTA CADA IMAGEN CON LA FRASE CORRECTA

  **1**  **2** **3**

Do you think we have enough money to buy this house?	The food was delicious, but there wasn't enough of it.	Bob was too tired to concentrate on cooking the meal.	If you're too cold, close the window.

104.2 COMPLETA LOS ESPACIOS CON LAS EXPRESIONES DEL RECUADRO

Dan's _____*old enough*_____ to remember the 1960s.

1 I'm not _____ to afford those shoes.

2 Michael is _____ to watch that movie.

3 The water is _____ to go for a swim.

4 My neighbor always plays his music _____ .

5 This bookcase is _____ for me to move.

6 My French isn't _____ to understand Pierre.

7 The exercise was _____ for a total beginner.

too hard
rich enough
too loudly
~~old enough~~
too young
too heavy
good enough
warm enough

104.3 ESCRIBE DE NUEVO LAS FRASES PONIENDO LAS PALABRAS EN EL ORDEN CORRECTO

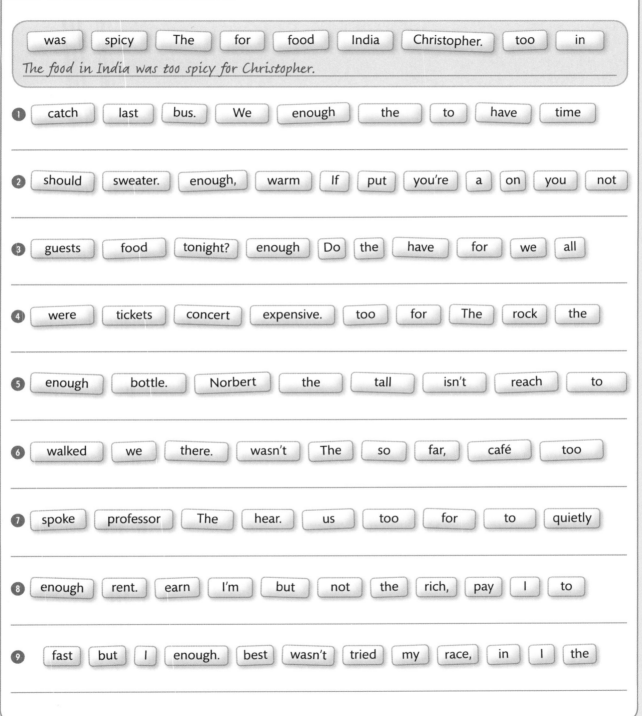

was | spicy | The | for | food | India | Christopher. | too | in

The food in India was too spicy for Christopher.

❶ catch | last | bus. | We | enough | the | to | have | time

_____

❷ should | sweater. | enough, | warm | If | put | you're | a | on | you | not

_____

❸ guests | food | tonight? | enough | Do | the | have | for | we | all

_____

❹ were | tickets | concert | expensive. | too | for | The | rock | the

_____

❺ enough | bottle. | Norbert | the | tall | isn't | reach | to

_____

❻ walked | we | there. | wasn't | The | so | far, | café | too

_____

❼ spoke | professor | The | hear. | us | too | for | to | quietly

_____

❽ enough | rent. | earn | I'm | but | not | the | rich, | pay | I | to

_____

❾ fast | but | I | enough. | best | wasn't | tried | my | race, | in | I | the

_____

105 Preposiciones

Las preposiciones son palabras que sirven para mostrar la relación entre las distintas partes de una cláusula, como las relaciones de tiempo, lugar o causa.

105.1 CONECTA CADA IMAGEN CON LA FRASE CORRECTA

The meeting is on Monday morning.

He was so scared that he jumped up onto a chair.

There's a café by the church.

Peter works at the local airport.

Julie gave her teacher her homework after the lesson.

Mia was nervous before going in to speak to her boss.

Dan put the flowers on the table.

105.2 MARCA LAS FRASES QUE SEAN CORRECTAS

Since quit her job, she's been happier. ☐
Since quitting her job, she's been happier. ☑

① Before leaving for work, I wash the dishes. ☐
Before to leave for work, I wash the dishes. ☐

② I have an English class on Tuesdays. ☐
I have an English class at Tuesdays. ☐

③ I don't know what to listen. ☐
I don't know what to listen to. ☐

④ Al passed without study for the exam. ☐
Al passed without studying for the exam. ☐

⑤ Kumi's listening the radio. ☐
Kumi's listening to the radio. ☐

⑥ Emma's house is by the park. ☐
Emma's house is for the park. ☐

⑦ Their office is next the library. ☐
Their office is next to the library. ☐

⑧ After finishing work, I go swimming. ☐
After to finish work, I go swimming. ☐

⑨ Jon wants to studying Spanish. ☐
Jon wants to study Spanish. ☐

⑩ I live with Pete, with Dan, and with Ed. ☐
I live with Pete, Dan, and Ed. ☐

105.3 COMPLETA LOS ESPACIOS CON LAS PREPOSICIONES DEL RECUADRO

There are lots of great restaurants _____ by _____ our hotel.

Box: of   at   ~~by~~   at   near   of

1 My aunt is really good _____ making her own clothes.

2 My new house is _____ the National Museum.

3 In spite _____ the bad pay, Eleni loves her job.

4 You've been looking _____ that phone all morning.

5 Instead _____ going to college, I became a carpenter.

105.4 ESCRIBE DE NUEVO LAS FRASES Y CORRIGE LOS ERRORES

Michael and Amanda are looking forward **to go out** for dinner tonight.
Michael and Amanda are looking forward to going out for dinner tonight.

1 I'm not used **to wake up** so early each morning.

_____

2 My son is planning **to going** to college in New York.

_____

3 I'm sorry I haven't got around **to reply** to your email yet.

_____

4 Jean-Pierre used **to driving** a red sports car.

_____

5 Martin decided **to quitting** his job at the library.

_____

6 Virginie confessed **to steal** the bottle of wine.

_____

106 Preposiciones de lugar

Las preposiciones de lugar se utilizan para relacionar la posición o la localización de dos cosas. El uso de distintas preposiciones suele modificar el significado de una frase.

106.1 TACHA LAS PALABRAS INCORRECTAS DE CADA FRASE

Katie is ~~in~~ / ~~at~~ / on a bus to London.

1. The dinner is in / at / on the table.

2. Julian lives in / at / on the United States.

3. Mesut wasn't in / at / on the party.

4. I went to meet Ula in / at / on the airport.

5. Carmen works in / at / on France.

6. I bought it in / at / on the supermarket.

7. Mary stayed in / at / on bed all morning.

8. There are 20 rooms in / at / on the building.

9. Put the toys back in / at / on their box.

10. We went to London in / at / on the train.

11. Marta's left her keys in / at / on home.

12. Ben is sitting in / at / on the sofa.

13. The students are all in / at / on their desks.

106.2 CONECTA EL INICIO Y EL FINAL DE CADA FRASE

There's a great selection of movies — playing at the theater downtown.

1. Marina works at Z-Tech, the | posters on your kitchen wall.

2. You have some lovely | number 16, Nelson Avenue.

3. My uncle Tony lives at | software company on Park Street.

4. We keep the lawnmower | on the ninth and tenth floors.

5. The college library can be found | the bakery across the road.

6. I usually buy my bread at | in the shed behind the house.

106.3 OBSERVA LAS IMÁGENES Y COMPLETA LAS FRASES
CON LAS PREPOSICIONES DEL RECUADRO

We have a lovely photograph hanging
_____*above*_____ the couch.

④ Ian put his bag on the seat
_____ .

① The castle sits _____
some ugly modern buildings.

⑤ There's a lovely park _____
my house.

② I placed the final box of books
_____ the others.

⑥ The library is _____
the bank and the café.

③ Alan is working in the garage
_____ a car.

⑦ I found Craig and Robin hiding
_____ a tree.

on top of	behind	under	near
between	~~above~~	in front of	opposite

107 Preposiciones de tiempo

Las preposiciones de tiempo suelen utilizarse para hablar de agendas y rutinas. Dan información sobre cuándo ocurre algo, y sobre cuánto dura.

107.1 CONECTA CADA IMAGEN CON LA FRASE CORRECTA

During the week I wake up at 7am.

Canada gets very cold in winter.

We'd better hurry. Our flight leaves in two hours.

I'm free on Wednesday and Thursday this week.

Jan has a bath in the evening before she goes to bed.

I usually make coffee when I get up in the morning.

It often gets far too hot in the summer in the city.

107.2 MARCA LAS FRASES QUE SEAN CORRECTAS

Ted has plans on the afternoon. ☐
Ted has plans in the afternoon. ☑

① I'm meeting Eliana at 6pm. ☐
I'm meeting Eliana on 6pm. ☐

② Joe has his final exam at Friday. ☐
Joe has his final exam on Friday. ☐

③ She started working here on August. ☐
She started working here in August. ☐

④ I go to Angelo's café at lunchtime. ☐
I go to Angelo's café in lunchtime. ☐

⑤ Pat works from home at Thursdays. ☐
Pat works from home on Thursdays. ☐

⑥ I always have a nap in the afternoon. ☐
I always have a nap on the afternoon. ☐

⑦ Their wedding is on August the 15th. ☐
Their wedding is in August the 15th. ☐

⑧ The performance starts in 4 o'clock. ☐
The performance starts at 4 o'clock. ☐

⑨ Maria usually goes skiing in winter. ☐
Maria usually goes skiing on winter. ☐

⑩ My daughter was born at 1996. ☐
My daughter was born in 1996. ☐

107.3 CONECTA EL INICIO Y EL FINAL DE CADA FRASE

I always pick my children up → from school at 3pm.

Independence Day on July 4.

1. Americans celebrate
   a barn owl is at night.

2. The best time to spot
   from school at 3pm.

3. I often go walking in spring,
   on Sunday morning.

4. I usually clean my apartment
   her family at Christmas.

5. Magda usually stays with
   when the weather improves.

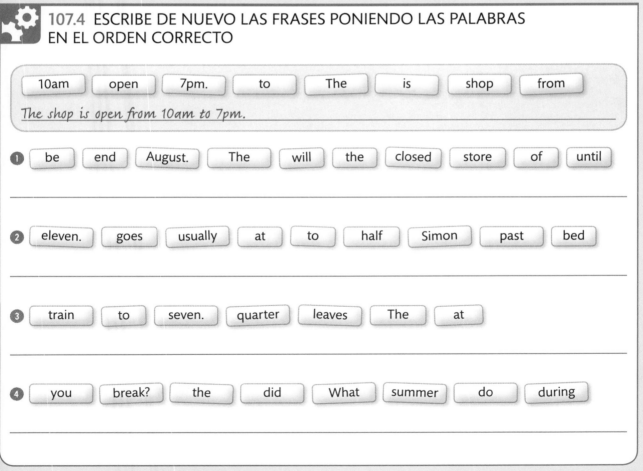

107.4 ESCRIBE DE NUEVO LAS FRASES PONIENDO LAS PALABRAS EN EL ORDEN CORRECTO

| 10am | open | 7pm. | to | The | is | shop | from |

The shop is open from 10am to 7pm.

1. be | end | August. | The | will | the | closed | store | of | until

   _____

2. eleven. | goes | usually | at | to | half | Simon | past | bed

   _____

3. train | to | seven. | quarter | leaves | The | at

   _____

4. you | break? | the | did | What | summer | do | during

   _____

261

107.5 COMPLETA LOS ESPACIOS CON LAS EXPRESIONES DEL RECUADRO

Wendy has been on vacation _____ *for* _____ three days.

until	during
~~for~~	since
between	by

1 I usually go for lunch _____ 1 and 2pm.

2 I'm planning to work here _____ I retire.

3 Martin has worked here _____ October.

4 I lived in Spain for a couple of years _____ the 1970s.

5 Guests should leave their rooms _____ 11:30am.

107.6 ESCRIBE DE NUEVO LAS FRASES Y CORRIGE LOS ERRORES

Yasmin **is** a student here since last year.
Yasmin has been a student here since last year.

1 The café is open **for** 8am and 6pm.

_____

2 I'll be writing this essay **to** 10pm.

_____

3 I've been working here **since** about five months.

_____

4 We're traveling around Mexico from July **and** September.

_____

5 Mabel's lived in Madrid **from** she was a child.

_____

6 Camilla **is** my manager here since July.

_____

108 Otras preposiciones

Las preposiciones también sirven para expresar relaciones distintas del lugar o la hora, como por ejemplo el origen, la propiedad o la ausencia.

 108.1 CONECTA CADA IMAGEN CON LA FRASE CORRECTA

We went for a walk with our children this afternoon.

Elsa shouldn't have left the house without an umbrella.

My aunt's written a book about the town where she grew up.

I get a lot of work done when I travel by train.

 108.2 TACHA LAS PALABRAS INCORRECTAS DE CADA FRASE

I've just written a book ~~by~~ / ~~with~~ / about the history of European royalty.

1. *Macbeth* was written by / without / about William Shakespeare in the early 1600s.

2. Takumi went to the theater by / with / about his wife last night.

3. We found our way to the castle by / without / about too much difficulty.

4. I ordered boiled potatoes by / with / about my steak.

5. Most tourists travel around Tokyo by / with / without metro.

6. We need to talk by / without / about employing some more staff.

7. Sarah managed to finish the project by / without / about any help.

108.3 CONECTA EL INICIO Y EL FINAL DE CADA FRASE

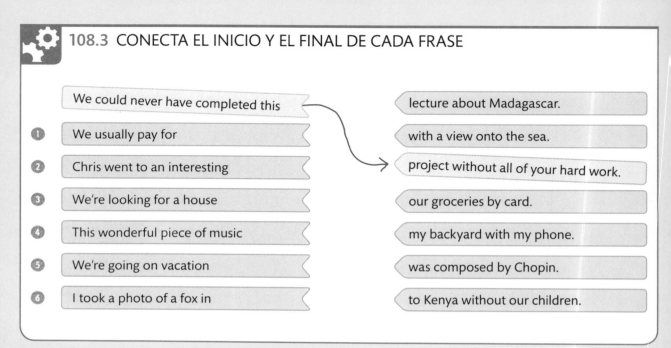

We could never have completed this — project without all of your hard work.

1. We usually pay for — our groceries by card.
2. Chris went to an interesting — lecture about Madagascar.
3. We're looking for a house — with a view onto the sea.
4. This wonderful piece of music — was composed by Chopin.
5. We're going on vacation — to Kenya without our children.
6. I took a photo of a fox in — my backyard with my phone.

108.4 ESCRIBE DE NUEVO LAS FRASES PONIENDO LAS PALABRAS EN EL ORDEN CORRECTO

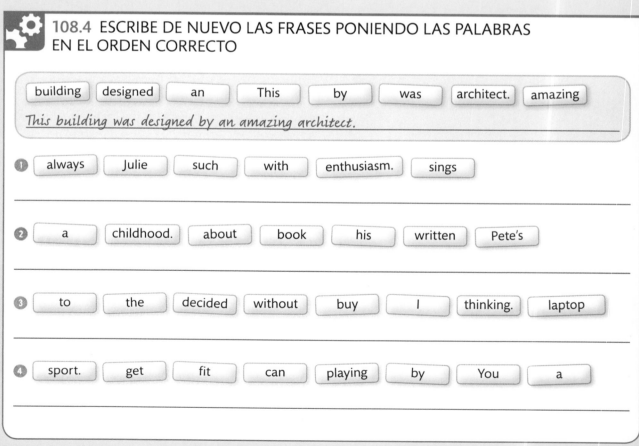

building | designed | an | This | by | was | architect. | amazing

This building was designed by an amazing architect.

1. always | Julie | such | with | enthusiasm. | sings

_____

2. a | childhood. | about | book | his | written | Pete's

_____

3. to | the | decided | without | buy | I | thinking. | laptop

_____

4. sport. | get | fit | can | playing | by | You | a

_____

264

109 Preposiciones dependientes

Ciertas palabras deben ir seguidas por una determinada
preposición, que se conoce como preposición dependiente.
Dichas palabras pueden ser adjetivos, verbos o sustantivos.

109.1 CONECTA CADA IMAGEN CON LA FRASE CORRECTA

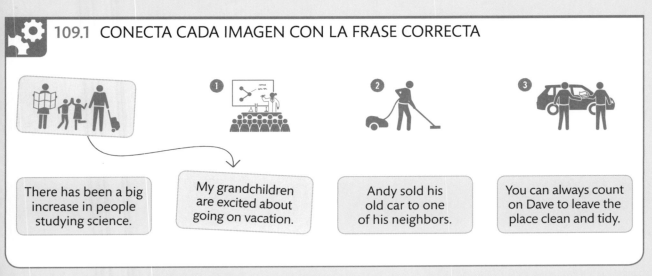

There has been a big
increase in people
studying science.

My grandchildren
are excited about
going on vacation.

Andy sold his
old car to one
of his neighbors.

You can always count
on Dave to leave the
place clean and tidy.

109.2 ESCRIBE DE NUEVO LAS FRASES PONIENDO LAS PALABRAS EN EL ORDEN CORRECTO

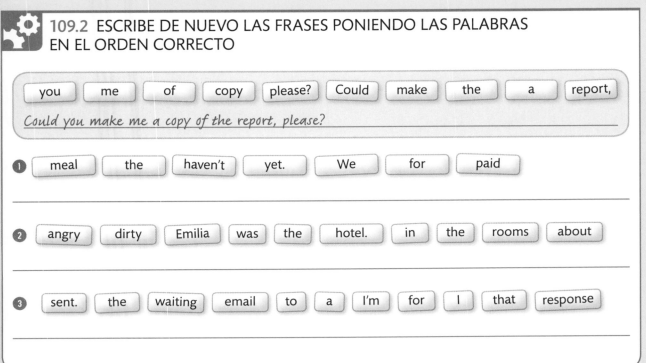

you · me · of · copy · please? · Could · make · the · a · report,

Could you make me a copy of the report, please?

① meal · the · haven't · yet. · We · for · paid

_____

② angry · dirty · Emilia · was · the · hotel. · in · the · rooms · about

_____

③ sent. · the · waiting · email · to · a · I'm · for · I · that · response

_____

109.3 TACHA LA PALABRA INCORRECTA DE CADA FRASE

 What do you think about / ~~on~~ my new haircut?

① I was so proud of / with Katie when she passed the test.

② There are lots of advantages by / to working from home.

③ This company is advertising of / for a new secretary.

④ Is everyone ready for / of the big exam tomorrow?

⑤ Stephanie has a very positive attitude at / toward her work.

⑥ The roadwork caused problems for / with many drivers.

⑦ I was so impressed of / by the room service.

⑧ My boss told us to / about be more punctual in future.

⑨ I don't agree to / with my husband about many things.

⑩ My son is afraid of / with spiders.

⑪ They've found another problem for / with my car.

⑫ Esther has talked to / about moving abroad for years.

109.4 COMPLETA LOS ESPACIOS CON LAS EXPRESIONES DEL RECUADRO

My daughter's asked _____*for*_____ a new laptop for her birthday.

~~for~~	in
to	about
with	to

1. I saw Leonard talking _____ a police officer yesterday.
2. There's been an increase _____ the number of thefts.
3. These animal toys should appeal _____ children.
4. Sangita is annoyed _____ her housemates.
5. My grandfather loves to talk _____ his childhood.

109.5 ESCRIBE DE NUEVO LAS FRASES Y CORRIGE LOS ERRORES

Will you have time to reply **at** my email today?
Will you have time to reply to my email today?

1. Ella is really upset **with** losing her mother's necklace.

_____

2. Bill is anxious **for** giving a speech at the conference.

_____

3. I have an excellent relationship **between** my manager.

_____

4. My teacher asked me what I know **for** Roman history.

_____

5. Erik has sold his bicycle **for** one of his cousins.

_____

6. I've been having a lot of problems **for** my internet router.

_____

110 Conjunciones copulativas

Las conjunciones copulativas unen palabras, frases o cláusulas que tienen igual importancia. Deben aplicarse ciertas normas al utilizar las comas con las conjunciones copulativas.

110.1 CONECTA CADA IMAGEN CON LA FRASE CORRECTA

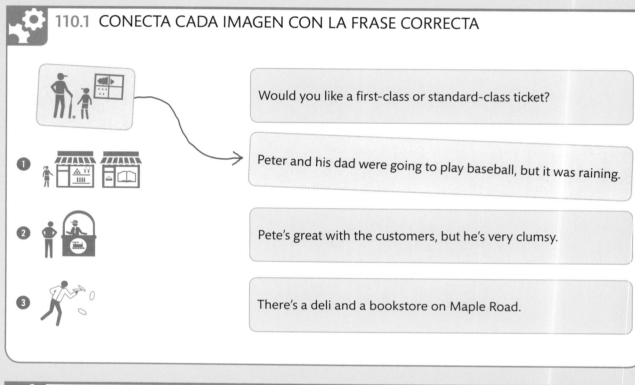

Would you like a first-class or standard-class ticket?

Peter and his dad were going to play baseball, but it was raining.

Pete's great with the customers, but he's very clumsy.

There's a deli and a bookstore on Maple Road.

110.2 CONECTA EL INICIO Y EL FINAL DE CADA FRASE

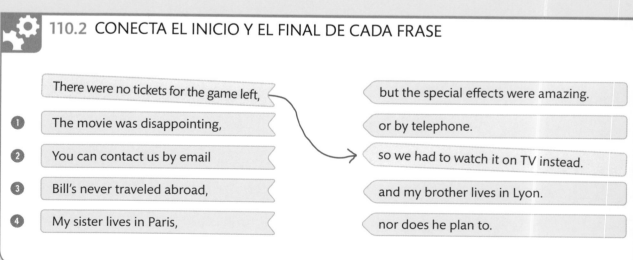

There were no tickets for the game left,

① The movie was disappointing,

② You can contact us by email

③ Bill's never traveled abroad,

④ My sister lives in Paris,

but the special effects were amazing.

or by telephone.

so we had to watch it on TV instead.

and my brother lives in Lyon.

nor does he plan to.

110.3 COMPLETA LOS ESPACIOS CON LAS CONJUNCIONES COPULATIVAS DEL RECUADRO

It's only 10am and _____*yet*_____ I've already got all my errands done.

1 I've been to Ottawa, _____ I've never been to Vancouver.

2 It was raining, _____ we decided to go to the art gallery.

3 While walking, we saw an eagle, a puma, _____ a bear.

4 Ben has to choose between studying math, art, _____ psychology.

5 I did not like the food at the restaurant, _____ did I like the decor.

| and | ~~yet~~ | but | nor | or | so |

110.4 ESCRIBE DE NUEVO LAS FRASES PONIENDO LAS PALABRAS EN EL ORDEN CORRECTO

can | or | to | We | the | center. | go | leisure | shopping

We can go shopping or to the leisure center.

1 bed. | to | so | tired, | Kim | went | feeling | was | she

_____

2 nor | live | at | doesn't | son | My | my | daughter. | home, | does

_____

3 planning | I | was | go | I | my | forgot | but | to | swimsuit. | swimming,

_____

4 grandchildren. | still | 76, | yet | his | with | he | soccer | Len's | plays

_____

111 Conjunciones subordinantes

Las conjunciones subordinantes se utilizan para unir palabras, frases y cláusulas de distinto nivel de importancia. Sirven para decir por qué, dónde o cuándo sucede algo.

111.1 CONECTA EL INICIO Y EL FINAL DE CADA FRASE

Jeremy started his own business — so that he could work for himself.

1 The children ran out to play — because he likes bird-watching.

2 We bought Jim some binoculars — even though he worked hard for it.

3 Adam failed his test, — as soon as it stopped raining.

4 Someone stole my purse — when he gets home from work.

5 Sam usually eats — while I was at the restaurant.

111.2 TACHA LAS PALABRAS INCORRECTAS DE CADA FRASE

You need to enter your password in order to / ~~so that~~ access your account.

1 Eli decided to go jogging, so that / even though it was raining.

2 Ella put on some sunscreen because / so that she didn't get sunburned.

3 When / While I finish this report, I'll give you a hand.

4 You need a passport in order to / so that enter most countries.

5 Even though / Because I prefer coffee, I decided to have a cup of tea.

6 Paolo decided to have a nap although / because he was feeling tired.

7 I made the dinner when / while my wife cleaned our apartment.

111.3 COMPLETA LOS ESPACIOS CON LAS CONJUNCIONES SUBORDINANTES DEL RECUADRO

Regina called her parents _____*as soon as*_____ her boyfriend proposed.

~~as soon as~~	
When	
even though	
while	
so that	
until	

1. I read a newspaper _____ I was waiting for the train.

2. My dad bought some paint _____ he can decorate the kitchen.

3. I'm not going out _____ I've finished my homework.

4. Sally's moving to Spain, _____ she can't speak Spanish.

5. _____ you've written the report, can you send me a copy?

111.4 ESCRIBE DE NUEVO LAS FRASES Y CORRIGE LOS ERRORES

Yuri got burned so he stayed in the sun too long.
Yuri got burned because he stayed in the sun too long.

1. The concert begins as soon as the singer will arrive.
_____

2. Even although I arrived early, there were no tickets left.
_____

3. Miguela is learning to juggle in order for impress her friends.
_____

4. Can you give me a call when you will arrive?
_____

5. I usually eat while my roommate gets home.
_____

6. I went to the supermarket for buy some groceries.
_____

Son varias las palabras que pueden utilizarse para indicar la relación entre dos frases o dos partes de una frase, ya sea de causa, efecto, énfasis, contraste o comparación.

112.1 CONECTA CADA IMAGEN CON LA FRASE CORRECTA

Bill loves going fishing, just like his dad.

My trip to the Azores was ruined because of the bad weather.

Andy is tall, whereas his cousin is quite short.

I like visiting the mountains, especially in the winter.

112.2 CONECTA EL INICIO Y EL FINAL DE CADA FRASE

I love reading novels,

just as her grandmother did.

1 Selma has curly brown hair,

all the trains this afternoon are delayed.

2 Due to the bad snow,

especially murder mysteries.

3 As no one bought any tickets,

whereas we drive on the right here.

4 Andy hated the movie,

because of the icy conditions.

5 People in Japan drive on the left,

we've canceled tonight's show.

6 We had to drive slowly

though I thought it was okay.

112.3 TACHA LAS PALABRAS INCORRECTAS DE CADA FRASE

> I love to travel, especially / ~~notably~~ to hot countries.

❶ Lianne loves football, whereas / hence her brother hates it.

❷ I was late for the interview because / because of the traffic.

❸ The professor was sick. As a result / Especially, the lecture was postponed.

❹ Frank is a zookeeper, yet / since he is terrified of mice.

❺ I get on well with Saul, so / because we are going on vacation together.

112.4 OBSERVA LAS IMÁGENES Y COMPLETA LOS ESPACIOS CON LOS CONECTORES DEL RECUADRO

Ellie prefers to wear smart clothes, _____whereas_____ Dan likes to dress casual.

❸ There are a lot of environmental problems _____ the bad pollution.

❶ Magda loves gardening, _____ in the spring.

❹ _____ her music teacher, Selma became a great pianist.

❷ Omar visited Rome _____ he loves ancient history.

❺ I wanted to come this morning, _____ the tickets had sold out.

| because | ~~whereas~~ | Thanks to | especially | because of | but |

113 Conjunciones: repaso

Las conjunciones son conectores que describen la relación entre dos partes de una frase. Pueden ser copulativas o subordinantes.

113.1 ESCRIBE LOS CONECTORES DEL RECUADRO EN LOS GRUPOS A LOS QUE CORRESPONDAN

CONJUNCIONES COPULATIVAS

or
_____
_____
_____
_____

CONJUNCIONES SUBORDINANTES

_____
_____
_____
_____
_____

nor	in order that	after	so	and
even though	but	~~or~~	because	although

113.2 INDICA EL USO DE LAS CONJUNCIONES EN CADA FRASE

Go home **as soon as** you're finished.
motivo ☐   **condición** ☐   **tiempo** ☑

1 I was an actor **before** I worked here.
condición ☐   **tiempo** ☐   **contraste** ☐

2 Take a sweater **so** you don't get cold.
tiempo ☐   **causa** ☐   **motivo** ☐

3 I got a hot dog **because** I was hungry.
contraste ☐   **causa** ☐   **motivo** ☐

4 Jo reads **while** she travels to work.
tiempo ☐   **motivo** ☐   **causa** ☐

5 I wore a hat **so that** I don't get burned.
contraste ☐   **tiempo** ☐   **motivo** ☐

6 Paula took a map **in case** she got lost.
causa ☐   **contraste** ☐   **condición** ☐

7 We will go running **unless** it rains.
motivo ☐   **condición** ☐   **tiempo** ☐

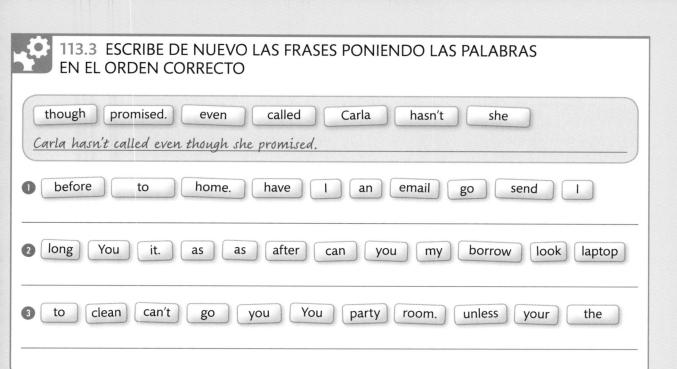

113.3 ESCRIBE DE NUEVO LAS FRASES PONIENDO LAS PALABRAS EN EL ORDEN CORRECTO

though | promised. | even | called | Carla | hasn't | she

Carla hasn't called even though she promised.

1 before | to | home. | have | I | an | email | go | send | I

_____

2 long | You | it. | as | as | after | can | you | my | borrow | look | laptop

_____

3 to | clean | can't | go | you | You | party | room. | unless | your | the

_____

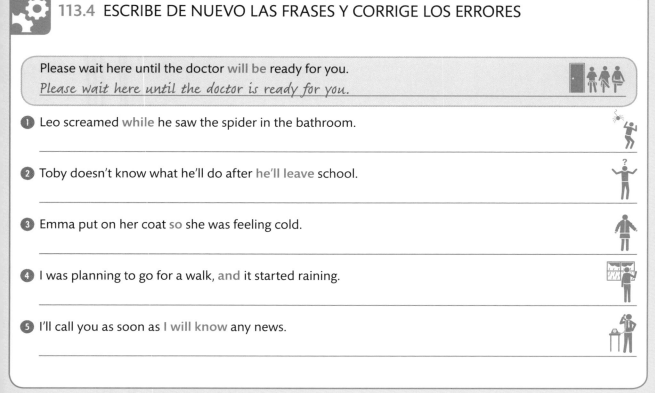

113.4 ESCRIBE DE NUEVO LAS FRASES Y CORRIGE LOS ERRORES

Please wait here until the doctor **will be** ready for you.
Please wait here until the doctor is ready for you.

1 Leo screamed **while** he saw the spider in the bathroom.

_____

2 Toby doesn't know what he'll do after **he'll leave** school.

_____

3 Emma put on her coat **so** she was feeling cold.

_____

4 I was planning to go for a walk, **and** it started raining.

_____

5 I'll call you as soon as **I will know** any news.

_____

Los prefijos son pequeños grupos de letras que pueden añadirse al principio de muchas palabras para darles un significado distinto.

114.1 CONECTA CADA IMAGEN CON LA FRASE CORRECTA

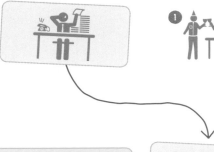

I much prefer nonfiction, such as biographies, to fiction.	I'm worried about John. He's really overdoing it at work.

My girlfriend disapproves of me eating fast food.	I had a lot of fun with my coworkers at the office party.

114.2 TACHA LAS PALABRAS INCORRECTAS DE CADA FRASE

It's impossible / ~~unpossible~~ to start your own business without making sacrifices.

1. The police are looking for a man in his mid-twenties / post-twenties.

2. I've misplaced / displaced my glasses. Have you seen them?

3. The actor's performance was prestandard / substandard.

4. It was inresponsible / irresponsible to drive so quickly.

5. Clara is trying to disprove / misprove the allegations against her.

6. The teacher said their behavior was unacceptable / inacceptable.

7. The student's handwriting was quite inlegible / illegible.

114.3 COMPLETA LOS ESPACIOS CON LOS PREFIJOS DEL RECUADRO

The book is coming out next week, but you can _____pre_____ order it now.

im	
dis	
~~pre~~	
under	
ir	
un	
il	
re	
mis	

1 We found Alexandra's cakes totally _____resistible.

2 I _____read your name. I thought it said Davies, not Davis.

3 Les failed the exam, but he can _____sit next semester.

4 Andy was _____honest about being fluent in Portuguese.

5 Emily was struggling to _____tie her shoelaces.

6 It's _____legal to drive without wearing a seat belt.

7 This cake is really _____cooked. It's almost raw inside.

8 Don't be so _____patient. The train will come soon.

114.4 ESCRIBE DE NUEVO LAS FRASES Y CORRIGE LOS ERRORES

Katia is so unpolite. She never says "please."
Katia is so impolite. She never says "please."

1 I realized I had the wrong key when I couldn't dislock the door.

_____

2 Ed's so inreliable. He's always late.

_____

3 You can preapply for the course next year.

_____

4 Ola was incertain what to think about Jim's haircut.

_____

5 I think she overcharged us. It should have cost more.

_____

115 Sufijos

Los sufijos son pequeños grupos de letras que pueden añadirse al final de muchas palabras para darles un significado distinto.

115.1 CONECTA EL INICIO Y EL FINAL DE CADA FRASE

We were all mystified by

1 This wooden box should be

2 Karl's dog looks dangerous,

3 Our accountant has been

4 The evening's entertainment

5 My brother's a pessimist

really useful for storing our documents.

accused of incompetence.

my uncle's sudden disappearance.

and thinks things will deteriorate.

but it's actually quite harmless.

included some wonderful music.

115.2 ESCRIBE LOS SUFIJOS DEL RECUADRO EN LOS GRUPOS A LOS QUE CORRESPONDEN

ADJETIVOS
-able / -ible

VERBOS

SUSTANTIVOS

-al /-ial   -en   -ate   -able/-ible   -ist /-ian   -less   -ism   -ance/-ence

-ity/-ty   -ful   -ify   -ic/-tic/-ical   -dom   -ize   -ous   -er/-or

115.3 TACHA LAS PALABRAS INCORRECTAS DE CADA FRASE

 Winning the lottery is a rare occurrence / ~~occurence~~.

① Alan works for a managment / management recruitment company.

② The café serves a selection of seasonnal / seasonal vegetables.

③ The fish are plentiful / plentyful in local rivers.

④ Kids love taking inflatable / inflateable toys to the beach.

⑤ I found the music festival very enjoiable / enjoyable.

⑥ She always shows great committment / commitment to her students.

115.4 ESCRIBE DE NUEVO LAS FRASES PONIENDO LAS PALABRAS EN EL ORDEN CORRECTO

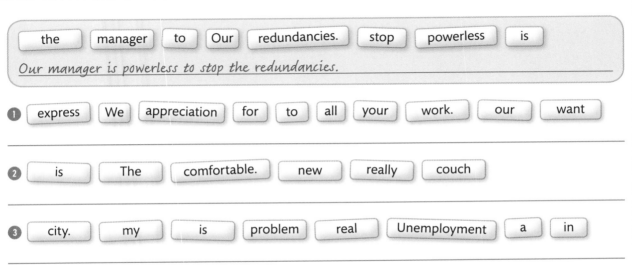

| the | manager | to | Our | redundancies. | stop | powerless | is |

Our manager is powerless to stop the redundancies.

① express | We | appreciation | for | to | all | your | work. | our | want

_____

② is | The | comfortable. | new | really | couch

_____

③ city. | my | is | problem | real | Unemployment | a | in

_____

116 Expresiones que se confunden

En inglés, hay expresiones que se parecen o que suenan de manera similar pero que tienen significados distintos. Es importante no confundir unas con otras.

116.1 CONECTA EL INICIO Y EL FINAL DE CADA FRASE

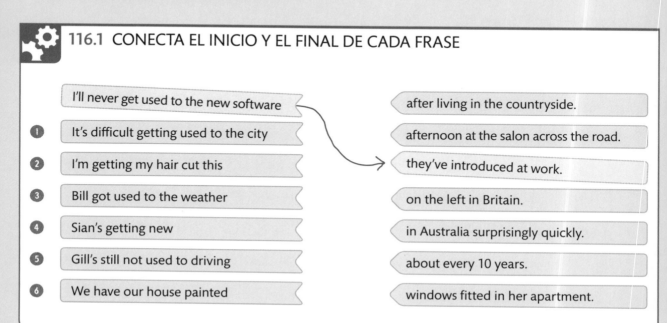

I'll never get used to the new software → they've introduced at work.

1. It's difficult getting used to the city — after living in the countryside.

2. I'm getting my hair cut this — afternoon at the salon across the road.

3. Bill got used to the weather — in Australia surprisingly quickly.

4. Sian's getting new — windows fitted in her apartment.

5. Gill's still not used to driving — on the left in Britain.

6. We have our house painted — about every 10 years.

116.2 CONECTA CADA IMAGEN CON LA FRASE CORRECTA

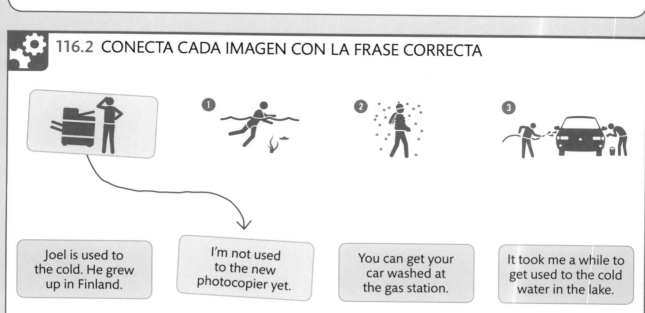

Joel is used to the cold. He grew up in Finland.

I'm not used to the new photocopier yet.

You can get your car washed at the gas station.

It took me a while to get used to the cold water in the lake.

116.3 MARCA LAS FRASES QUE SEAN CORRECTAS

Will you get your car fixed before the trip? ☑
Will you get your car fix before the trip? ☐

1️⃣ I hated working nights at first, but then I got used to it. ☐
I hated working nights at first, but then I am used to it. ☐

2️⃣ Olga grew up in Moscow, so she used to cold winters. ☐
Olga grew up in Moscow, so she's used to cold winters. ☐

3️⃣ I am used to work as a lab technician before I became a teacher. ☐
I used to work as a lab technician before I became a teacher. ☐

4️⃣ Nico has his hair cut at the barbershop on Main Street. ☐
Nico has cut his hair at the barbershop on Main Street. ☐

5️⃣ I got my locks changed after our place was broken into. ☐
I got changed my locks after our place was broken into. ☐

116.4 ESCRIBE DE NUEVO LAS FRASES PONIENDO LAS PALABRAS EN EL ORDEN CORRECTO

| living | isn't | on | own. | his | used | Alfie | to |

Alfie isn't used to living on his own.

1️⃣ | a | on | delivered | gets | Sheila | Fridays. | pizza | always |

_____

2️⃣ | living | in | country. | not | I'm | to | a | used | rainy |

_____

3️⃣ | cleaned | a | I | once | teeth | month. | have | hygienist | my | the | by |

_____

117 Ordenar y organizar

El inglés dispone de una serie de palabras y expresiones que ayudan a explicar el orden de los acontecimientos. Pueden utilizarse también para organizar el texto y hacerlo más fácil de comprender.

117.1 COMPLETA LOS ESPACIOS CON LAS PALABRAS DEL RECUADRO

overall = *in conclusion*

1 for example = _____

2 furthermore = _____

3 next = _____

4 first of all = _____

| then | to begin with | for instance | ~~in conclusion~~ | moreover |

117.2 CONECTA EL INICIO Y EL FINAL DE CADA FRASE

First of all, I find my recipe → book and kitchen utensils.

1 Then I switch on the — in a bowl and mix them together.

2 Next, I put all the ingredients — into a baking pan.

3 After that, I pour the mixture — oven and find my ingredients.

4 You can add extra ingredients, — the oven for about 25 minutes.

5 Finally, put the cake into — such as nuts or dried fruit.

117.3 ESCRIBE DE NUEVO LAS FRASES PONIENDO LAS PALABRAS EN EL ORDEN CORRECTO

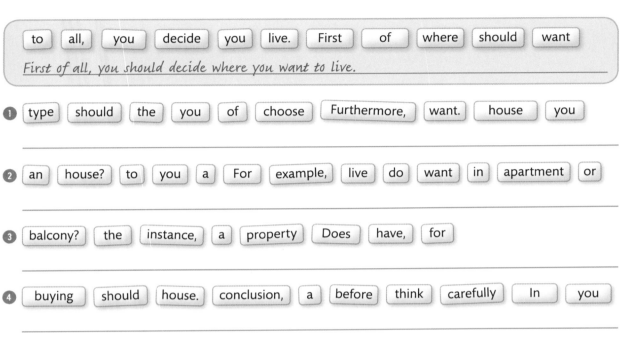

to · all, · you · decide · you · live. · First · of · where · should · want

First of all, you should decide where you want to live.

1 type · should · the · you · of · choose · Furthermore, · want. · house · you

_____

2 an · house? · to · you · a · For · example, · live · do · want · in · apartment · or

_____

3 balcony? · the · instance, · a · property · Does · have, · for

_____

4 buying · should · house. · conclusion, · a · before · think · carefully · In · you

_____

117.4 TACHA LAS PALABRAS INCORRECTAS DE CADA FRASE

~~Firstly of all~~ / First of all, forests are home to so many local species.

 1 Additional / Additionally, they provide employment to many people in the region.

 2 Farthermore / Furthermore, many species are in danger of extinction.

 3 Meantime / Meanwhile, the logging companies continue to destroy vast areas.

 4 In conclusion / By conclusion, forests are in need of urgent protection.

Corregir y cambiar de tema

Ciertas palabras y expresiones se utilizan para corregir a alguien o discrepar de su opinión, cambiar de tema o bien aceptar un argumento del interlocutor. Suelen ir al principio de la frase.

118.1 CONECTA LAS AFIRMACIONES CON LAS RESPUESTAS CORRECTAS

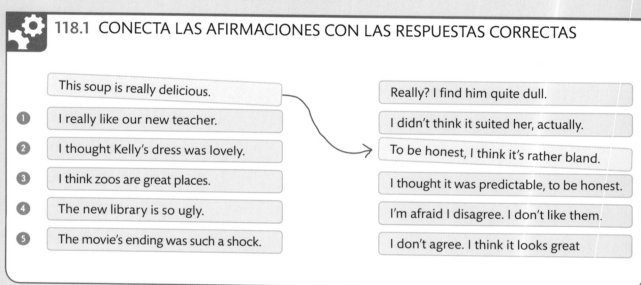

This soup is really delicious. → To be honest, I think it's rather bland.

1 I really like our new teacher.

2 I thought Kelly's dress was lovely.

3 I think zoos are great places.

4 The new library is so ugly.

5 The movie's ending was such a shock.

Really? I find him quite dull.

I didn't think it suited her, actually.

To be honest, I think it's rather bland.

I thought it was predictable, to be honest.

I'm afraid I disagree. I don't like them.

I don't agree. I think it looks great

118.2 INDICA LA MEJOR RESPUESTA PARA CADA AFIRMACIÓN

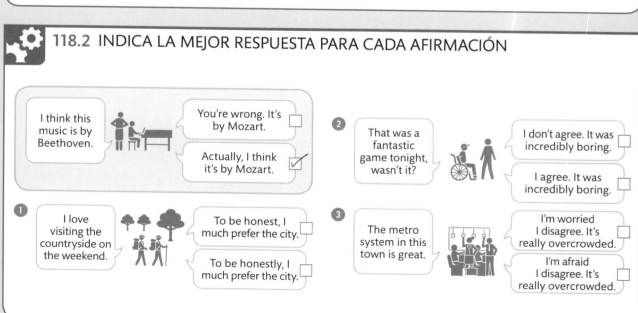

I think this music is by Beethoven.

You're wrong. It's by Mozart. ☐

Actually, I think it's by Mozart. ☑

1 I love visiting the countryside on the weekend.

To be honest, I much prefer the city. ☐

To be honestly, I much prefer the city. ☐

2 That was a fantastic game tonight, wasn't it?

I don't agree. It was incredibly boring. ☐

I agree. It was incredibly boring. ☐

3 The metro system in this town is great.

I'm worried I disagree. It's really overcrowded. ☐

I'm afraid I disagree. It's really overcrowded. ☐

118.3 ESCRIBE DE NUEVO LAS FRASES PONIENDO LAS PALABRAS EN EL ORDEN CORRECTO

was | long, | be | thought | I | novel | to | latest | honest. | too | Claudia's

I thought Claudia's latest novel was too long, to be honest.

1 a | really | she's | still | Anyway, | writer. | good

_____

2 don't | I | I'm | she | think | is. | afraid

_____

3 was | very | is | As | saying, | I | she | talented. | I | think

_____

4 think | agree | you, | with | actually. | don't | I | I

_____

5 have | read | way, | her | By | novel? | the | first | you | ever

_____

6 much. | point | a | You | costing | about | have | too | books | her

_____

7 was | thought | Actually, | awful. | character | main | the | I

_____

8 about | see | character. | your | main | point | the | I

_____

9 Claudia's | you | told | new | novel! | like | I | wouldn't | I

_____

119 Decisiones y matices

El inglés cuenta con una serie de palabras y expresiones para plantear los distintos aspectos de un argumento o hacer que las frases tengan un tono menos definitivo.

 119.1 CONECTA CADA IMAGEN CON LA FRASE CORRECTA

It seems my car has broken down again.

Fishing is arguably the most relaxing activity in the world.

I don't like modern art. However, I don't mind this picture.

It would appear that the cat has knocked over the vase.

 119.2 CONECTA EL INICIO Y EL FINAL DE CADA FRASE

In spite of the terrible weather,

nearby, I rarely eat there.

① Although the restaurant is

are made using the finest ingredients.

② However, whenever I go there,

I will go to the restaurant.

③ Of course, all the dishes

but on the other hand, it's good quality.

④ On the one hand, it's very expensive,

I always have a good time.

⑤ I might go out tonight.

I decided to go out with my friends.

⑥ Despite feeling tired,

Alternatively, I could relax in front of the TV.

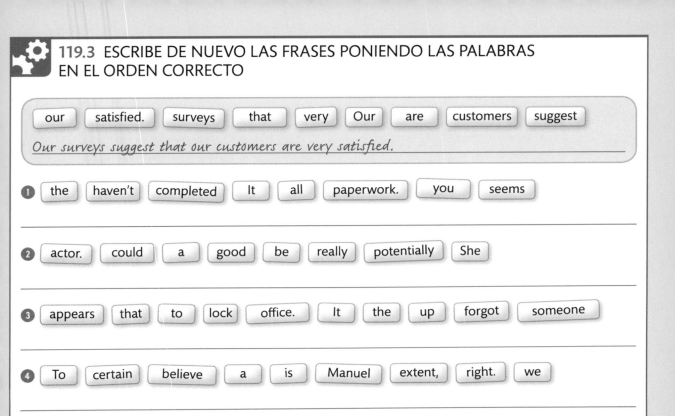

119.3 ESCRIBE DE NUEVO LAS FRASES PONIENDO LAS PALABRAS EN EL ORDEN CORRECTO

| our | satisfied. | surveys | that | very | Our | are | customers | suggest |

Our surveys suggest that our customers are very satisfied.

1. the | haven't | completed | It | all | paperwork. | you | seems

_____

2. actor. | could | a | good | be | really | potentially | She

_____

3. appears | that | to | lock | office. | It | the | up | forgot | someone

_____

4. To | certain | believe | a | is | Manuel | extent, | right. | we

_____

119.4 MARCA LAS FRASES QUE SEAN CORRECTAS

It looks that the thief entered through that window. ☐
It seems that the thief entered through that window. ☑

1. The figures suggest that we are losing a lot of customers. ☐
The figures recommend that we are losing a lot of customers. ☐

2. Despite of the delays, I enjoyed myself thoroughly. ☐
Despite the delays, I enjoyed myself thoroughly. ☐

3. In the one hand, I'm rich. In the other hand, I'm not very happy. ☐
On the one hand, I'm rich. On the other hand, I'm not very happy. ☐

4. To some extend, crime has increased in the past year. ☐
To some extent, crime has increased in the past year. ☐

120 Mantener una conversación

Son muchas las palabras en inglés que sirven para hacer más fluida una conversación. Estas técnicas pueden ser de organización, retroalimentación o dilación.

120.1 INDICA LA MEJOR RESPUESTA PARA CADA AFIRMACIÓN

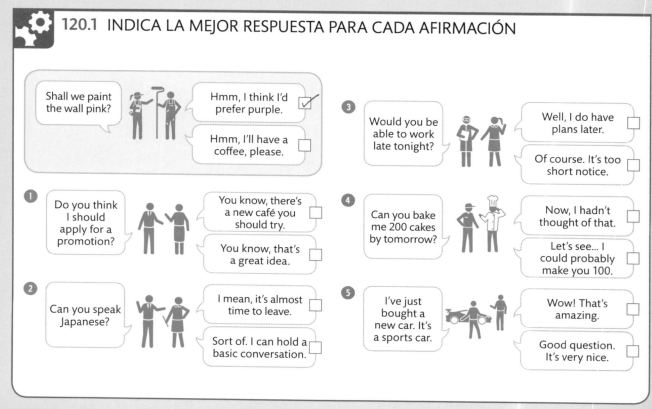

Shall we paint the wall pink?
- Hmm, I think I'd prefer purple. ✓
- Hmm, I'll have a coffee, please.

1 Do you think I should apply for a promotion?
- You know, there's a new café you should try.
- You know, that's a great idea.

2 Can you speak Japanese?
- I mean, it's almost time to leave.
- Sort of. I can hold a basic conversation.

3 Would you be able to work late tonight?
- Well, I do have plans later.
- Of course. It's too short notice.

4 Can you bake me 200 cakes by tomorrow?
- Now, I hadn't thought of that.
- Let's see... I could probably make you 100.

5 I've just bought a new car. It's a sports car.
- Wow! That's amazing.
- Good question. It's very nice.

120.2 CONECTA EL INICIO Y EL FINAL DE CADA FRASE

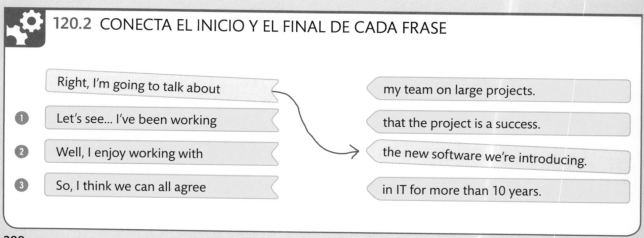

Right, I'm going to talk about — the new software we're introducing.

1 Let's see... I've been working — in IT for more than 10 years.

2 Well, I enjoy working with — my team on large projects.

3 So, I think we can all agree — that the project is a success.

120.3 ESCRIBE DE NUEVO LAS FRASES PONIENDO LAS PALABRAS EN EL ORDEN CORRECTO

| thinking | I'm | of | Paris. | to | moving | So, |

So, I'm thinking of moving to Paris.

1 | to | What | going | Really? | there? | you | are | do |

_____

2 | I'd | work | a | as | waiter. | like | to | Well, |

_____

3 | work. | know, | be | that | might | You | hard |

_____

4 | will | French. | I | practice | suppose | I | my | but | so, |

_____

5 | French? | Of | speak | But | course. | do | you | any |

_____

6 | like | Good | question. | I'd | but | yet, | Not | to. |

_____

7 | to | right. | do? | else | do | What | want | you | Oh |

_____

8 | travel | like | to | France. | I'd | see. | Let's | around |

_____

9 | sounds | Wow! | great | idea. | That | a | like |

_____

Respuestas

NOTA: Algunas de las siguientes respuestas pueden escribirse de distintas formas, por ejemplo con o sin contracciones.

01

1.1
1. Tony **makes** a huge breakfast for his family on Sundays.
2. I usually **eat** my lunch at 1pm at an Italian restaurant.
3. Fiona **meets** her friends at a café on Thursday evenings.
4. We sometimes **play** tennis with our friends on Saturday mornings.
5. My cousin **starts** work at 6am every morning.
6. The shop assistant **leaves** work at 6pm in the evening.
7. You **drink** a lot of coffee every morning.
8. Paolo usually **reads** a book in the evenings.

1.2
1. Greg works in a factory.
2. My dad watches TV every evening.
3. Michel plays the piano beautifully.
4. Jane brushes her hair in the morning.
5. Selma goes shopping after work.
6. Imran washes his clothes on Sunday.
7. Mary teaches French at a college.

1.3
1. I **am** a doctor at the local hospital.
2. Vicky **is** my eldest child.
3. We **are** from a town in Scotland.
4. Both my parents **are** lawyers.
5. You **are** a very good friend.
6. I **am** an American.
7. That policeman **is** so tall.
8. She **is** twenty-three years old.
9. It **is** cold outside.
10. I **am** fifteen today.
11. Our cat **is** black and white.
12. We **are** very excited.
13. They **are** students from France.
14. Jim **is** an architect.
15. My sister-in-law **is** from Japan.
16. I **am** so hungry!
17. You **are** very lazy.
18. My children **are** so tired.
19. I **am** forty-three years old.
20. They **are** late for work.
21. Claudia and Paolo **are** Italian.
22. My grandfather **is** retired.
23. We **are** from Pakistan.
24. Paul **is** disappointed.

1.4
1. Jack **has** a new car.
2. Jennifer **has** Abbie's bag.
3. We **have** a beautiful farm.
4. I **have** three sisters.
5. Bob **has** toothache.
6. My house **has** a large garage.
7. They **have** a new laptop.
8. We **have** so many books.
9. My dad **has** red hair.
10. You **have** an old phone.
11. My neighbors **have** a daughter.
12. Juan's house **has** three floors.
13. That bird **has** big eyes.
14. I **have** a new baby.
15. We both **have** headaches.
16. They **have** the same dress.
17. My grandparents **have** chickens.
18. You **have** a friendly cat.
19. My town **has** two museums.
20. Yuko **has** a painful back.
21. Our dogs **have** lots of toys.
22. We **have** an English class tonight.
23. Vineetha **has** a new haircut.
24. I **have** dinner at 6pm every day.

1.5
1. Brad goes camping in the forest every summer.
2. Hannah takes beautiful photos of the places she visits.
3. Emil leaves the office at 6pm each day.

1.6
1. I **start** work at 9am during the week.
2. You **are** an engineer.
3. Maria **has** coffee with Jules in the morning.
4. They **go** to work by train.
5. My dad **is** 67 years old.
6. Robert **finishes** work at 7pm.
7. We **have** an English lesson later.
8. Paul often **watches** a film in the evening.
9. Emma **goes** to bed early on Sundays.

02

2.1
1. She is not a doctor.
2. We are not from New Zealand.
3. My dad is not American.
4. They are not my dogs.
5. You are not Egyptian.
6. This is not my computer.
7. I am not an engineer.

2.2
1. You **do not** work in the library.
2. He **does not** eat meat.
3. Val **does not** watch TV in the evening.
4. I **do not** play football very often.
5. We **do not** get up early on Saturdays.
6. My grandparents **do not** have a car.
7. Nico **does not** work in the factory.
8. She **does not** go to work on Fridays.
9. I **do not** go to restaurants very often.
10. You **do not** have a cat.
11. They **do not** work outside.

2.3
1. He's not a teacher.
   He isn't a teacher.
2. Carla's not very tall.
   Carla isn't very tall.
3. You're not from Australia.
   You aren't from Australia.
4. They're not farmers.
   They aren't farmers.
5. We're not happy.
   We aren't happy.
6. You're not lawyers.
   You aren't lawyers.
7. She's not a doctor.
   She isn't a doctor.
8. It's not very cold outside.
   It isn't very cold outside.

2.4
1. I don't like Sam's cooking.
2. You don't look very happy.
3. Antonio does not live in Madrid.
4. Phil doesn't drive a car.
5. I'm not a doctor.
6. Diana doesn't have a computer.
7. I don't like cats.
8. Paolo does not get up at 6am.
9. My dad doesn't feel well.
10. They aren't from China.
11. My friends don't like chess.

2.5
1. Amy **doesn't work** as a receptionist in our office.
2. I **don't like** going to the health center.
3. Your company **isn't** very successful.
4. You **don't play** the violin very well.
5. Jean **doesn't cook** the dinner in the evening.
6. This TV show **isn't** very interesting.
7. Sonia and Rick **don't live** in Paris.
8. My son **isn't** a firefighter.
9. Our house **isn't** very big.
10. Sandra **doesn't work** late on Fridays.
11. My husband and I **don't relax** on weekends.
12. Edith and Sam **don't like** dancing in their free time.

03

3.1
1. **Are** you the new teacher?
2. **Is** she your sister?
3. **Are** we nearly home?
4. **Am** I on the list?
5. **Are** your dogs friendly?
6. Where **is** the front door?
7. **Is** Carlo still a teacher?
8. **Are** we late for the party?
9. Where **are** my shoes?
10. **Is** that Shelly's new car?
11. Who **is** the manager here?
12. **Am** I too late for the concert?
13. When **is** your birthday?
14. **Is** he here for the presentation?
15. Where **is** the bathroom?
16. **Am** I supposed to be at work?

⑰ Why **are** they angry?
⑱ **Is** it time to eat yet?
⑲ **Are** they coming to the seminar?

3.2
① **Does** Laura have a brother?
② **Do** they know your address?
③ **Does** Craig still live in Dublin?
④ Where **does** your mother work?
⑤ **Do** they know your father?
⑥ **Does** the restaurant serve fish?
⑦ **Do** you still have my book?
⑧ **Does** your house have a garage?
⑨ **Do** we have enough time?
⑩ How **does** Ben travel to work?
⑪ **Do** your parents have a car?
⑫ When **does** the lesson end?
⑬ **Do** you work on Saturdays?
⑭ **Does** she play any instruments?
⑮ What **do** you want for dinner?
⑯ **Do** I need to wear a dress?
⑰ What **does** he want this time?
⑱ **Do** they know what time it is?
⑲ Where **does** she buy her clothes?

3.3
① Does Danielle play baseball very often?
② Do you know how to play the electric guitar?
③ Does your daughter know how to drive a car?
④ What time do you get up in the morning?

3.4
① Does she like going to the theater?
② Does Carlo like Chinese food?
③ Do you like gardening?
④ Does he know how to play chess?
⑤ Does Cleo have breakfast every morning?
⑥ Does Jim have a lot of homework this weekend?
⑦ Do they live in London?
⑧ Does it rain often here?
⑨ Does Peter enjoy taking photos?
⑩ Does Sally know how to swim?
⑪ Do they play golf on Saturdays?

04

4.1
① Michelle is visiting a gallery.
② Pedro is hiking in the mountains.
③ Martin is cooking dinner for his family.

4.2
① You **are wearing** a beautiful red dress.
② Matilda **is reading** a travel book about Brazil.
③ My cat **is climbing** the apple tree.
④ I **am reading** such an interesting book.
⑤ Hetty and Paula **are drinking** some orange juice.
⑥ Phil **is practicing** for his piano lesson.

4.3
① Clara **is trying** on some new shoes.
② I **am writing** a letter to my girlfriend.
③ Sanjay **is learning** to drive.
④ Mel and Tim **are getting married** today.

⑤ Robin **isn't studying** for the French exam this afternoon.
⑥ Sam and Ashwin **are playing** baseball at the park.
⑦ My sister's friend **is performing** on stage now.

4.4
① Sam and Pete aren't playing cards in the living room.
② The children eat pizza once a week.
③ Julian is wearing a suit for the meeting.

4.5
① Are they going **to the festival?**
② What are we **eating for dinner?**
③ Is it **snowing outside?**
④ Why is Lisa **wearing such fancy clothes?**

4.6
① Chris isn't playing football today.
② Are your kids watching a football game?
③ My wife is visiting her friend this afternoon.
④ Where is Selma living at the moment?
⑤ Joe isn't wearing a tie today.

4.7
① Are they driving to the beach?
② Are you going swimming?
③ Is she watching a movie?
④ Is Nelson going shopping?
⑤ Is Ben listening to classical music?
⑥ Is Chrissie climbing the tree?
⑦ Are Sven and Olly singing?
⑧ Are you drinking apple juice?
⑨ Are they are playing tennis?
⑩ Is my son reading a book?
⑪ Is Pavel speaking Russian?
⑫ Are you are wearing a dress?

4.8
① I'm not going to the zoo.
② The dog isn't chasing a cat.
③ They aren't walking their dog.
④ Angela isn't wearing a dress.
⑤ We aren't playing chess.
⑥ I'm not eating Chinese food.
⑦ James isn't wearing your shirt.
⑧ You aren't reading a book.
⑨ She isn't cleaning her room.
⑩ Ed and Gus aren't watching a movie.
⑪ I'm not speaking French.
⑫ It isn't raining outside.

05

5.1
① Annabelle **explores** caves in her free time.
② João **doesn't like** dogs. He's really scared of them.
③ Is Dimitri still **building** the garage wall?
④ Brendan **loves** watching comedies on TV in the evenings.
⑤ Sid and Les **work** at the beauty salon.

5.2
① Kit **goes** scuba-diving with her friends on Fridays.
② Ben and Kelly **are dancing** at the club tonight.
③ Sai **puts** the dishes in the dishwasher each evening.
④ Bruce **is waiting** to go for a walk.

5.3
① Mary **doesn't send** letters often, but she **is writing** one to her mother now.
② I **am working** from home today, but usually I **work** in an office.
③ We usually **go** to Spain on vacation, but this year we **are going** to Mexico.
④ Helen **works** in a primary school. **She's teaching** math right now.
⑤ I **don't eat meat** very often, but tonight **I'm having** a steak.
⑥ It **doesn't rain** often in California, but today **it's pouring.**
⑦ My cousin **is performing** on stage now. I **love** her voice.
⑧ Rajiv **is wearing** a T-shirt now, but he always **wears** a shirt at work.
⑨ My dad **is sleeping** now. He **is** tired after the journey.
⑩ Juan normally **starts** work at 8am, but today **he's going** to the dentist.
⑪ Bob **is taking** a taxi to work today, but he usually **takes** the bus.

5.4
① My brother doesn't **work on Friday afternoons.**
② My mom usually bakes **a cake on the weekends.**
③ Where is your sister **living at the moment?**
④ Tom's new girlfriend **lives in a resort in Spain.**
⑤ What's dad cooking **in the kitchen?**
⑥ How often do you **play golf with your colleagues?**

5.5
① Do you play soccer on the weekend?
② Is Paula studying French at college?
③ Why is your dad wearing a suit today?
④ Clarissa usually works at home on Fridays.

5.6
① Lou wakes up at 7am each morning.
② Henry is performing at a country and western club tonight.
③ Tanya doesn't feel well, so she's not coming to the party.

5.7
① Steve **reads** in bed before he **goes** to sleep.
② Lisa and Tim **go** to the gym after work.
③ My mom **is playing** golf with her friend this afternoon.
④ Vernon **doesn't like** snakes. He really **hates** them.
⑤ We often **go** to the café by the park.
⑥ Craig **is walking** in the mountains with Rob this week.

06

6.1
write, draw, run, help, take, give, start, begin, work, send, listen, turn, come, read, smile

6.2
1 Be careful on the wet floor!
2 Take the second road on the right.
3 Don't sit there! It's Andrew's chair.
4 Let me help you with your bags, Vera.

6.3
1 Turn right **at the crossroads.**
2 Eat your **breakfast, Greg!**
3 Give the cake **to Layla.**
4 Please close **the window.**
5 Let's go to **the theater.**
6 Don't walk on **the grass.**
7 Take the first **road on the left.**
8 Don't touch **that vase!**

6.4
1 Turn left after the library.
2 Just give me a minute, please.
3 Let's go to the swimming pool.
4 Go straight ahead at the crossroads.
5 Please close the door.
6 Give the book to your brother.
7 Don't sing so loudly!

07

7.1
1 I **cleaned** my bedroom this morning.
2 We **played** football in the afternoon.
3 After his dinner, Alex **watched** a movie on TV.
4 My wife **visited** her parents yesterday.
5 Lucia **danced** with her friends at the party.

7.2
1 Terry usually takes the metro to work, **but yesterday he walked instead.**
2 I arrived at work early **so I checked my email.**
3 In the morning we walked to **the old town and visited the museum.**
4 Angela cried when she **heard the sad news.**
5 We usually go to France **but last year we traveled around Russia.**
6 Jemma washed the dishes **after she finished her dinner.**
7 Roger listened to some music **then started reading his new book.**

7.3
1 Amy felt sick, so she went to the doctor.
2 I usually walk to the café, but yesterday I drove.
3 Mia laughed when she heard Martin's joke.

7.4
1 Simone **tried** to open the door, but it was completely stuck.
2 Elena **decided** to wear a nice dress to the dinner party that evening.
3 Chan **washed** the dishes after she and Dan had eaten.
4 Stephan and Klara **hurried** to catch the last train home.
5 The waiter **dropped** the dishes onto the floor.
6 Megan **carried** the files into the office.

7.5
1 Marilyn **went** with Clive to the exhibition at the gallery.
2 I **saw** Phil and Dan at the party last night.
3 Sheila **swam** across the lake to the island.
4 I **drank** a large bottle of water after the race.
5 We **drove** to a beautiful resort in the mountains.
6 Carol **put** her cup down on the table.
7 Seb **did** his homework on the bus to school.
8 Omar **bought** a scarf for his wife at the market.
9 She **drew** a beautiful picture of a cherry tree.

7.6
1 You **were** at Paulina's party on Saturday.
2 Joanna **was** very tired after the flight to Australia.
3 My parents **were** delighted when I passed all my exams.
4 There **were** so many people waiting to buy a ticket.
5 I **was** upset when I lost my purse.
6 Liam **was** a pilot for more than 40 years.
7 There **was** a loud bang in the kitchen.
8 My cousins **were** famous dancers in the 1990s.
9 We **were** at the convention last year.

7.7
1 Robin **wanted** to go skiing in the winter.
2 Julie and Scott **drank** a lot of coffee at the café.
3 Eli **went** camping in the woods last summer.
4 Jon **played** rugby on Saturday afternoon.
5 I **watched** TV dramas until late last night.
6 We **went** to a jazz club to listen to live music.
7 Sadiq's dog **barked** in the yard all evening.
8 The pollution in my city **was** very bad.
9 Angelo **ate** an apple for his lunch.
10 Kyle **made** his bed after getting up in the morning.
11 Tina **played** the piano with her little brother.

08

8.1
1 Emily didn't go to the party **because she felt tired.**
2 The sports car cost a huge amount, **so we didn't buy it.**
3 Ben was upset because **Jenny didn't call him on his birthday.**
4 My uncle didn't enjoy the film **because he hates science fiction.**
5 The teacher shouted at me **because I didn't do my homework.**
6 Katie is very shy, so **she didn't talk to anyone at the party.**

8.2
1 Zehra didn't play football yesterday. She went fishing.
2 Michael did not like the burger he ordered, so he sent it back.
3 I didn't go out last night; I stayed in and watched TV instead.

8.3
1 There **weren't** enough sandwiches for everyone.
2 I **did not finish** mowing the lawn because I was tired.
3 The book **wasn't** interesting, so I watched TV instead.
4 Joe **didn't make** enough potatoes for everyone.
5 The students **didn't understand** the teacher.
6 There **weren't** many people at the concert last night.
7 It **wasn't** very warm outside, so we stayed at home.
8 My brother **didn't enjoy** the movie very much.

8.4
1 We **didn't speak** to Ellen.
2 They **were** happy.
3 They **weren't** late.
4 I **waited** for Carl.
5 Lola **did not understand**.
6 Brendan **was** there.
7 They **didn't pay** the bill.
8 Hugh **talked** to me.
9 Claire **didn't eat** the cake.
10 She **went** swimming.

09

9.1
1 Did Salvador win the lottery?
2 Did Peter take a shower earlier?
3 Did they drink all the juice?
4 Did Nick wash the dishes?
5 Did Sam buy a sports car?
6 Did they build a new house?

9.2
1 Was it very windy on the island?
2 How was your band practice yesterday?
3 Why was Xander late for the meeting?

9.3
1 Did you take the dog for a walk?
2 How did you get home last night?
3 What was the food like in Greece?

9.4

1. **Why were you** both so late for work this morning?
2. **Was Katie** pleased with the present you got her?
3. **Did you take** any good photos while you were on vacation?
4. **What was the weather like** while you were in Greece?
5. **Where did you buy** that lovely suit, Vincent?

10

10.1

1. This time last year, Craig was on vacation in Hawaii.
2. I was decorating the kitchen on Wednesday evening.
3. I was mowing the lawn when you tried to call.

10.2

1. We **were sunbathing** when it **began** to rain.
2. When I **met** Tracy yesterday, she **was wearing** a lovely dress.
3. It **was** a beautiful day and the birds **were singing** in the trees.
4. I **heard** a loud bang when I **was watching** TV last night.
5. It **started** to rain while I **was talking** on the telephone.

10.3

1. We **were hiking in the Alps** this time last year.
2. Colm **was driving to work when he saw** a deer.
3. Who **were you talking to when I saw you** yesterday?
4. It was cloudy yesterday, but at least **it wasn't raining again**.

10.4

1. Mia **visited** Sydney while she **was traveling** around Australia.
2. The children **were reading** when I **entered** the classroom.
3. Ravi **saw** an old castle when he **was walking** through the forest.
4. The sun **was shining** when we **set off** on the journey home.

11

11.1

1. Daria **has** baked a delicious cake for everyone at the office.
2. My parents **have** decided to buy a little cottage in the country.
3. Ola **has** taken the day off and **has** gone to the new gallery in town.
4. We **have** decided when we're going to get married.

11.2

1. Hank **hasn't opened** the letter from his college yet.
2. My children **have washed** the car at last.
3. Kelly still **hasn't cleaned** her bedroom. It's so messy!
4. Danny **has painted** the bedroom and the living room.
5. Jess **has visited** Peru and Ecuador so far this year.

11.3

1. Fran and Leo **have gone** to the fair together.
2. Angelo **has not cooked** dinner for his family yet.
3. Jenny **has cleaned** all the windows in her apartment.
4. I **have not met** Nick's new girlfriend yet.
5. Morgan **has watched** this movie at least six times already.
6. Mr. Fernandez and his son **have left** the building.

11.4

REGULAR:
wanted, watched, helped, walked, asked
IRREGULAR:
given, done, seen, swum, put

11.5

1. I studied French in college a long time ago.
2. I haven't lived in Venezuela since 2009.
3. Kevin first visited Munich in 1997.
4. Enzo finished the report on Friday.
5. Sebastian has worked as a chef for 10 years.

11.6

1. Owen **started** work here in 2017.
2. I **have spoken** to Tina about this twice today already.
3. How many countries **have you visited** so far?
4. Gloria **has never tried** windsurfing before.
5. Fabio **has lived** in England for more than 15 years.

11.7

1. I've just been to the dentist for a filling.
2. They've gone to the library.
3. Yes, she's been shopping with her friends.
4. Yes, I've just been for a run.
5. No, she's gone for a walk with the dog.

11.8

1. Of course, I've visited it many times.
2. Yes, I tried it when I went to Athens last year.
3. Yes, I moved here in 1997.
4. Yes, I saw *Macbeth* when I went to London.
5. Yes, I've tried it twice since I've been in Malaysia.

12

12.1

1. Val has been learning to dance tango **for more than six months.**
2. Jess has been running today **and looks very tired.**
3. Have you been living at this **address for a long time?**
4. I've been eating too much cake lately, **so I want to go on a diet.**
5. I haven't been running for ages, **so I don't feel very fit.**

12.2

1. Colin has been looking for a new house all year.
2. My brother's been painting the kitchen since Sunday.
3. It's been raining for more than a week.

12.3

1. I **have been cleaning** the house because my parents are coming tomorrow.
2. You **have been building** that wall all day. Are you nearly finished?
3. Joe **has been fishing** all afternoon, but he hasn't caught anything yet.
4. We **haven't been playing** tennis together for very long.
5. How long **have** you **been training** for the marathon, Jon?
6. Josh **has been painting** a lovely landscape this afternoon.
7. Matt and Heather **have been studying** for their exam all evening.
8. I **haven't been reading** this book for very long.
9. Jane **has been traveling** all summer.
10. **Has** Robin **been walking** all day? He looks exhausted.
11. I **have been trying** to cook a new recipe today.
12. Ed **hasn't been feeling** well, so I told him to go to the doctor.
13. My friend **has been touring** Europe with his band.
14. My manager **has been sleeping** at his desk all afternoon.

13

13.1

1. The play **had started** by the time we arrived at the theater.
2. Ben liked Sal, even though he **had met** her only a few times.
3. I **hadn't eaten** Indian food before, so I didn't know what to expect.
4. Justin called his sister, but she **had gone** to bed.
5. Edith **hadn't seen** her niece for years so was delighted when she visited.
6. Amber felt so happy that she **had passed** her exam.

7 My uncle was upset because I **hadn't called** him recently.

8 Christine worked late, because she **hadn't finished** her project yet.

9 There were a lot of delays because a bus **had broken down**.

10 When we arrived at the station, we discovered the train **had left**.

11 Amy couldn't take her flight because she **had forgotten** her passport.

12 My son looked bored because he **had been** inside the house all day.

13 The house looked shabby because we **hadn't painted** it in years.

14 Jane was excited about going to Rome. She **hadn't been** to Italy before.

13.2

1 Pete had almost finished tiling the wall by the time I got home.

2 I had just sat down with my drink when it started to rain.

3 Janine felt really cold because she'd been outside too long.

4 Tony had called for a taxi an hour earlier, but it still hadn't arrived.

13.3

1 Craig **arrived** late to work because he **had missed** the train.

2 Marie **hadn't ridden** a bike for years, so she **found** it difficult.

3 Dana **was** delighted that she **had passed** her driving test at last.

4 James **had prepared** breakfast when Caitlin **got up.**

5 She **had visited** San Francisco once before, when she **was** seven.

6 I **hadn't met** Karl before, but we **had** lots in common.

7 We **had seen** the play once before, but we **enjoyed** it anyway.

14

14.1

1 Maya had been working here for five years when I started.

2 It had been raining for a week before the sun came out.

3 I got sunburned because I'd been lying in the sun all day.

4 We went to see that movie everyone had been talking about at work.

5 Vlad had been studying English for a year when he moved to Toronto.

6 My computer hadn't been working properly for ages, so I bought a new one.

7 We only found the hotel after we'd been driving for more than an hour.

8 I'd been training for years before I won my first marathon.

9 Carol had been cooking all morning, so she was exhausted.

10 I went to the doctor because I hadn't been feeling well all week.

14.2

1 Marion had been learning Spanish **for six months before she went to Spain.**

2 The forest looked beautiful because **it had been snowing all night.**

3 Kelly had been practicing all week, **so her performance was perfect.**

4 Clive had been complaining **about the bad smell all week.**

14.3

1 Nina **had been shopping** all morning and **needed** a coffee.

2 Carla **had been living** in Paris for 10 years when she **met** Liam.

3 Chris **felt** exhausted because he **had been playing** football all day.

4 Phil **had been watching** TV when the telephone **rang**.

5 Jill **had been feeling** ill all day, so she **went** to bed early.

6 The kids **had been watching** TV all afternoon because it **was** so cold outside.

7 Jo **had been studying** for years before she **passed** the exam.

8 Ahmed **had been working** for hours before he finally **left** the office.

15

15.1

1 I **used to live** in London, but I moved to Paris 10 years ago.

2 When I was a teenager, I **would go** fishing on Saturdays. Now I prefer photography.

3 There **didn't use to be** any factories here. There were beautiful woods.

4 When I worked, I **would get up** at 5am. Now I relax in the morning.

5 Did you **use to ride** a bike when you were a child?

15.2

1 Dana used to play soccer with her friends when she was a child.

2 Chris didn't use to have such long hair.

3 I visited Prague three times when I was a child.

4 Maria used to believe in ghosts when she was little.

5 I used to know Andre well when I was a student.

15.3

1 I would **try** to save money when I was at college.

2 My brother **used** to read comics when he was a kid.

3 Did **you use to** play computer games when you were young?

4 I **didn't use** to read novels, but I really enjoy them now.

16

16.1

1 When I saw Sam earlier this morning, he **was mopping** the floor.

2 Ron and Tim **have worked** at the salon for more than 10 years.

3 Danny **didn't understand** what the man was saying.

4 When I was a kid, I **used to be scared** of spiders.

5 I love travel, but I **haven't been** to New York before.

6 I discovered the loggers **had cut down** almost all the trees.

7 Pavel went outside and **built** a snowman in the park.

8 We were delayed, and the concert **had started** by the time we arrived.

9 Ash **had been studying** Spanish for years before he moved to Madrid.

10 We **have been hiking** all morning. Let's have a break, shall we?

11 It was a beautiful day, and the sun **was shining** through the window.

16.2

1 How long have you **been studying English?**

2 Pedro has been living in his apartment **for more than six months.**

3 It had been raining all night, **and the garden was flooded.**

4 Chrissie loves trying new dishes, **but she's never tried Vietnamese food.**

5 Peter was walking home **when he bumped into an old school friend.**

6 Did you go to the new exhibition **at the museum last weekend?**

16.3

1 Aditya wasn't feeling well, so he went home.

2 You used to go to my school, didn't you?

3 How long have you been working in this office?

4 Ed had been working here for ages when I met him.

16.4

1 When I arrived at the venue, I realized I **hadn't brought** the tickets.

2 By the time we arrived at the theater, the play **had begun.**

3 I **haven't seen** that movie yet. Jon told me it's great.

4 Sophie **has been cooking** all morning. She's exhausted.

5 Harry looked great. He **was wearing** his new suit.

6 Natalia **was sunbathing** when she noticed a monkey in a tree.

7 I **didn't go** to the party on Friday. I was at a concert.

8 Len **has been decorating**. He has paint on his clothes.

9 Jamie **had been practicing** for months before yesterday's show.

⑩ I **called** my dad this morning to wish him a happy birthday.

⑪ Bill **was taking** a bath when he heard a knock at the door.

16.5

① I was sleeping soundly when my alarm clock rang.

② After we'd eaten, Marco helped me to clear the table.

③ I've been dreaming of going abroad all year. •

16.6

① It **was** my gran's birthday yesterday.

② I **used to** like mathematics, but now I prefer chemistry.

③ When I walked into the room, Juan **was talking** on the phone.

④ We were sailing to Crete when I **saw** a dolphin.

⑤ You look hot, Karen. **Have** you **been running?**

⑥ When Dan **had finished** the cleaning, he went to the park.

⑦ We **were** lost for three weeks before the helicopter spotted us.

⑧ **Have** you **lived** in this house for a long time?

⑨ I **cycled** all the way to London yesterday.

⑩ We **were walking** through the woods when we saw a bear.

⑪ When Ben was a child, he **wanted** to be an astronaut.

⑫ **Did** you **enjoy** your vacation last week?

17

17.1

① Predicción
② Plan futuro
③ Predicción
④ Plan futuro
⑤ Plan futuro
⑥ Predicción
⑦ Plan futuro

17.2

① Ted told me he's going to travel around Egypt next year.

② Ben's brought his guitar. I think he's going to sing.

③ Cal has the ball. Is he going to score?

④ I think Angela is going to fall off the ladder!

⑤ Oh dear! The waiter's going to drop all the plates.

⑥ Sam's writing on the wall. His dad's going to be furious.

⑦ Look at those clouds. I think it's going to rain.

17.3

① Is Gerald going to win the race?

② Is Aziz going to sail to Ireland?

③ Is Fiona going to teach us about statistics?

④ Are we going to run out of milk soon?

17.4

① My son **is going to cook** for us tonight.

② **Is** Jess **going to study** French at college?

③ Katie **isn't going to** teach us next year.

④ It looks like it **is going to** rain again.

⑤ **Are** they **going to** sing another song for us?

⑥ I**'m going to** sell my bike. I never use it.

⑦ Emily **is going to** fix the shower for us.

⑧ Pete **isn't going to play** rugby with us today.

⑨ Dad**'s going to get** perfume for Mom's birthday again.

18

18.1

① Ronaldo **won't go** to bed before midnight.

② The kids **will have** a great time in Florida next summer.

③ You **will love** the new coat I just bought for the winter.

④ Mia **won't eat** anything with meat in it.

⑤ My car broke down, so I **will take** the train to work today.

⑥ Eric **will want** to eat steak and fries for his dinner.

⑦ Noah **will win** the 400m race at the track competition.

⑧ My children **won't like** that flavor of ice cream.

⑨ Charlotte **will marry** her boyfriend this year.

⑩ I **will stay** at home and watch TV tonight.

⑪ Arnie **will go** swimming with Bob and Sue.

18.2

① Decisión
② Predicción
③ Promesa
④ Oferta

18.3

① I know he will win the competition.

② I will definitely wear a warm coat if it's cold.

③ The new office will certainly be an improvement.

19

19.1

① Presente
② Futuro
③ Presente
④ Presente
⑤ Futuro
⑥ Futuro
⑦ Presente
⑧ Futuro
⑨ Futuro
⑩ Presente

19.2

① The exam **is** next week. I'm nervous!

② The bus to London usually **departs** at 5pm.

③ Phil **is taking** his children to the library tomorrow.

④ Lech won't be at work tomorrow. He **is traveling** to Berlin.

⑤ I can't come to the meeting tomorrow; I **have** a doctor's appointment.

⑥ Mel and Phil **are getting** married this weekend.

19.3

① We **are going** to a party later if you want to join us.

② The train from Glasgow **arrives** at 10:15pm.

③ I **am going** fishing with my father this afternoon.

④ Terry **is working** all next weekend to earn a bit of extra money.

20

20.1

① Will you be coming into college later? **I need some help with my project.**

② In the year 3000, I think **people will be living on the moon.**

③ I can give you a lift. I'll be **driving past the library anyway.**

④ Will we be having a meeting **about the new company logo?**

⑤ I'm sure people won't be driving **flying cars in 20 years' time.**

⑥ Mia is going to be bringing her **new boyfriend to the party tonight.**

⑦ I'm working as a waiter now, but I hope **I'll be running my own restaurant in 10 years.**

⑧ Will you be playing soccer **with us this weekend?**

⑨ Enzo's studying French. He hopes **he'll be working as a translator in a few years.**

⑩ I can post your letter. I'll be going **to the post office this afternoon anyway.**

⑪ In 10 years' time, I hope **I'll be living in a nice house in the country.**

⑫ Tomorrow evening, Femi's band **are going to be performing at Funky Joe's.**

⑬ I guess Liz won't be coming to work **today. She looked terrible yesterday.**

⑭ Marco hopes that he'll be working **as an actor in a few years' time.**

⑮ Sophie will be traveling to Paris next **Thursday to see her mother.**

20.2

① Petición
② Pregunta neutra
③ Pregunta neutra
④ Pregunta neutra
⑤ Petición

20.3

① I**'ll be living** in a villa by the time I'm 40.

② Marie is **going to be talking** about the sales figures.

③ We**'ll** all **be relaxing** on the beach next week!

④ Cas **will** probably **be earning** lots of money before too long.

⑤ Is Martin **going to be playing** any of his new songs?

⑥ I think humans **will be exploring** other planets by 2050.

21.1

① Amelia **will have moved** to Cairo by the end of September.

② By the end of this year, we **will have been living** here for 25 years.

③ **Will** Pedro **have finished** the painting by the time we return?

④ The paint **will have dried** by tomorrow morning.

⑤ By four o'clock, we **will have been waiting** here for two hours.

⑥ I'm sure he **will have won** more than 10 medals by the end of the year.

⑦ I think by the end of the year Rio **will have asked** Yukio to marry him.

⑧ By the time she's 22, Suzy **will have finished** college.

⑨ We **will have completed** the project by the end of May.

⑩ Sam **will have graduated** by this time next year.

⑪ **Will** you **have finished** the assignment by early October?

⑫ How many countries **will you have visited** by the time you're 40?

⑬ By the time I'm 25, I **will have been studying** for six years.

⑭ I **will have left the country** by the time you get here.

⑮ Dan **will have retired** by the time he's 60.

⑯ By this time next week, we**'ll have been** married for a year!

⑰ Sam **will have been cooking** all day by the time the dinner's ready.

⑱ By the end of tonight, I**'ll have written** this essay.

21.2

① Don't worry. I'm sure we'll have put up the tent by sunset.

② Will Dan have made that chair by the time we come back?

③ It looks like they won't have finished the building by next month.

21.3

① Anika **will have been acting** for 10 years by the end of the year.

② I'm afraid I **won't have painted** the kitchen by the time you return.

③ By December, I **will have been** learning the piano for six months.

④ The guests **will have eaten** all the food by the time Tom arrives.

⑤ Leroy **will have turned** 18 by the end of next month.

⑥ In a year's time, Katie **will have been living** in Rome for 20 years.

22.1

① I thought Hugo would have been promoted by the end of the year.

② Pari was going to buy a kitten for her daughter.

③ Did you think you'd still be working here in 2021?

④ I thought Sam would pass the final English exam.

⑤ Penny was going to clean her house if she had time.

⑥ I knew Michelle would become a successful singer one day.

⑦ Beccy wasn't going to do the English course, was she?

22.2

① Christopher **thought he would go** traveling when **he finished** college.

② Farouk **was going to start** cycling to work in the new year.

③ I **was going to cook** dinner when I **got** home from work.

④ Pablo **had** the ball. I **thought he was going to** score.

⑤ I **was** sure Danny **would finish** the wall soon.

⑥ I **thought** Ania **would win** the athletics competition.

⑦ My sister **was going** to get a cat when she **moved** house.

⑧ The radio **said it was going to snow** tonight.

⑨ Craig **thought** he **would visit** Japan in the summer.

⑩ **We were going to see** a new band playing at Club 9000.

⑪ I **was** sure **he was going to talk** about the company's problems.

⑫ Kelly **was** sure she **was going to see** some dolphins on vacation.

23.1

① Are you meeting my sister for dinner this evening?

② They will have finished the stadium by the end of the year.

③ By August, I will have been working here for one year.

④ It's clear that Petra isn't going to win.

⑤ Derek thought he would study engineering at college.

⑥ Does the lesson begin at half past three?

⑦ In 10 years' time I'll be living in Spain.

23.2

① I thought I was going to be late, **but I made it to work just on time.**

② Tomorrow's lecture about **volcanoes will be very interesting.**

③ Tim thought the meeting **would have started by now.**

④ Sorry, I'm busy at the moment, but **I will have finished in 10 minutes.**

23.3

① Sue tells me she **is going** to start learning Spanish next year.

② You look tired. **I'll** get you some coffee.

③ Look at those clouds. **It's going to** rain soon.

④ **I'll** help you with those bags, Edith.

⑤ Look! He **is going to** ask his girlfriend to marry him.

⑥ I **am going to** see a play at the theater. I've already got the tickets.

⑦ In the future, I think people **will** travel to other planets.

⑧ **I'll** have the chocolate cake on the right, please.

23.4

① The forecast said it was going to rain later.

② If you're not careful, you'll smash a window.

③ I hope Silvia's going to sing all her hits tonight.

23.5

① Our company **is not going to** make a profit this year.

② I don't think my son **will be** an artist when he grows up.

③ I can't meet you tomorrow. **I'm playing** tennis with Antoine.

④ **We're going to miss** the beginning of the play. Let's hurry!

⑤ Sal **will have been working** at the diner for 10 years in August.

⑥ I **was going to eat** another piece of cake, but I remembered I was on a diet.

23.6

① My son thinks we will be driving flying cars in the future.

② Seb won't have finished the decorating by the time you get back.

③ Look! That child's going to fall off that wall.

④ It's Angie's party tonight. I'll bring some snacks and cakes.

⑤ The train had broken down, so I knew I was going to be late.

⑥ I'm going to buy that house I saw a couple of times last week.

⑦ Suki is joining us for dinner at the Hotel Bristol.

⑧ When I turn 40, I will have been living in Lisbon for 20 years.

⑨ I am traveling to Paris by train this afternoon.

⑩ I know! I'll buy my grandmother a new scarf.

⑪ John knew there were going to be bad delays on the trains.

⑫ Do you think you'll have finished the essay by the time I arrive?

⑬ This time next year, I hope I'll be studying medicine at college.

24

24.1
1 The alarm **is tested** once a month at my workplace.
2 The sculpture **is displayed** in the main hall.
3 The Eiffel Tower **is visited** by millions of tourists each year.
4 Lunch **is eaten** in the college cafeteria.
5 The band **is expected** to perform its greatest hits.

24.2
1 This program is used by many students.
2 Her new dress is being made by a famous designer.
3 Our apartment is cleaned every Thursday.
4 The train is usually driven by Martin.

24.3
1 The game is usually played in Central Park each September.
2 The play is being performed on stage later tonight.
3 Solar panels are being used by an increasing number of people.

24.4
1 English **is not understood** by many people here.
2 A new shopping mall **is being built** near the park.
3 Some shows **are watched** by millions of people each day.
4 The food **is being prepared** at home today.
5 The castle **is surrounded** by dense forests.
6 Our products **are** usually **dispatched** within two days.
7 Latin **is not studied** by many young people.
8 Guests **are** always **provided** with a complimentary lunch.
9 My computer **is being repaired** at the moment.
10 Kelvin **is being taugh**t how to juggle today.
11 The children **are** always **supervised** by two adults.
12 A lot of old factories **are being knocked down**.
13 The crime **is being investigated** by the police.
14 Students **are expected** to be punctual at all times.
15 I'm staying with Claire while my house is **being decorated**.
16 The play **is being performed** in French tonight.
17 That course **is** usually **taught** by Eduardo.
18 All our plastic and glass **is recycled** by the council.
19 Ron **is being investigated** for fraud.
20 My hair **is cut** by a stylist from Ecuador.
21 The car **is being washed** right now.
22 Karim's performance **is being recorded** tonight.

25

25.1
1 The temple in my town was built in 1482.
2 We couldn't use the kitchen because it was being painted.

3 Patrick was surrounded by all the books he had to read.
4 The roof was repaired by my father.
5 I was taught how to drive by my aunt.
6 John's birthday cake was made by his grandmother.
7 Our cat was being looked after by a friend.

25.2
1 When we got home, **we discovered the house had been broken into.**
2 Karen was so upset **because she hadn't been invited to the party.**
3 I hadn't been told it was Rajiv's birthday, **so I didn't have a present for him.**
4 Many houses have been damaged **by the recent hurricane.**
5 Have all the staff been informed **about tomorrow's meeting?**
6 Has your car been fixed yet? **It's been in the auto repair shop for ages!**

25.3
1 The play **was interrupted** by the smoke alarm. We had to evacuate the theater.
2 Dan's room was filthy. It **hadn't been cleaned** in weeks.
3 That old factory near my house **has been demolished**.
4 All of the plants on the balcony **have been watered**.
5 The mail **hasn't been delivered** yet. I'm still waiting.
6 Most of the forest **was cut down** last year.
7 The spy **was being followed** by two men in hats.
8 Malcolm **has been fired**. He was so lazy!

25.4
RESPUESTAS DE EJEMPLO
1 All of the cake that Jemima had made was eaten.
2 All the money from the bank's safe was stolen.
3 My brother was injured in a car accident yesterday.
4 All the tables in the restaurant have been booked.
5 Lots of tower blocks were being built in the suburbs.
6 That part of the country hadn't been explored before.
7 They were so happy that their cat had been found.
8 I wasn't informed that the office was closed on Friday.
9 All the tickets for tonight's movie have been sold.
10 That mountain has never been climbed before.
11 A lot of buildings have been destroyed by the earthquake.
12 It's cold. The window has been left open.

26

26.1
1 The new stadium **will be opened** by the president.
2 All the food **will be cooked** by our new chef, Luigi.
3 Our house **won't be finished** by the end of the year.
4 The prisoner **will be released** after 30 years.
5 **Will** the show **be presented** by a new DJ?
6 My latest novel **will be published** in January.
7 The water **will be turned off** on Thursday morning.
8 The lecture **will be given** by Professor O'Brien.
9 Dinner **will be served** in the dining room between 7 and 9pm.
10 All the laundry **will be done** by the time you get back.
11 **Will** the students **be given** a test at the end of the course?

26.2
1 I hope my house will have been sold by next month.
2 I'm sure we'll have been visited by aliens by 2100.
3 Will the dress have been altered before her wedding day?

26.3
1 By 2030, intelligent robots **will have been developed**.
2 I'm sure our car **will have been repaired** by the beginning of next week.
3 The computer **will have been replaced** before you start work.
4 I think Jane **will have been fired** by this time next year.
5 By 2050, many more galaxies **will have been discovered**.
6 Do you think the criminals **will have been caugh**t by then?
7 All our staff **will have been trained** by the end of the week.
8 **Will** the project **have been completed** by the time we return?
9 All the issues **will have been resolved** before we release the product.
10 I hope the kitchen **will have been painted** by the time we move in.
11 Our new bed **will have been delivered** by the end of the month.
12 The decision **will have been made** by Friday evening.

27.1
1. All computers should be turned off before leaving the office.
2. Protective glasses must be worn at all times.
3. We should have been told about the exam.
4. Can the meeting be postponed until later in the week?
5. All the tourists should be given a guidebook.
6. You could have been killed running across that street!
7. Our car should have been repaired weeks ago.

27.2
1. All the floors must be mopped at the end of the day.
2. That ugly building should have been demolished years ago.
3. The mountain can be climbed with the help of ropes.
4. Our forests must be protected from destruction.
5. You wouldn't have been stung if you'd remained calm.

27.3
1. Bicycles should only be ridden **if you are wearing a helmet.**
2. The dentist told me that **one of my teeth must be removed.**
3. Clara should have been given **more time to finish her assignment.**
4. Everyone should be warned that **a tiger has escaped from the zoo.**
5. The dish could have been improved **if we'd used better ingredients.**
6. The steak should be fried **for one minute on each side.**
7. The accident might have been avoided **if the car hadn't been going so fast.**

28.1
1. It has been revealed that the company is losing a lot of money.
2. That old house across the road is said to be haunted.
3. The movie star is rumored to be in a relationship with her co-star.
4. The new gallery is reported to contain a lot of modern art.
5. The mountain is known to be dangerous to climb.
6. It has been reported that many houses have been destroyed.
7. There are said to be many beautiful temples in Japan.

28.2
1. I'm hoping that I will **get promoted** to senior manager soon.
2. My colleague often **gets criticized** for the quality of her work.
3. The bedroom's **getting redecorated** next week.
4. My aunt's car **got stolen** from the parking lot at work.
5. Samantha **got bitten** by a dog in the local park.

28.3
1. This store **is known** to sell high-quality shoes.
2. It **has been reported** that Ella is going to start performing again.
3. The grass **gets cut** once a month by our gardener.
4. It **is rumored** that we are going to have an exam today.
5. All the dishes **got washed** by Danny.

29.1
1. Food tastes awful when you add too much salt.
2. If my dog gets hungry, he barks loudly.
3. If you misbehave, you get sent to detention.

29.2
1. When it gets too cold, **we light the fire.**
2. If you squeeze a balloon hard enough, **it explodes.**
3. Water boils if you **heat it long enough.**
4. Eggs usually break when **you drop them.**
5. If you keep cooling water, **it eventually freezes.**
6. If you don't pay your bills on time, **you get fined.**

29.3
1. If the phone rings, please **answer** it.
2. **Let me know** if you have any problems at all.
3. **Don't eat** it if you don't like it.
4. When you buy something expensive, always **keep** the receipt.
5. If it's sunny tomorrow, **make sure** to use sunscreen.

29.4
1. If it **stops** raining, I'll finish painting the fence.
2. If Janine works very hard, she **will pass** her exams.
3. If I **don't get** the job, I'll be very upset.
4. Sally **will lose** her job if she keeps missing deadlines.
5. If it doesn't rain tomorrow, we **will have** a picnic.
6. If I **get** a raise, I'll definitely go on an expensive vacation.
7. Sarah will go fishing on Saturday if she **has** time.
8. If we take this path, we **will get** there more quickly.

29.5
1. Phil would buy a new television if he had more money.
2. If I didn't have a headache, I'd definitely come to the party.
3. I'd visit you more often if I had more time.
4. If I was young again, I would go traveling around the world.

29.6
1. Tony would buy a villa if he won the lottery.
2. If we had more money, we would start our own business.
3. I'm sure David would help you if you asked him.
4. If Ania went traveling, she'd go to Vietnam.

29.7
1. If Fleur **had gone** to bed earlier, she **wouldn't have felt** tired all day.
2. Simon **would have gone** to jail if the police **had caught** him.
3. If Marco **had known** there was a test, he **would have studied** for it.
4. I **would have brought** an umbrella if I **had known** it was going to rain.
5. If Chris **hadn't scored**, we **wouldn't have won** the championship.
6. If I **had known** you were coming, I **would have cleaned** the apartment.
7. I **would have bough**t you a present if I **had known** it was your birthday.
8. Dom **wouldn't have been** alone on his birthday if he **had invited** his friends.
9. If I **hadn't slept** through my alarm, I **wouldn't have** arrived late for work.
10. Abbie **would have studied** art if she **had gone** to college.
11. If we **had arrived** early, we **wouldn't have missed** the train.
12. Libby **would have won** the race if she **had been** faster than Nina.
13. We **would have gone** camping if **we'd known** it was going to be so hot.
14. If Lou **hadn't worked** so hard, the project **wouldn't have been** such a success.

29.8
1. If I hadn't brought the umbrella **I'd be very wet now.**
2. If Ed had scored higher on his tests, **he'd going to a good college now.**
3. I'd be at work now **if I hadn't missed the 7am train.**
4. Chloe wouldn't be sitting outside now **if she'd remembered her key this morning.**
5. Gordon wouldn't be in prison **if he hadn't stolen the painting from the gallery.**

29.9
1. Jemma **wouldn't be** so tired now if she'd gone to bed earlier.
2. If they **had finished** the decorating, we wouldn't be sleeping in a camper.
3. If Emma **had listened** to our advice, she would be more successful now.
4. I wouldn't be such a good athlete if I **hadn't trained** so hard.
5. If Len had fixed my car, I **wouldn't be walking** to work today.
6. Tim **would love** it here if he had decided to join us.
7. Karen wouldn't have to stand if she **had reserved** a seat.
8. If I hadn't lost my job, I **wouldn't be living** with my sister.
9. If you **had kept** practicing, I'm sure you'd be a famous singer today.

29.10

1 If I **had to** make a choice, I would say I prefer dogs.

2 I **would have graduated** by now if I'd continued with my studies.

3 If you **don't hurry up**, you're going to be late for school.

4 You would have had a great time at the party if you **had come**.

5 We'd be on vacation now if we **hadn't missed** the flight.

6 When water **gets** hot enough, it boils.

7 I **will go** to the doctor if my leg still hurts tomorrow.

8 The soup **would taste** better if I had added more salt.

9 I always drink plenty of water if I **get** too hot.

10 It **would have been** a perfect party if the dog hadn't eaten the cake.

11 I **will repair** the roof this afternoon if the weather's good.

12 I **would be** very scared if I ever saw a UFO.

30

30.1

1 You **can have** an ice cream if you're really good.

2 If you'd asked her to marry you, she **might have said** yes.

3 We **could go** camping if I take a few days off work.

4 If she had practiced more, Helena **could have been** a great singer.

5 If I have some free time later, I **might do** some gardening.

30.2

1 Unless you get up now, **you're going to be late.**

2 She'll leave the firm **unless we start paying her more.**

3 Unless you turn the music down, **the neighbors will complain.**

4 You'll get sunburned **unless you wear sun protection.**

5 Unless you start working harder, **you're not going to graduate on time.**

6 Angelica will get annoyed **unless you reply to her email.**

7 Unless there's bad weather, **we'll reach the summit before noon.**

30.3

1 Had business been better, the company wouldn't have gone bankrupt.

2 Had Pamela been richer, she would have bought a larger house.

3 Had you studied harder, the exam wouldn't have been so difficult.

4 Had Paul attended the meeting, he would have known about the new project.

5 Had the weather been better, their trip would have been more enjoyable.

31

31.1

1 Second
2 First
3 Zero
4 Third
5 First
6 First
7 Zero
8 Second
9 Third
10 Second

31.2

1 If I had more money, I'd go on vacation to Rome.

2 We would have packed warmer clothes if we'd known it was so cold here.

3 They could play baseball if it stopped raining.

4 If you keep practicing, you will win the championship.

31.3

1 I would have passed the test if I'd studied.

2 If Mia had more time, she'd start a hobby.

3 If it's sunny tomorrow, I'll go swimming.

4 If you heat ice, it turns into water.

5 I'd have caught the bus if I hadn't overslept.

6 If my team doesn't win, I'll be disappointed.

7 If Mel won the lottery, she'd buy a villa.

8 If I had seen Rob, I would have said hello.

9 If I'm late again, my boss will be so angry.

10 If she had asked me, I would have helped her.

11 If you went to bed earlier, you'd feel less tired.

32

32.1

1 Probable
2 No ha sucedido
3 No ha sucedido
4 Improbable
5 No ha sucedido
6 Improbable
7 Improbable
8 Probable
9 Probable
10 Improbable

32.2

1 What if Vicky became a famous actress? **She really enjoys drama, after all.**

2 Suppose you lost your job at the café. **Where do you think you'd work?**

3 Suppose we get lost in the forest. **We may not be able to find the path.**

4 Let's prepare some more food **in case more people arrive.**

5 Take some water with you **in case you get hot while you're jogging.**

6 I'm nervous about going on stage tonight. **What if the audience don't like me?**

32.3

1 Check the gallery's website in case it is closed on Mondays.

2 Suppose the factory closed. What would the town do?

3 What if we come across a bear? There are lots of them in the mountains.

4 It's your interview tomorrow. Set an alarm in case you don't wake up.

5 What if we won the lottery? What would we do with the money?

6 Take a good book in case you get bored waiting.

33

33.1

1 I wish I had a job where I could work outside.

2 Simone wishes she'd remembered to bring her camera.

3 Martin wishes he knew how to ski.

4 Pete wishes he had a better car.

5 Ronaldo wishes he hadn't broken his guitar.

6 Joan wishes she had a lawn mower.

7 We wish it was sunny, so we could go to the beach.

33.2

1 Ya no podría suceder
2 Ya no podría suceder
3 Aún podría suceder
4 Ya no podría suceder
5 Aún podría suceder

33.3

1 I wish I **didn't work** so late all the time. I'm so tired in the evenings.

2 We're lost! We **should have planned** our route a little better.

3 Ed, I wish **you would** stop singing out of tune all the time.

4 If only **I could** cook! Everything I make is a disaster.

34

34.1

1 Are the children waiting?
2 Is there a good restaurant on Park Street?
3 Can Fu speak fluent French?
4 Is Jean going to win the game?
5 Should Peter tell Amy about the party?
6 Has Kelly bought a gift for her dad?

34.2

1 Did Anthony start his new job at the bank?
2 Does Wayne want to come to the zoo with us?
3 Did Harleen work for us a few years ago?
4 Does Henry like classical music?
5 Do Lara and Michael go to the same school?
6 Do they own the bookstore by the park?

34.3

1. Does Tina still work at the boutique?
2. Do you prefer cats or dogs?
3. Did the children enjoy the fair?
4. Did you manage to move that box?
5. Does Selma go jogging often?
6. Did you help clean up after the party?
7. Do you often go abroad on vacation?
8. Doesn't Clara have two large dogs?
9. Have you ever read *Little Women*?
10. Don't you like fast food, Phillippe?
11. Have you ever had a driving lesson?
12. Did you enjoy the art exhibition?
13. Did you remember to feed the dog?

34.4

1. **Does** Dora work in a bank?
2. **Are** your colleagues coming to the party?
3. **Do** we start work at 10am on Fridays?
4. **Does** Marlon really live in a mansion?
5. Did Bill **work** for the government?
6. **Were** there many animals in the forest?
7. **Does** Marcel come from Argentina?
8. Did you **go** to the theater last night?
9. **Have** you seen Anika's new car?
10. **Is** Tom going to finish the report today?
11. Did Bruce **live** in Glasgow?
12. **Was** John at the airport to meet you?
13. **Do** you take a shower in the evening?
14. **Is** there any juice left?
15. **Have** we got enough time left?
16. **Is** your brother coming later?
17. **Do** Claire and Sam have any children?
18. **Does** Tim play soccer on the weekend?
19. **Are** those your tools on the table?
20. Did Elsa **have** a boyfriend named Gus?
21. **Does** Ash still work at the café?
22. **Is** your daughter still in college?
23. **Has** Sheila seen your new house yet?

34.5

1. Has she finished the painting yet?
2. Have you been to India?
3. Are you coming to the party later?
4. Is Jackie still a teacher?
5. Did you remember to lock the door?

34.6

1. Has Ed lived in New York for more than 10 years?
2. Are Katia and Pavel getting married in June?
3. Did Claudia take a flight to Rio de Janeiro?
4. Does Mia go swimming every evening after work?
5. Did you remember to buy some water?
6. Are Ron and Lily playing tennis this afternoon?

35

35.1

1. **What** did you buy at the market?
2. **Why** is Lena laughing so much?
3. **Which** of these bags is yours?
4. **How** does your dad feel today?
5. **Who** is going to teach the course?
6. **Whose** car is parked outside?
7. **How** quickly can you finish it?

8. **Where** does your cousin live?
9. **When** does the hardware store close?
10. **Whose** diary is on the desk?
11. **When** did you last see Maria?
12. **How** many times has he been to Kenya?
13. **Why** did she quit the course?
14. **Where** is the entrance?
15. **Who** did you invite to the party?
16. **How** long does it take to get there?
17. **Which** car should I buy?
18. **Where** did I put my glasses?

35.2

1. Where is the classroom?
2. Whose phone is this?
3. Why did you do that?
4. How long did you wait?
5. Who did you meet earlier?
6. Which house is yours?
7. When does the movie start?

35.3

1. When did you start playing the guitar, Tom?
2. How does the soup taste, Gustav?
3. Which way do you think we should go?

35.4

1. What is the date today?
2. What's the name of your business?
3. Which train are you taking, the 1pm or the 3pm?
4. Which do you prefer, skiing or snowboarding?
5. What time are they arriving?
6. If you had to choose between dogs and cats, which would you choose?

35.5

1. How often do you read?
2. When can we have our meeting?
3. When is the movie being released?
4. How often do you perform in public?
5. When do you finish work?

35.6

1. How many people work **in your department?**
2. Where are they going **to build the new airport?**
3. Whose coat has been left **on the back of that chair?**
4. Which way is it **to the bus station?**
5. What time does **the concert start?**
6. When does the train **to Glasgow leave?**

36

36.1

1. **What would you do** if you saw a ghost?
2. **When do you think** you will finish building the house?
3. **How do you feel** after the race?
4. **How often do you** water your plants?
5. **Why do you both** look so happy?

36.2

1. What time does the train leave?
2. What is your name?
3. How was the movie?

4. When did you get this dog?
5. Why did you phone me earlier?
6. Who can speak English here?
7. Who should I call to complain?
8. When do you start work?
9. What is this button for?
10. Which dress do you prefer?
11. Why aren't you at work today?
12. What do you eat for breakfast?
13. Where does David live?

36.3

1. What **is she going** to sing for us next?
2. Where **did you buy** that lovely dress?
3. What **happened** to your leg, Paul?
4. **Whose** bicycle is that in the yard?
5. Why **do you have to** watch so much TV?
6. How **do you feel** about losing your job?
7. Where **do you cycle** to on Sundays?
8. How many times **have you visited** New York?
9. Why **are you** so angry, Anthony?
10. How old **are the twins** today?
11. What time **do you eat** your lunch?
12. When **did you last go** camping, Sam?

37

37.1

1. I went with an old friend from school.
2. An artist from Australia painted it.
3. It was a present from my boyfriend.
4. We saw a play by William Shakespeare.
5. I'm going to have fish and chips.
6. Angelica. She has so much experience.
7. There was a terrible storm last week.

37.2

1. Pregunta de sujeto
2. Pregunta de sujeto
3. Pregunta de objeto
4. Pregunta de sujeto
5. Pregunta de sujeto
6. Pregunta de objeto
7. Pregunta de objeto

37.3

1. Who **played golf** with you yesterday?
2. What **did you see** at the movies last night?
3. Who **married** Sonia at the end of the movie?
4. What **did you catch** while fishing yesterday?

37.4

1. Who **did I see** you playing golf with on Sunday?
2. Who **stole** the money from the bank?
3. Who **left** this terrible mess?
4. What **are you going** to wear to the wedding?
5. Who **lives** in that huge castle?
6. What **did you give** the cat to eat?
7. Who **won** the race this afternoon?

38

38.1
1. Do you know **what time the lesson begins**?
2. Do you know **where the bus station is**?
3. Could you tell me **how to get to the national gallery**?
4. Do you know **how much a ticket to Oslo costs**?
5. Could you tell me **if breakfast is still being served**?
6. Could you tell me **why this is so expensive**?
7. Do you know **whether the train goes to Swansea**?

38.2
1. Could you tell me where Lizzy lives?
2. Do you know why the school is closed?
3. Do you know if the course has begun yet?
4. Could you tell me why you did that?

38.3
1. Do you know if Emma has brushed the yard?
2. Could you tell me whose that old car is?
3. Do you know if the car will be ready by 5pm?
4. Could you tell me where the station is?
5. Do you know when you will finish the report?

39

39.1
1. Brian was a Spanish teacher, **wasn't he?**
2. Mark is Mike's cousin, **isn't he?**
3. There aren't any tickets left, **are there?**
4. There's a nice café near the park, **isn't there?**
5. That was such an exciting movie, **wasn't it?**
6. It's not going to rain today, **is it?**

39.2
1. Your grandmother likes tea, **doesn't she?**
2. Gerald has finished the gardening, **hasn't he?**
3. Luca didn't pass the English exam, **did he?**
4. Carla worked in a bakery, **didn't she?**
5. We should buy a new fridge, **shouldn't we?**
6. You haven't seen my glasses, **have you?**
7. Mike can swim, **can't he?**

39.3
1. The hat on the left is gorgeous, **isn't it?**
2. That ride was really scary, **wasn't it?**
3. You're Daniel's cousin, **aren't you?**
4. I think our team's going to win, **isn't it?**
5. We aren't going to catch our plane, **are we?**
6. You've read that book before, **haven't you?**
7. The guests don't look very happy, **do they?**
8. Bill plays the guitar really well, **doesn't he?**
9. Chloe will do the shopping for you, **won't she?**
10. I should have brought an umbrella, **shouldn't I?**
11. Martin doesn't like cooking much, **does he?**
12. Paul looks absolutely exhausted, **doesn't he?**
13. We've been waiting here for 30 minutes, **haven't we?**
14. You're not listening to anything I say, **are you?**

40

40.1
1. Does he?
2. Did you?
3. Isn't it?
4. Have you?
5. Did she?
6. Is she?
7. Hasn't he?
8. Was it?
9. Is he?

41

41.1
1. Yes, there is.
2. No, I don't.
3. No, we won't.
4. Yes, I do.
5. Yes, we are.
6. Yes, there were.
7. Yes, he can.
8. No, I haven't.
9. No, I wouldn't.

42

42.1
1. Is Joe playing tennis on Thursday?
2. Have they knocked down the apartment block?
3. Is Jean-Paul learning to cook?
4. Is Rob going to win the race?
5. Does Chrissy do exercises each morning?
6. Will they play all their greatest hits?
7. Did Claire and Ben get married last week?
8. Does Aziz work late every evening?
9. Did Jessica take the dog for a walk?

42.2
PREGUNTAS DE SUJETO:
Who wrote this book?
What happened next?
Who called earlier?
Who drove you to work?
PREGUNTAS DE OBJETO:
Who did you invite?
What did you buy?
Who do you live with?
What does John do for work?

42.3
1. Pregunta abierta
2. Pregunta cerrada
3. Pregunta cerrada
4. Pregunta abierta
5. Pregunta cerrada
6. Pregunta cerrada

43

43.1
1. Emilia said she wanted to come to the park with us.
2. She said her husband was from Alabama.
3. He said it was extremely hot in Adelaide.
4. She told me that she was a lawyer.
5. My son said he wanted to quit school.
6. Our boss told us we had to work harder.
7. They told me they owned a villa in Spain.

43.2
1. She told me she was a Canadian citizen.
2. Rob said he had won a huge amount of money.
3. Ella said that Phil's 18th birthday party was great fun.
4. Ted told me he went backpacking around Europe last year.

43.3
1. She **said** that she **traveled** around the world a lot for work.
2. She **told** me that her new boyfriend **was** from Ethiopia.
3. Silvio **told** Maria that he **lived** in Milan with his family.
4. Mike **said** that he **felt** sick, so he went home.
5. She **told** me that her brother **worked** in a travel agency.

44

44.1
1. Jan said she would give me a call later that evening.
2. Benedict said he was seeing his grandma later that day.
3. George told me he'd arrived at the hotel hours earlier.
4. Matt and Mable said they were going to the movies to see a thriller.
5. Danny said he couldn't afford to come on vacation with us this summer.
6. Gemma told me that my new dress looked great.
7. Katie said she'd give the camera back to me the next day.

44.2
1. Archie told me that his car had broken down.
2. Betty said she'd seen a wolf in the woods last year.
3. Malcolm told Mel that he works in a salon.

44.3
1. Cath told me she **had** posted the letter a few days ago.
2. The weather forecast said it **was** going to be sunny yesterday.
3. Angela told me she **had** already mowed the lawn.
4. Miles told us that the company **was** losing money before it went bankrupt.

5 In February, Lisa told me that she **had had** a great idea for a vacation.
6 Emil said he **would** visit me in Japan that summer.

44.4
1 Harry told me they were going to the zoo on Thursday.
2 The shop assistant told me they didn't have a shirt in my size.
3 Michelle said she didn't want to go to the party last night.
4 The manager said the hotel was fully booked in July.
5 Jenny told me that she'd worked on a farm when she was a student.
6 Billy's mom said he would pass all his exams.
7 Robert told me he was writing a novel set in Ancient Rome.
8 She said that she lives in a house near the bus station.
9 Carlo said he was going to buy a new car that afternoon.

45

45.1
1 Don **reminded me to buy** some milk on the way home.
2 My parents **encouraged me to study** medicine in college.
3 Tina's sister **explained that she would be** late to the recital.

45.2
1 Wayne admitted that it was the first time he'd made pancakes.
2 Archie's boss threatened to fire him if he didn't work harder.
3 Sergio asked me to marry him while we were on vacation.

46

46.1
1 Pedro explained that he **didn't work on Fridays.**
2 Paul's mom told him **not to draw on the walls.**
3 Monika reminded me **not to forget my passport.**
4 I said that I didn't want **to drive to the restaurant.**
5 I told my brother I couldn't **come because I was feeling ill.**

46.2
1 My colleague mentioned that the printer wasn't working.
2 Mark explained that he didn't like dogs.
3 Myra phoned to say that she wasn't coming to the meeting.
4 Jon tried to persuade me not to eat any more cake.

47

47.1
1 The artist asked us what we thought of his painting.
2 Georges asked me if I'd ever been to Paris.
3 Dave asked if I'd like to go fishing with him.
4 Jon asked me why I was dressed as a clown.
5 Mom asked if I'd done the dishes yet.
6 My stylist asked me what I wanted.
7 The waiter asked me what I wanted to drink.

47.2
RESPUESTAS DE EJEMPLO
1 He asked me **where you live.**
2 Sue asked me **what I think.**
3 Amy asked us **if she should bring something.**
4 Paul asked **why I left.**
5 They asked me **where I had been.**
6 The girl asked me **where the station is.**
7 She asked **where the exit was.**
8 Mia asked me **if I own a car.**
9 They asked me **who he is.**

47.3
1 Peter asked **if you were coming to the** performance later.
2 My teacher asked **me if I'd decided to** study math at college.
3 Lou asked **me where I wanted to go** on Saturday.
4 The waiter asked **if we wanted to order** more drinks.
5 Susan asked **me what time we usually have** our lunch break.
6 She asked **me if I wanted to go to the** movies with her.
7 Claire asked **her kids if they wanted mint or** strawberry ice cream.
8 Fran asked **how long we had lived in** San Francisco.
9 Pete asked **whether I could help him move house** this weekend.

47.4
1 Paul asked if he **could** borrow my T-shirt.
2 Danny wanted to know if it **is raining / was raining** here.
3 Hiroshi asked whether you **are coming** to the lecture later today.
4 Shona asked me if I **would post** this letter for her.
5 My granddaughter asked me how long **have been knitting / I had been knitting** for.
6 Antonia asked me where you **are living** at the moment.
7 Greg asked me who the singer **is / was** in the band we saw last night.
8 I asked the architect if he knew when they **are going to finish / were going to finish** the block.
9 Ella asked me who **won / had won** the marathon yesterday.
10 My children asked me today if I **believe / believed** in ghosts.
11 Patsy wanted to know who **directed / had directed** the new comedy.

48

48.1
1 Steph told me that she really missed her friends and family.
2 Les told me Christine had paid for lunch the previous week.
3 Rohan tells me he really doesn't want to work this Saturday.
4 Mia told Dan that her daughter dreamed of becoming an actor.
5 Jiya once told me she'd be a famous singer by 2015.
6 Lou told me they were going to the theater the following day.
7 Angela tells me she's never been to the Tower of London.

48.2
1 Ruth explained why the results were so bad.
2 Phil said he'd finish the garden last Wednesday.
3 Carla asked whether she could leave the office early.
4 Liam told me he had visited Paris the previous year.
5 Ken asked Katie if she wanted to dance with him.

48.3
1 Karen told me she was going to Vietnam for her honeymoon.
2 Mike said he wanted to be a police officer when he was a kid.
3 Sophia mentioned that she has a spare ticket.

49

49.1
1 Principal
2 Auxiliar
3 Auxiliar
4 Auxiliar
5 Principal
6 Principal
7 Auxiliar
8 Principal
9 Auxiliar
10 Principal

49.2
1 You **should** call your grandma. It's her birthday.
2 The students **have** all handed in their papers.
3 Sandra **isn't** coming to the party tonight.
4 My son **could** already swim when he was three.
5 I **had** already left by the time Jim arrived.
6 I **didn't** like her boyfriend. He was rude.
7 You **mustn't** speak so loudly in the library.

49.3

TRANSITIVOS:
want, bring, throw
INTRANSITIVOS:
arrive, come, smile

50

50.1

1. Acción
2. Estado
3. Acción
4. Acción
5. Estado
6. Estado
7. Acción

50.2

1. We **know** Jenny very well.
2. This soup **tastes** awful.
3. Chris **wants** an ice cream.
4. Our vacation **cost** a lot of money.
5. Craig **understands** Spanish.
6. I **recognized** that man.
7. My son **hates** vegetables.
8. Dom's pie **smelled** great.
9. Your book **sounds** interesting.

50.3

VERBOS DE ACCIÓN:
try, read, eat, kick, drive
VERBOS DE ESTADO:
be, contain, know, hear, own

50.4

1. Fatima **is writing** a book about her childhood.
2. It **is raining** outside. Let's watch something on TV.
3. Marco **is playing** guitar on stage now.
4. Rosita **has** two sisters, who live in the United States.
5. Claude **hates** all salad and vegetables.
6. I **am reading** a travel guide to Los Angeles.

51

51.1

1. **plan** planning **planned**
2. play **playing played**
3. **do** doing **done**
4. **like** liking **liked**
5. **find finding** found
6. **write writing** written
7. finish **finishing finished**
8. **buy buying** bought
9. read **reading read**
10. **tell telling** told
11. **hope hoping** hoped
12. swim **swimming swum**
13. **go going** gone
14. **cry** crying **cried**
15. **begin** beginning **begun**
16. **say saying** said
17. **love** loving **loved**

51.2

1. Carla has **finished** all of her assignments.
2. Marsha's **planning** a surprise party for Ed.
3. Marion is **going** to get married this fall.
4. We hadn't **planned** to stay in, but it started raining.
5. We want **to go** to the art exhibition tomorrow.

51.3

1. **Writing** new vocabulary in a notebook helps me to remember it.
2. Tim's English teacher asked if he'd **done** his homework.
3. My husband keeps **forgetting** his keys. It's so frustrating.
4. My children don't **want to go** to school this morning.
5. I go **swimming** most weekends with my friends.
6. Everyone had **sung** Happy Birthday by the time I arrived.

52

52.1

1. I finally **managed** to buy a house after saving for years.
2. Alberto has **finished** painting the landscape.
3. We **arranged** to meet for a drink after work.
4. My brother **considered** buying a sports car when he turned 40.
5. I really **enjoyed** meeting your friends at the party.

52.2

1. My dad has decided to start studying Spanish.
2. My colleague offered to help me finish the report.
3. I really enjoy running on the weekend.

52.3

1. Carlo enjoys **going** to the theater each Friday.
2. Rob and Phil intend **to buy** a house this year.
3. Ellie is planning **to visit** Sydney while she's in Australia.
4. I don't feel like **playing** football this evening.
5. Margo refused **to eat** the ice cream Jed offered her.
6. My boss agreed **to let** me go home early from work.

52.4

1. I wish I hadn't told Jon about my job.
2. I was driving home when I decided to stop for a cup of coffee.
3. I will remember to pick Angela up later from the airport later.
4. Do you remember the time you first met Paul at the conference?
5. I used to drink coffee, but I decided to stop a long time ago.

6. The professor thanked the organizers and then talked about the experiment.
7. You were supposed to meet Paul. Did you remember to do that?
8. I'll always remember when I saw Angela for the first time.
9. The professor was talking about the experiment and continued to do so.

53

53.1

1. Alfred spends a lot of time playing golf after work.
2. Janice watched the kids playing in the park.
3. Marco tried to sell his old car to me.
4. My boss wants me to work more quickly.
5. Helena heard people talking in the room next door.
6. My aunt borrowed a lot of money from my dad.
7. My mom wants me to clean my room immediately.
8. Hanif asked me to help him use the new software.
9. Yuri bought an ice cream for his girlfriend.
10. Tom reminded Peter to buy some tickets for the concert.

53.2

1. My parents expect me to keep my room clean.
2. Gus's boss allows him to finish early on Fridays.
3. Danny watched the children playing on the lawn.
4. Don reminded me to phone my grandmother.
5. The principal told us to walk more slowly.
6. I can imagine Katie becoming an actor one day.
7. Ravi spent his summer lying on the beach.
8. Eleanor wants her dog to be more friendly.
9. Mona asked me to buy some milk from the store.

54

54.1

1. Emma is talking **about** quitting her job.
2. Ania finally admitted **to** stealing the jewelry.
3. My dad tried to prevent me **from** studying art in college.
4. Our company believes **in** doing the best possible job.
5. Frank apologized **for** forgetting my birthday.
6. I want to ask my tutor **about** doing the exam again.
7. We congratulated Sandra **on** winning the competition.
8. Paul objected **to** Danny eating a burger in the office.
9. We decided **against** buying a house in the country.

⑩ We're all looking forward **to** visiting you soon.
⑪ I need to concentrate **on** passing all my exams this spring.
⑫ Peter is worrying **about** his interview tomorrow.
⑬ The council banned people **from** taking dogs onto the beach.
⑭ Chloe accused me **of** stealing her idea for the presentation.
⑮ Leo's parents tried to stop him **from** marrying the girl he loved.

55

55.1
① It's taken me a long time to get over this cold.
② Tony works out at the local gym each evening.
③ My mother takes care of my sons on Fridays.
④ We checked into the hotel and went to our room.
⑤ I've heard from Bill. He's got some shocking news.
⑥ I get along very well with my brother.
⑦ I meet up with my friends most weekends.

55.2
① Jen and Hugo eat out very often.
② You should try it on before buying it.
③ The music was loud so I turned it down.
④ I've always looked up to my brother.
⑤ We've run out of milk.
⑥ We checked into the hotel at noon.
⑦ Rob meets up with Nina on Fridays.
⑧ Does Pete always show up on time?
⑨ I was annoyed because he woke me up.
⑩ I'm staying in to watch the game tonight.
⑪ Sharon handed in her essay early.
⑫ The caterpillar turned into a butterfly.
⑬ It's heavy. Please help me pick it up.

55.3
① Ramon is **getting over** the flu.
② It was lovely **to hear from you.**
③ She told the children **to sit down.**
④ Here's your coat. **Put it on please.**
⑤ We need **to check into the hotel.**
⑥ I spotted a coin and **picked it up.**
⑦ Riku **gets up** at 9:30am on Saturdays.
⑧ The baby's crying. **You woke him up.**
⑨ I love cooking so I **don't eat out often.**
⑩ The café has **run out** of coffee.
⑪ Femi **grew up** in New York.
⑫ The airplane **takes off** in one hour.

55.4
① I work out in the gym most evenings.
② Camila really looks up to her English teacher.
③ Rachel takes after her father.
④ It's so hard to keep up with Libby.
⑤ We ran out of food so I made some more.
⑥ I didn't get on with my brother when we were young.
⑦ We got back from our trip to Wales on Thursday.
⑧ I usually get up later on the weekend.
⑨ My dad's car is always breaking down.

55.5
SEPARABLES:
turn on, **throw away**, **fill up**, **wake up**
INSEPARABLES:
do without, **get through**, **go over**, **come across**

55.6
① A break on the coast sounds like the ideal **getaway.**
② There has been another **outbreak** of the disease in the city.
③ The café was a **rip-off**! We paid $20 for a bowl of soup.
④ After the **downpour**, the sun came out again.
⑤ It's important to make a **backup** of any work you do.
⑥ There have been so many **dropouts** from the course this year.
⑦ All the students were given a **handout** with important information.
⑧ Following her **break-up** with Charlie, Ola was very unhappy.
⑨ We haven't had **snowfall** like this for years. There's snow and ice everywhere.

56

56.1
① You should learn how to use a computer.
② Could I have another piece of cake?
③ You must not run in the corridor.
④ My sister can speak four languages fluently.
⑤ Can I give you a hand with your shopping?
⑥ Could you lend me your pen for a moment?
⑦ That letter must be from Ken's college.

56.2
① You mustn't be late for work again.
② Can I get you a drink?
③ Can I help you with your bag?

56.3
① Can I help you clean up?
② Should Phil study math in college?
③ Can Graham play the violin?
④ Does Peter have to go to the meeting?
⑤ Can she have another chocolate?
⑥ Could Angela drive us to the party?

56.4
① Leroy can't repair your oven.
② My grandma couldn't speak Welsh.
③ You shouldn't eat more red meat.
④ Louisa can't swim well.
⑤ Students don't have to wear uniforms.
⑥ You can't have another piece of cake.

57

57.1
① Jamie can't lift that box. I'll help him.
② Emma can make beautiful dresses.
③ I can't solve this. It's too difficult.
④ Chris can repair your car.
⑤ I can't climb that mountain.
⑥ Rita can cook the most amazing dishes.
⑦ Chloe can speak three languages.

57.2
① Jonathan can play the guitar.
② We can't open the door.
③ Amy can sing really well.
④ Lizzie cannot drive a car.
⑤ Femi can climb trees.
⑥ Marion can speak five languages.
⑦ Derek can't move that piano.

57.3
① My grandmother could **make wonderful cakes.**
② I couldn't fix your phone. **You need a new one.**
③ When I was a child, **I could run much faster.**
④ Martha could play the piano **when she was four years old.**
⑤ I couldn't come to the party **because I felt ill.**
⑥ When she was six, **Jen could already speak six languages.**

57.4
① I'll be able to speak it fluently by the summer.
② I won't be able to take my flight without it.
③ In the future we'll be able to travel to other planets.
④ I'm hoping I will be able to fix it soon.

58

58.1
① Formal
② Informal
③ Formal
④ Informal
⑤ Formal
⑥ Formal
⑦ Informal

58.2
① Petición
② Ofrecimiento
③ Petición
④ Ofrecimiento
⑤ Petición
⑥ Petición
⑦ Ofrecimiento

58.3
① Can I take your coat?
② May I take your order?
③ Shall I carry it for you?

58.4
1. **Could I sit** here, please?
2. **May I make** an appointment, please?
3. **Could I have** a piece of your pizza?
4. **Can I get** you something to drink?
5. **Can I have** the chicken and a salad, please?
6. **Could you tell** me the way to the museum?

59

59.1
1. You should take it out for a walk.
2. You should put on some sunscreen.
3. You should try talking to a native speaker.
4. He should join a club or take up a hobby.
5. She should try to relax before bed.
6. You could make a little card for her as a gift.
7. He should eat less cake and exercise more.
8. You should go home and get some sleep.
9. You should try to save money regularly.

59.2
1. It's going to rain. You **had better** take an umbrella.
2. The train's been cancelled. We **had better** take a taxi.
3. It's icy outside. You **had better not** drive tonight.
4. I'm late for the meeting. I **had better** call my boss.

59.3
1. If I were you I'd try jogging.
2. You really must visit the castle.
3. You ought to go to the barbershop.
4. He should get a cat. They're quite independent.
5. You could wear jeans and a shirt.

60

60.1
1. You have to go. It's about the new IT system.
2. You must call her right away!
3. You won't have to do any when the summer break comes!
4. In that case, you don't have to take your medication any longer.
5. The council must do something to stop people from littering.
6. I have to keep to the speed limit.
7. Yes, all our workers must wear a helmet at all times.
8. He had to go home because his daughter's unwell.
9. You must not lift anything heavy for two weeks.

60.2
1. I **don't have to** wear a suit for work, but I wear one anyway.
2. I'm staying in bed because I **don't have to** go to work today.
3. You **must not** stay in the sun too long. You'll get burned.
4. You **must not** touch that pan. It's hot.
5. You **don't have to** be great at tennis to enjoy it.
6. I have a secret, but you **must not** tell anyone else.

60.3
1. Everyone will have to leave before 5pm.
2. You will have to inform your manager.
3. Brenda will have to go home early today.
4. She will have to pay for the damage.

60.4
1. The managers had to apologize.
2. Greg had to eat all the broccoli.
3. Joe had to work very hard today.
4. I had to rest all this week.

61

61.1
1. It looks like Sam could win this race.
2. Look! Janet must have passed her driving test.
3. He can't be the plumber. He's wearing a suit.

61.2
1. Alina drank all the water. She **must** have been really thirsty.
2. I can't read this. I **might** need new glasses.
3. Ben **can't** have stolen the vase. He was with me all evening.
4. The journey home takes ages. The children **must** be so bored.
5. I can't find my wallet. I **must** have dropped it somewhere.

61.3
1. I can't find my purse. I **might have left it on** the bus.
2. I keep sneezing. I think I **might have a** cold.
3. Veronika is crying. She **must have failed** her test.
4. What's that animal with brown fur? It **could be a bear**.

61.4
1. That must be so interesting.
2. There might be a burglar downstairs.
3. It must have cost a lot of money.
4. She can't be feeling very happy.
5. You can't have followed the recipe properly.

62

62.1
1. It looks like my team **might win** tonight's game!
2. I **might take** some driving lessons if I can afford them.
3. I think the train **might have been** canceled.
4. I can't find my keys. I **might have left** them at work.
5. If you don't hurry you **might miss** the deadline!

6. I think we **might be** lost. We had better ask someone.
7. I **might not finish** the building by the end of the year.

62.2
1. I might have forgotten to turn off the iron.
2. The forecast said it might snow later.
3. Karl might not come to the party this evening.
4. Jon may have gone away for the weekend.

62.3
1. I might not be able to come to the movies.
2. I might go to the zoo next weekend.
3. Sue might be delayed because of the traffic.
4. It looks like it might rain later.

63

63.1
1. Russia is **a** huge country. It took me seven days to cross it by train.
2. While hiking in Scotland, I spotted **an** eagle soaring above us.
3. Bill took me on **a** date to **the** most expensive bar in town.
4. Where can you get **a** good cup of coffee in **the** evening?
5. **The** food in Italy was absolutely delicious.
6. When I was **a** child, I wanted to be **an** actor.
7. **The** first train to Madrid leaves at 4:30 from platform 4.
8. It's going to rain this evening. Don't forget to take **an** umbrella.
9. Do you live in **a** house or **an** apartment?
10. I saw **a** wolf and **a** bear in Canada. **The** bear was catching fish.
11. Neil Armstrong was **the** first man to set foot on **the** moon.
12. Last week, I went to see **a** show with my cousin.
13. My brother used to be **a** chef. He's **an** optician now.
14. While I was in Rome, I visited **the** Colosseum.
15. **The** cakes in that bakery are the best in town.
16. I had **a** cup of coffee and **a** croissant. **The** coffee was cold, though.
17. Is there **a** good hotel where I can stay in your town?
18. **The** book that I just finished was really interesting.

63.2
1. **There are some mugs** in the dishwasher.
2. I have **some pencils** here.
3. **There are some sandwiches** for you.
4. Mary has **some beautiful dresses**.
5. Hassan caught **some big fish**.
6. **There are some cafés** in town.
7. There **are some watches** on the counter.
8. Marco climbed **some high mountains**.
9. **There are some bags** in the kitchen.
10. **There are some people** running outside.
11. There **are some big hotels** by the shore.
12. Ola sang **some beautiful songs**.

63.3

1. Clara works in **an** office.
2. Do you have **any** brothers or sisters?
3. There are **some** banks on my street.
4. There aren't **any** cookies in the cupboard.
5. Is there **a** hospital near here?
6. We visited **an** interesting exhibition today.
7. Are there **any** good restaurants nearby?
8. London is **a** very big city.
9. Is there **a** swimming pool in your town?
10. There aren't **any** students in the classroom.
11. There are **some** nice cafés near my house.
12. I tasted **the** best pasta while I was on vacation.

63.4

1. The president is visiting the **north of the country next week.**
2. The rich always complain **that they don't earn enough.**
3. The buildings in the **capital are really beautiful.**
4. The coffee in this café **is the best in town.**
5. I had a great trip, but **the weather was disappointing.**
6. The press were waiting **outside the star's apartment.**

63.5

1. Children start school when they are seven in my country.
2. The children wanted to know the way to the school.
3. Bears often visit people's yards to look for food.
4. Residents were warned that there could be a flood soon.

63.6

1. My sister-in-law is a doctor at the local hospital.
2. The perfume you bought for your wife is in my bag.
3. Try not to get water all over the bathroom floor.
4. I'm going to climb the highest mountain in my country.
5. You really should go to bed. You're exhausted.
6. The food was excellent during our trip to Morocco.
7. The phone has been ringing all morning.
8. Is there a museum I can visit in your town?
9. I rode an elephant when I visited India last year.
10. You might see lions while you're on safari.
11. Christopher has a hot dog for lunch every day.
12. I ride my bike to the office each morning.
13. Only rich people can afford to go to that restaurant.

64

64.1

1. It's so warm outside. I'm going to invite **some** friends over for a barbecue.
2. **The** new secretary seems good but doesn't have much experience.
3. I read **some** really good books during my last vacation.
4. What happened in **the** kitchen? It's such a mess.

5. The shirt Liam bought for **the** party cost more than $80.
6. My cousin has **a** really friendly dog.
7. While walking in the park, I spotted **a** rare bird.
8. I have **a** lot of friends who still live with their parents.
9. Paula has left **some** money on **the** kitchen table for you.
10. I think Brazil would be **a** fascinating country to visit.
11. I've just baked **some** cupcakes. Would you like to try one?
12. **The** cake you made for the fair was absolutely delicious.
13. My family's big. I have three brothers and a sister.
14. **The** blue whale is **the** biggest animal that has ever existed.
15. I asked **the** waiter for **a** large cup of coffee.
16. **The** saxophone is **a** difficult instrument to play.
17. India is **the** country I'd most like to visit.
18. We saw **a** bear on our trip through **the** mountains.

64.2

1. I don't go to work on Fridays. I look after my young son.
2. My son rides **a** bike to school each day.
3. In my country, people usually retire when they're about 60.
4. Colm works as **a** scientist at a large research centre.
5. You should make sure you get plenty of sleep before **the** exam tomorrow.
6. Irma buys her paint from the store by **the** café.
7. Bill got married to **a** woman he met at work.
8. **The** band I went to see last night was awful.
9. I'm still in touch with the friends I made while on vacation.
10. My aunt thought she saw **a** wolf in the woods today.
11. **The** shoes I bought yesterday are far too big.
12. My mom says that cats are much cleaner than dogs.
13. While I was traveling in Australia, I saw **a** kangaroo.
14. **The** president gave **a** long speech at the conference.

65

65.1

1. **This** is my new boyfriend, Dan.
2. **That** book is so interesting.
3. **That** was such a tasty pizza!
4. I'd like **those** grapes, please.
5. Do you like **this** shirt?
6. I want to see **that** movie tonight.
7. **These** are your glasses, right here.
8. Where did you buy **those** jeans?
9. Is **this** my cup of coffee?
10. **Those** shoes look great on you!
11. **This** is the perfect car for a family.
12. Is **that** your new motorcycle, Andy?

13. Who made **these** cakes?
14. **These** are my parents, Anna and Charles.
15. **This** wardrobe's so heavy!

65.2

1. That is my new house. It's just by the ocean.
2. This is your desk and computer.
3. That was an amazing goal. You should have seen it!

65.3

1. Those boots really suit you.
2. This is one of the best books I've read.
3. I'm sure I've seen this movie before.
4. I don't think this meat is cooked properly.

65.4

1. That is one of the most beautiful **castles that I've ever seen.**
2. I'll have a half kilo of those potatoes and **a bag of these apricots, please.**
3. Your most important role is **that of spokesperson for our company.**
4. The cars we drive today are safer **than those our parents used to drive.**
5. I like these jeans here, but I prefer **those with the stripe on them over there.**
6. This is the best coffee I've **ever had. It's absolutely delicious.**

66

66.1

1. We had no time to make lunch, so we went out for burgers instead.
2. I've missed the train again. I'm having no luck this week!
3. None of the clothes I tried on suited me.
4. We wanted a room with a view, but the receptionist said that there were none available.
5. I couldn't call you because there was no reception where I was.
6. I wanted to order apple pie, but there was none left.
7. None of my friends believed I saw a ghost.

66.2

1. There **aren't any** free seats.
2. I **have no** money left.
3. There **weren't any** more tickets.
4. Kinga **doesn't have any** friends at work.
5. It **takes no** time to get there.
6. There **was no** doubt that he did it.

66.3

1. **No** vegetarian food had been ordered for the convention.
2. There are **no** places left on the English course.
3. **None** of the staff wanted to work on Saturdays.
4. Amelia wanted to buy salad, but there wasn't **any** in the shop.
5. There was **no** time to think about the exam questions.
6. I called five hotels, but **none** had a free room for tonight.

7 There wasn't **any** milk left, so I went to the shops.
8 I had **no** energy left after work, so I watched some TV.
9 **None** of my friends wanted to go see a movie with me.
10 There weren't **any** seats free on the train home.
11 I wanted to try one of Sarah's cakes, but there were **none** left.
12 **No** dentists were available to see me, so I went home.

67

67.1
1 David and his wife visit the Poconos every March.
2 I go to the Indian restaurant in town every Monday.
3 Each of us was given a sandwich and a drink.
4 Every morning, Luis buys a coffee before work.
5 This shampoo works for every type of hair.
6 Each member of the team was given a prize.
7 Maddy gave each of her children a thousand dollars.

67.2
1 I go hiking with my dog every summer.
2 Mona has a different type of earring in each ear.
3 Our boss spoke to each employee in turn about the redundancies.
4 Each player was given a medal by the president.

67.3
1 Our manager has spoken to **each employee about the factory closing.**
2 We gave every child at the party **a present and some cake.**
3 My sister loves jewelry and **wears a bracelet on each wrist.**
4 Every Thursday, I play golf **with one of my work colleagues.**
5 Oscar makes sure he does **some exercise every morning.**
6 The bakery near my house sells **every kind of bread you can think of.**
7 Each city we visited in Spain **had incredibly beautiful architecture.**
8 Every time I hear that song, I **remember the first time I heard it.**
9 I love that author. I've read **every one of her books.**

68

68.1
1 **Neither** Dan nor Belinda could remember the way to the theater.
2 **Both** of my brothers go hiking in the hills on the weekend.
3 **Neither** of us could resist another piece of cake.
4 Janet could afford to buy **either** the skirt or the dress.

5 I invited **both** Sheila and Bill to my apartment in Paris.
6 **Both** Steve and Louis work really hard in their English class.
7 Let's eat out **either** on Wednesday or Thursday.
8 **Neither** of the managers were at the meeting, unfortunately.
9 I had to take **both** the cat and the dog to the veterinarian.
10 Ramon can play **both** the electric and acoustic guitar.
11 Chetana didn't really like **either** of the paintings on sale.

68.2
1 Neither Gabriela nor Carlos came **to the party last night.**
2 My niece wants to be either an **actress or an accountant.**
3 Lisa wants both a puppy **and a laptop for her birthday.**
4 Neither the apple pie nor **the cheesecake appealed to my aunt.**
5 I want to see either an action film **or a comedy tonight.**
6 Both my brother and sister **still live with our parents.**
7 Neither the electricity nor the water **works properly in my new house.**

68.3
1 Either my cousin or my parents **are** going to pick you up from the airport.
2 Neither Paula's car nor her bike **is** working properly.
3 I hope either the steak or the fish **is** on the menu today.
4 Both the food and the drink **were** really overpriced.
5 Neither my brother nor my sister **is** coming tomorrow.
6 Either a cat or a dog **makes** a great pet for a family.
7 Neither of us **wants** to go to the conference.
8 I don't really like either of the **dresses** she bought.
9 Neither the boss nor the workers **were** pleased about the deal.
10 We're thinking about adopting both of the **puppies** we saw.

69

69.1
1 car
2 castle
3 chess
4 thought
5 waterfall

69.2
NOMBRES COMUNES:
town, flower, hope, scissors
NOMBRES PROPIOS:
France, September, George, Jupiter

69.3
1 When I finished my dinner, I washed all the **dishes**.
2 I bought my new **watch** in Switzerland.
3 A lot of **people** were waiting on the platform.
4 We need to protect endangered **species**.

69.4
1 Tim asked to borrow the **dictionary**.
2 The **trains** always **leave** on time.
3 The **women were** talking about the past.
4 The mayor visited the **factory** in our city.
5 I think there **is a mouse** in the kitchen.
6 **Those stories were** wonderful.
7 The **sheep was** standing in the road.
8 The **boxes are** full. We need to buy more.
9 Carla rested her **foot** on a cushion.
10 Ellie asked the **man** for directions.
11 Maria put her **babies** into the **cots**.

70

70.1
CONTABLES:
question, apple, city
INCONTABLES:
sugar, knowledge, money

70.2
1 Is there a bag of rice in the pantry?
2 Can you get a carton of juice?
3 Would you like a piece of cheese?

70.3
1 **There's some** milk in the fridge.
2 I **didn't buy any** eggs at the store.
3 We **didn't see any** bears in the mountains.
4 **There's some** juice left.
5 I **got some** gifts for my birthday.
6 I **don't have any** fruit in my bag.
7 We **have some** important information.
8 There **isn't any** rice in the cupboard.
9 I **have some** money saved for the vacation.

70.4
1 How much meat is there?
2 How many cups of tea are there?
3 How much coffee have you made?
4 How many bars of chocolate do we have?
5 How many jars of jam are there?
6 How much juice will we need?
7 How much milk is there?
8 How many bowls of cereal are there?
9 How many bananas do you have?
10 How many bags of flour did you buy?
11 How many cartons of milk are there?

71.1

1 Athletics **consists of a number of sports**, such as running and the high jump.
2 I think the news **is really boring**, but my parents always watch it.
3 The United States **has a population** of more than 300 million people.
4 Measles **is an illness** that usually affects children rather than adults.
5 *The Adventures of Sherlock Holmes* **is my favorite book**. I read it every summer.

71.2

1 The Netherlands **is** one of the world's biggest exporters of fresh flowers.
2 Gymnastics **wasn't** my first choice of sport.
3 *The Three Musketeers* **has** remained a popular novel since its publication in 1844.
4 Mathematics **was** my favorite subject when I was at school.

71.3

1 My family usually gets together each Christmas.
2 The company have hired a couple of new managers.
3 The government is refusing to reveal any details.
4 All the staff are going out for a meal after work.

72.1

1 Pablo has so many qualifications, **but he has almost no experience.**
2 We had quite a bit of difficulty finding **our way to the right block.**
3 Chiara has great ideas, **but not enough money to develop them.**
4 Don's had plenty of success, **and he's won three awards this year.**

72.2

CONCRETOS:
pencil, car, tree, table
ABSTRACTOS:
happiness, love, time, belief

72.3

1 I met people from many different **cultures** at college.
2 After a lot of **thought**, I've decided to quit my job.
3 Being able to play an instrument is a great **skill** to have.
4 I've visited the museum a few **times** this year.
5 Don't give up **hope**! Your team might win.
6 I have a terrible **memory** for people's names.
7 It takes a lot of **time** to learn a foreign language.
8 Venice is famous for its **culture** and history.
9 Trisha loves to share her **memories** of the past.

10 There's a lot of **space** in my new apartment.
11 My uncle is always driving everywhere at high **speed**.
12 I made some lasting **friendships** while traveling.
13 There isn't enough **time** to finish the project.

73.1

1 During the heat wave, we kept the air-conditioning switched on all day.
2 My mother-in-law had her birthday party in the town hall.
3 I went to pick up my theater tickets from the ticket office.
4 Sally had a terrible headache, so she asked her boyfriend to get her some painkillers.
5 Marc looked at the night sky as he relaxed on his camping trip.
6 Alberto stood at the front door with his suitcase, waiting for the taxi.
7 As Ellie felt the first raindrops fall, she regretted not bringing a raincoat.

73.2

1 We've been waiting at this **bus stop** for an hour.
2 Graham cleans his **bathroom** on Saturday morning.
3 I like your new **haircut**, Ed. It looks great.
4 My **sister-in-law** works in the main hospital.
5 You'll need a **bottle opener** for those drinks.

73.3

1 The police are investigating the break-in at the bookstore.
2 The teapot fell onto the kitchen floor.
3 I bought some toothpaste at the drugstore.
4 I got up at sunrise and had a bowl of breakfast cereal.
5 Darren bought a birthday card for his son.

74.1

1 cardinal
2 ordinal
3 cardinal
4 cardinal
5 ordinal
6 ordinal
7 cardinal

74.2

1 nine thousand
2 848
3 417
4 six thousand, five hundred
5 nine hundred and fifty-eight
6 97
7 three thousand, five hundred and ninety
8 three hundred and fifty-nine

74.3

1 six million, eight hundred and forty thousand, two hundred and fifty
2 fourteen million, two hundred and twenty thousand, nine hundred and two
3 ninety million, three hundred and ten thousand

74.4

1 twelve point five
2 twenty-seven point five percent
3 two-thirds
4 thirty-two percent
5 six and three-quarters
6 fourteen point nine five
7 nineteen percent
8 two-fifths
9 six point three four
10 eight and a third
11 seventy-nine point four percent
12 eight and a half

75.1

1 **Lots of students** also have a part-time job.
2 Only **a few of my friends** came to my barbecue on Saturday.
3 There are **some good bands** performing tonight.
4 I sent **a few postcards** while I was traveling.
5 There is **lots of juice** in the fridge if you want some.

75.2

1 There **isn't** enough sugar to make a birthday cake.
2 The burger costs six euros? I'm afraid that's **too much.**
3 Do we have **enough** money to buy a car?
4 There are **too many** people on the bus this morning.
5 There **isn't enough** chicken to make dinner for everyone.
6 I bought **too much** fruit. Please take some!
7 **Is** there enough orange juice in the fridge for breakfast?
8 There are only two seats left. There are **too many** of us here.

75.3

1 **A lot of** people visit the mountains on the weekend.
2 I'm not rich, but I try to donate **a little** money to charity every month.
3 Sadly, there are **few** Sumatran tigers left in the world today.
4 I met **quite a few** new clients at the conference.
5 I have **little** patience for people who are always late. I'm always on time!
6 There's **quite a bit of** snow. Let's build a snowman!
7 **Lots of** people came to Craig's 40th birthday party.
8 Do you need some help with that report? I have **a little time** I can spare.
9 Be careful! That vase is worth quite **a bit of** money.

⑩ There are **a few** paintings in the museum I haven't seen. Can we stay a bit longer?

⑪ There are very **few** people I would lend money to, but my brother is one of them.

⑫ I don't have lots of friends, but I've got **a few** who I'm really close to.

75.4

① I spent **less** time on this essay than I did last time.

② The lecture was almost empty. There were **fewer** than 10 students there.

③ I'm earning **less** money with my new job, but the conditions are better.

④ **Fewer** people eat meat today in comparison with a decade ago.

⑤ The train leaves in **less** than half an hour. We should hurry!

⑥ There was much **less** traffic than usual on the way to work.

⑦ There are **fewer** than 5,000 black rhinos left in the wild.

⑧ **Fewer** young people are studying languages than in the past.

⑨ It's **less** than 10 minutes' walk to the historic part of the city.

75.5

① We didn't go shopping because we didn't have enough money.

② The weather was awful, but at least I made a few friends there.

③ There is much less traffic in the city than 15 years ago.

④ A male African elephant can weigh more than seven tons.

⑤ I received a lot of presents for my 30th birthday.

75.6

① Marco was making **far too much noise**, so Ellie went out to the café.

② I'm afraid it's bad news. Our company is making **less money than** it did last year.

③ Unfortunately **very little** can be done about the bad weather.

④ Do we have **enough pasta** to make lunch for all the family?

⑤ We have **lots of things** to pack. Do you think there's room in the box?

⑥ **Few people** come to the restaurant on a Monday evening. It's almost empty.

⑦ There are **quite a few sandwiches** left. Help yourself to one!

⑧ There were a **lot of people** waiting on the platform for the train.

⑨ There were **quite a few clothes** I liked, but I didn't buy any.

⑩ **Fewer than 10 people** work for our company. It's very cozy here.

⑪ The safari park costs **less than $5** to visit. It's a real bargain.

⑫ We have **quite a bit of time** before we need to leave.

76

76.1

① Almost all our customers are happy with the service they receive.

② About half of the students failed the exam this year.

③ Just under a third of all people own a cat in my country.

76.2

① There are as many as two exams **each month on my college course.**

② Well over half of the country **consists of mountains and forests.**

③ Almost none of the money is left **following the expensive carnival.**

④ Approximately 75% of Earth's **surface is covered in water.**

⑤ As many as 7 out of 10 people **can speak a second language.**

76.3

① You could be fluent in English in as little as two months.

② In most cases, people recover quickly from food poisoning.

③ The children have eaten almost all the cakes.

④ About half the students failed the final exam.

⑤ As few as one in ten applications are successful.

⑥ Well over three-quarters of students use social media.

⑦ In a minority of cases, people go to prison.

⑧ There are as many as 25 public parks in my city.

⑨ My house is just under a mile away from the station.

77

77.1

① us
② you
③ him
④ she
⑤ it
⑥ they

77.2

① Kelly's so angry with him.
② Paula asked me to marry her.
③ Do you know what happened to them?
④ Mike gave her the money.

77.3

① They went to the same music festival as last year.

② I play soccer with my friends every weekend.

③ We visited Venice for our 20th wedding anniversary.

77.4

① She saw him working in a shop in Edinburgh.
② He gave us a ride to the movie theater.
③ He offered her a flower.

77.5

① Jane cooked a new dish, but **it** tasted awful. **She** was so disappointed.

② Tom asked Roger to water the plants. **He** watered **them** and went home.

③ The commuters waited for the train. **They** were angry because **it** was delayed.

④ Mike told his parents he wanted to study drama. **They** replied that **it** was a great choice.

⑤ Shona bought a coffee for Brian. **He** thanked **her** for **it**.

78

78.1

① yourself
② yourselves
③ him
④ her
⑤ itself
⑥ ourselves
⑦ them

78.2

① I asked **myself** if I should leave my job.

② You should pride **yourself** on your work, Phil.

③ Did Daniel injure **himself** when he fell off the wall?

④ Ed and Flora are teaching **themselves** to cook.

⑤ Sarah is preparing **herself** for the interview.

⑥ Did you and Claire enjoy **yourselves** at the party?

78.3

① Tim **shaves** when he gets up in the morning.

② Angela **cut herself** while she was chopping the onions.

③ The door **opened**, and my uncle walked into the room.

④ Chan **hurt himself** when he slipped on the ice.

⑤ Janet **feels** better after her illness.

78.4

① I baked the cake myself. I hope you like it.

② Most stores close at 5pm in my town.

③ Did the children behave themselves during the class?

④ Annie asked Peter and me to move the boxes.

⑤ The child sat by himself reading a book.

⑥ How was the party? Did you enjoy yourselves?

⑦ We were talking to each other when the phone rang.

78.5

1. My wife is going to paint the house herself.
2. Carlos admired himself in the mirror before leaving.
3. The CEO herself offered to help clean the office.
4. I enjoyed the evening, but the movie itself was bad.

78.6

1. My grandpa is a carpenter and **built this table himself.**
2. My cats hate each other **and fight almost every day.**
3. Betty is very selfish and **only thinks about herself.**
4. My sister and I call each other **every day to share the latest gossip.**
5. The children played in the park, **throwing snowballs at one another.**
6. Lee and Ben are helping **each other with their homework.**

78.7

1. Sharon is teaching **herself** how to knit.
2. It's hard to tear **yourself** away from a really good book.
3. Martin shaves each morning when he gets up.
4. I made some tea while the cake baked in the oven.
5. We found **ourselves** in a strange part of town. We were lost.
6. My grandparents have convinced **themselves** to go swimming each day.
7. How was the fair? Did the children enjoy **themselves** there?
8. The truck started to reverse, so we moved out of the way.
9. I'm familiarizing **myself** with the new software.
10. Jim and Ula are decorating their new house **themselves.** It's so much cheaper.
11. My arm really hurts. I hope I haven't broken it.
12. Our café prides **itself** on its excellent service.
13. I find it so hard to concentrate with all that noise.
14. It looks like the weather is improving. Let's go out.

79

79.1

1. What would you prefer? Tea or coffee?
2. There's a meeting in room 10.
3. I'm not feeling very well at all.
4. It was nothing. Probably just the cat playing.
5. Yes, it's half past five
6. Of course. Pass it here.
7. No one's heard of him, sorry.

79.2

1. Everyone's asking why you're not at the party!
2. Did you buy anything when you were at the grocer's?
3. I was exhausted after checking everything.

79.3

1. I know absolutley **nothing** about electronics.
2. Libby doesn't want **anything** to eat at the moment.
3. I don't get on with my brother. We have **nothing** in common.
4. I didn't buy **anything** while I was at the store.
5. There's **nothing** to do here. I'm bored!
6. I think I just heard **something** downstairs.

80

80.1

1. **you** your **yours**
2. he **his his**
3. **she her** hers
4. **it** its **its**
5. we **our ours**
6. **they their** theirs

80.2

1. I saw the children playing with their dog.
2. You look very excited with your new present.
3. There's Silvia taking her dogs for a walk.

80.3

1. Where is their house?
2. This desk is yours.
3. Is that my charger there?
4. These books aren't theirs.
5. That is her coat.
6. Are these his glasses?
7. Which of these cups is mine?

80.4

1. **Their** IT system is modern, but **ours** needs replacing soon.
2. These earrings are **mine**, but that bracelet is **hers**.
3. **My** bag is the yellow one. Which one is **yours**?
4. The large boxes are **theirs**, but these small ones are **ours**.
5. **Her** parents live in the countryside, while **mine** live in the city.
6. If this is **yours**, then I don't know which laptop is **mine**.
7. Stacey put **her** lunch in the fridge. Are these sandwiches **yours**?
8. Katya parked **her** car by the park. Where did your parents park **theirs**?
9. We drive **our** cars on the right, whereas they drive **theirs** on the left.
10. **Your** father drives a sports car, but **mine** rides a bike.

80.5

1. Mary and Don's uncle
2. Ben's son
3. The students' grades
4. Sam and Ayshah's cat
5. Debbie's house
6. My parents' dog
7. Marco and Kate's car
8. My grandparents' house

9. Elsa's grandchild
10. Beth's parrot
11. The people's choice

80.6

1. The women's clothes are downstairs.
2. Pick the babies' toys up, please.
3. Your car's new, while mine is old.
4. That book is yours, and this one is mine!
5. Tom's computer is slow.
6. Hurry up! It's time you left for work.
7. My town is bigger than yours.
8. The children's food is here.
9. That bag over there is yours.
10. These are the ladies' coats.
11. My parents' house is small.
12. The men's changing room is there.
13. The dog can't find its home.

80.7

1. I don't have any money **left to go on vacation this year.**
2. The nearest town has a swimming pool **and a bowling alley.**
3. Have you got any free time **to help me with this project?**
4. My dad hasn't got a phone or **an email account.**
5. My wife's from a big family and has **two brothers and two sisters.**
6. Has your brother got **red hair and a long beard?**
7. I'm very worried that my son **doesn't have any friends at college.**

80.8

1. Yes, I do. How can I help?
2. No, she hasn't. Why do you ask?
3. Yes, I do. It's in my bag.
4. No, we don't. There's one tomorrow.
5. Yes, it has. There are two lines.

81

81.1

1. I met a man who has sailed around the world.
2. The book that you lent me was really exciting.
3. The dessert that Misha ordered looks delicious.
4. Laura invited some people who she knows from college.
5. The palace that I was hoping to visit was closed.
6. Sanjay is moving to a house that is close to the sea.
7. I loved the band which performed on stage.

81.2

1. My son has a camera which takes wonderful photos.
2. The milk that you bought yesterday has turned sour.
3. The woman who was just speaking to you is incredibly rich.
4. Where did you get the hat you're wearing?

81.3
1. Ben works for a company **which produces kitchen equipment.**
2. Do you like the shirt **that I bought at the market today?**
3. Fatima showed me the dog **that she wants to adopt.**
4. Betty is playing a woman **who dreams of becoming an astronaut.**
5. This is the villa **which we're planning to buy.**
6. There are only two stores **that sell that particular part.**
7. My dad studied with the woman **who lives over the road.**
8. Does Mira have an umbrella **that she could lend me?**

82

82.1
1. Den has a new sports car, **which** he spent all his savings on.
2. The Statue of Liberty, **which** is on a small island, is popular with tourists.
3. Sam has a lovely dog, **which** he takes for a walk each morning.

82.2
1. My new sweater, **which is** made of wool, cost $40.
2. I teach many international students, many of **whom** are Indian.
3. David's cat, **which is** usually very calm, just scratched me!
4. My wife, **who** is an optician, enjoys her job very much.
5. He has two daughters, both of **whom** are lawyers.

82.3
1. I've recently bought a house, **which** I'm now decorating.
2. My nephew, **who** is only seven years old, is learning to play the violin.
3. The singer thanked her fans, many of **whom** were at the event.
4. My car, **which** I only bought last week, has already broken down.
5. Jill, **who** has worked here for 15 years, is extremely reliable.

82.4
1. Definida
2. Indefinida
3. Indefinida
4. Definida

83

83.1
1. I'll never forget that afternoon **when** Paula told me she wanted to move to another country.
2. Jane, **whose** sister you work with, is giving the speech this afternoon.
3. A long break and some sunshine is exactly **what** Kelly needs right now.
4. Toni's café, **where** you worked as a student, has closed down.
5. I'm interviewing a woman **whose** brother used to work here.
6. I'm looking forward to a time **when** we don't have to work so late.
7. That sofa is just **what** we need for the living room.
8. The companies have an agreement **whereby** they share customer data.

83.2
1. I thought it was Monday **when** Manuela was supposed to come.
2. I have no idea **what** he's bought me for my birthday.
3. We visited the part of India **where** my parents grew up.
4. Liam, **whose** report you've just read, is an excellent lawyer.
5. Stratford-upon-Avon, **where** Shakespeare was born, is lovely.

83.3
1. In 2008, when I got my first job here, I worked in the warehouse.
2. This is Miguel, whose sister works in the HR department.
3. I'm not sure what this is, but I know I like it.
4. I've already broken the phone that I bought last week.

83.4
1. 2013 was the year **when I decided to study art**.
2. This is the store **where we buy our groceries**.
3. That singer, **whose songs Jane loves**, is performing tonight.
4. This dress is exactly **what I need for Abigail's party**.

84

84.1
1. I want to finish this puzzle, **however long it takes.**
2. Catrina said she'd support me, **whichever decision I make.**
3. You can wear whatever you like **for John's birthday dinner tonight.**
4. Tony tries to visit his parents **whenever he gets the chance.**
5. Whoever was in the kitchen last **has left a terrible mess.**

84.2
1. **Whatever** did Jon do to make you so angry with him?
2. We're going to be late, **whichever** route we take.
3. Elsie told me that she'd be there to help **whenever** I needed her.
4. The engagement's not a secret. You can tell **whoever** you want.
5. **Whoever** won first prize must be a really good artist.
6. **Whenever** I hear that music, I always think of Paris.
7. My new kitten follows me **wherever** I go in the house.

84.3
1. I'm going to study drama, **whatever** my parents say.
2. John's in front of the TV **whenever** I go to see him.
3. **Wherever** Andy's gone, he's forgotten his wallet.
4. **Whoever** painted this clearly has a vivid imagination.
5. I do some gardening **whenever** I have a spare moment.
6. **Whichever** student answers this question will win a prize.
7. I'm going to finish this novel, **however** long it takes!
8. **Whatever** it is John's cooked, it tastes absolutely terrible.
9. **However** much Anthony earns, he always wants more.

85

85.1
1. There was such a mess after the party.
2. There's been an explosion at the laboratory.
3. There's going to be a jazz band at the concert hall tonight.
4. There are some lovely hats for sale in that store.
5. There was some awful pollution on the beach.
6. I'm afraid there isn't any chocolate cake left.

85.2
1. There **is** still some milk in the fridge.
2. There **were** huge crowds yesterday.
3. There **hasn't been** an inspection so far.
4. There **aren't** any cakes left, sorry.
5. There **was** a storm last night.
6. There **will be** a presentation tomorrow.
7. There **is** a heatwave at the moment.
8. There **have been** no thefts since June.
9. There **will be** rain later today.

85.3
1. There have been a lot of complaints **about the poor service at the restaurant.**
2. There will be a meeting to **discuss the forthcoming redundancies.**
3. There's going to be a party **to celebrate our silver wedding anniversary.**

④ There weren't many **cars in my village when I was a child.**

⑤ There are not enough **seats for all the people here.**

85.4

① There **were** a lot of visitors at yesterday's exhibition.

② There **aren't** any tickets for the show this evening.

③ There **is** a lot of sugar in the recipe for Cathy's cake.

④ **Is there** a party to celebrate Olive's 90th birthday tomorrow?

⑤ There **is** going to be a soccer match this afternoon.

⑥ **Was** there enough room for all the guests?

⑦ Do you know if there **is** another train tonight?

⑧ There **has been** some terrible weather recently.

⑨ There **weren't** many students at the lecture.

⑩ Bill's so busy at work. There **is** a deadline soon.

⑪ There **is** water all over the floor. What happened?

⑫ I'm sure there **won't be** another unexpected election this year.

85.5

① There's plenty of food in the fridge.

② There is a large dog in the street.

③ Are there any good cafés in your town?

④ There are a lot of people selling fruit and vegetables.

⑤ There won't be another bus today.

⑥ Do you know if there is any rice left?

⑦ There are lots of people waiting outside.

⑧ Will there be an exam at the end of the course?

⑨ Is there going to be a meeting this afternoon?

86

86.1

① Awful! It's pouring.

② It was in 1564, I think.

③ It's quarter to three.

④ No, it's just a five-minute walk.

86.2

① Distancia

② Día / Fecha / Mes / Año

③ Climatología

④ Hora

86.3

① It is essential that all candidates **arrive 15 minutes before the interview.**

② It's often said that **absence makes the heart grow fonder.**

③ If you don't start working harder, **it's unlikely you'll pass the exam.**

④ It was so nice to meet **you and your husband at the party.**

⑤ It is difficult for foreigners to **pronounce some words in my language.**

⑥ It is dangerous to drive **too fast on the highway.**

⑦ It would be great if **we could meet for coffee next weekend.**

⑧ It's been impossible for me **to find a free moment to call you.**

⑨ It's such a shame that it **rained every day on our vacation.**

⑩ It was a surprise to discover **that we share the same birthday.**

⑪ It is wonderful to lie in a field **and look up at the stars.**

⑫ It's been 40 minutes. It looks **like the bus isn't coming.**

86.4

① It is true **that** being a doctor involves a lot of hard work.

② It is important **to** lock all the doors when you go out.

③ It is useful **to** write down important information in a notebook.

④ It is possible **that** Andre forgot that the party is tonight.

87

87.1

① It's honey, not sugar, that **you should add to the cake.**

② It was the manager, not the intern, **who broke the photocopier.**

③ It was Neil Armstrong, not Buzz Aldrin, **who first walked on the moon.**

④ It was Poland that I visited, **not Germany.**

⑤ It's on Tuesday that we're meeting, **not Thursday.**

⑥ It was James, not John, who **I saw at the theater.**

87.2

① What I really hate is people singing out of tune.

② What Karen needs is to get more sleep.

③ What I enjoyed most were the fascinating ruins.

87.3

① **The person** I admire most in the world is my grandfather.

② **The one thing** I'll never forget is when I won the national prize.

③ **The reason** they gave for firing me was ridiculous.

④ **The country** I loved visiting most was Montenegro.

⑤ **The subject** I enjoyed most at school was history.

87.4

① It's the location that I like most about my home.

② What I want to do is travel around the world.

③ The animal I'd like to see while on safari is the tiger.

④ What Dave disliked most was the bad acting.

⑤ It was my neighbor who told me about the flood.

88

88.1

① Hardly had it stopped raining when the children ran out to play.

② Only after my departure did I realize that I had forgotten to say goodbye.

③ No sooner had I arrived at the airport than I decided I wasn't going to leave the country.

④ Never before have we achieved such amazing results.

⑤ Little did we know that the boy would one day become president.

⑥ Rarely have I had such a positive response to a proposal.

⑦ Only when I opened the letter did I realize that I was going to college.

88.2

① **Not since the 1980s have I known such** a hot summer.

② **Only sometimes do you witness such** kindness from strangers.

③ **No sooner had we finished the project** than the next one began.

④ **Little did they suspect how expensive** the vacation would be.

88.3

① Neither do I! ② So am I. ③ So do I.

89

89.1

① Ella woke up before dawn and **made herself a strong cup of coffee.**

② I need to tell my parents I'm leaving college, **but I'm not sure how.**

③ We need to hire a new mechanic **but don't know where to find one.**

④ I'd like to cook something special **for dinner, but I can't decide what.**

⑤ I hope Jamie comes to the wedding, **but I don't think he will.**

⑥ Someone with real talent painted **this, but we don't know who.**

89.2

① Neither of them, to be honest.

② At the market on Church Road.

③ A bit tough, actually.

④ Monday morning, 9am.

89.3

① I asked Charlie to stop playing soccer, but he didn't.

② I'm trying to make an omelet, but I don't know how.

③ I want to move to a new area, but I don't know where.

④ I really enjoy skiing, but my brother doesn't.

⑤ Someone's left a present, but I'm not sure who.

⑥ I want to buy one of these laptops, but I'm not sure which.

⑦ Catalina said she'd come to the party, but I don't think she will.

⑧ There is a museum somewhere, but I'm not sure where.

⑨ I tried to lift the box, but I wasn't strong enough.

⑩ My wife can swim really well, but I can't.

⑪ I want to study something at college, but I'm not sure what.

⑫ Anne and Si passed the exam, but Matt didn't.

90

90.1
① There are fewer factories here than there used to be.

② I was going to buy some shoes but couldn't afford to.

③ I tried to fix the bathtub but wasn't able to.

90.2
① There aren't as many cars on the streets **as there used to be.**

② I meant to call my grandma on her birthday, **but I completely forgot to.**

③ Sean could have studied at Oxford University, **but he chose not to.**

④ Liz hasn't completed as much work **as she intended to.**

⑤ I've eaten much more cake **than I meant to.**

90.3
① He didn't want to.

② Yes, she's determined to.

③ Yes, she seemed to be.

④ That's right. He promised.

⑤ There's no need to be.

90.4
① This software is more complicated than it needs to be.

② Mia didn't come to the party even though she promised.

③ I'd love to try hang gliding, but I don't have the courage.

90.5
① Maurice wasn't at the convention, even though he had hoped to be.

② I was thinking of studying French at college but decided not to.

③ Shelly isn't at school today, but she ought to be.

④ I wasn't able to go on the trip, but I did want to.

⑤ The dish isn't vegetarian, even though it's supposed to be.

90.6
① Lisa invited me to visit Spain, and I told her I'd love to.

② We asked Mario to play golf with us, but he didn't want to.

③ I wanted to see you this summer, but I won't be able to.

91

④ We can alter the dress for you. Would you like us to?

⑤ I've never seen the Great Wall of China, but I'd love the chance to.

⑥ Gerard doesn't have a motorcycle now, but he used to.

⑦ Mary was going to buy a dog, but she decided not to.

⑧ I dream of buying that apartment, but I can't afford to.

91.1
① There aren't any cafés here, but **there are some nice ones by the park.**

② The computers at work are much **slower than the ones in my old office.**

③ If you need to borrow a raincoat, **you can take one of mine.**

④ I don't own a drill, I'm afraid, **but my brother-in-law does.**

91.2
① Cathy refuses to get a phone, though her boyfriend **has got one.**

② I really don't like this sofa, but I **like the red one** over there.

③ There isn't any juice left, but I think **there's some** in the fridge.

④ I love your boots. I saw **some similar ones** in the boutique by the park.

⑤ I liked the look of the cakes in the bakery, so I **bought some**.

91.3
① My car is ruined. I need to buy a new one.

② We don't like fishing, but our dad does.

③ We'd like a dessert. Could you recommend one?

④ I really like cooking, and so does my husband.

⑤ If that dress is too expensive, we have cheaper ones, too.

⑥ Zhao liked the artwork, but I didn't.

⑦ I own few books myself, but there are lots at the library.

⑧ That looks delicious. Can I try some?

91.4
① We'd prefer it if you did.

② I don't think so, sorry.

③ I'm afraid I don't.

④ I hope so.

⑤ I'm afraid not.

⑥ I did it this morning.

92

92.1
① My boyfriend gave me a **beautiful gold** necklace for my birthday.

② My grandma's knitting me a **dark-green woolen** sweater.

③ We went to see the **ancient Aztec** ruins while in Mexico.

④ We adopted a **cute friendly** kitten from the shelter.

92.2
TAMAÑO:
little, **tiny**, **massive**
FORMA:
diamond-shaped, **round**, **square**
EDAD:
young, **ancient**, **old**
COLOR:
pink, **light-blue**, **red**
NACIONALIDAD:
Argentinian, **Vietnamese**, **French**
MATERIAL:
china, **cotton**, **steel**

92.3
OPINIÓN GENERAL:
awful, **good**, **nasty**, **wonderful**,
OPINIÓN ESPECÍFICA:
clever, **friendly**, **delicious**, **beautiful**

92.4
① I read this exciting new French novel while on vacation.

② That small old brown dog belongs to Harry.

③ Ebru made this lovely white silk dress.

92.5
① Claude has a **beautiful old Indian** rug in his living room.

② Nigel's bought himself a **big red American** sports car.

③ Catalina keeps her jewelry in a **small black wooden** box.

④ My granddaughter is engaged to a **charming tall young** man.

92.6
① Everyone found the presentation extremely **boring**.

② The instructions are so **confusing**. I don't know what to do.

③ Selma and Bob are **interested** in wildlife.

④ We were all **amazed** when Sharon won the race.

93

93.1
① Ola is a very talented cook.

② It was boiling hot outside.

③ They were ecstatic when they won the tournament.

④ My new shoes are not very comfortable at all.

⑤ Our plumber is not particularly reliable.

⑥ Marty was really hungry and ordered two hamburgers.

93.2
① Extremo

② Absoluto

③ Clasificador

④ Extremo

93.3

GRADUABLES:
interesting, cold, intelligent, large
NO GRADUABLES:
awesome, square, perfect, wooden

93.4

1 The weather was extremely **bad. It rained every day.**
2 The cookies that Ellie made **were not very tasty.**
3 I found the exam almost **impossible to finish in time.**
4 Our business is reasonably **successful, but it could do better.**
5 This antique vase is quite **unique. There are no others like it.**
6 Martin was absolutely **terrified when he saw the bear.**

93.5

1 The food at the wedding wasn't particularly impressive.
2 Hikaru speaks fairly good English, but she makes mistakes.
3 The rooms in the hotel were really awful.
4 Our old car is still in reasonably good condition.

93.6

1 I can't criticize his cakes. They're absolutely **perfect**.
2 The clothes here are of good quality and **reasonably** priced.
3 The concert was absolutely **awful**. She simply can't sing!
4 There's a wonderful **medieval** castle in my town.
5 The software is **fairly** easy to use and won't cause too many problems.
6 It's **freezing** outside! Make sure you wear a hat.

94

94.1

1 Al's new car is faster than mine.
2 The weather was colder than we'd hoped for.
3 Mount Everest is higher than K2.
4 The festival was better than I had expected.
5 Our house is larger than our neighbor's.
6 The Eiffel Tower is taller than the Statue of Liberty.

94.2

1 faster 2 more beautiful 3 happier
4 hotter 5 younger 6 thinner 7 colder
8 more complicated 9 earlier 10 more tiring
11 worse 12 more popular 13 bigger 14 lazier
15 better 16 angrier 17 closer 18 more difficult

94.3

1 Danny's dog is much **larger than mine.**
2 The wedding was more **extravagant than I'd expected.**
3 Karen is only slightly **older than her husband.**

4 Going to work by bike is **less stressful than taking a train.**
5 Electric cars are much more **common than they were 10 years ago.**
6 I'm less sporty than my **elder brother. I prefer reading to football.**
7 My daughter is much more **sensible than she used to be.**

94.4

1 The countryside is far **more quiet** than the city.
2 The Caspian Sea is **more shallow** than the Black Sea.
3 The new software we have to use couldn't be **more simple.**
4 The road was **more narrow** than I thought, and I scratched the car.
5 Jane is really mad with you. I've never seen anyone **more angry**.

94.5

1 Lisbon is much farther than Seville.
2 The Sahara Desert is hotter than the Atacama.
3 I feel happier since I moved to Barcelona.
4 The weather in California is much better than in Montana.
5 A cheetah is faster than a lion.
6 Tom is only slightly taller than his brother, Joe.
7 These jeans are much tighter than my old ones.
8 The old buildings in my town are more beautiful than the modern ones.
9 My new apartment is slightly smaller than my old one.
10 My city has a worse transportation system than yours.
11 The staff in this hotel are much more friendly than in the other one.
12 This book is much more interesting than the last one I read.

94.6

1 The castle is **quite a bit older** than the skyscrapers.
2 She was **just a bit quicker** than me in the race.
3 The weather was **much better** than was forecast.
4 A salad is **a lot healthier** than a hamburger.
5 My colleagues are **much more experienced** than me.
6 A cruise liner is **a lot bigger** than a sail boat.
7 I go to bed **slightly earlier** on Sunday evenings.

95

95.1

1 The more responsibility I take on, **the more stressed I get.**
2 The faster he drove, **the more scared she became.**
3 The more I earn, **the more I seem to spend.**
4 The longer I live here, **the more I want to move away.**
5 The more you study, **the easier the exam will be.**

6 The farther Joe walked, **the more tired he became.**
7 The colder it gets, **the more clothes you should wear.**

95.2

1 The **bigger the cake**, the more there will be to eat.
2 Ola's getting **more and more skilled** at the guitar.
3 It's getting **colder and colder**. Don't forget your scarf!
4 The faster you work, the **earlier you'll finish** the project.
5 My nephew gets **taller and taller** every time I see him.

95.3

1 The more, the merrier.
2 The sooner, the better.
3 The stronger, the better.
4 The more glamorous, the better.

95.4

1 Everyone is getting more and more concerned about climate change.
2 Philip's sunflowers keep growing taller and taller.
3 The exam gets harder and harder each year.
4 Robots are becoming more and more sophisticated.

96

96.1

1 I'm sure your pasta will be as tasty as usual.
2 Dogs are not so easy to look after as cats.
3 I hope the movie is as good as the book.
4 This hat is twice as expensive as the other one.
5 The results are not as good as we had hoped.
6 I hope the new chef is as talented as Jean-Louis.

96.2

1 I'm not as confident as I was before.
2 The food wasn't half as good as we'd hoped.
3 Rome is nowhere near as big as Paris.
4 He told us to finish as quickly as possible.
5 It's not quite as cold as last winter.
6 Ula doesn't call as much as she used to.
7 The journey took twice as long as usual.
8 Ben was as quiet as a mouse.
9 Ed is almost as old as my aunt.
10 It cost just as much as it did last time.

96.3

1 The exam was just **as** hard as I had expected.
2 The skyscrapers here are nowhere near **as** big as in Shanghai.
3 This restaurant is **twice as** expensive as the others.
4 The café is **almost as** big as the church.
5 The house is **not quite** as easy to find as we thought.
6 The singer was nowhere **near** as good as I hoped.
7 The play lasted twice **as** long as I expected.

8 It's **not nearly** as cold as we'd imagined.
9 The supermarket was not **quite** as busy as I feared.
10 The dress is **twice as** big as I thought it would be.
11 The other buildings are nowhere near **as** tall as the clock tower.
12 The company results were not quite **so** good as last year's.
13 The new store will be as popular **as** the others.
14 This was **not nearly** as easy to make as I expected.

97

97.1
1 The pianist played the most beautiful music I've ever heard.
2 The Eiffel Tower is still the tallest structure in Paris.
3 Parrots are some of the most intelligent animals.

97.2
1 Pablo has the strangest **taste in music in our class.**
2 Glasgow is the biggest **city in Scotland.**
3 Ania has the curliest hair **in my family.**
4 China has the largest **population in the world.**
5 Our soccer team was the least **successful in the league.**

97.3
1 sweetest **2** most frightening **3** best
4 slowest **5** easiest **6** happiest
7 most careful **8** worst **9** thinnest **10** dirtiest
11 smartest **12** heaviest **13** biggest
14 most boring **15** most beautiful
16 most dangerous **17** tidiest **18** newest
19 most expensive

97.4
1 That café is one of the most expensive places to eat.
2 We bought this vase because it was the most attractive.
3 My grandma always says the sweetest things about me.

97.5
1 The Mississippi is the longest river in the United States.
2 The sailfish is the fastest fish in the ocean.
3 Death Valley is the hottest place on earth.
4 Bungee jumping is the most exciting thing I've ever done.
5 Mont Blanc is the highest mountain in France.
6 My sister is the most creative person I know.
7 I felt like the luckiest person alive when I won the lottery.
8 Some of the oldest paintings can be found in local caves.

97.6
1 This is the **worst** coffee I've ever drunk.
2 Daniel is the **fastest** boy in my class.

3 I think this has been the **hottest** day of the year so far.
4 This feels like the **slowest** train I've ever been on.
5 Ashalata is the **friendliest** manager at work.
6 This is the **least** expensive car we have on sale at the moment.
7 That's the **most exciting** news I've heard today.
8 Mr. Clarke is the **strictest** teacher in school.
9 Michael lives the **farthest** away from our office.
10 That was one of the **saddest** movies I've ever seen.

97.7
1 Elvira was **the fastest** cyclist in the race.
2 I chose **the least expensive** drink on the menu.
3 This is **by far the tastiest** hamburger I've ever eaten.
4 The Burj Khalifa is one of **the tallest** buildings in the world.
5 It's **the worst** summer I've ever known.
6 This is **the best book** I've read for ages.
7 Paul **is the happiest** person I know.
8 Anna is **the most worried** of us all about tomorrow's inspection.
9 London is **the biggest** city in England.
10 Don is **easily the tallest** person in our class.
11 Feng is **one of the most talented** musicians I know.
12 Claire's is **by far the cheapest** salon in town.

98

98.1
1 Tim **kindly** helped Jo with her bags.
2 The kids played **happily** with the dog.
3 This bus is moving so **slowly**!
4 Charles **greedily** ate all the chocolate.
5 It started to rain **heavily**.
6 Carla shouted **angrily** at her computer.
7 Ed's mom thinks he drives too **quickly**.
8 My doctor told me to eat **healthily**.
9 Magda waited **nervously** for her results.

98.2
1 noisily **2** reluctantly **3** well **4** shyly
5 happily **6** long **7** calmly **8** straight
9 easily **10** hard **11** softly **12** dangerously
13 repeatedly **14** clumsily **15** late **16** badly
17 fast **18** stylishly

98.3
1 That child has been waiting **patiently for more than an hour.**
2 Anne advised me to arrive **early for the interview tomorrow.**
3 George left the room quietly, **so as not to wake up the baby.**
4 The number of people studying **English has increased rapidly.**
5 Alina is doing fine after **her operation last week.**
6 I think I answered all **the questions in the test correctly.**
7 I worry a lot about how **fast my daughter rides her bike.**

98.4
1 Ella **gently** stroked her new kitten.
2 Marvin played the piano **beautifully** last night.
3 Louis has worked **hard** to improve his English.
4 An eagle flew **high** above the ruined castle.
5 My stapler has **mysteriously** disappeared.
6 Kathy sang very **well** at the performance.
7 Tim shouted **angrily** at the TV when his team lost.
8 Sangita wasn't **badly** injured in the accident.
9 I went **straight** to my boss's office to talk to her.
10 Claudio passed the final test **easily**.

99

99.1
1 Ola played the most beautifully **of all the musicians.**
2 Carlo speaks English more **fluently than he does German.**
3 You've been working harder **since you got the promotion.**
4 Ahmed drove more carefully **when it started to snow.**

99.2
1 earlier / earliest
2 faster / fastest
3 more regularly / most regularly
4 harder / hardest
5 better / best
6 more stylishly / most stylishly

99.3
1 I usually get up earlier during the week.
2 A cheetah can run much faster than a human.
3 Juan comes here less frequently than he used to.

99.4
1 I should have looked **more closely** at my contract.
2 My employees **work less efficiently** when they're tired.
3 Who **performed better** in the test, you or your sister?
4 Joan gets up **the earliest** in our family.
5 My teacher said I should **try harder** in class.
6 Lena has to **travel the farthest** to get to our office.
7 Our cat can **jump much higher** than our dog.

100

100.1
1 Juan's cake was very popular. Everyone wanted more.
2 The two vases were only slightly different to each other.
3 Eric thought the test was fairly straightforward.
4 Phil's feeling remarkably fit considering how ill he was.

⑤ I don't think it's a particularly difficult mountain to climb.

⑥ The house at the end of the road looks really unusual.

100.2
MÁS FUERTE:
remarkably, **really**, **extremely**, **very**
MÁS DÉBIL:
fairly, **slightly**, **barely**, **not particularly**

100.3
GRADUANTES:
slightly, **fairly**, **very**, **not particularly**
NO GRADUANTES:
completely, **totally**, **absolutely**, **utterly**

100.4
DEL TODO:
totally, **thoroughly**, **completely**, **utterly**
CASI DEL TODO:
largely, **mainly**, **mostly**, **virtually**

100.5
① Marta's painting is virtually complete.
② I thought the lecture was fairly interesting.
③ Beatriz was absolutely thrilled to hear my news.
④ Craig looks completely different from his brother.

100.6
① Unfortunately, the hotel we stayed in was utterly awful.
② We found the music festival completely brilliant this year.
③ The students' handwriting was barely legible.
④ The food in the canteen is remarkably good.
⑤ It was nearly impossible, but we reached the summit in the end.

100.7
① The play had almost started **by the time we found the theater.**
② It's perfectly acceptable to **wear jeans to work on Fridays.**
③ This old phone is absolutely **useless without its charger.**
④ We were completely exhausted **when we reached the summit.**
⑤ Jon is extremely talented **and should study art at college.**
⑥ Timothy has essentially finished **writing his PhD thesis.**

101

101.1
① It looks like Sanchez is about to score!
② I've just knocked over that vase. I'm so sorry.
③ We've already packed everything for the move.
④ The chicken's not ready. It's still cooking in the oven.
⑤ Sarah looked like she was about to fall asleep.
⑥ The bus hasn't arrived yet. I'm going to be home late.

101.2
① Futura
② Pasada
③ Pasada
④ En curso
⑤ En curso

101.3
① I have **just** received a letter from an old friend.
② Mizuho has **already** been to Paris three times before.
③ Have you been introduced to Tonia's parents **yet**?
④ The judges are **about to** reveal the winner of the competition.
⑤ I've **just** finished my final exam. It's such a relief.
⑥ I haven't finished the book you lent me **yet**.
⑦ Maria has **just** told me she is quitting her job.
⑧ The concert had **already** begun by the time we arrived.
⑨ Lisa has **just** returned from her trip around South America.
⑩ I was **about to** leave, when I remembered the oven was still on.
⑪ The new block on Park Street isn't finished **yet**.
⑫ Hurry up, everyone! The train is **about to** leave.
⑬ I've **already** told Anna that the meeting has started.

101.4
① Vanessa is still working **for the bank, isn't she?**
② We have already spent **all the money we saved.**
③ Has Zahra visited **the National Gallery yet?**
④ Giuseppe's restaurant **is still the best in town.**
⑤ Clive looks like he's **about to give a speech.**
⑥ We still haven't heard **back from the plumber.**

101.5
① Mesut still hasn't given back the $30 I lent him.
② Leroy is still the best player on the team.
③ Has Timo shown you around the new office yet?
④ The guests have already eaten all of the birthday cake.
⑤ I've just seen your brother walking out of the police station.
⑥ Jess is still living in Aberdeen, isn't she?

102

102.1
① Ola goes to the gym **very often**.
② It **hardly ever** rains in the desert.
③ I **regularly** visit my gran.
④ I **usually** go shopping on Saturday.
⑤ She **frequently** goes running.
⑥ We **always** go to France on vacation.

102.2
SIEMPRE O CASI SIEMPRE:
nearly always, **very often**, **usually**
A VECES:
regularly, **sometimes**, **occasionally**
CASI NUNCA O NUNCA:
rarely, **hardly ever**, **almost never**, **never**

102.3
① Karen is hardly ever in the office on Fridays.
② I visit my parents about once a year.
③ The photocopier at work is nearly always broken.
④ Mira goes to the gym three times a week.

102.4
① Benny's very reliable and **is almost never late for work.**
② Carlita goes swimming at **least five times a week.**
③ Ella often stays at work **until after 10pm.**
④ I come from central Australia, **where it hardly ever rains.**
⑤ When do you usually **finish work in the evening?**
⑥ Ania plays badminton with her cousin **every Sunday morning.**

103

103.1
① It was so windy **that we couldn't fly a kite.**
② You children are so **much better behaved than mine.**
③ The bride wore such **a stylish dress for the wedding.**
④ It was so hot that we **all decided to go swimming.**
⑤ I've never seen such a **beautifully decorated cake before.**

103.2
① The cake Carlos made for the party was so tasty.
② Your exam results are so much better this year.
③ This store sells such lovely clothes.
④ Your brother owns such a beautiful villa.

103.3
① Colm's job looks **so** interesting, but it's very badly paid.
② My new phone's **so much** better than my old one.
③ Everyone had **such a** great time at the school reunion.
④ Hank is **so** generous. He gave me a watch for my birthday.
⑤ The new intern works **so much** harder than the old one.
⑥ It was **such a** shock when our boss said he was leaving.
⑦ Lorna's **such a** talented musician.
⑧ The weather was **so** bad that we decided to cancel the barbecue.

103.4
① My little sister is **such a** good dancer. She should take classes.
② The match was **so** disappointing. No one scored.
③ The weather is **so much** warmer in Florida. You should move here.
④ Kirsty's **so** funny. She always makes me laugh.
⑤ Sandra is **such a** good cook. Everything she makes is delicious.

104

104.1
1. If you're too cold, close the window.
2. Do you think we have enough money to buy this house?
3. Bob was too tired to concentrate on cooking the meal.

104.2
1. I'm not **rich enough** to afford those shoes.
2. Michael is **too young** to watch that movie.
3. The water is **warm enough** to go for a swim.
4. My neighbor always plays his music **too loudly**.
5. This bookcase is **too heavy** for me to move.
6. My French isn't **good enough** to understand Pierre.
7. The exercise was **too hard** for a total beginner.

104.3
1. We have enough time to catch the last bus.
2. If you're not warm enough, you should put on a sweater.
3. Do we have enough food for all the guests tonight?
4. The tickets for the rock concert were too expensive.
5. Norbert isn't tall enough to reach the bottle.
6. The café wasn't too far, so we walked there.
7. The professor spoke too quietly for us to hear.
8. I'm not rich, but I earn enough to pay the rent.
9. I tried my best in the race, but I wasn't fast enough.

105

105.1
1. There's a café by the church.
2. The meeting is on Monday morning.
3. Mia was nervous before going in to speak to her boss.
4. Dan put the flowers on the table.
5. Peter works at the local airport.
6. Julie gave her teacher her homework after the lesson.

105.2
1. Before leaving for work, I wash the dishes.
2. I have an English class on Tuesdays.
3. I don't know what to listen to.
4. Al passed without studying for the exam.
5. Kumi's listening to the radio.
6. Emma's house is by the park.
7. Their office is next to the library.
8. After finishing work, I go swimming.
9. Jon wants to study Spanish.
10. I live with Pete, Dan, and Ed.

105.3
1. My aunt is really good **at** making her own clothes.
2. My new house is **near** the National Museum.
3. In spite **of** the bad pay, Eleni loves her job.
4. You've been looking **at** that phone all morning.
5. Instead **of** going to college, I became a carpenter.

105.4
1. I'm not used to waking up so early each morning.
2. My son is planning to go to college in New York.
3. I'm sorry I haven't got around to replying to your email yet.
4. Jean-Pierre used to drive a red sports car.
5. Martin decided to quit his job at the library.
6. Virginie confessed to stealing the bottle of wine.

106

106.1
1. The dinner is **on** the table.
2. Julian lives **in** the United States.
3. Mesut wasn't **at** the party.
4. I went to meet Ula **at** the airport.
5. Carmen works **in** France.
6. I bought it **at** the supermarket.
7. Mary stayed **in** bed all morning.
8. There are 20 rooms **in** the building.
9. Put the toys back **in** their box.
10. We went to London **on** the train.
11. Marta left her keys **at** home.
12. Ben is sitting **on** the sofa.
13. The students are all **at** their desks.

106.2
1. Marina works at Z-Tech, the **software company on Park Street.**
2. You have some lovely **posters on your kitchen wall.**
3. My uncle Tony lives at **number 16, Nelson Avenue.**
4. We keep the lawnmower **in the shed behind the house.**
5. The college library can be found **on the ninth and tenth floors.**
6. I usually buy my bread at **the bakery across the road.**

106.3
1. The castle sits **in front of** some ugly modern buildings.
2. I placed the final box of books **on top of** the others.
3. Alan is working in the garage **under** a car.
4. Ian put his bag on the seat **opposite**.
5. There's a lovely park **near** the castle.
6. The library is **between** the bank and the café.
7. I found Craig and Robin hiding **behind** a tree.

107

107.1
1. Jan has a bath in the evening before she goes to bed.
2. During the week I wake up at 7am.
3. We'd better hurry. Our flight leaves in two hours.
4. It often gets far too hot in the summer in the city.
5. I'm free on Wednesday and Thursday this week.
6. I usually make coffee when I get up in the morning.

107.2
1. I'm meeting Eliana at 6pm.
2. Joe has his final exam on Friday.
3. She started work here in August.
4. I go to Angelo's café at lunchtime.
5. Pat works from home on Thursdays.
6. I always have a nap in the afternoon.
7. Their wedding is on August the 15th.
8. The performance starts at 4 o'clock.
9. Maria usually goes skiing in winter.
10. My daughter was born in 1996.

107.3
1. Americans celebrate **Independence Day on July 4.**
2. The best time to spot **a barn owl is at night.**
3. I often go walking in spring, **when the weather improves.**
4. I usually clean my apartment on **Sunday morning.**
5. Magda usually stays with **her family at Christmas.**

107.4
1. The store will be closed until the end of August.
2. Simon usually goes to bed at half past eleven.
3. The train leaves at quarter to seven.
4. What did you do during the summer break?

107.5
1. I usually go for lunch **between** 1 and 2pm.
2. I'm planning to work here **until** I retire.
3. Martin has worked here **since** October.
4. I lived in Spain for a couple of years **during** the 1970s.
5. Guests should leave their rooms **by** 11:30am.

107.6
1. The café is open **between** 8am and 6pm.
2. I'll be writing this essay **until** 10pm.
3. I've been working here **for** about five months.
4. We're traveling around Mexico from July **to** September.
5. Mabel's lived in Madrid **since** she was a child.
6. Camilla **has worked / has been working** here since July.

108

108.1
1 We went for a walk with our children this afternoon.
2 I get a lot of work done when I travel by train.
3 My aunt's written a book about the town where she grew up.

108.2
1 *Macbeth* was written **by** William Shakespeare in the early 1600s.
2 Takumi went to the theater **with** his wife last night.
3 We found our way to the castle **without** too much difficulty.
4 I ordered boiled potatoes **with** my steak.
5 Most tourists travel around Tokyo **by** metro.
6 We need to talk **about** employing some more staff.
7 Sarah managed to finish the project **without** any help.

108.3
1 We usually pay for **our groceries by card.**
2 Chris went to an interesting **lecture about Madagascar.**
3 We're looking for a house **with a view onto the sea.**
4 This wonderful piece of music **was composed by Chopin.**
5 We're going on vacation **to Kenya without our children.**
6 I took a photo of a fox in **my backyard with my phone.**

108.4
1 Julie always sings with such enthusiasm.
2 Pete's written a book about his childhood.
3 I decided to buy the laptop without thinking.
4 You can get fit by playing a sport.

109

109.1
1 There has been a big increase in people studying science.
2 You can always count on Dave to leave the place clean and tidy.
3 Andy sold his old car to one of his neighbors.

109.2
1 We haven't paid for the meal yet.
2 Emilia was angry about the dirty rooms in the hotel.
3 I'm waiting for a response to the email that I sent.

109.3
1 I was so proud **of** Katie when she passed the test.
2 There are lots of advantages **to** working from home.
3 This company is advertising **for** a new secretary.
4 Is everyone ready **for** the big exam tomorrow?
5 Stephanie has a very positive attitude **toward** her work.
6 The roadwork caused problems **for** many drivers.
7 I was so impressed **by** the room service.
8 My boss told us **to** be more punctual in future.
9 I don't agree **with** my husband about many things.
10 My son is afraid **of** spiders.
11 They've found another problem **with** my car.
12 Esther has talked **about** moving abroad for years.

109.4
1 I saw Leonard talking **to** a police officer yesterday.
2 There's been an increase **in** the number of thefts.
3 These animal toys should appeal **to** children.
4 Sangita is annoyed **with** her housemates.
5 My grandfather loves to talk **about** his childhood.

109.5
1 Ella is really upset **about** losing her mother's necklace.
2 Bill is anxious **about** giving a speech at the conference.
3 I have an excellent relationship **with** my manager.
4 My teacher asked me what I know **about** Roman history.
5 Erik has sold his bicycle **to** one of his cousins.
6 I've been having a lot of problems **with** my internet router.

110

110.1
1 There's a deli and a bookstore on Maple Road.
2 Would you like a first-class or standard-class ticket?
3 Pete's great with the customers, but he's very clumsy.

110.2
1 The movie was disappointing, **but the special effects were amazing.**
2 You can contact us by email **or by telephone.**
3 Bill's never traveled abroad, **nor does he plan to.**
4 My sister lives in Paris, **and my brother lives in Lyon.**

110.3
1 I've been to Ottawa, **but** I've never been to Vancouver.
2 It was raining, **so** we decided to go to the art gallery.
3 While walking, we saw an eagle, a puma, **and** a bear.
4 Ben has to choose between studying math, art, **or** psychology.
5 I did not like the food at the restaurant, **nor** did I like the decor.

110.4
1 Kim was feeling tired, so she went to bed.
2 My son doesn't live at home, nor does my daughter.
3 I was planning to go swimming, but I forgot my swimsuit.
4 Len's 76, yet he still plays soccer with his grandchildren.

111

111.1
1 The children ran out to play **as soon as it stopped raining.**
2 We bought Jim some binoculars **because he likes bird-watching.**
3 Adam failed his test, **even though he worked hard for it.**
4 Someone stole my purse **while I was at the restaurant.**
5 Sam usually eats **when he gets home from work.**

111.2
1 Eli decided to go jogging, **even though** it was raining.
2 Ella put on some sunscreen **so that** she didn't get sunburned.
3 **When** I finish this report, I'll give you a hand.
4 You need a passport **in order to** enter most countries.
5 **Even though** I prefer coffee, I decided to have a cup of tea.
6 Paolo decided to have a nap **because** he was feeling tired.
7 I made the dinner **while** my wife cleaned our apartment.

111.3
1 I read a newspaper **while** I was waiting for the train.
2 My dad bought some paint **so that** he can decorate the kitchen.
3 I'm not going out **until** I've finished my homework.
4 Sally's moving to Spain, **even though** she can't speak Spanish.
5 **When** you've written the report, can you send me a copy?

111.4
1 The concert **will begin** as soon as the singer **arrives.**
2 **Even though** I arrived early, there were no tickets left.
3 Miguela is learning to juggle **in order to** impress her friends.
4 Can you give me a call when **you arrive**?
5 I usually eat **when** my roommate gets home.
6 I went to the supermarket **to buy** some groceries.

318

112

112.1
1. Andy is tall, whereas his cousin is quite short.
2. I like visiting the mountains, especially in the winter.
3. Bill loves going fishing, just like his dad.

112.2
1. Selma has curly brown hair, **just as her grandmother did.**
2. Due to the bad snow, **all the trains this afternoon are delayed.**
3. As no one bought any tickets, **we've canceled tonight's show.**
4. Andy hated the movie, **though I thought it was okay.**
5. People in Japan drive on the left, **whereas we drive on the right here.**
6. We had to drive slowly **because of the icy conditions.**

112.3
1. Lianne loves football, **whereas** her brother hates it.
2. I was late for the interview **because of** the traffic.
3. The professor was sick. **As a result**, the lecture was postponed.
4. Frank is a zookeeper, **yet** he is terrified of mice.
5. I get on well with Saul, **so** we are going on vacation together.

112.4
1. Magda loves gardening, **especially** in the spring.
2. Omar visited Rome **because** he loves ancient history.
3. There are a lot of environmental problems **because of** the bad pollution.
4. **Thanks to** her music teacher, Selma became a great pianist.
5. I wanted to come this morning, **but** the tickets had sold out.

113

113.1
CONJUNCIONES COPULATIVAS:
or, nor, so, and, but
CONJUNCIONES SUBORDINANTES:
after, because, although, in order that, even though

113.2
1. tiempo
2. motivo
3. causa
4. tiempo
5. motivo
6. condición
7. condición

113.3
1. I have to send an email before I go home.
2. You can borrow my laptop as long as you look after it.
3. You can't go to the party unless you clean your room.

113.4
1. Leo screamed **when** he saw the spider in the bathroom.
2. Toby doesn't know what he'll do after **he leaves** school.
3. Emma put on her coat **because** she was feeling cold.
4. I was planning to go for a walk, **but** it started raining.
5. I'll call you as soon as **I know** any news.

114

114.1
1. I had a lot of fun with my coworkers at the office party.
2. I much prefer nonfiction, such as biographies, to fiction.
3. My girlfriend disapproves of me eating fast food.

114.2
1. The police are looking for a man in his **mid-twenties**.
2. I've **misplaced** my glasses. Have you seen them?
3. The actor's performance was **substandard**.
4. It was **irresponsible** to drive so quickly.
5. Clara is trying to **disprove** the allegations against her.
6. The teacher said their behavior was **unacceptable**.
7. The student's handwriting was quite **illegible**.

114.3
1. We found Alexandra's cakes totally **irresistible**.
2. I **misread** your name. I thought it said Davies, not Davis.
3. Les failed the exam, but he can **resit** next semester.
4. Andy was **dishonest** about being fluent in Portuguese.
5. Emily was struggling to **untie** her shoelaces.
6. It's **illegal** to drive without wearing a seatbelt.
7. This cake is really **undercooked**. It's almost raw inside.
8. Don't be so **impatient**. The train will come soon.

114.4
1. I realized I had the wrong key when I couldn't **unlock** the door.
2. Ed's so **unreliable**. He's always late.
3. You can **reapply** for the course next year.
4. Ola was **uncertain** what to think about Jim's haircut.
5. I think she **undercharged** us. It should have cost more.

115

115.1
1. This wooden box should be **really useful for storing our documents.**
2. Karl's dog looks dangerous, **but it's actually quite harmless.**
3. Our accountant has been **accused of** incompetence.
4. The evening's entertainment **included some wonderful music.**
5. My brother's a pessimist **and thinks things will deteriorate.**

115.2
ADJETIVOS:
-able/-ible, -al/-ial, -ful, -ic/-tic/-ical, -less, -ous
VERBOS:
-ate, -en, -ize, -ify
SUSTANTIVOS:
-ance/-ence, -dom, -er/-or, -ism, -ist/-ian, -ity/-ty

115.3
1. Alan works for a **management** recruitment company.
2. The café serves a selection of **seasonal** vegetables.
3. The fish are **plentiful** in local rivers.
4. Kids love taking **inflatable** toys to the beach.
5. I found the music festival very **enjoyable**.
6. She always shows great **commitment** to her students.

115.4
1. We want to express our appreciation for all your work.
2. The new couch is really comfortable.
3. Unemployment is a real problem in my city.

116

116.1
1. It's difficult getting used to the city **after living in the countryside.**
2. I'm getting my hair cut this **afternoon at the salon across the road.**
3. Bill got used to the weather **in Australia surprisingly quickly.**
4. Sian's getting new **windows fitted in her apartment.**
5. Gill's still not used to driving **on the left in Britain.**
6. We have our house painted **about every 10 years.**

116.2
1 It took me a while to get used to the cold water in the lake.
2 Joel is used to the cold. He grew up in Finland.
3 You can get your car washed at the gas station.

116.3
1 I hated working nights at first, but then I got used to it.
2 Olga grew up in Moscow, so she's used to cold winters.
3 I used to work as a lab technician before I became a teacher.
4 Nico has his hair cut at the barbershop on Main Street.
5 I got my locks changed after our place was broken into.

116.4
1 Sheila always gets a pizza delivered on Fridays.
2 I'm not used to living in a rainy country.
3 I have my teeth cleaned by the hygienist once a month.

117

117.1
1 for instance 2 moreover 3 then
4 to begin with

117.2
1 Then I switch on the **oven and find my ingredients.**
2 Next, I put all the ingredients **in a bowl and mix them together.**
3 After that, I pour the mixture **into a baking pan.**
4 You can add extra ingredients, **such as nuts or dried fruit.**
5 Finally, I put the cake into **the oven for about 25 minutes.**

117.3
1 Furthermore, you should choose the type of house you want.
2 For example, do you want to live in an apartment or a house?
3 Does the property have, for instance, a balcony?
4 In conclusion, you should think carefully before buying a house.

117.4
1 **Additionally**, they provide employment to many people in the region.
2 **Furthermore**, many species are in danger of extinction.
3 **Meanwhile**, the logging companies continue to destroy vast areas.
4 **In conclusion**, forests are in need of urgent protection.

118

118.1
1 Really? I find him quite dull.
2 I didn't think it suited her, actually.
3 I'm afraid I disagree. I don't like them.
4 I don't agree. I think it looks great.
5 I thought it was predictable, to be honest.

118.2
1 To be honest, I much prefer the city.
2 I don't agree. It was incredibly boring.
3 I'm afraid I disagree. I think it's really overcrowded.

118.3
1 Anyway, she's still a really good writer.
2 I'm afraid I don't think she is.
3 As I was saying, I think she is very talented.
4 I don't think I agree with you, actually.
5 By the way, have you ever read her first novel?
6 You have a point about her books costing too much.
7 Actually, I thought the main character was awful.
8 I see your point about the main character.
9 I told you I wouldn't like Claudia's new novel!

119

119.1
1 It seems my car has broken down again.
2 It would appear that the cat has knocked over the vase.
3 I don't like modern art. However, I don't mind this picture.

119.2
1 Although the restaurant is **nearby, I rarely eat there.**
2 However, whenever I go there, **I always have a good time.**
3 Of course, all the dishes **are made using the finest ingredients.**
4 On the one hand, it's very expensive, **but on the other hand, it's good quality.**
5 I might go out tonight. **Alternatively, I could relax in front of the TV.**
6 Despite feeling tired, **I decided to go out with my friends.**

119.3
1 It seems you haven't completed all the paperwork.
2 She could potentially be a really good actor.
3 It appears that someone forgot to lock up the office.
4 To a certain extent, we believe Manuel is right.

119.4
1 The figures suggest that we are losing a lot of customers.
2 Despite the delays, I enjoyed myself thoroughly.
3 On the one hand, I'm rich. On the other hand, I'm not very happy.
4 To some extent, crime has increased in the past year.

120

120.1
1 You know, that's a great idea.
2 Sort of. I can hold a basic conversation.
3 Well, I do have plans later.
4 Let's see... I could probably make you 100.
5 Wow! That's amazing.

120.2
1 Let's see... I've been working **in IT for more than 10 years.**
2 Well, I enjoy working with **my team on large projects.**
3 So, I think we can all agree **that the project is a success.**

120.3
1 Really? What are you going to do there?
2 Well, I'd like to work as a waiter.
3 You know, that might be hard work.
4 I suppose so, but I will practice my French.
5 Of course. But do you speak any French?
6 Good question. Not yet, but I'd like to.
7 Oh right. What else do you want to do?
8 Let's see. I'd like to travel around France.
9 Wow! That sounds like a great idea.

CAPTAIN AMERICA
WHO WON'T WIELD THE SHIELD

WRITERS: **JASON AARON, MATT FRACTION** & **STUART MOO**
ARTISTS: **MIRCO PIERFEDERICI, BRENDAN McCARTHY** & **JOE QUINON**
COLORISTS: **HOWARD HALLIS** & **JAVIER RODRIGU**

LETTERS: **TODD KLEIN** • COVER ART: **GERALD PAF**
ASSISTANT EDITOR: **TOM BRENNAN** • EDITOR: **STEPHEN WACK**

"MERRY FREAKIN' CHRISTMAS

WRITER: **FRED VAN LENTE** • PENCILER: **SANFORD GREE**
INKER: **NATHAN MASSENGILL** • COLORIST: **JOHN RAU**

LETTERS: **JEFF ECKLEBER**
EDITOR: **SEBASTIAN GIRN**

COLLECTION EDITOR: **CORY LEV**
EDITORIAL ASSISTANTS: **JAMES EMMETT** & **JOE HOCHST**
ASSISTANT EDITORS: **MATT MASDEU, ALEX STARBUCK** & **NELSON RIBE**
EDITORS, SPECIAL PROJECTS: **JENNIFER GRÜNWALD** & **MARK D. BEAZ**
SENIOR EDITOR, SPECIAL PROJECTS: **JEFF YOUNGQU**
SENIOR VICE PRESIDENT OF SALES: **DAVID GABR**
SVP OF BRAND PLANNING & COMMUNICATIONS: **MICHAEL PASCIU**

EDITOR IN CHIEF: **AXEL ALON**
CHIEF CREATIVE OFFICER: **JOE QUESA**
PUBLISHER: **DAN BUCKL**
EXECUTIVE PRODUCER: **ALAN F**

DEADPOOL: DEAD HEAD REDEMPTION. Contains material originally published in magazine form as DEADPOOL #900, DEADPOOL #1000 and CAPTAIN AMERICA: WHO WON'T WIELD THE SHIELD? First p 2011. ISBN# 978-0-7851-5649-9. Published by MARVEL WORLDWIDE, INC., a subsidiary of MARVEL ENTERTAINMENT, LLC. OFFICE OF PUBLICATION: 135 West 50th Street, New York, NY 10020. Cop © 2009, 2010 and 2011 Marvel Characters, Inc. All rights reserved. $15.99 per copy in the U.S. and $17.50 in Canada (GST #R127032852); Canadian Agreement #40668537. All characters featured issue and the distinctive names and likenesses thereof, and all related indicia are trademarks of Marvel Characters, Inc. No similarity between any of the names, characters, persons, and/or institutions magazine with those of any living or dead person or institution is intended, and any such similarity which may exist is purely coincidental. **Printed in the U.S.A.** ALAN FINE, EVP - Office of the President, M Worldwide, Inc. and EVP & CMO Marvel Characters B.V.; DAN BUCKLEY, Publisher & President - Print, Animation & Digital Divisions; JOE QUESADA, Chief Creative Officer; JIM SOKOLOWSKI, Chief Operating Of

DEADPOOL #900 VARIA

by Dave Joh

Some jobs are just too tough for your average fast-talkin' high-tech gun-for-hire. Sometimes…to get the job done right…you need someone crazier than a sack'a ferrets. You need Wade Wilson. The Crimson Comedian. The Regeneratin' Degenerate. The Merc with a Mouth…

DEADPOOL

Well it's been a long time coming (I'M PRETTY SURE EVERY HERO/VILLAIN HAS KILLED US AT LEAST ONCE. Probably.) but we're finally here at the BIG issue #900 (HOW FITTING THAT M SERIES IS THE FIRST COMIC EVER TO HIT THAT NUMBER, BABY! Must have been all the weekl shipping during my three picture movie career.)! But now that we've reached the BIC #900 and after all those years of carrying second-rate heroes on my shoulders, onc again it's me (AND ME), good ol' Wade Wilson, starring in his own series (I DIDN'T LIKE YO GUYS ANYWAY!).

But instead of getting on with this BIG issue I'll briefly recap my recent team-u issues, as if everyone wasn't buying them religiously (THAT'S RIGHT, I'M TALKING TO YOU! For the past one hundred and sixty-eight issues I've been side by side with the likes c Wolverine (YES, HE SMELLS), Captain America ("I COME BACK FROM THE DEAD ALL THE TIM AND NO ONE CARES!"), Thor (DOES ANYONE STILL WEAR A CAPE?), and Spider-Man (RED LOOK BETTER ON ME).

Then there was the woman who stole my heart (LITERALLY). I never thought I'd lov again after Black Widow (DUDE, SHE CHOPPED US INTO PIECES…I'm easy), but then Lad Deadpool came along! I never found out who she was but I'll never forget that smokir body (PRETTY SURE IT WAS JARVIS…Impossible, I'd recognize Jarvis' figure anywhere And who could forget my brief stint as a teen in those Young Deadpool years pairing u with Power Pack, the New Warriors, and Franklin Richards…what a kid…(DID YOU KNOW H HAS PSYCHOTIC POWERS? Psionic powers, psionic.)

Now that all of you lazy bums are caught up we can get on with the show! By the wa did I mention this issue is HUGE??? Enjoy it, folks (OR ELSE), this is the once in a lifetime never before seen in comics history issue #900 of a comic! Wahooo! I can't wait…why ar you waiting? Start turning those pages (IMMEDIATELY!).

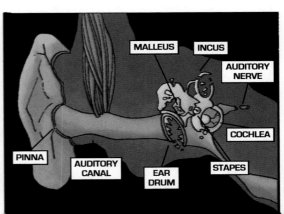

LUCKY THAT GEEK DIDN'T SEE I WAS PALMING *THIS* OFF HIS NECK AS I FLIPPED OVER HIM.

HEY! MY *EARDRUMS* GREW BACK AFTER THAT EXPLOSION BLEW 'EM OUT!

WHOOPEE! NOW WE GET TO HEAR YOU TALK AGAIN.

GUESS I SHOULD RETURN THESE LI'L DOOHICKEYS TO THE *INSTITUTE*, COLLECT MY *FEE*...

...THOUGH THEY DO COME IN HANDY. MAYBE I SHOULD ARRANGE FOR ONE OF 'EM TO GO "MISSING," HEH-HEH...

Wait. If our eardrums were blown out just *now*, why was the *flashback* silent, too?

EH. I WASN'T REALLY LISTENING TO ANYTHING THAT OLD GEEK WAS SAYING...

SILENT BUT *DEADLY*

FRED VAN LENTE WRITER **DALIBOR TALAJIC** ARTIST

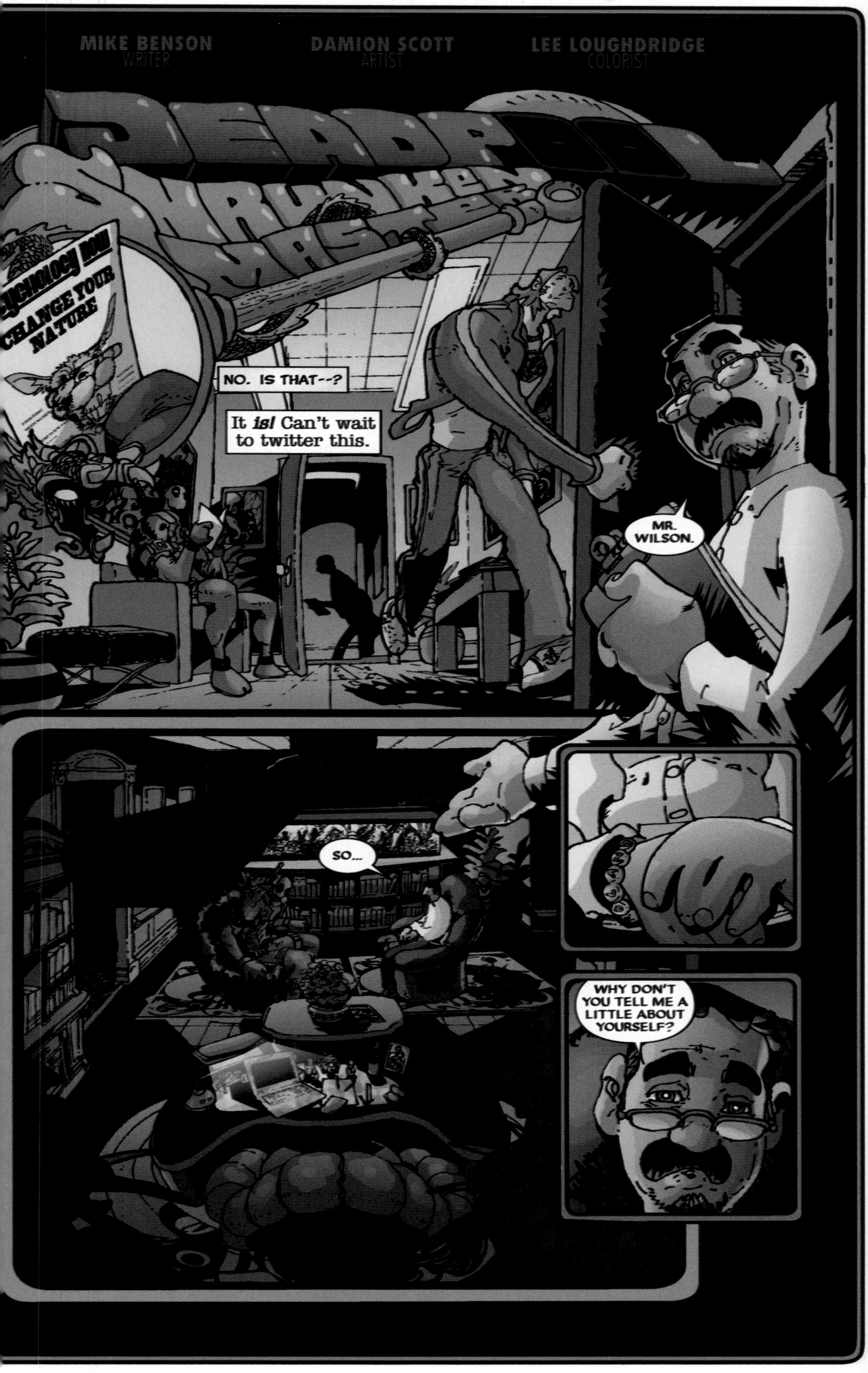

MIKE BENSON
WRITER

DAMION SCOTT
ARTIST

LEE LOUGHDRIDGE
COLORIST

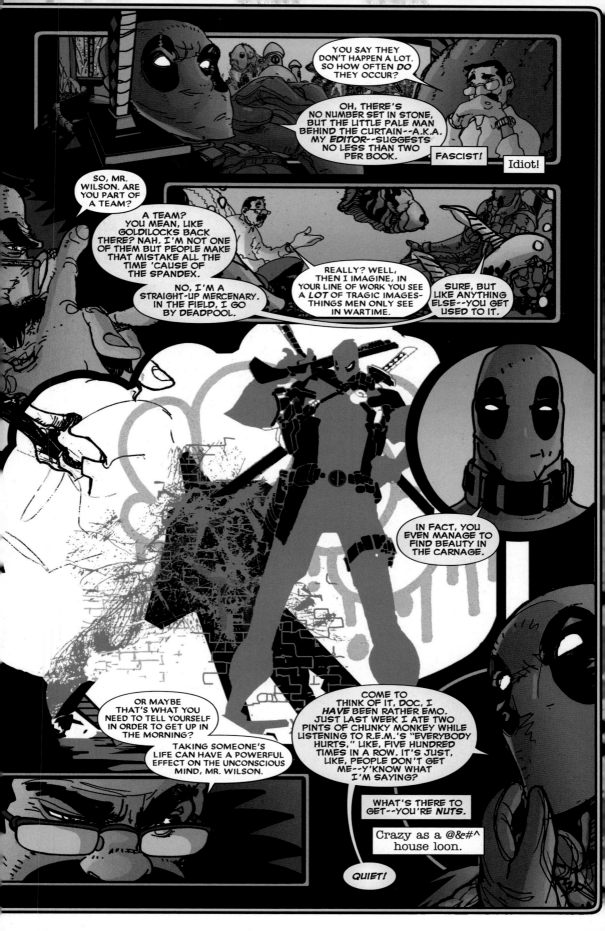

THE END

What Happens in Vegas...

DUANE SWIERCZYNSKI
WRITER

SHAWN CRYSTAL
ARTIST

LEE LOUGHRIDGE
COLORIST

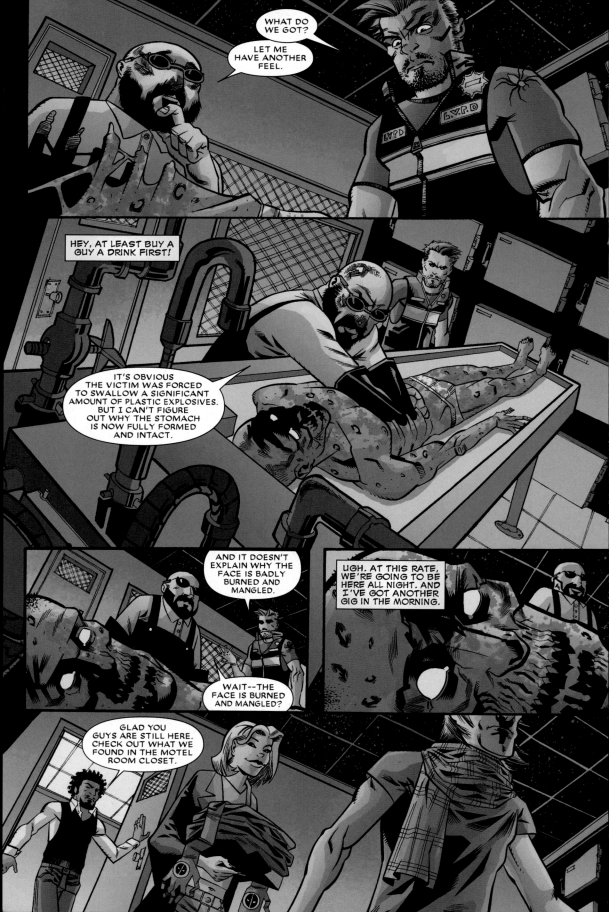

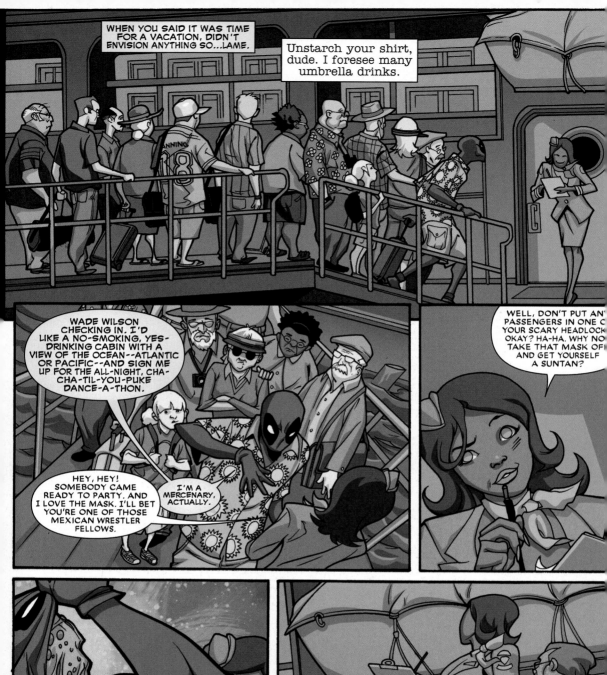

WHEN YOU SAID IT WAS TIME FOR A VACATION, DIDN'T ENVISION ANYTHING SO...LAME.

Unstarch your shirt, dude. I foresee many umbrella drinks.

WADE WILSON CHECKING IN. I'D LIKE A NO-SMOKING, YES-DRINKING CABIN WITH A VIEW OF THE OCEAN--ATLANTIC OR PACIFIC--AND SIGN ME UP FOR THE ALL-NIGHT, CHA-CHA-TIL-YOU-PUKE DANCE-A-THON.

HEY, HEY! SOMEBODY CAME READY TO PARTY. AND I LOVE THE MASK. I'LL BET YOU'RE ONE OF THOSE MEXICAN WRESTLER FELLOWS.

I'M A MERCENARY, ACTUALLY.

WELL, DON'T PUT AN[Y] PASSENGERS IN ONE [OF] YOUR SCARY HEADLOCK[S], OKAY? HA-HA. WHY NO[T] TAKE THAT MASK OF[F] AND GET YOURSELF A SUNTAN?

I GUESS A LITTLE SUN MIGHT BE NICE, AND--

PUT IT BACK ON! PUT IT BACK ON!

I'D LIKE TO BE ON THE OTHER SIDE OF THE SHIP FROM HIM, PLEASE.

LIKE THIS!

AND I COULD HAVE SWORE I WANTED TO START--

That's just silly.

AS OPPOSED TO...?

THIS?

It's funny.

IT'S EMBARRASSING.

Humanizing.

I'M NOT KILLING ANYONE!

AND HOW DOES THAT MAKE YOU FEEL?

DON'T YOU START!

I mean, can you get through a whole story without killing anyone?

WHY THE #### WOULD I?

So we can learn something new about you. Depth.

I'M AN UNKILLABLE KILLER. DEPTH ISN'T AT ISSUE.

IS IT SUPPOSED TO BE CLEVER HAVING ME HIDE OUR ###?

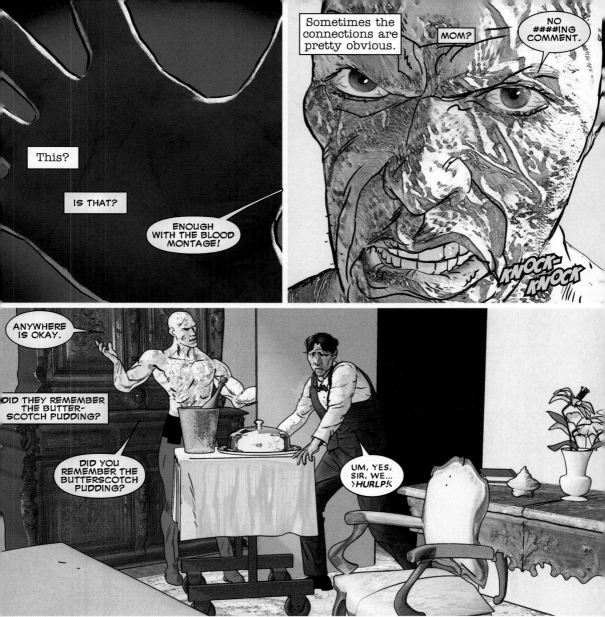

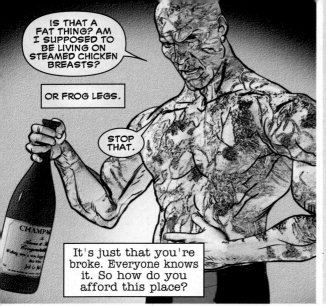

Aren't you tired of that kind of thing?

NOPE.

...oesn't it ever ...el redundant?

CAN'T SAY THAT IT DOES.

Like maybe it'd be interesting to do something new?

LIKE HAVING MY ### WASHED ON A BIDET?

It was a new experience anyway.

SO WAS WATCHING A GUY PUKE IN HIS OWN MOUTH.

NOPE, SEEN THAT BEFORE.

But the bidet did feel nice.

WELL...

IT WAS...

REFRESHING.

See!

THEN I'M THE EGG.

WHOA! THAT IS. MY MIND IS BLOWN ALL OVER THE PLACE.

Yeah, but obviously you didn't lead to me.

THAT SO?

SO IF I WASN'T HERE WOULD YOU BE WRITING THIS?

EXCUSE ME, THAT'S OUR--

WHAT'S HER PROBLEM?

That's their car.

IF YOU DON'T WANT ME TO TAKE IT, GIVE ME MY OWN.

SO PEAKS THE EGG.

THIS IS SO MUCH BETTER THAN THE BUS.

Kind of over the top.

BOK-BOK-BOK.

Will you stop that! I mean, what is the point?

HE WANTS TO KNOW THE POINT.

THE POINT IS THAT EVERYTHING HAS A REASON.

TURN, TURN, TURN.

I LOVE THAT SONG.

NO YOU DON'T.

THEN WHY DID I JUST...?

Chicken! Egg!

RIGHT.

IF YOU ELIMINATE A THING'S SOURCE.

OR REASON FOR BEING.

YOU KILL IT.

Yeah, okay. But.

OTHERWISE...

OTHERWISE, IT CAN BE HARD TO KILL A THING.

DON'T

I

KNOW

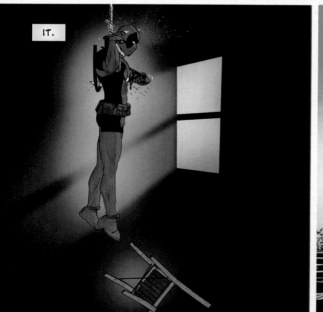

IT.

I still don't...

MY BODY IS A GIANT SELF-HEALING SCAR.

YUCKY. MAKES PEOPLE MOUTH-PUKE.

MAKES ME MOUTH PUKE.

IF YOU WERE THOUGHTFUL, YOU MIGHT HAVE REALIZED A LITTLE SOMETHING ABOUT ME.

THE BASICS.

LIKE THE FACT THAT I WANT TO DIE.

FOR KEEPSIES.

Well I could just--

WHAT? PUSH ME DOWN THE STAIRS?

WOULDN'T LEAVE A SCRATCH.

AND SAY YOU DROWN ME IN ACID AND I BOIL AWAY TO GREASE. WHAT THEN?

I'LL TELL YOU WHAT.

AS SOON AS THERE'S ENOUGH DEMAND TO SEE ME BACK, I'LL BE RESURRECTED BY SOME CLONE MASTER WITH A SCRAP OF MY DNA.

THE HIGH EVOLUTIONARY!

CAN WE MAINTAIN COMPOSURE FOR JUS ONE MINUTE HERE?

PROBABLY NOT.

MAXIMUM EFFORT.

NO PROMISES.

POINT IS, AS LONG AS ANYONE WANTS TO READ ME, I'M NOT GOING TO GET ANY PEACE.

NOT THAT THE NUMBERS ARE HUGE.

RESPECTABLE! THEY'RE RESPECTABLE. I HAVE A SMALL BUT DEVOTED FOLLOWING.

CULT!

MAN, I'LL SAY. HAVE YOU SEEN MY WIKIPEDIA ENTRY? IT'S LONGER THAN ####ING SPIDER-MAN'S!

IT'S A COLLECTOR'S ITEM NOW.

ONE DOWN. FORTY SEVEN THOUSAND, NINE HUNDRED AND SIXTY-ONE TO GO.

I'm never going to work again.

ONE DOWN

CHARLIE HUSTON WRITER   KYLE BAKER ARTIST

DEADPOOL 900

Cover Gallery 1-100

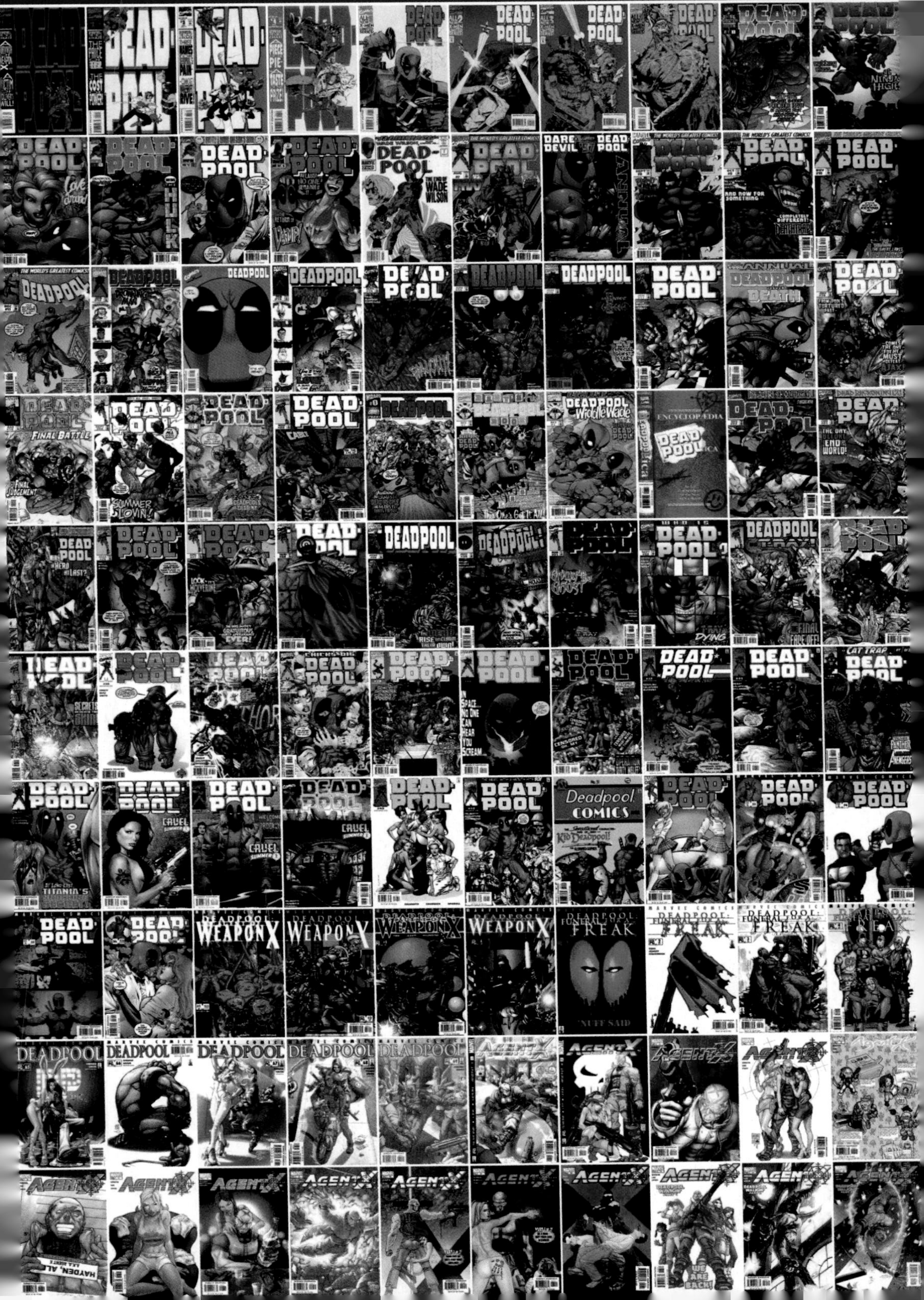

Design: Spring Hoteling • Production: Ryan Devall • Special Thanks to Japh Yc

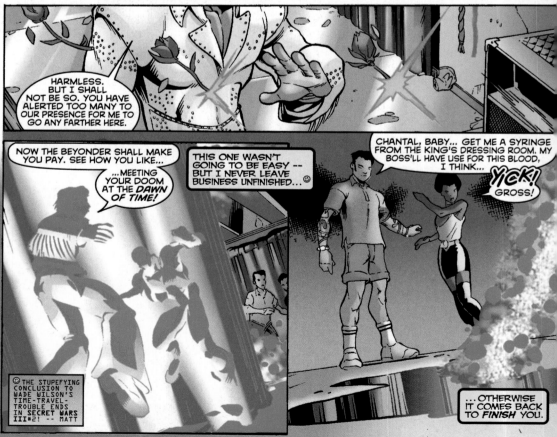

<NOW THIS WAS THE WORK OF ONE SICK PUPPY -- TAKE IT FROM THE MAC-DADDY WISHBONE OF SICK PUPPIES.>

<YOU GOIN' TO BURY THIS GUY OR GIVE HIM TO SOMEONE'S GRANNY FOR A JIGSAW PUZZLE?>

<WHO WAS THE POOR SLOB? THIS WAS ONE BODY, RIGHT?>

<HE WAS MY RIGHT-HAND MAN. MY LIEUTENANT. TONIGHT I HAVE TO TELL HIS WIFE, CHANTAL, WHAT... HAPPENED.>

<LIEUTENANT? IS IT HARD TO REPLACE ONE OF THOSE?>

<SEE THIS HAND? IN MY PROFESSION, YOU LOSE ONE JOINT OF A FINGER FOR EVERY MISTAKE YOU MAKE.>

<SHIGERU... MY LIEUTENANT -- HE WAS MISSING NO FINGERS. BECAUSE OF MISTAKES HIS FATHER MADE, HE DID NOT ALLOW HIMSELF TO MAKE MISTAKES. UNTIL NOW.>

<HE WAS IRREPLACEABLE. JUST LIKE THESE MISSING JOINTS OF MINE.>

<THIS IS THE OYAKATA. A COACH OF RIKISHI -- WHAT YOU CALL SUMO WRESTLERS. HE IS THE KILLER'S NEXT TARGET. STOP THE KILLER.>

<FOR ME. FOR SHIGERU.>

<TH-THIS... IS THE TARGET... YOU WANT...SAVED? UH...WHO IS THIS KILLER? ANY CLUES?>

<NO QUESTIONS, SIR! THAT IS OUR ARRANGEMENT. THE PHOTO -- YOU'RE..! YOU WILL REMEMBER WHAT THE OYAKATA LOOKS LIKE?>

<YEAH... YEAH... I WON'T FORGET THE GUY.>

CRUMPLE

HAHAHAHAHAHAHAHAHAHA

HIT BY *16 TONS*, GOING *50MPH*, AND THE THING IS *STILL* LAUGHING. ONLY ONE GUY CAN PLAY A SHOW LIKE THAT AND IT'S *ME*. USED TO BE ONLY ME.

THE MUNCHKIN'S GOING TO BE *BACK*... AND *EXPECTING* ME.

<I OFFER HEARFELT THANKS FOR YOUR ASSISTANCE TONIGHT, STRANGELY GARBED MAN.>

<THANK YOU! THANK YOU, NO APPLAUSE NEC->

<ONLY ONE FOOL BOWS LIKE THAT! CHIYO! YOU CAME BACK, MY BOY!>

I DON'T WHAT YOU'RE TALKING ABOUT! *LEGGO*, YOU *LARD-BUTT!*

GREAT. I WAS AFRAID HE'D *RECOGNIZE* ME...

<C'MON! C'MON! STOP SPEAKING ENGLISH. YOU CAN'T FOOL ME! ADMIT IT OR I'LL TELL MY BOYS ABOUT THE TWO WOMEN IN OSAKA WHO YOU DISCOVERED WEREN'T EXACTLY WOMEN...>

<OKAY! OKAY!>
<I'M SORRY, OYAKATA. I-I'VE BEEN THROUGH A LOT. YOU WERE ANOTHER TIME...>

<NEVER MIND THAT. YOU'RE SKIN AND BONES! WHAT HAVE THEY BEEN FEEDING YOU?! AND TAKE OFF THAT SILLY MASK.>

<YOU'VE BEEN PROFESSIONAL WRESTLING, HAVEN'T YOU? ONE OF MY BOYS IN THE PACIFIC TERROR WRESTLING LEAGUE -- CAN YOU IMAGINE..?>

WHAP

DON'T TOUCH THE MASK! EVER.

<POP, I JUST GOT BACK FROM THE RESTAURANT AND HEARD WHAT HAPPENED! DON'T SNEAK OUT LIKE THAT!>

<WHO'S THE PERVERT IN THE LEATHER SUIT?>

<IT'S CHIYO! CHIYO'S RETURNED AFTER ALL THESE YEARS! ISN'T THAT GREAT?!>

<HEY, SAZAE. YOU AIN'T FAT ANYMORE...>

<THAT A GIANT FIBERGLASS WEENIE OR ARE YOU JUST HAPPY TO SEE ME?>

<DON'T YOU EVER GO NEAR MY POP AGAIN, YOU CREEP!>

THOK

NOTE TO SELF...

I QUICKLY BECAME THE STAR *RIKISHI* IN THE STABLE AND IT CAME TIME FOR ME TO CHOOSE A *SHIKONA* -- A TRADITIONAL NAME TO BE USED IN COMPETITION.

SAZAE, THE OYAKATA'S YOUNG DAUGHTER, GAVE ME MY NAME. *"CHIYONOSAKE"* -- *"THE WOLF OF THE RICE WINE."*

I *LOVED* THAT NAME. NOT BECAUSE I GOT DRUNK, BUT BECAUSE... *WELL,* WHEN LADIES GIVE ME A NAME, IT'S USUALLY NOT THAT KINDLY, IF YOU KNOW WHAT I MEAN?

IT WAS A *GOOD* LIFE. BEING WAITED ON HAND AND FOOT. A CLEAR OPPONENT -- A WORLD OF *RULES* AND *ORDER.*

SAZAE USED TO DO THE COOKING IN THE HEYA, SINCE THE OYAKATA'S WIFE HAD DIED IN SOME ACCIDENT.

SHE TOOK A LIKING TO THIS UP-AND-COMING RIKISHI WHO SEEMED TO TREAT HER WORLD LIKE IT WAS ALL SOME KIND OF FUN RIDE.

SHE USED TO SNEAK ME *CURRY UDON* TO GET ON MY GOOD SIDE. AND THE WHOLE TIME THE OYAKATA'S TURNING A BLIND EYE TO IT ALL, LIKE SOME MATCH-MAKING *GRANDMA.*

IT WAS EVENTUALLY ARRANGED THAT WHEN SAZAE WAS OF AGE, SHE WOULD MARRY ME -- CHIYO. I'D INHERIT THE HEYA, *CHARGE* OF THE PUPILS... AND EVERYTHING VALUABLE TO THE OYAKATA.

MOST *IMPORTANTLY,* I'D BE ENTRUSTED WITH SAZAE'S WELFARE -- NO ONE ELSE WOULD THE OYAKATA TRUST WITH HIS DEAREST TREASURE.

I CAN TELL YOU, IT WAS ABOUT AS CLOSE AS A FELLA LIKE ME COULD COME TO THE *WHITE PICKET* FENCE ROUTINE. ALL COZY. *UNTIL...*

MY LITTLE MISTAKE WAS THAT I THOUGHT I COULD LEAVE BEHIND ALL THE UNHAPPINESS AND UGLINESS IN MY LIFE.

ONE SUNNY MORNING, THERE WAS A *MESSAGE* IN MY CREME-FILLED *DWINKEE.* IT WAS TIME FOR ME TO DO WHAT I WAS BEING PAID FOR.

AND WHAT WAS THAT? *SURPRISE.*

"KILL THE OYAKATA."

FOR ONCE IN MY LIFE, I SAID *"ENOUGH."* FOR THE FIRST TIME EVER, I WAS WALKING AWAY FROM A JOB -- *LEAVING* BEFORE I COULD HURT ANYBODY EXCEPT *MYSELF.*

SHE WOULDN'T MAKE IT *EASY,* THOUGH. THEY *NEVER* DO.

I TOLD HER THAT I COULDN'T EXPLAIN WHY I WAS RUNNING AWAY. THAT SHE WOULDN'T *WANT* TO KNOW WHY.

<I DON'T *CARE* WHY! YOU *CAN'T* GO...OR... OR...I'LL SCREAM!>

AND I COULDN'T *HAVE THAT...*

THUMP

I HAD TO KNOCK HER UNCONSCIOUS BEFORE SHE KNEW WHAT HIT HER. I *HAD* TO.

THEN I DID WHAT I DO SO WELL -- I *DISAPPEARED.*

<CHIYO! STOP! WHERE ARE YOU GOING?>

AND IT WAS A LONG, *LONG* TIME UNTIL THERE WAS A MORNING I DIDN'T WONDER WHAT SHE DID WHEN SHE WOKE UP. IF SHE WAS *SAD* OR *ANGRY*...OR JUST AS DISAPPOINTED IN ME AS I WAS.

<POP, YOU OKAY?! GET *OFF* HIM, CHIYO -->

<-- BEFORE I **CHOP** YOU *OFF!*>

<KEEP HER AWAY FROM MY **G-R-O-I-N!**>

<SOMEONE'S TRYING TO KNOCK OFF YOUR POP, BUT IT *AIN'T* ME.>

<I *STILL* TRUST HIM, SAZAE. YOU DON'T *KNOW* HIM LIKE *I* DO.>

<I KNOW HIM *TOO* WELL. THAT'S THE *PROBLEM,* POP.>

<OKAY. TAKE THE FAMILY FEUD *OUTSIDE.* I GOTTA *SLEEP,* AND I DON'T WANT TO REVEAL TO MERE MORTALS WHERE THE *FLY* IS ON THIS JOY-SUIT.>

<REST UP. THAT MUNCHKIN WON'T ATTACK UNTIL *TOMORROW* NIGHT.>

<HE *WON'T?* HOW DO YOU KNOW?!>

<TRADE SECRET.>

YEAH, I *KNOW.* AT FIRST I THOUGHT THAT THING MIGHT HAVE JUST BEEN *STALKING* ME, DRESSING UP IN MY SHRUNKEN THROW-AWAYS. BUT HE'S GOT MY *MOVES.*

AND HIM LIVING THROUGH THAT TRUCK *SETTLED* IT -- HE'S ALSO GOT MY *ACCELERATED HEALING FACTOR.* HE'S *ME,* WITH *HALF* THE CALORIES.

WEIRD, BUT NO WEIRDER THAN ANYTHING ELSE ON THIS FIELD TRIP -- AND THAT'S A NICE BON-BON TO GO TO SLEEP ON...

IT WAS A STRANGELY *QUIET* NIGHT FOR THE NEIGHBORHOOD. YOU COULDN'T EVEN HEAR THE *TRUCK HORNS* FROM THE FREEWAY.

IT'S KIND OF... *SCARY* NOT TO HEAR ANY NOISE THIS DEEP IN THE CITY -- JUST WAITING FOR *DEATH* TO CREEP UP.

HE'S GONE. PROBABLY RAN *AWAY AGAIN*, THE BIG COWARD.

<POLICE FILES?>

<YAKUZA ASSASSINATIONS...?>

<GIMME THOSE!>

<SAZAE! I WAS JUST COMING TO... I JUST WANTED TO SAY I'M...>

<LOOK. I WAS LYING. IT WAS A MEAN, STUPID THING TO SAY ABOUT YOUR DAD -->

<YOU USED TO BE THE ONLY ONE WHO NEVER LIED TO ME.>

<PROMISE ME YOU WILL BE THAT PERSON AGAIN -->

<-- THE ONE PERSON I CAN TRUST IN THE WORLD...>

<LOOK OUT BELOW -- WHOOPS!>

HAHAHAHA!

<LOOKS LIKE FALL'S HERE!>

<NEED A LITTLE HELP?>

<UH-OH...>

I BURIED THE LITTLE FELLA IN A LOCAL PLAYGROUND WHERE I ONCE SAW A LITTLE BOY BURY HIS *CAT* AT MIDNIGHT.

IT'S A BETTER GRAVE THAN I'LL PROBABLY GET WHEN *MY* DAY COMES.

<...SAZAE'S GOT HER HANDS FULL RUNNING THE *CHANKO-NABE* RESTAURANT -- THAT'S HOW WE KEEP THE MONEY COMING IN DURING THE *LOSING SEASONS.*>

<BEEN A *LONG TIME* SINCE THEY CUT MY HAIR -- TOO LONG TO GO BACK IN THE RING. *HALF* OF MY MEN ARE IN THE HOSPITAL. THE OTHER HALF ARE IN THE *MORGUE.*>

<IT'LL TAKE ME A FEW YEARS TO TRAIN UP A NEW BATCH OF *RIKISHI.* I WANT YOU TO *COME BACK* TO SUMO.>

<YOU *ANSWER* ME -- YOU COMING BACK TO FIGHT? *ANSWER* ME OR I DON'T WANT TO SEE YOU HERE AGAIN... *EVER.*>

<WE'RE NOT TALKING ABOUT *THAT* NOW. I WANT TO KNOW IF YOU -- IF *WE'RE* -- GOING AFTER THE BOSS. HE HIRED SOMEONE TO *KILL YOU!*>

<AND HE HIRED *YOU* TO *SAVE ME.* THAT MAKES IT *OKAY.* THAT'S HOW WE... HOW *THEY* WORK. BUSINESS OUTSIDE IS *DIFFERENT* THAN IN HERE.>

<YOU *DISAPPOINTED* IN YOUR *OYAKATA,* HUNH? 'CAUSE HE *KILLED* TO KEEP THIS PLACE OPEN -- TO KEEP YOU *FAT?*>

<I *NEVER* SAID ANYTHING WHEN YOU *LEFT* YEARS AGO. I NEED YOU *NOW,* THOUGH.>

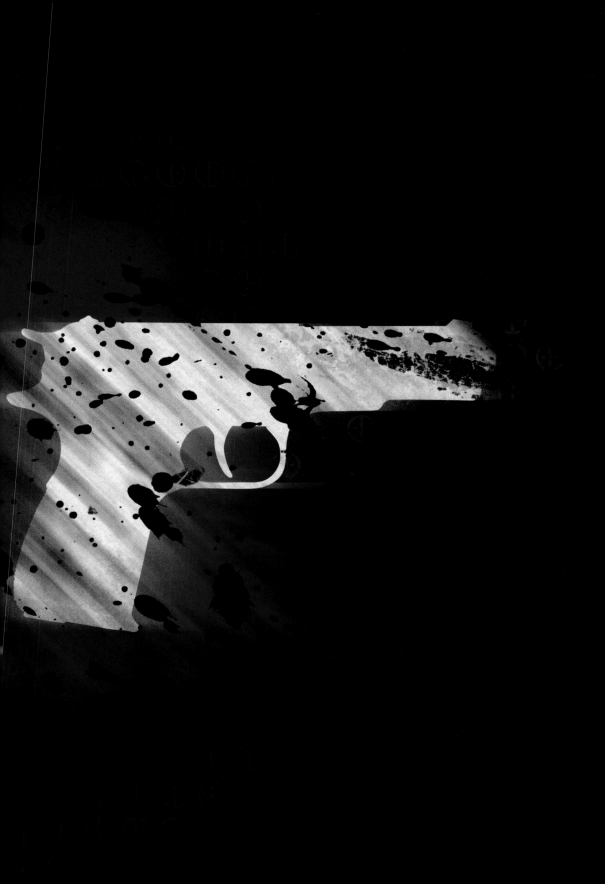

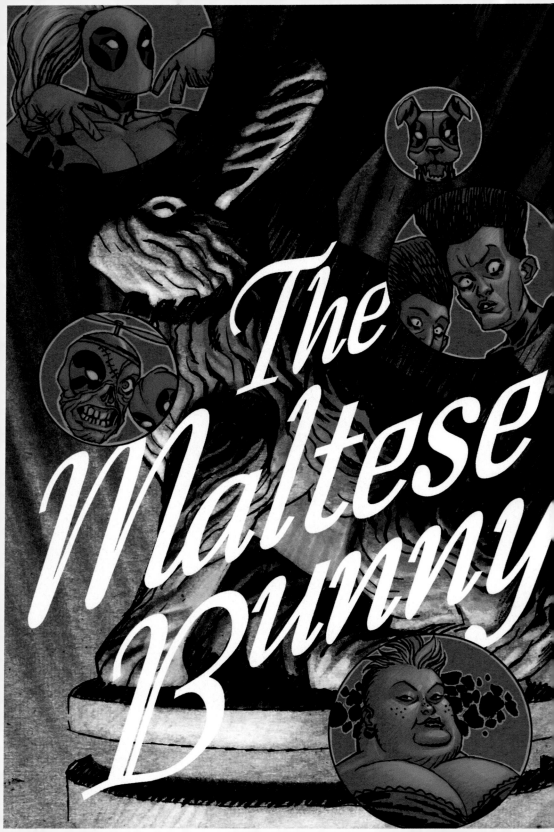

THE END

INEZ? MY NAME IS *O'WONDERFUL*. AND PLEASE DON'T CALL ME CRAZY AGAIN, OR I'LL RIP OUT YOUR SPLEEN.

MAYBE SHE HAS AMNESIA. BEST PLAY ALONG.

GOTCHA.

OKAY, MISS O'WONDERFUL. WHAT SEEMS TO BE YOUR PROBLEM?

IT'S MY DOG. I LOST IT.

IT'S A CHOCOLATE DOG. WITH BIG BUNNY EARS.

WHAT KIND OF DOG? IF IT'S A POODLE, WE CHARGE EXTRA.

NIPPERS THAT THEY ARE.

HYDRA BOB WILL PERSONALLY OVERSEE THE CASE.

DO I GET PAID FOR THIS?

NO, BUT YOU GET TO KEEP YOUR TOES.

IT'S FOR MY NEPHEW FOR EASTER, AND I SIMPLY MUST GET IT BACK.

IS THIS ENOUGH MONEY?

OKAY, MISS O'WONDERFUL. TAKE ME TO WHERE YOU LAST SAW THIS CHOC--

BLAM

UGH!

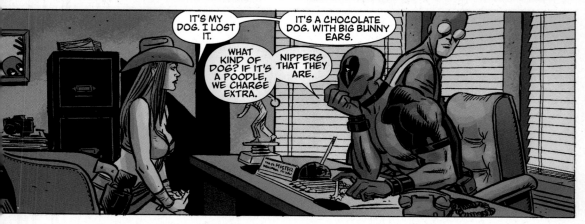

HA, HA. I LIKE YOU, MR. DEADPOOL. CLEARLY YOU LIKE TO TALK.

AND I'M A MAN WHO LIKES TO TALK TO A MAN WHO LIKES TO TALK.

YOU'RE NOT EVEN A *MAN*, MAN!

FISK WAS SICK.

HAVE YOU EVER HEARD OF THE MANDARIN, SIR? A PERSON MOST FOUL.

LIKE THE LITTLE ORANGES.

UGH, I DON'T LIKE THOSE. TOO SWEET.

ME EITHER.

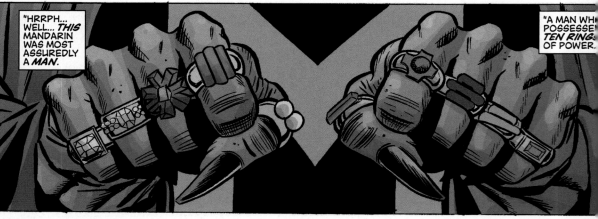

"HRRPH... WELL... *THIS* MANDARIN WAS MOST ASSUREDLY A *MAN*.

"A MAN WHO POSSESSED *TEN RINGS* OF POWER.

ONE RING COULD FIRE AN *ICE RAY* THAT COULD CHILL YOUR SOUL AND YOUR MARTINI AT THE SAME TIME.

LORD, NOT THIS SPEECH AGAIN.

DEA!
PRIVATE IN

THE SECOND RING COULD INCREASE *MENTAL ACUITY* TO THE POINT WHERE ONE COULD HOLD SWAY OVER ANOTHER'S MIND.

YET A THIRD COULD PRODUCE ENOUGH *ELECTRICITY* TO POWER A SMALL CITY.

YOU *LOVE* ME...

STOP TOUCHING ME.

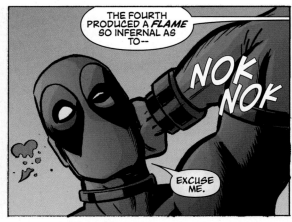

THE FOURTH PRODUCED A *FLAME* SO INFERNAL AS TO--

NOK NOK

EXCUSE ME.

BOB? YOU'RE NOT DEAD?

JUST A SCRATCH, BOSS, BUT LOOK WHAT SOME SEA CAPTAIN RANDOMLY DROPPED OFF FOR ME AT THE HOSPITAL.

IT'S THE DOG-- BUNNY-- THING!

LOOK, BOB. TRAGICALLY, I'M GOING TO HAVE TO PIN YOUR MURDER ON MY SOON-TO-BE FIANCE.

IT'S PROBABLY BEST IF YOU STAY DEAD...

AHHHHHHH!

...NINE. *DISINTEGRATION.* TRUE AND COMPLETE. I HAVE NEVER HEARD TELL OF RETURN FROM IT. HEH, HEH... *HAH... HAGHHH...* EXCUSE ME. NOW THE FINAL RING --

STOP ALL THE JAB-JAB-JABBERING. I HAVE THE DOG!

DEADPOOL

≋BURP≋ OR AT LEAST I KNOW WHERE I CAN GET IT...

YOU ATE IT? YOU IDIOT!

MMM... I HAVE A WEAKNESS.

RELAX. GET ME A BRAN MUFFIN AND GIVE IT ABOUT THREE HOURS -- HURP!

DEADPOOL

FOOM!

I'VE ALWAYS WANTED TO DO THAT.

HE HAS THE RINGS!

MAY I REMIND YOU, MR. DEADPOOL. YOU MAY HAVE THE DOG, BUT WE MOST CERTAINLY HAVE YOU.

WELL, YOU CAN'T HAVE ME. MY HEART BELONGS TO CRAZY INEZ.

THAT'S IT!

DON'T CALL ME CRAZY!

OOF!

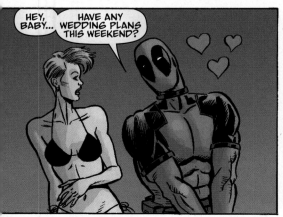

I'M COMIN', BOY!

SWIWOOSH

OOF!

FWUMPP

≥HUFF≤ OKAY... PAPA'S ON HIS WAY ≥HUFF≤

JUST... HOLD ON... ≥HUFF≤ GIMME A SEC...

≥FART≤

WAAAAAIT, A MINUTE...

THINK OUTSIDE THE BUN!

NOW PAPA GOT WHAT HE NEED TO MAKE THEM BAD GUYS BLEED!

NOT A BAD BATTLE CRY GIVEN MY BRAIN'S SOAKED IN HYDROGENATED HORMONE OIL AND SATURATED BUTTER FAT.

WE'RE RECEIVING A RED ALERT, YOUR DARKNESSHIP.

HMMM. ANOTHER GRINDER CLOG.

WHICH-EVER OF YOU CLEANS IT CAN FEED ON THE SWEET OBSTRUCTION WITHIN.

I DEMAND A REFUND!

SKLAMMM

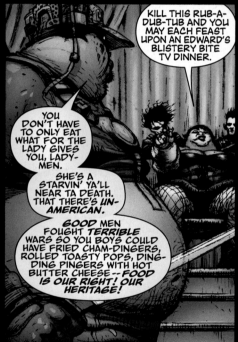

KILL THIS RUB-A-DUB-TUB AND YOU MAY EACH FEAST UPON AN EDWARD'S BLISTERY BITE TV DINNER.

YOU DON'T HAVE TO ONLY EAT WHAT FOR THE LADY GIVES YOU, LADY-MEN.

SHE'S A STARVIN' YA'LL NEAR TA DEATH. THAT THERE'S UN-AMERICAN.

GOOD MEN FOUGHT TERRIBLE WARS SO YOU BOYS COULD HAVE FRIED CHAM-DINGERS, ROLLED TOASTY POPS, DING-DING PINGERS WITH HOT BUTTER CHEESE -- FOOD IS OUR RIGHT! OUR HERITAGE!

THEY NEED ME TO STARVE THEM! THEY HUNGER FOR IT!

IF THEY GREW PLUMP AGAIN NO ONE IN THE VAMPIRE "SCENE" WOULD ESTEEM THEM. NOT EVEN SWEET STEVEN THE JUGALO!

ME, I THINK THAT'S SOCIAL LEVERING. THE KIND A SOCIALIST WOULD USE ON GOOD FOLKS TO DUST THEIR MINDS WITH THE CLOUDY LOGIC OF EVOLUTION!

PINKO COMMIE NONSENSE TALK! I DIDN'T BLOW OFF MY DINK-A-DILLY IN THE JUNGLE WAR OF CONTRA FOR THIS SHAMALAMA-DOO-DOO!!

ARE YOU GONNA TAKE THIS GUFF?

OR ARE YOU'RE GONNA KILL AND EAT THAT ANGST PASTRY!?

The *Ru-Bari* of the *Cygnus* system were a race noted for their profound depth of feeling...

...expressed in some of the most beautiful *music*, the most soul stirring *singing* the universe had ever heard.

So *secure* where the Ru-Bari in their own selves that they did not *flinch* when a member of the *Nova Corps*, too deep in his *cups*...

...dismissed their world as *"The Planet of the Celery People."*

Why is it that the most *innocent* are the most *vulnerable* to purest evil?

Why is it the purest and most *sublime* cultures are the ones most quickly *devolved* into the lowest and most despicable form of *performance art*?

How could that thoughtless appellation of *"Celery People"* be so horrifically *embraced* when the maddened Ru-Bari consumed each other with *bleu cheese dressing* and Buffalo wings?

And... most important of all:

EVEN *I'D* HEARD OF BERNARD'S OF GREAT NECK...

...ORGANIZED CRIME'S *FAVORITE* WEDDING, BAR MITZVAH, AND CONFIRMATION MILL...

...AND GOOD TASTE HAD *NOTHING* TO DO WITH IT.

YO, DEAD -- BEEN *TOO* LONG.

ABSOLUTELY.

WHO THE HELL IS THAT GUY...

...AND WHAT *IS* IT ABOUT A LIFE OF *CRIME* THAT MAKES PEOPLE SO *FAMILIAR?*

AH -- THE PROUD AND HAPPY BAR MITZVAH BOY'S *MOM* AND HER *INTENDED...*

...LILLIAN HOWARD AND AL SEGAL.

I KNEW LILLIAN'S LATE HUSBAND, PHIL...

...FOR A GREEDY, LOAN-SHARKING HOMICIDAL *HOODLUM,* PHIL WAS AN *OKAY* GUY...

...*WHICH,* IF I'M TO TAKE MY CLIENT AT HIS *WORD,* COULD NOT BE SAID FOR HER *FIANCE.*

"Today I Am Da Man!"

Written and Illustrated by Howard Chaykin

HEY, CHECK IT *OUT*--

-- SETH'S MOM HIRED A *CLOWN*.

YEAH -- BUT I'M SURE HE'S AN *IRONIC* CLOWN, RIGHT?

OH, YEAH -- -- WHEN IT COMES TO CLOWNING, I'M *ALL* ABOUT THE IRONY.

HEY, STICK *AROUND* -- -- I'M JUST ABOUT TO IRONICALLY *JUGGLE* FRANKS IN BLANKETS, CHOPPED LIVER AND CRUDITES.

WHAT A *JERK*.

NOW IS THAT *NICE*?

THAT'S JUST *AMBER* --

...SAME OLD SAME OLD.

SETH HOWARD REALLY **WAS** HIS FATHER'S SON.

WHEN HE *HIRED* ME TO DO THIS *GIG*, I ASSUMED IT WAS ABOUT THE *MONEY*.

I MEAN, IT'S *USUALLY* ABOUT THE MONEY, RIGHT?

BUT IN *THIS* CASE, IT WAS ALL ABOUT THE *LOVE*.

AL SEGAL IS A TOTAL *SCUMBAG*..

...TAKING **HIM** OUT IS ALMOST A PUBLIC **SERVICE**...

SKLUSSSH!

...WHICH IS **NOT** TO SAY I'M **WAIVING** THE BAR MITZVAH BOY'S **PAYCHECK**, FOR GOD'S SAKE...

...I AM A **PROFESSIONAL**, AFTER ALL.

'EY -- WHAT'D THE IRONIC CLOWN DO TO **AL**?

SETH'S MOTHER **LILLIAN** WAS PROBABLY GOING TO FEEL A TOUCH **SAD** FOR AWHILE --

-- BUT NOT FOR **LONG**...

CHANNGGK- CHANGGKK!

...I MEAN, LET'S **FACE** IT...

...ANY WOMAN WHO'D **MARRY** PHIL HOWARD AND **CONSIDER** MARRYING AL SEGAL...

BRATA- BLAMABRAKA- CHANGKK!

MARVEL BROMANCE COMICS PRESENTS:
"NO LONGER IN A RELATIONSHIP"
WRITTEN AND ILLUSTRATED BY TIM HAMILTON

AMUSING.

FACELESS BOOK
The networking site for disfigured sycophants

BARON ZEMO
JUST LEFT UPPER DECKER IN CAPTAIN AMERICA'S TOILET.

4 PEOPLE LIKE THIS.

DOOM!

DEADPOOL!

WHY DOOM?! WHY DID YOU DO IT!?

I GUESS IT WAS ONLY A MATTER OF TIME BEFORE YOU NOTICED. IT'S OVER BETWEEN US!

DUH! OUT OF THE FOUR PEOPLE ON FACELESS BOOK, YOU AND JIGSAW WERE THE ONLY TWO TO ACCEPT MY FRIEND REQUEST! DO YOU SEE WHAT JIGSAW POSTS ON HIS UPDATES? DO YOU?

PHOTOS OF HIS CAT. THAT'S IT.

AND THE CAT IS UGLY.

AND HE DRESSES THE CAT UP SOMETIMES.

AND I DON'T THINK IT'S REALLY A CAT.

DRASTIC MEASURES I KNOW. BUT I HAD TO UN-FRIEND YOU. I TIRED OF THAT WEB COMIC YOU FORCE ME TO READ WEEK AFTER WEEK.

THAT STORY LINE WITH THE UNICORNS AND THE RABBITS AND ALL THE BLOOD. JUST... STOP IT. IT'S PATHETIC.

NOW LEAVE ME. I MUST YET AGAIN PRESS THE "SHARE" BUTTON.

YOU WIN, DOOM... FOR NOW.

MY DOOM-I-CORNS! NOOOOOOO!

"THE NINJA RABBIT KILLS DOCTOR DOOM'S DOOMICORNS." Y-YES, MR. DEADPOOL THIS WILL MAKE A GREAT ON GOING COMIC BOOK!

AND I THINK YOU'RE RIGHT ABOUT THE ART. YOU'LL DO A MUCH BETTER JOB THAN JOHN ROMITA JR. WOULD.

MARVEL COMICS

COMICS

AXEL ALO

A WISE CHOICE MR. ALONSO, A WISE CHOICE.

TELL ME, MR. DEAD-POOL, WHAT DOES AMERICA HAVE THAT CANADA DOES NOT?

AMERICAN IDOL.

APART FROM THAT.

NANCY PELOSI, THE ABILITY TO WIN AT SPORTS OTHER THAN ICE HOCKEY, TAYLOR SWIFT, GUN CRIME, DON DELILLO, PHILADELPHIA, A REALLY BIG HIPPO AT SAN THE DIEGO ZOO...

PLEASE STOP NOW.

OK.

ZE ANSWER IS SUPER HEROES, MR. DEAD-POOL.

WAIT, THERE'S THOSE ALPHA FLIGHT DOOFUSES.

THEY, SADLY, MAY BE DEAD.

YEAH? WHO OFFED THEM?

Bendis.

ZAT IS NOT IMPORTANT, MR. DEAD-POOL.

WHAT IS IMPORTANT IS THAT CANADACORP™! BELIEVES THAT CANADA, OUR GREAT NATION, DESERVES ITS OWN CAPTAIN AMERICA.

A SUPREMELY FAMOUS SYMBOL OF ALL THAT IS GOOD ABOUT CANADA. SOMEONE WHO IS THE BEST THERE IS...

...GUYS.

JUST WANNA SAY...

FIRST PERSON MENTIONS WOLVERINE GETS AN EXTRA NOSTRIL.

'KAY?

NO, MR. DEAD-POOL!

IT IS YOU WHO WE ABSOLUTELY DESIRE AS OUR DEFINITE FIRST CHOICE! YOU WHO ARE CURRENTLY CANADA'S MOST HIGH-PROFILE SUPER-PERSON!

BECOME THE IDOL OF CANADA!

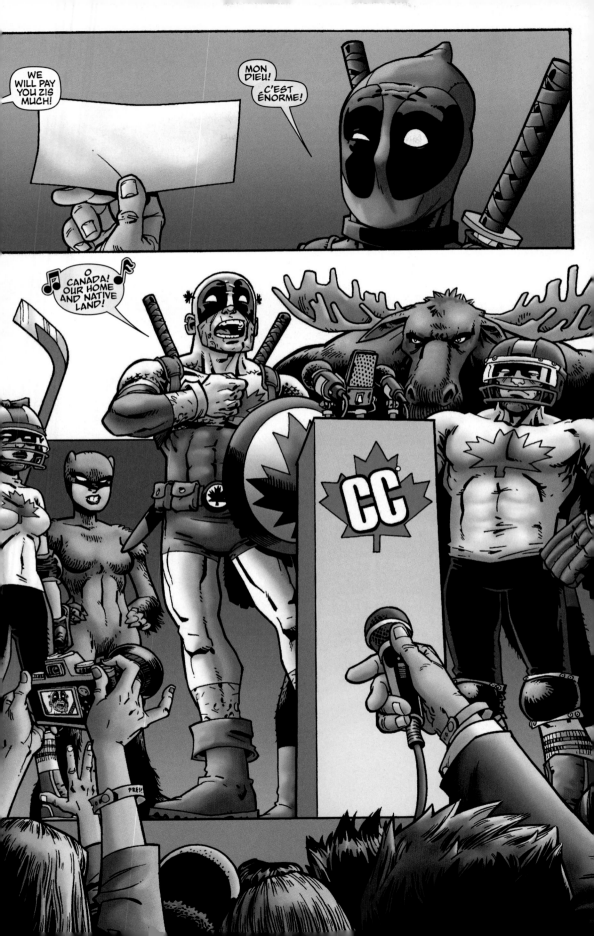

MOUTH
OF THE BORDER
Cullen Bunn: Writer • Matteo Scalera: Art
Matt Wilson: Colors

LATER.

YEAH, BUT IT WAS RIB NIGHT.

ABOUT THIRTY SECONDS OF "MY WORST" AND MR. BIG BAD GOAT SUCKER SANG LIKE A MUTILATED CANARY.

That wasn't your worst. I've seen you be more brutal at old country buffet.

AW... ARE YOU KIDDING ME?

GOAT GOAT SUCKERS!

HOW COME NO ONE EVER TOLD ME CHUPACABRAISM WAS CONTAGIOUS!?

GRRRRR!

BAAAH!

B-AAH! BAAAH!

THE END

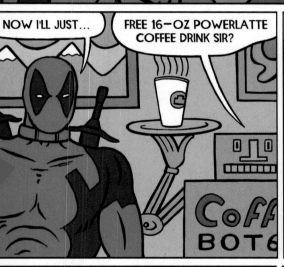

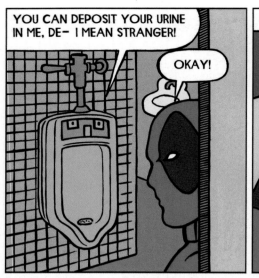

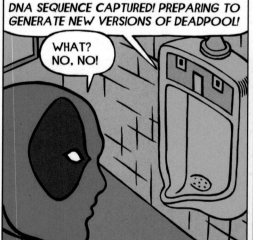

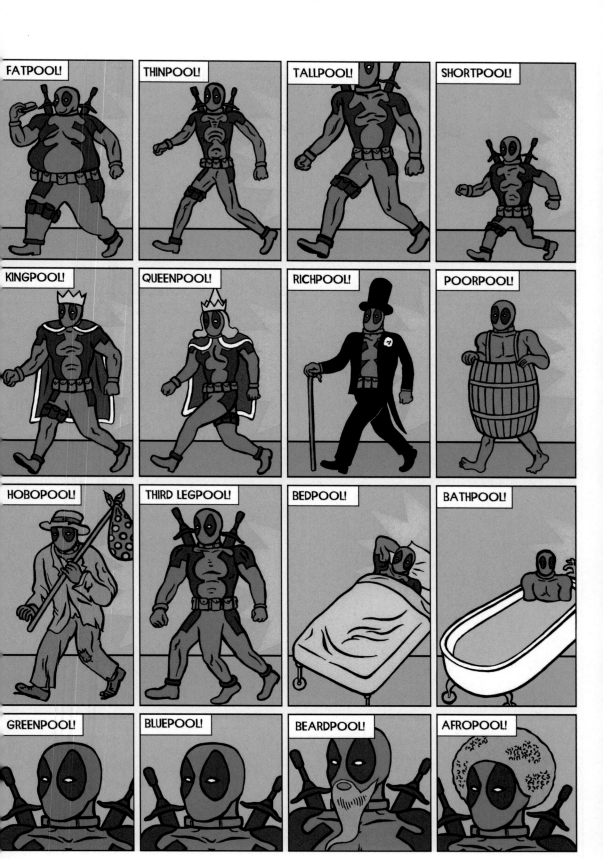

ROUNDPOOL!

BEEPOOL!

CARPOOL!

CHEFPOOL!

BEARD OF BEESPOOL!

YULEPOOL!

DROOLPOOL!

NORSEPOOL!

INVISIBLEPOOL!

FOOLPOOL!

BEARPOOL!

FROGPOOL!

PROFESSORPOOL!

MUSTACHPOOL!

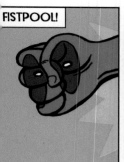

FISTPOOL!

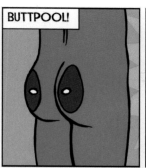

BUTTPOOL!

AND STICKPOOL!

LAME!!

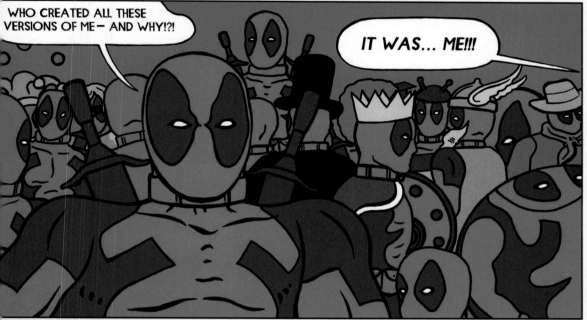

WHO CREATED ALL THESE VERSIONS OF ME — AND WHY!?!

IT WAS... ME!!!

HOT—PANTS ZEUS!

WHO?

I COME FROM AN ALTERNATE UNIVERSE... WHERE THE GREEK GODS WEAR HOT PANTS!

AND I CREATED ALL THESE VERSIONS OF DEADPOOL TO...

FIGHT!!!!!!

A NIGHTMARE on Elm Tree

Story & Art by Dean Haspiel
Colors by Joe Infurnari
Special Thanks to Reilly Brown

MISTER DEADPOOL, PLEASE SAVE MY LITTLE PUSSYCAT FROM FALLING OUT OF THAT BIG TREE!

OF ALL THE HIGH PROFILE GIGS I'VE BEEN HIRED TO DO AND ALL THE PIGGY BANKS MY SERVICES HAVE SMASHED, THIS ONE TAKES THE CAKE.

HSSSSS

QUIT YOUR FELINE FRENZY, TIGER, OR I'LL FRY YOU WITH MY LION-SIZED FLAME-THROWER!

MEOOWW-RRRR

THAT'S THE LAST TIME I ADVERTISE ON CRAIG'S LIST!

CAPTAIN AMERICA

WHO WON'T WIELD THE SHIELD?

THIS COMIC HAS NOTHING TO DO WITH
CAPTAIN AMERICA
REBORN

CAPTAIN AMERICA

WON'T

WHO WILL WIELD THE SHIELD?

This issue takes place AFTER the events of some comic on sale next month, completely blowing its ending.
And they still promoted Brevoort! The suckers.

MARVEL

To: Stephen Wacker, Senior Editor, Marvel Comics
From: Dave Althoff, Associate Counsel, Marvel Comics
Re: Captain America: Who Won't Wield the Shield

Steve,

We need to talk about this "Captain America: Who Won't Wield the Shield" nonsense. You can't be serious about publishing this book. I stopped by your office but Brennan says you're "in a meeting and won't come back until I leave you alone." How can you be in a meeting for sixteen days?! Is Brevoort leading a beard-trimming seminar or something?

I'm begging you – shelve the book. If not for me, then for my newborn twins. Look at them, Peter and Zachary – look at how happy they are. Now think of how they'll feel when this book gets us all canned. Think about it!

Look, I know you wanted me to name one of the kids Stephen. I'm prepared to do it – I'll get the birth certificate, change it up, and boom! Stephen Wacker Althoff. Just drop this book. Please? PLEASE?!

Regards,

Dave Althoff

Mr. Wacker,
When you wake
up, you should
probably read
this.

--Brennan

P.S. Spider-Man
stinks now!

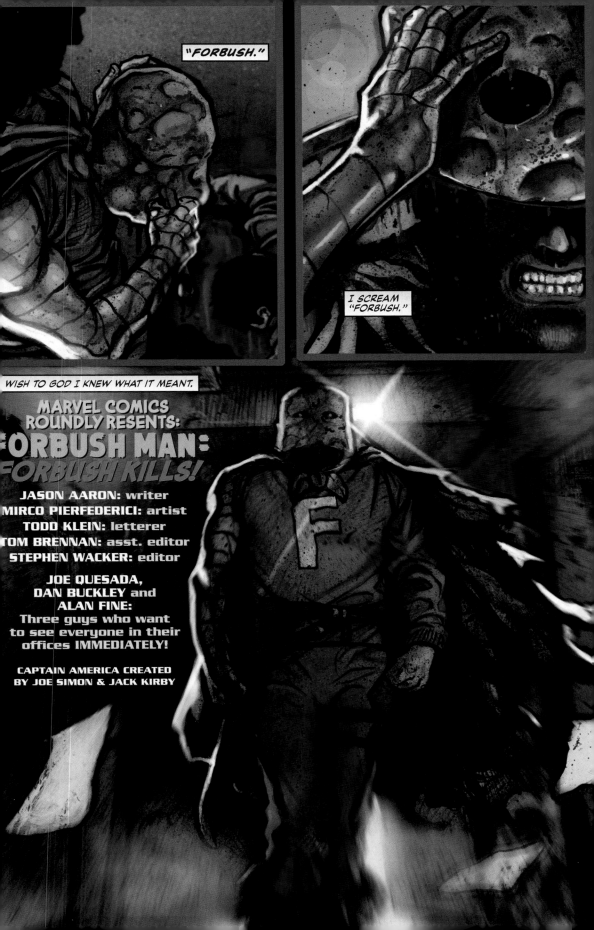

"FORBUSH."

I SCREAM "FORBUSH."

WISH TO GOD I KNEW WHAT IT MEANT.

MARVEL COMICS
ROUNDLY RESENTS:
FORBUSH MAN:
FORBUSH KILLS!

JASON AARON: writer
MIRCO PIERFEDERICI: artist
TODD KLEIN: letterer
TOM BRENNAN: asst. editor
STEPHEN WACKER: editor

JOE QUESADA,
DAN BUCKLEY and
ALAN FINE:
Three guys who want
to see everyone in their
offices IMMEDIATELY!

CAPTAIN AMERICA CREATED
BY JOE SIMON & JACK KIRBY

Later.
A small midwestern strip mall.

ELITE COMICS

SIGNING TODAY:
EISNER AWARD WINNING
COMIC BOOK SUPERSTAR:
ED BRUBAKER

AND ALSO
JASON AARON

UMM, SO AM I GONNA GET THAT COFFEE SOMETIME **SOON?** A GUY GETS THIRSTY WINNING ALL THESE **EISNERS.**

ED, I TOLD YOU BEFORE, I DON'T WORK HERE. IT'S **ME,** JASON AARON, REMEMBER?

UMM, YEAHHH. CAN I GET TWO SUGARS WITH THAT?

KRSH!

WHO THE... WHO THE HELL ARE YOU, PAL?

DON'T... DO I **KNOW** YOU?

NO.

BLAM

OH, MY GOD! THAT GUY JUST KILLED **NOMAD**!

WHO?

UMM...YEAHH, THAT'S IMPOSSIBLE. **I** KILLED NOMAD BACK IN CAP #3 (FIFTH SERIES)...YOU KNOW, RIGHT BEFORE I WON MY FIRST **EISNER.**

WHO THE HELL ARE YOU?

UM, HI, I'M JASON--

ASK ME ABOUT *CRIMINAL* AND *INCOGNITO* Available Now!

EEK

WHACK

NOT YOU. THIS ONE HERE WITH THE FUNNY LITTLE HAT.

HEY! YOU'RE ONE TO TALK!

YOU DID THIS? YOU **KILLED** CAPTAIN AMERICA?

YOU MEAN DID I WRITE THE HIGHEST SELLING COMIC BOOK OF 2007? YES, I DID. HERE, YOU WANNA TOUCH MY EISNERS, DON'T YOU?

SHUT UP BEFORE I PULL YOUR TONGUE OUT AND MAKE YOU **EAT** IT.

AND **YOU.** GOOD GOD, I DON'T EVEN KNOW WHAT TO MAKE OF THIS.

I KNOW, I'M SORRY.

I'M A VERY TROUBLED MAN.

I came through + came to, experiencing OCCULT AWARENESS for the first time... all my black-eyed "chakras" dialing open like apertures...I was reborn on the 13th day of the secret 13th month...

SAMO SAMO!

"JUMP CUT" TO TRAINING MONTAGE.

THAT SURE WAS A LOT OF TRAINING, BOSS!

THE BLACK PANTHERS APPROVE!

THE BLACK PANTHER BLACK PANTHERS APPROVE!

NOW MEET YOUR PARTNER.

'SUP?

The kitten purrs...the sound of infernal cogs spinning inside the devilish clockwork of spacetime...plot devices...narrative... the stuff of life...

I'M BAAL LEBUTTE THE GOAT BOY, AND I'M WAY BETTER THAN BUCKY BARNES BECAUSE I AM A GOAT THAT IS ALSO A BOY.

TOYETIC!

ACTION SCENE!

KROAKLE!

WATCH OUT, OLD CHUM--WHAT ARE THESE MYSTERY MONSTROSITIES?

TEEVEE EYES!!

POF!

ALTAMONT! The freak war wages on the west coast as the horrific affront of Woodstock is answered HERE AND NOW! Hippies and Hell's Angels swarm together in a tense miasma of riotous intent--!!

THE BROTHER GOT TA RAP! THE BROTHER GOT TA RAP! THE BROTHER GOT TA RAP! THE BROTHER GOT TA--

--HIT ME!

BAD VIBRATIONS! Not even the "Galactus of Soul" can keep a lid on it!

The Angels are directed by RICHARD MILHOUS MANSON, a.k.a. THE CRIMSON EUPHEMISM! Alongside him stalks BEBE REBEYONDER, the goddess of squaredelic cruelty!

THE NUCLEAR BOMB, DOES THAT BOTHER YOU?...I JUST WANT YOU TO THINK BIG, FOR *****-SAKE...*

*Richard Milhous Nixon, 25 April 1972.

"SOCK IT TO ME?"*

BAM!!

*Richard Mohawk Nixon, 16 September 1968.

If I fail, Meredith Hunter dies at dawn!

PING!

PANG!

"(18½ MINUTE GAP)"*

*Richard Mjolnir Nixon, 20 June 1972.

*Editor's Note: Calling those numbers could be a terrible idea for you.--Sexchattin' Steve

WITHOUT HIM, THE COMIC INDUSTRY GOES "BELLY UP"! THE MARVEL BULLPEN MAKES--*THE CALL!* BRING BACK *DOCTOR AMERICA!* A FREAK SÉANCE IS HELD AT THE TAR PITS! THE THICK SCENT OF *DITKIRBANKO ENERGY* SWARMS THE AIR!

DITKIRBANKODITKERBANKODITKERBANKO DITKIRBANKODITKERBANKODITKERBANKO DITKIRBANKODITKERBANKO DITKIRBANKO!

BLUBB BLUBB. BLUBB! BLUBB! BLUBB! BLUBB!

COMIC BOOKS ARE INCENSE TO SATAN!

STRANGE LIGHTS! POLYSYLLABIC, VOWEL-LESS GODWORDS! IT'S HAPPENING! *IT'S ALL HAPPENING!*

MEANWHILE, AT THE *WATERGATE HOTEL,* RICHARD MILHOUS MANSON MAKES HIS MOVE TO SEIZE THE "DREADLY" *ELEKTRIK KIRBY ACID KETTLE:*

"EACH MOMENT IN HISTORY IS A FLEETING TIME, PRECIOUS AND UNIQUE!

"BUT SOME STAND OUT AS MOMENTS OF BEGINNING, IN WHICH COURSES ARE SET THAT SHAPE DECADES OR CENTURIES!"*

*Richard Mnnnnnnn Nixon, 10 January 1969.

"WHEN THE PRESIDENT DOES IT, IT MEANS THAT IT IS NOT ILLEGAL!!"* **

*Frank Langella, 23 Jan., 2009.

**Untrue.--Steve Wicker, editor of CHAMP Magazine, 1943-1972

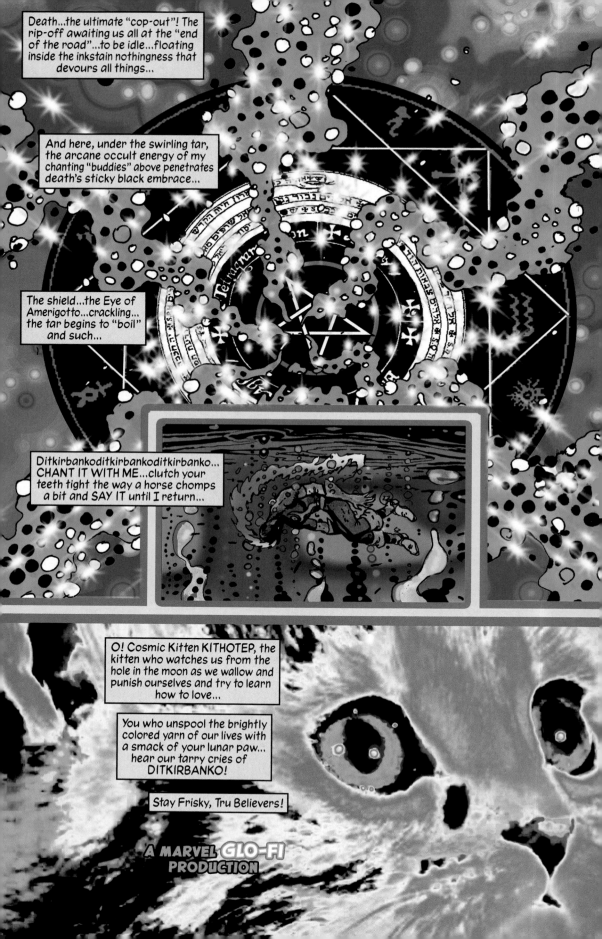

Death...the ultimate "cop-out"! The rip-off awaiting us all at the "end of the road"...to be idle...floating inside the inkstain nothingness that devours all things...

And here, under the swirling tar, the arcane occult energy of my chanting "buddies" above penetrates death's sticky black embrace...

The shield...the Eye of Amerigotto...crackling... the tar begins to "boil" and such...

Ditkirbankoditkirbankoditkirbanko... CHANT IT WITH ME...clutch your teeth tight the way a horse chomps a bit and SAY IT until I return...

O! Cosmic Kitten KITHOTEP, the kitten who watches us from the hole in the moon as we wallow and punish ourselves and try to learn how to love...

You who unspool the brightly colored yarn of our lives with a smack of your lunar paw... hear our tarry cries of DITKIRBANKO!

Stay Frisky, Tru Believers!

A MARVEL GLO-FI PRODUCTION

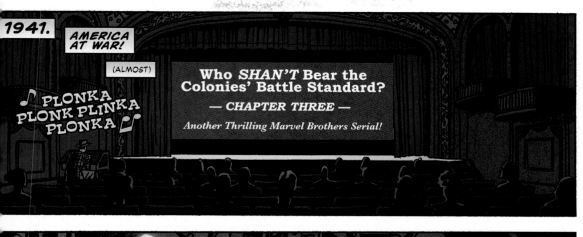

1941.

AMERICA AT WAR!

(ALMOST)

♪ PLONKA PLONK PLINKA PLONKA ♪

Who SHAN'T Bear the Colonies' Battle Standard?
— CHAPTER THREE —
Another Thrilling Marvel Brothers Serial!

IN A TOP SECRET GOVERNMENT LABORATORY, **DR. MYRON MACLAIN** DEDICATES ALL HIS ENERGY TO THE CAUSE OF LIBERTY!

BRAVELY, TIRELESSLY...DAY AFTER DAY HE LABORS, WITHOUT REST OR...OR...

Z

MACLAIN!!

UH! WHAT? I'M SORRY, KAISER!

GOD BLESS AMRRRICA!

HUH...THIS ALLOY OF VIBRANIUM AND STEEL. SOMEHOW, WHILE I WAS... RESTING MY *EYES*...IT ACHIEVED THE TENSILE STRENGTH I WAS HOPING FOR.

BETTER POUR IT INTO A MOLD BEFORE IT SETS...

THEN IT'S BACK TO THE...THE BUSINESS...

...OF FREEDOM...

OH, *COME ON!*

Z

BUT **WAIT!** WHO'S THIS SHADOWY FIGURE JUST ENTERING DR. MACLAIN'S TOP SECRET GOVERNMENT LAB?

Z

LOOKS LIKE HE'S TRYING TO STEAL AMERICA'S SECRETS!

WHO COULD HE BE?

WHY--IT'S--

The Golden Age
DEADPOOL

STUART MOORE: WRITES. "JAUNDICED" JOE QUINONES: DRAWS! JAVIER RODRIQUEZ: COLORS? TODD KLEIN: LETT3RS

WHOOPTY WHOOP!

BUY BONDS, YO!

AAAAAND...

...CUE SHORT FEATURE!

1917.

AMERICA AT WAR!

(FOR SURE THIS TIME)

♪ PLONKA PLONK PLINKA PLONKA ♪

THE SECRET ORIGIN OF THE GOLDEN AGE DEADPOOL

A MarvelToon Short Subject

AS THE U.S. ENTERS WORLD WAR I, PRESIDENT WOODROW WILSON SEES AN IDEAL CHANCE TO DISPOSE OF HIS EMBARRASSING NEPHEW...

...IT'LL BE GOOD P.R. FOR THE *FAMILY,* FREDDY.

DESPERATE TO ESCAPE THE FOXHOLES OF EUROPE, PRIVATE FREDERICK "WHEEZY" WILSON SEIZES ON A DARING PLAN: SMOKE HIS OWN WEIGHT IN CIGARS, THEN FAKE MUSTARD GAS POISONING. IN THE PROCESS, HE PERMANENTLY DAMAGES HIS LUNGS.

cough cough cough

TRY THIS ON, FREDDY.

THE MILITARY IS NOT FOOLED BY WILSON'S RUSE, BUT AGREES TO DISCHARGE HIM ANYWAY.

AND SO HE FINDS HIMSELF BACK IN THE STATES, PENNILESS, FORCED TO CARRY HIS GAS MASK AT ALL TIMES.

⸗COUGH⸗

AFTER A DECADE OF MENIAL JOBS, "WHEEZY" WILSON SPENDS MOST OF THE 1930S IN A STATE OF ABJECT POVERTY, WATCHING CARTOONS IN CUT-RATE THEATERS.

CUT OFF FROM ALL HUMAN CONTACT, HE STARES AT THE CRUDE, BIZARRE IMAGES DANCING ON THE SCREEN...

⸗COUGH⸗

...WHILE HIS MIND SLOWLY CRUMBLES.

NOW, THREE YEARS LATER...SHORTLY AFTER THE PUBLIC UNVEILING OF CAPTAIN AMERICA...

HEY, RAGGEDY ANDY!

STOP RIGHT THERE!

...VEAPON X HAS BEEN ACTIVATED!

UHHH!

BAM

BAM

BAM

BAM

UH, EXCUSE ME!

MISTER FIFTH COLUMNIST, SIR!

PLEASE RETURN THAT SPECIMEN, I'M BEGGING YOU!

IT'S...IT'S THE RIGHT THING TO DO...

COURAGEOUS DR. MACLAIN!

APPEALING TO A RUTHLESS KILLER IN THE NAME OF AMERICA...OF ALL THAT IS JUST, DECENT, AND FREE...

IF GENERAL GARVEY FINDS OUT HOW MUCH TIME I SPEND SLEEPING IN TOP SECRET GOVERNMENT LABS, HE'LL LOCK ME UP TILL THE *NEXT* WORLD WAR.

THAT'S FIVE YEARS, AT LEAST!

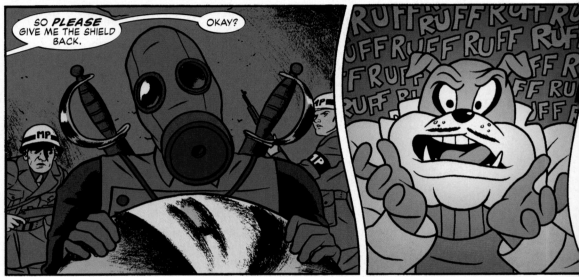

SO *PLEASE* GIVE ME THE SHIELD BACK.

OKAY?

RUFF RUFF RUFF RUFF RUFF RUFF RUFF RUFF RUFF RUFF

COME ON, BUDDY.

LET'S GET A LOOK UNDER THAT TURRET--

YO, DON'T *TOUCH* THE *HAIR!*

:UHH!:

:WHOOF!:

YOU... SAVED MY LIFE. WHY?

HEY... IF ANYBODY RUINS XMAS AROUND HERE, IT'S GONNA BE ME!

THAT'S *CHRISTMAS*, YOU HEATHEN!

HEH! *LOVE* IT WHEN YOU SAY THAT...

WHAT ARE WE *FIGHTING* FOR, ANYWAY?

WELL... I'M PULLING DOWN SEVEN FIGURES FROM A GUY NAMED *RASS BANKIN*...

OF COURSE. THE NOTED INTERNATIONAL *SCUMBAG*.

HE'S SICK OF GETTING *COAL* FROM YOU EVERY YEAR... ...SO HE HIRED ME TO UPLOAD THIS *WORM* ONTO YOUR MAINFRAME...

...THAT'D SWITCH HIS NAME FROM "NAUGHTY" TO "NICE!"

DEADPOOL! AND YOU *AGREED?* BUT YOU *MAKE* THE LIST EVERY DECEMBER!

YEAH, I *KNOW...* BUT...

I WRITE YOU *EVERY YEAR...* AND YOU *NEVER* BRING ME WHAT I *REALLY* WANT!

HO, HO... THEN I HAVE A *SURPRISE* FOR YOU!

THE COMPLETE *"MONSTERS OF COMMUNISM"* PEZ DISPENSER SET! AT LAST!

YOU TRULY ARE THE *KING OF KINGS.*

UM. YEAH. YOU'RE CONFUSING ME WITH *SOMEONE ELSE...*

"...BUT DO WE HAVE AN *UNDERSTANDING* HERE, OR..."

THUMP THUMP THUMP

OH! I HEAR ON THE ROOF...

...THE *PRANCING* AND *PAWING* OF EACH LITTLE *HOOF!*

I CAN'T WAIT...

SORRY, BANKIN.

YOU GOT OUTBID.

BLAM!

BLAM!

BLAM!

BLAM!

BLAM!

MERRY FREAKIN CHRISTMAS!!

WRITER: FRED VAN LENTE
ARTISTS: SANFORD GREENE
& NATHAN MASSENGILL
COLOR: JOHN RAUCH
LETTERS: JEFF ECKLEBERRY

AVENGERS: THE INITIATIVE #3
by David Yardi

CAPTAIN AMERICA #603
by Gerald Parel

DARK AVENGERS #14
by Mike Deodato

DARK WOLVERINE #83
by Juan Doe

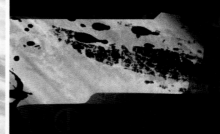

FANTASTIC FOUR #576
by Alan Davis

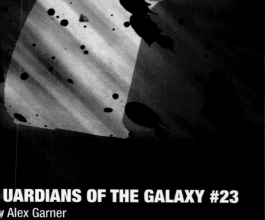

GUARDIANS OF THE GALAXY #23
Alex Garner

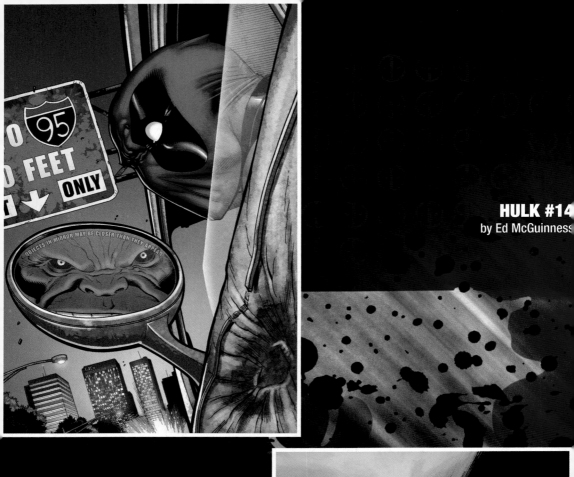

HULK #14
by Ed McGuinness

HULK #16
by Ed McGuinness

Matt Fraction
Salvador Larroca
Frank D'Armata

The Invincible

IRON MAN

Stark: Disassembled *4 of 5*

INVINCIBLE IRON MAN #23
by Salvador Larroca

MIGHTY AVENGERS #34
by Khoi Pham

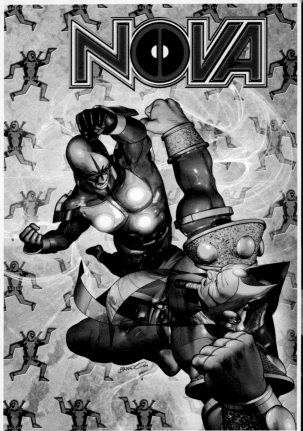

NOVA #34
by Brandon Peterson

SECRET WARRIORS #13
by Khoi Pham

TAILS OF THE PET AVENGERS #1
by Chris Eliopoulos

THOR #607
by Juan Doe

WEB OF SPIDER-MAN #5
by Phil Jimene

WOLVERINE ORIGINS #45
by Jacob Chabot

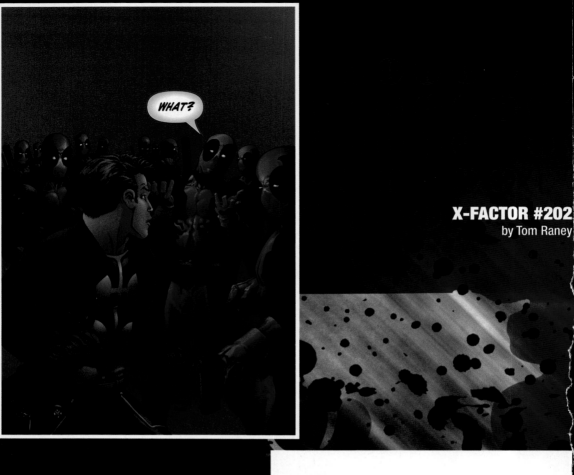

X-FACTOR #202
by Tom Raney

X-MEN LEGACY #233
by Giuseppe Camuncoli